ETHICS AND SOCIAL JUSTICE

CONTEMPORARY PHILOSOPHIC THOUGHT

The International Philosophy Year Conferences At Brockport

ETHICS
AND
SOCIAL JUSTICE

Edited by Howard E. Kiefer and Milton K. Munitz

STATE UNIVERSITY OF NEW YORK PRESS

ALBANY

PUBLISHED BY STATE UNIVERSITY OF NEW YORK PRESS
THURLOW TERRACE, ALBANY, NEW YORK 12201

LIBRARY OF CONGRESS CATALOG CARD NUMBER 69-14640
STANDARD BOOK NUMBER 87395-054-2
MANUFACTURED IN THE UNITED STATES OF AMERICA

DESIGNER: RHODA C. CURLEY

CONTENTS

PREFACE

This fourth volume of *Contemporary Philosophic Thought* is unlike the other three volumes in organization, in that its contents have not been divided into separately titled sections which correspond to like topics dealt with at individual conferences of the International Philosophy Year program. Instead, major papers drawn from four conferences (Philosophy of Practice, Ethics, Philosophy of Social Science, and Philosophy of Human Rights) have been grouped together under the general covering title of the volume, *Ethics and Social Justice*.

This minor organizational difference is deliberate, and reflects the view that the contents of Volume IV should be considered as interrelated in ways not entirely applicable to the various topics grouped together in the other three volumes; that is to say, the relationship between ethical problems and problems of social justice is more intimate and perhaps less arbitrary than some of the other problem groupings contained in the other three volumes of the anthology. But however important or unimportant it may be to accept this view about the relationship between ethical problems and problems of social justice, it is possible to argue that ethical problems are more theory-oriented than problems of social justice, which are practice-oriented. This topic deserves some discussion, because it leads us directly to one of the major issues dealt with in these pages.

The theory-practice dichotomy is an ancient one, supposedly supported alike by the *soi-disant* practical man, impatient with whatever may seem too far removed from realistic realms of action, and by the dedicated theoretician, whose questions about implications and meanings seem to require their detailed analysis. By contrast, so-called "pure" scientific research, frankly pursuing understanding rather than the

ix

achievement of practical ends, reportedly has earned popular, if grudging, respect, not for whatever intrinsic merit it may possess, but rather because it has become generally accepted as an essential prolegomenon to the eventual solution of practical human problems. The philosopher's perennial concern with ethical problems, however, enjoys no such reputation; indeed, the apparent absence of substantial evidence that what philosophers do with such problems makes an important difference in the world, seems to contrast sharply with the increasingly acknowledged relationship between "pure" scientific investigation and the fruits of successful scientific engineering.

Thus, some may consider the dual title of this volume to be appropriately descriptive of two related, but apparently discrete domains of human activity: on the one hand, the consideration of ethics in theory, and on the other, the consideration of ethics in practice. According to this view, problems of meta-ethics, sources of ethical judgments, the identification of the good and the good life, and the other almost endless concerns of moral philosophers, are considered as constituting an area of intellectual concern which may be contrasted appropriately with another area consisting of problems such as those of the practical administration of justice, the dilemmas which may arise out of consistent rule application, conflicts arising between cases involving the exercise of individual rights and the protection of social interests, and so on. Others may consider the volume title essentially redundant, on the grounds that meaningful ethical judgments always are judgments about human actions and intentions within a social context. I take it that "meaningful," as used in the sentence above, has more of a pragmatic flavor than a logical or epistemological one, and—to borrow Austin's phrase—its use may imply the view that it is wise to let sleeping dogmatists lie.

The nature of the relationships which obtain between theory and practice, taken together with the roles played by theoreticians and practitioners, becomes an appropriate starting point for the consideration of problems of ethics and social justice. Professor Charles Frankel begins the discussion of the philosophy of practice by noting problems which arise out of the relationship between "intellectuals" and "those called or miscalled members of the establishment," and argues that the main problem for the practitioner comes when he is confronted with a situation which cannot be analyzed in terms of the definitions and generalizations he is used to dealing with in his professional capacity. Indeed, because of this, many judgments come to be made that are based on "no particular domain of practice." It is just at this juncture, Frankel argues, that there may be a place for a philosophy of practice which would serve to clarify discussion, sort out issues, analyze assumptions, and indicate appropriate relationships between practical decisions and ideals. In response, Professor Walter Kaufmann is generally sympathetic to Frankel's aims, but focuses his criticism on what he takes to be Frankel's "strategy." He reaffirms the Socratic mission of rigorous questioning, and doubts that philosophers will meet their responsibilities by creating another "philosophy of something." He argues that the splintering of philosophy and the proliferation of so many subfields are "among the symptoms of a new scholasticism." He notes the most interesting and important work in philosophy often cuts across the subfields, and he urges a rebirth of the Socratic ethos in the old fields rather than the creation of a new one.

Professor Francis Sparshott distinguishes between four senses of "practice" in order to see which sense may have some philosophic relevance. He claims that "practice," as used in the phrase "philosophy of practice," should not be taken to mean (1) the whole domain of human action, nor (2) the rehearsal of action for purposes of perfecting it, nor (3) accepted standard operating procedures. He concerns himself with practice in another sense, as contrasted with theory—in fact, as a term that is correlative with theory, a theory being what justifies or explains a practice and a practice being the application of the relevant theory. He discusses the types of relations between theory and practice that are possible in principle, and argues that "theory is the theory of a certain practice, and practice is the practice of a certain theory." In response, Professor James Gutmann urges consideration of reciprocity of theory and practice, and cites the philosopher as playing a central role in the critical examination of various practices.

Professor Walter Kaufmann distinguishes three phases of the current crisis in morality: the growth of moral skepticism, skepticism about law, and doubts about justice. He concerns himself with seeking criteria by which a particular social practice can be morally justified. In addition, he attacks as confused both the material and formal conception of distributive justice, arguing that rewards and punishments may be unjust, but never, except in simplistic cases, just. In response, Professor Sidney Hook claims that we cannot know what it is to be unjust in practice, if we cannot know what it is to be just in practice. Thus, Professor Hook argues, it cannot be claimed that there is both no clear concept of justice and that distributions can be seen to be unjust.

United States Senator George McGovern contends that a philosophy of practice as proposed by Professor Frankel is vital in today's world of politics and diplomacy, so that the spirit of philosophy and the practice of politics may be mutually reinforcing. He cites as urgent (1) that more rigorous standards of truth be applied to the formulation and enunciation of public policy, (2) that scholars in government maintain the intellectual and moral claims of their own disciplines in the face of the suspicion of some politician who may regard them as "impractical" or "idealistic," (3) that channels of discussion, inquiry, and dissent be kept open, and (4) that an order of priorities and values in public policy be sought by the application of a philosophy of practice.

Professor Kurt Baier argues against the widely held theory that value judgments cannot be considered to be either true or false, as is the case with empirical, factual statements, because he holds consideration of "the anatomy of value judgments" shows that they are a species of empirical, factual statements. He argues that basic concrete value claims involve three different assertions: (1) that someone tried to attain an end, (2) something was an aid to him in trying to attain that end, and (3) the attempt to attain that end with the aid of that thing constituted a benefit. He then discusses the way in which appraisals differ from other types of orderings, explicating the ways in which his account of value judgments differs from rival theories.

Professor Anthony Quinton considers features distinguishing actions and values that are specifically moral from those that are non-moral. To this end, he examines four criteria: (1) that moral evaluations are categorical, (2) that moral decisions are autonomous, (3) that moral judgments are universal, and (4) that moral considerations are always overriding. He argues that all of these are inadequate, suggesting rather that a suitable criterion might be one which distinguishes those actions as moral which diminish suffering.

Professor Paul W. Taylor discusses the principle of universalizability, that if the exemplification of the characteristics of an object or act in one case is accepted as a reason for saying that an object is good or that an act ought to be done, then consistency requires that the same be said of any other object or act that exemplifies those properties. He recognizes that universalizability is a purely formal principle, true of all normative statements, and considers the traditional objection that moral prescriptions cannot be made to follow from a purely formal principle alone. He goes on to argue that by a special application of a purely formal principle to a certain class of cases, the rational ground for a universal, cross-cultural standard of social justice can be established. He goes on to state that if this argument is sound, it provides a justification for the adoption of the basic norm of "justice as fairness," i.e., that all men have an equal right to a fulfillment of their interests. In response, Professor Joseph Gilbert argues that the universalizability requirement, role reversal, and the principle of mutual acknowledgment have little moral and far less rational import than hitherto thought.

Professor H. L. A. Hart turns to Kelsen's doctrine of the unity of law, that all valid laws necessarily form a single system and that valid laws cannot conflict. He attempts to show that Kelsen's doctrine of the unity of all valid laws and its conclusions concerning the possible and actual relationships between international law and municipal laws, are mistaken. He holds, however, that the effort to criticize these doctrines is rewarding, because it reveals (1) that a good deal of unfinished business remains for analytical jurisprudence, including a much-needed clarification of the meaning of the common assertion that laws belong to or constitute a system of laws, and (2) that the present familiar forms of deontic logic may not be adequate in dealing with the logic of norms and their interrelationships.

In response, Professor Ronald M. Dworkin claims that Hart's argument ignores the complexity of Kelsen's writings by conflating two issues that Kelsen separates, (1) the identification of the science of law and its distinction from the science of sociology, and (2) the dynamics of legal reasoning in the application of a particular analysis of validity to a problem for which it was not intended.

Professor Graham Hughes discusses the implications of acts of civil disobedience for the political-question doctrine, which holds that some actions, practices, or determinations by legislature or executive are not reviewable in the courts. He argues that when the courts refuse to grant certiorari, their decision should be accompanied by a reasoned opinion, where the legality of a particular government action is concerned. He holds this view for several reasons, including the weight of legal precedence involving a political question, the possible interpretation that a mere statement denying certiorari may imply that the challenged actions of the executive are legal, and the possibility that such proceedings may tend to undermine confidence in the courts.

Professor Ronald M. Dworkin considers the question of how the state should respond when a person, out of conscience, breaks a criminal law the constitutionality of which is unclear. After arguing that, in general, the state has a "responsibility of leniency" in such cases of civil disobedience, due to the traditional practice of encouraging people to use their own best judgment when a law is not clear, he goes on to consider the several ways in which the state might handle cases of this sort in a manner consistent with other state policies.

Mr. Justice Tom C. Clark discusses the nature of the law and its relationship to law-givers and jurists, maintaining that from their actions, legal philosophies, theories and systems have evolved. He considers the problem of civil disobedience and the right to dissent, and considers these issues in connection with established legal proceedings and the role of the United States Supreme Court.

Professor Sidney Hook turns to the consideration of human rights, and notes that their history exemplifies the point that social and political theory often lags far behind social and political practice. He argues that human rights, when considered as morally justifiable claims made in behalf of all men, are defensible because of the consequences of acting upon them. Although granting there may be a wide disparity between official declarations of human rights and the practices of the society which officially proclaims them, he argues that such declarations have an educational influence that in time undercuts political maneuvering and hypocrisy, noting that when opposition movements develop against dictatorial practices or regimes in countries that formally profess allegiance to Bills of Rights, they can make headway by appealing to these official declarations.

Professor Raymond Aron is concerned with the place that declarations of the Rights of Man have in today's world, taking as his point of departure a comparison between the first French declaration of 1789 and the 1948 declaration of the United Nations General Assembly. He concludes that there have been important changes in the expressed character of rights especially in the economic and social area. He argues that the drafters of the 1948 declaration, without being fully aware of it, were prepared to give all powers to the state in order that it might assure the security and the standard of living of all. He notes that the 1948 declaration criticizes liberal society in the name of the socialist ideal, and socialist society in the name of the liberal ideal, and raises the question as to which of the two societies offers the greater resistance to this criticism.

Professor Richard McKeon asserts that human rights have a philosophy as well as a history, and that the acquisition, extension, increase, and exercise of human rights depends on the historical situation in which they are asserted and achieved, and on the views and convictions which make statements of them, and actions in accordance with them, possible. He recounts what was involved in the development of the history and philosophy of human rights leading to the formulation of the United Nations declaration in 1948. Professor Jeanne Hersch closes the discussion of human rights by concerning herself with the question of whether or not such declarations represent a Western concept. She describes the work of the UNESCO Division of Philosophy in gathering information from both Eastern and Western nations which support the view that the concept of human rights is a universal one.

H. E. K.

PHILOSOPHY OF PRACTICE

Charles Frankel

I

It will be no news to anyone that one of the vexatious problems of the moment is the relationship, or lack of relationship, of intellectuals to public affairs. The air is filled with irritable accusations. More and more intellectuals appear to regard those who hold power as ignorant or conscienceless. And more and more, those who hold positions of power indicate by their words or tone of voice or, perhaps most of all, by their silent refusal to be drawn into debate, that they regard intellectuals as naive or irresponsible.

It is not part of my business here to discuss the immediate causes of this conflict or to assess the rights and wrongs of the issues on which it turns. What I would point out about it is only that this conflict is not a new one. It is a central theme of philosophy, on which variations have been composed by philosophers from Socrates to Karl Marx, and from John Dewey to Jean-Paul Sartre. What the practical man today says about intellectuals echoes the remark of the Thracian handmaid, who said of Thales that he was so eager to know what was going on in heaven that he could not see what was before his feet. And the response of the intellectuals echoes that of Socrates:

But, O my friend, when the philosopher draws the [practical man] into the upper air, and gets him out of his pleas and rejoinders into the contemplation of justice and injustice in their own nature . . . , or [takes him from his] commonplaces about the happiness of a king or a rich man to the consideration of government and of human happiness and misery in general—what they are, and how a man is to attain the one and avoid the other—when that narrow, keen, little legal mind is called to account about all this, he gives the philosopher his revenge; for dizzied by the height at which he is hanging, whence he looks down into space, which is a strange experience to him, he being dismayed, and lost, and stammering broken words, is laughed at, not by Thracian handmaidens . . . but by every man who has not been brought up a slave.[1]

Yet the relationship between intellectuals and wielders of power has been characterized by more than mutual disrespect. On one side, although philosophers and intellectuals have perennially despised and distrusted power, this has not prevented them from talking about it and giving a good many signs that they would like to have it, if only in self-defense. On the other side, although practical men who hold power have been perennially suspicious and contemptuous of intellectuals, this has not prevented them from wanting the approval of intellectuals and resenting their disapproval. Nor has it prevented them from turning to intellectuals for help, if only in self-defense.

Indeed, if philosophy is a series of footnotes to Plato, as White-head believed, then the strange, ambiguous relationship between intellect and power—the condition of mutual need and mutual repulsion which has at once bound the two together and set them apart—may well be a main source of philosophy as such. Certainly, much of Plato's philosophy is motivated by his indignation that society should condemn philosophers to futility and death, and by his search for a program of philosophical and social reform that would give philosophy the governing role in the affairs of the commonwealth. The present conflict between those we call (or miscall) "intellectuals" and those we call (or miscall) "members of the Establishment" has at least some of the characteristics of the conflict between contemplation and action rehearsed in the Platonic dialogues and in Plato's own personality and career. It is part of an ancient debate over the relation of philosophy to power, and, more generally, over the relation of theory to something known as "practice." And the main drift of this larger debate does much to explain, I think, the character and temper—including the bad temper—of the present debate about intellectuals and their relation to the life of action.

What philosophers have traditionally said about the relation of philosophy and practice has exercised an influence not only over the nature of philosophy but over the attitudes of mind of both intellectuals and practical men. It is therefore an important political and historical fact, at once full of consequences in itself and symptomatic of a larger dislocation in society as a whole, that the main drift of philosophic debate has produced a situation in which the very phrase "philosophy of practice" is likely to puzzle those who hear it.

What have been some of the principal answers of philosophers to the question of the relation of philosophy to practice? One has been the view that the philosopher must turn his mind away from practice if he is to achieve true understanding. Thus, when Descartes consciously chose to be guided in daily life by practical conventions which he would not examine, he made this choice so that he could be free to pursue, untroubled, his radical philosophical doubts. Again, Kant taught that considerations of practical expediency lead to precisely the wrong answers in morals. And even Hume warned that the uncertainties about sensory experience which he uncovered as a philosopher had no relation to, or influence on, the practical certainties he felt when he walked on the street.

A second sort of answer to the question of the relation of philosophy to practice has resembled the first in its preference for the presumed consistency and clarity of philosophical theory over the capriciousness and ambiguities of practice. But it has not been indifferent to practice. Instead, it has sought to improve practice by introducing into it some of the virtues of intellectual enterprises. Thus, philosophers of this persuasion, like Plato or Hobbes, have usually proposed models for the analysis and control of practice derived from theoretical enterprises like mathematics or physics.

Utilitarianism is probably the prime example in recent philosophy, and the problems it raises are perhaps indicative of the problems raised by this general approach. Although the obvious intention of utilitarianism is to sharpen practical judgment and to bring it the help of scientific knowledge, the principle of utility is of limited utility in making practical judgments. Even if we set aside the questions that can be asked about its standing as a first principle in ethics, and also ignore the discomfort provoked by the fact that moral and political judgments, as a matter of daily experience, appear to involve the weighing of incommensurables, the principle of utility still leaves us without definite guidance in the field of practice. The reason for this is that weighing alternatives by determining which promises more satisfaction or utility involves placing them on a scale of satisfactions or utilities, and that the principle of utility does not in itself tell us what scale to employ.

Of course, approaches like utilitarianism serve important purposes, both theoretical and practical. They have value when they are employed within an already defined and accepted context, such as that in which economists, working with a price system, conduct their inquiries. While I do not have the time to discuss the merits of such approaches, I do not mean to dismiss them as wasted efforts. But they derive their value precisely from their use within such specialized and well-defined contexts of theoretical inquiry, and they become systematically misleading when they are used outside such contexts or when it is assumed that they can by themselves yield practical judgments.

A third sort of philosophical answer to the relation of theory and practice has expressed a tendency rather characteristic of a good deal of philosophy—namely, to go to the other extreme. It has embraced practice body and soul. This approach to the issue accepts the fact that there are radical differences between practice and theory. But it goes on to argue that an analysis of practice offers the path to a truer and more peculiarly philosophical understanding of reality. The philosophy of Bergson, phenomenology, existentialism, and the pragmatism of William James are different examples of this approach. Thus, to take perhaps the simplest case, James argued that while abstract theoretical appraisals of the evidence commonly leave the mind unable to answer certain momentous questions, the human will, which is practical, not only insists upon an answer to them but also provides an answer if we follow its lead. In sum, the ideal that philosophy shall be the guide to practice is dropped in favor of the principle that practice shall be the guide to philosophy. Practice is proclaimed not as a domain in which the mind uses or needs evidence or forms of rational, discursive thought continuous with those employed in other domains, but as the domain in which truths that evidence or discursive thought do not by themselves support can nevertheless be established.

Against this background, it is perhaps not surprising that philosophers have done so much less to illuminate the problems of practical men than many philosophers and practical men have hoped. At any rate, it is surely unmistakable that there is today a widespread feeling, shared by many scholars outside philosophy as well as by judges, legislators, diplomats, teachers, and other practitioners, that philosophy has somehow let them down. And when philosophers tell such people that they misunderstand philosophy and should not expect it to solve their practical problems, these not wholly unintelligent observers remain unconvinced and dissatisfied. They are likely to reply that they are faced by inescapable practical questions about what to believe, and, even more, about what to do, that they need enlightenment about such questions, and that no matter what the name of the discipline is, there is a need for these questions to be examined in a disciplined way.

Moreover, the situation is not one in which no answers of any sort are provided. Prejudice and convention provide plenty. So do theologians in their way, and politicians in their way, and business men, novelists, psychiatrists and bureaucrats—all in their own ways. And philosophers too, despite their unresolved doubts about the relation of theory to practice, have leaped into the breach, blessing commonplace intuition, or offering answers to practical questions derived from all-inclusive metaphysical systems, or preaching a general gospel of engagement and commitment while providing only the most elusive clues as to the logical processes that ought to be employed in choosing any specific commitments.

To be sure, there have been some correctives to this situation. Vigorous tendencies in twentieth-century philosophies of law and science have turned to the actual practice in these enterprises to find a base for the critical interpretation of them. More generally still, logical empiricism and pragmatism, particularly the latter, have stressed the connections of theory and practice, and Wittgenstein and his followers, employing linguistic analysis as a basic tool of philosophy, have stressed that the meaning of terms lies in their use, and have explored the variety of meanings that given terms have in different contexts of use.

Yet all of these philosophical efforts still leave a vast field of possible endeavor largely unexplored. Positivism and pragmatism take their lead from scientific inquiry. When they speak of ideas as "instruments," they mean primarily their use as leading principles in procedures of thought whose ends-in-view are statements that can be pronounced true or false. The "practice" which these philosophies have mainly in mind is controlled experimentation. Undoubtedly, questions of truth and falsehood and the model of scientific experimentation are relevant, but it is at the very least an open question whether the route to the understanding and criticism of practical judgment lies exclusively in the analysis of scientific discourse and practice. Nor is the analysis of what is known as "ordinary usage" the only available alternative, particularly when this ordinary usage is examined mainly as a linguistic phenomenon. Another alternative is to go to practice directly, to analyze its distinctive features, and to determine whether there is a role for philosophical criticism in connection with it.

It is with this general possibility that the remainder of this essay is concerned. Does "practice" offer a field of philosophical inquiry which has been unduly neglected? Does the analysis of practice offer a potential vocation for philosophy which might refresh and reinvigorate it, and which, even if it does not supplant other established philosophical enterprises, would be a source of illumination to them? More specifically, is it possible for a philosophy of practice to exist? What would it be if it did?

Obviously, these are large questions, and what I shall say in this brief essay is offered as only the beginning of an answer. Let us turn first to an account of some of the distinguishing features of practice. And, so that we can know with some definiteness what it is that we are talking about, let us take as our models the identifiable professions, such as law, medicine, engineering, teaching, politics, and public administration. The idea of "practice" is not exhausted by what such professions are and do.

But because they have more or less stable and definite features, we can move with greater assurance into a discussion of practice if we know that we have them centrally in mind.

(1) The first obvious characteristic of practice is that it presents *forced options*. You know that you are dealing with a practical question when you have no choice but to choose. When you are confronted by a theoretical scientific question, you are always free to hold off giving an answer or to circumscribe your answer with words like "probably." Practice offers no such latitude. In this sense, if in no other, it is like mathematics or formal logic. You have to say yes or no. And practice goes beyond mathematics or formal logic because there is nothing hypothetical about the assent or denial you give. It does not depend on your accepting the terms of the argument. Even if you do not like any of the options given to you in practice, you must nevertheless take one of them (unless, of course, you can find or make some new ones). If you are irresolute and refuse to choose, then you have simply chosen that option which will prevail without your intervention.

This fundamental difference between theory and practice allows us to keep the two apart in our minds even though they are, in fact, very often simply different aspects of a single process. Purely theoretical pursuits invariably have a practical side. There is chemical theory, but there is also the practice of chemistry, which runs the gamut from washing bottles through mediating the human problems among members of a research team to choosing the most economical or fruitful strategy of research. But while theories are themselves the products of practices of specific kinds, and while theoreticians are all also practitioners, the product which validates their activity is a true statement, whereas the primary product of the model practitioner is a decision or action affecting some specific state of affairs.

(2) A second obvious characteristic of practice, implicit in what has already been said, is that practice is concerned with action. This statement, however, has an evident redundancy about it, and is also somewhat misleading, for it requires us to assign a broader meaning to "action" than is normal if we are to accept it as true. For sound practical judgment (in medicine, for example) may often recommend inaction—doing nothing. It is less misleading to say that practice has to do with *change*, and that it is *future-oriented*. The object of practice is to achieve a desired state of affairs, either by producing a change, preventing a change, or letting a change take place. The mark of what we know as "practicality," accordingly, is sage judgment about what does not change, and about what changes can or cannot be affected by human effort.

A closely connected point is that practical judgment cannot be satisfied with purely general or abstract considerations. I do not mean that practice does not lean on such considerations. We shall turn to them subsequently. But the purpose of practice is not to yield statements to which specific times and places are irrelevant. When verbal utterances are involved at all in practical decisions, their primary significance lies in the role they play as elements in a process of intervention in a specific set of changes, and their meaning has to be interpreted accordingly—a point Aristotle made in another connection in considering the role of general statements in works of art. In brief, practice is concerned with doing or not doing something. In deciding what to do, a man may well ask hypothetically what would happen *if* he did this or that. But the more he is interested simply in exploring hypothetical alternatives, and the more these alternatives are formulated so that they encompass all possible situations, the less practical the process of inquiry is. This is one source of the tension that exists between abstract moralists and practical men. The practical man, who makes no effort to connect his present decision with any principle or policy, abandons the claim to rationality. The theoretical man, who makes no effort to connect his principles to what happens to exist and what happens to be possible here and now, abandons all claims to relevance or, indeed, to human compassion. Fortunately, most reflective men fall somewhere between these two extremes.

(3) A third plain characteristic of practice, in the light of what has been said, is its relation to human desires. It is an effort to reach desired ends, and rests on or actively involves value-judgments. But this is a bare and highly abstract statement. When the analysis of practice by philosophers ends with this proposition, as it so often does, we are left with little information either about practice or about the elements that go into human decisions. What characterizes practical value-judgments within the professions, for example, is that they are made within highly determinate social contexts in which *certain matters must be largely, though not entirely, taken as given.* Among the matters that must be taken for granted are a *machinery of action,* a *set of inherited ends or purposes,* and a *professional doctrine,* tacit or explicit.

3.1 A generally accepted machinery of action is a conspicuous feature of all organized practices. Lawyers are bound to the courts, politicians to the election system, foreign affairs policy-makers to a system of embassies and representation at a distance. The creative or ingenious practitioner can break through this accepted machinery of action at one point or another. To the extent, however, that his goals are limited and his time span restricted, he is forced to work with most of the machinery he inherits. Indeed, even if his goals are very broad, and he is brave enough or intellectually arrogant enough to work in a time span of a generation or more, he will have to develop and lean on new machinery that will be characterized by stability. And he will still have to work perforce with some of the machinery he inherits, simply because it has a momentum of its own.

In other words, the practitioner cannot, as a practitioner, indulge in wholesale Cartesian doubt—a point that Descartes himself accepted for practice even if he did not accept it for theory. Of course, in certain respects, as the mention of Descartes may remind us, the practitioner's situation is not different from the theorist's. Neither logically nor psychologically is it possible to erase all assumptions, or to begin a process of thought with an absolutely blank mind. Moreover, the theories accepted in his discipline are the primary machinery employed by the theorist to formulate and solve his problems. There is always a prima facie pragmatic case to be made for preserving this machinery as far as possible and for bringing new problems within the framework of existing theories if this can be done. Yet there remains a significant difference between the theorist and the practitioner, if only in degree. Theoretical inquiry is indoctrinated with the idea of change and reform: Descartes' systematic doubt is an expression of this ethic. And the replacement of basic theoretical machinery by new theoretical machinery is not only easier to accomplish on paper but easier to accomplish in social action since it requires only the assent of other trained specialists working within the same language and ethic. The practitioner's situation is hardly comparable in these respects.

Moreover, in determining what machinery he must accept and what he should reject, the practitioner cannot employ, as the theoretician can, only the test of efficiency with respect to the solution of his specific problems. He also has to take into account the fact that some social machinery is impregnable to change whatever its efficiency. To put it simply, he has to take human inertia and human irrationality into account. Indeed, he may be forced to go further. He may be forced to accept them, in actual operation, as ends or goals. For since the machinery of action on which the practitioner leans is a condition for his work, the maintenance of that machinery can become an ongoing requirement for him, so that actions which are likely to break the machinery become inadvisable. Thus, the maintenance of a political party, created as a means to certain ends, usually becomes itself an end. The commonplace criticisms of the professional politician, the legalistic lawyer, and the bureaucratic administrator have a certain injustice about them, at least from this point of view. Such people, whose primary commitment is to the machinery of action, serve a function. They are the price we pay for having any machinery of social action at all. I would wish to add, however, that the price we are presently paying for this service is somewhat inflated.

This basic difference between the conditions of practical and theoretical inquiry helps explain why something like a dialogue of the deaf so often takes place between the intellectual and the official, or the layman and the professional. The intellectual is on the outside, the official on the inside of the decision-making process. The official, faced with a practical decision, is enmeshed in present circumstances. The intellectual is freer to disregard the existing machinery of action. So neither talks in the terms that make sense to the other. Indeed, I cannot help but mention to this audience that this difference between the conditions of practical and theoretical judgment may help explain why professors are so often vaultingly ambitious in their opinions and advice about public affairs while they remain incongruously conservative in their practical decisions regarding their own departments and universities.

3.2 Practice involves not only a machinery of action but, usually, a set of given *ends or purposes*. Thus, the physician's work takes place within a framework of activities overwhelmingly committed to the principle of the sanctity of life. Only within very narrow limits, if at all, is he free to make judgments about the desirability of prolonging life. More generally still, it is a characteristic of much practice that it can be routinized so that little conscious thought or deliberate choice is required. Farming, carpentering or driving a car are all examples. But these routines themselves involve some implicit and settled ordering of social values. And these values do not emerge from the practice itself, but set its limits. Thus, to take a homely example, a carpenter does not usually give conscious thought to whether he should use a ruler in making a measurement. The decision is, in effect, made for him by established routines. But the degree of precision required by these routines is set not simply by the task he is trying to accomplish, but by the importance attached to precision in such a task by the environing social group which calls upon him to be a carpenter.

Accordingly, when we speak of "a practice" we mean, among other things, a set of more or less accepted routines and disciplines which bear the stamp of standards and values that emanate from outside the practice itself. The practitioner is an agent of purposes that are not entirely "practical"—of purposes, that is to say, whose character cannot be specified or justified unless we bring in considerations that go beyond the requirements of the practice itself. Thus, the current practice of penology cannot be explained so long as we take into account only the practical requirements that must be met in the management of prisons. In explaining or appraising what is actually done, even the mention of such often-stated purposes as the incarceration and rehabilitation of offenders or the deterrence of other potential violators of the law is not enough. The revulsion that is felt by the outside community in the face of certain crimes and the desire or need for revenge are also an indispensable part of the story.

In consequence, there is an ineffaceable amateur quality in practice —at any rate when it rises above the merely routine. For when a practice's accepted routines run into difficulties, the cure may necessitate or provoke the reordering of moral attitudes that are not the exclusive monopoly of the practice itself. The practitioner may have something relevant and competent to say about such attitudes, but he does not have the only relevant or competent word. This amateur quality is most pronounced in the practices which we call the "higher professions," and is one of the characteristics that differentiate them most sharply from the simpler crafts. For it is in these professions that the structure of settled value-judgments is likely to come under the steadiest and severest attack, as the result of developments in science, the general evolution of moral sentiments, and the emergence of problems with no clear and unambiguous precedent.

Thus, the development of medical science's capacity to prolong human life has itself helped to change the value traditionally attached to the principle of the sanctity of life, and has raised ethical questions for doctors which they did not face before. In these new circumstances, doctors can of course take refuge in the inherited moral code, and argue that the "larger ethical questions" pose imponderables which they, as doctors, need not resolve. But adjustments of medical practice are nevertheless taking place, even though the ethical and legal codes that surround medical practice may remain officially unchanged.

The amateur quality of practice also differentiates it from the primarily cognitive or theoretical disciplines. To be sure, theoreticians also have the problem of breaking away from settled routines. Moreover, it is undeniable that the influence exerted over their work by external social and practical considerations is often considerable even though it may be hidden. However, the specialist in a theoretical discipline has considerably greater freedom to remain a specialist than does the reflective practitioner. His findings and decisions can be stated in the language special to his discipline. He is not pushed by the day-to-day pressures of his job, in the way that the practitioner is, to deal with issues that cannot be formulated from the standpoint of his own professional competence alone. A practice represents, in part, the convergence of interests and purposes which cannot be stated or evaluated in the special, professional terms of the practice. Theory, in contrast, is the product of the isolation of subject matter and the ascetic withdrawal from issues irrelevant to it.

3.3 A third element which enters into a practice is its possession of what might be called a *"professional doctrine"*—a set of basic propositions which are taken, for practical purposes, either as descriptive of "reality" [2] or as rules for formulating such a description. Thus, the operative position of most social workers with regard to the question of the individual's responsibility for his behavior is broadly deterministic; the operative position of the judge, in contrast, is voluntaristic. Again, for most professional practitioners in the field of international affairs, the working view of "reality" is that international relations consists in the relations of independent states each seeking to defend or enhance its own power. The operative view of scientists concerned with the practical affairs of the scientific community is likely to be that national frontiers are artificial and destructive fictions, and that cooperation is as conspicuous a feature of international relations as competition.

Of course, a professional doctrine is not always explicit. The degree of its explicitness depends on the state of professional education and of critical reflection in the profession. Moreover, a practice may become a field for the contest of competing doctrines, particularly when the practice is under pressure to meet new demands and to respond to alternative values. Nevertheless, at any particular time and for any particular practitioner, it is possible to say that his decisions are at least in part the product of inferences governed, tacitly or explicitly, by doctrinal considerations.

Once again, therefore, we touch on the amateur quality that is potentially present in professional practice. It is potentially present for at least two reasons. The first is that the practitioner may come to problems which cannot be analyzed with the help only of the generalizations and definitions available to him as part of his professional point of view. He has to invoke generalizations about human behavior or society whose standing, if they have any at all, is derived from their acceptance by some other group of practitioners or by theoreticians. Moreover, he is very often forced to fall back on general ideas about human behavior or social causation that belong to no particular domain of practice or theory at all, but only to that vague domain known as "common sense" or "common judgment" where superstition and wisdom flourish side by side. It is impressive to note how many of the biggest and riskiest decisions that practitioners make in the courts, in foreign policy, or in domestic politics turn tacitly or explicitly on judgments of this sort. The professional expert, more often than not, takes a back seat. At any rate, it is his nonexpert judgments, whether recognized or not, that give him the ticket to a front seat when he occupies one.

There is a second reason as well why a professional doctrine may take the practitioner into waters that are deeper than he realizes. There is an imperial thrust in most professional doctrines. They fade easily into professional *ideologies*, becoming definitions of reality that incorporate and sanctify basic value-judgments, thus justifying the existence of a profession and lending warrant to the assertion that its doctrine should be given preeminence over other doctrines when they come into conflict in the analysis of public issues.

One of the prime examples is the doctrine of "political realism," which has a dominant position as the working professional doctrine in the study and practice of international relations. In the ambitious version of this doctrine developed by Professor Hans Morgenthau,[3] the key concept is "the concept of interest defined in terms of power." The concept is crucial, according to Professor Morgenthau, for the following reasons:

It sets politics as an independent sphere of action and understanding apart from other spheres, such as economics, ethics, aesthetics, or religion. Without such a concept a theory of politics, international or domestic, would be altogether impossible, for without it we could not distinguish between political and nonpolitical facts, nor could we bring at least a measure of systematic order to the political sphere.

It is common, in theoretical inquiries, to introduce such basic concepts in order sharply to separate and limit the subject matter of inquiry. But the result is a descriptive theory, not a doctrine that is normative. Yet it is plain that Professor Morgenthau, for all his "realism," has normative purposes in mind as well:

Political realism [he writes] contains not only a theoretical but also a normative element. . . . It shares with all social theory the need, for the sake of theoretical understanding, to stress the rational elements of political reality; for it is these rational elements that make reality intelligible for theory. . . . At the same time political realism considers a rational foreign policy to be good foreign policy; for only a rational foreign policy minimizes risks and maximizes benefits and, hence, complies both with the moral precept of prudence and the political requirement of success. . . . Aware of the inevitable gap between good—that is, rational—foreign policy and foreign policy as it actually is, political realism maintains not only that theory must focus upon the rational elements of political reality, but also that foreign policy ought to be rational in view of its own moral and practical purposes.[4]

In brief, "political realism" is not only a recommendation for inquiry but a recommendation for practice. Its key concept—"interest defined in terms of power"—is intended, in Professor Morgenthau's own language, to establish international politics as an independent sphere of both "action and understanding." This illustrates a fallacy which has been historically characteristic of political realism. First, the theory picks out distinctive features of political action, and insists that, when we try to explain behavior in this domain, we recognize that it has its own laws, and is not to be understood in the way that, say, family relations are to be understood. Then it converts this description into a *recommendation* to political practitioners, who are told that they are "irrational" unless they rule out all considerations except those that figure in the theory. Political realism thus changes into a professional ideology. Although its protagonists may not intend such a consequence, its latent function is to give protective intellectual coloration to the well-known tendency of professional practitioners in all fields to develop what Veblen called a "trained incapacity" to attend to matters outside their normal ken.

Against the background of these observations about practice, let us turn back and consider the questions I asked at the beginning of these remarks about the nature, possibility, and utility of a branch of philosophy that might be known as "the philosophy of practice." What I have said about practice is painfully sketchy in its details and obviously incomplete taken as a whole. Yet I believe that it gives us some clues to the answers to these questions.

In essence, if I am right in what I have said up to this point, the function of a philosophy of practice is to insure that practice keeps its amateur standing. To be sure, professional specialization is clearly necessary. I do not argue that point, nor do I deplore the efforts being made to introduce scientific methods and findings into many fields of professional education and practice. On the contrary. Nevertheless, an analysis of practice supports the truth, I believe, of Protagoras' basic position that where knowledge of virtue is concerned there are no experts. For there are questions that arise within specific practices which practitioners, locked within the practice, may not normally detect or may be incompetent to assess in all their dimensions.

Practice is that aspect of human endeavor in which values enshrined by certain routines clash with values that stem from the outside. It is that aspect of endeavor where, for better or worse, common sense ideas that belong to every man's domain and to no man's are employed. It is that aspect of endeavor where the doctrines that grow out of and that give shape to daily routines clash with doctrines rooted in other routines. Scientific methods and scientific knowledge can enlighten practice, but they are not sufficient by themselves to provide disciplined and responsible answers to the questions that emerge under these conditions.

At this point, what is also needed is an intellectual activity whose function is to sort out the issues, clarifying the terms of discussion and indicating the relationship between practical decisions made amidst the urgencies of the moment and more far-reaching ideals of human excellence and possibilities. The potential task of a philosophy of practice is to associate itself with organized practices, devoting itself to the specification and criticism of the values that compete for attention in practical judgment, and to the analysis of the common-sense and doctrinal assumptions that play a part in practical inferences. So conceived, the philosophy of practice would be practice's gadfly, alerting practitioners to the premises and the larger nonprofessional implications of their thinking.

It would be, I should add, a Socratic rather than a high Platonic discipline. Although it would take another paper to argue the point fully, nothing that I have said supports the claim, so far as I can see, that it is possible to develop an architectonic philosophy of practice, a discipline that could pull all fields of practice together in the service of a single *summum bonum* which it alone discovered and decreed. The philosophy of practice is, in my opinion, a critical and evaluative activity, not a science in pursuit of special truths. It would operate essentially in the interstices between different domains of practice; it would offer to the practitioner, who becomes an amateur when he moves into these interstices, not an authoritative and preemptive answer to his problems, but only the illumination of a disciplined outsider's point of view.

Such a philosophy of practice would not replace other established branches of philosophy. I do not call attention to this sphere of possible philosophical activity in the belief that there is no validity in what philosophers do in other spheres. Nor do I argue that philosophers are not presently doing anything in this sphere. Although they are not doing much, they have obviously been active to some extent, particularly in the philosophy of law. It is at least possible, however, that analyses of practical judgments will throw significant new light on philosophical issues that have long been debated within other contexts. There is a never-ending character to philosophical arguments which is in part the product of the circumstance that so few of these arguments have a defined subject matter that holds the discussion in bounds. The philosophy of science has made progress because its subject matter is reasonably definite. The analysis of practice might serve a similar function with regard to many of the problems now debated by philosophers of language and morals.

Can contemporary philosophers perform this task? The answer is both yes and no, and the equivocation in my answer is due to certain well-known equivocations in the meaning of the word "can." The contemporary philosopher, with some exceptions, is like the man who has never tried to putt a golf-ball into a hole. He cannot do so, and yet he could if he learned. Without the proper training and experience, philosophers will obviously have little of value to contribute to the analysis and illumination of practice. Philosophical education and philosophical careers would have to be substantially changed if any noticeable proportion of philosophers were to devote themselves usefully to the analysis and criticism of practice. What the philosopher will offer of value will depend on the degree to which he can combine philosophical discipline and sophistication with a reasonably intimate understanding of some particular domain of practice. The obstacles in the way of providing such training and experience are not inconsiderable.

Yet the effort seems to me worth making. It was Aristotle's view that politics was the most authoritative art, the master art—"for politics uses the rest of the sciences, and legislates as to what we are to do and what we are to abstain from, so that the end of this science must include those of the others." Aristotle looked to the moral and political philosopher to develop this science. The ideal of such a supreme art or science is not one that a philosopher can adopt today. Apart from the philosophical reasons, there is the elementary practical consideration that no man today can aim without naïveté at an all-embracing kind of knowledge. But it is odd to use such an argument to support the abandonment of the ancient philosophical effort to sift values and clarify human choices. This would be the function of a contemporary philosophy of practice. It would offer a vocation for philosophy which could invigorate it, and would justify a passionate commitment to it.

NOTES

1. *Theaetetus.*
2. I use this notorious word in full recognition of its tendency to combine a normative and a descriptive function. It is the appropriate word in this context.
3. Hans Morgenthau, *Politics Among Nations*, 2nd ed. (New York, Alfred A. Knopf, 1954).
4. *Ibid.*

A PLEA FOR SOCRATES' HERITAGE

(A RESPONSE)

Walter Kaufmann

I

In *Authors Take Sides on Vietnam*, W. H. Auden says: "Why writers should be canvassed for their opinion on controversial political issues I cannot imagine. Their views have no more authority than those of any reasonably well-educated citizen. Indeed, when read in bulk, the statements made by writers, including the greatest, would seem to indicate that literary talent and political common sense are rarely found together."

Our concern here is with philosophers, not writers; but there are many people, including a large segment of the philosophical community both in the United States and abroad, who would say without hesitation that Auden's dictum applies to philosophers. There is certainly much evidence for saying that philosophical talent and political or, more generally, practical common sense enjoy no natural affinity.

Plato argued that until philosophers become rulers or rulers philosophers, men would continue to be badly governed; but those who mistrust philosophers when they give practical advice have never hesitated to cite Plato as a witness for the prosecution—not a willing witness, to be sure, but an important one.

Those of us who believe in the relevance of philosophy to politics and practice need not take our stand with Plato. Nor need we insist that the genius of philosophy is usually accompanied by an uncommon share of practical common sense. Rather, a training in philosophy might lead us to question common sense, to stand apart from the consensus of the moment, to oppose what Freud and Ibsen called the "compact majority," and to cultivate conscientious independent judgment and a greater sensitivity to intellectual and moral scruples than most men have.

This conception of philosophy is Socratic rather than Platonic. Most contemporary philosophy is neither Socratic nor Platonic but at best Aristotelian and for the most part Neo-Scholastic. There are many schools, as there usually are in scholastic ages, but most competent philosophers belong to one or another of these and take little interest either in rival schools or in the relevance of their own work to questions of practice. Those who take this line can and often do plead the example of the sciences. But while indifference to moral questions may have facilitated the spectacular rise of modern science, the cliquishness of so much contemporary philosophy suggests that philosophy has become scholastic rather than scientific.

Even so it may be argued, and often is, that philosophers, like scientists, ought to aspire toward purity and not worry about practical relevance, as first-rate theoretical work is apt to have quite unforeseen and unforeseeable applications. This is, on the whole, excellent advice, and perhaps it should be followed in nine cases out of ten.

The trouble is that questions of faith, morals, and practice remain, have to be resolved here and now, and *are* resolved—most of the time haphazardly, without the benefit of any rigorous Socratic questioning. If most philosophers did little but busy themselves with questions of that sort, giving unsought advice, one might recall them to other tasks and perhaps also remind them that to earn the right to be heard with respect on any question one has to work hard to gain the necessary competence. But what philosophers need to be told in the present situation is this: If the philosophers do not keep Socrates' heritage alive, who will? If none of us apply our hard-won skills to questions of faith and practice, we abdicate one of our crucial responsibilities. But if we apply ourselves and gain the necessary competence in the fields concerned, we have every reason to suppose that our voices will be heard.

Some philosophers are preachers *manqué*, and some are scientists *manqué*. Some, like Plato, exemplify both tendencies. But Plato and Socrates also compared the philosopher to a physician. There is no need for all philosophers to do the same thing. But let not all who are not preachers try to emulate pure scientists! Let there be a few who don't spurn practice and who don't assume that the only way to take an interest in practice is by preaching!

One can be a brilliant mathematician or logician by the time one reaches twenty. To become a great diagnostician and surgeon takes much longer. It makes little sense for all young men to say, rightly, that they lack the competence to do that kind of work, and to let it go at that. If humanity desperately needs some work to be done, then some people should apply themselves until they have the necessary skills and knowledge. If everybody begs off, humanity will be at the mercy of quacks, faith healers, and witch doctors.

But why, you may ask, should the *philosophers* do this work? While there is no reason why *all* philosophers or *only* philosophers should do it, there are good reasons why *some* philosophers should. First and most important, a training in philosophy is an excellent foundation for a sustained critical scrutiny of beliefs, value systems, and decisions. Secondly, there is no other profession or academic discipline with an equally remarkable and old tradition of such work. Finally, there is no other equally or better prepared group in sight that might take over this task.

II

It should be obvious by now how much I am in overall agreement with Charles Frankel's paper. Where there is such sympathy with a man's central concern, it would be perverse to focus your attention on tangential points. And it would be tedious to recount the ways in which we two agree.

The reservations I wish to voice concern not his aims but his strategy—or perhaps only what some might take him to propose. I am not wholly enthusiastic about his plea for what he calls "philosophy of practice." I doubt that what we need most if we want to meet our responsibilities is another "philosophy of something." The splintering of philosophy and the proliferation of so many subfields are among the symptoms of the new Scholasticism. Plato's *Republic* and Spinoza's *Ethics*, Hume's *Treatise* and Kant's *Critique of Pure Reason* did not fit into any of the numerous pigeonholes of our present-day curricula, and were the better for it. Nowadays we have logic and the history of philosophy, metaphysics and epistemology, ethics and theory of value, social and political philosophy, and the philosophy of art, of education, of history, of language, of law, of mathematics, of mind, of religion, and of science. But the most interesting and important work often cuts across these fields.

Charles Frankel and I share some central concerns and are trying to summon the same energies. The question remains whether these energies should be channeled into yet another subfield. This suggestion strikes me as a symptom of our age, in line with current thought and fashion.

To organize a conference like ours, or to gain support for a project, a label like "philosophy of practice" is invaluable, and some such tag is almost indispensable. What foundation would support a man who said he wished to do what Socrates did? And no man in his senses would submit a project for a book that cut across as many fields as *The Republic* or Spinoza's *Ethics* did. "Philosophy of practice" is the kind of label that may win respect from the foundations and from deans and chairmen. Indeed, it sounds as innocuous as "philosophy of education" or "ethics." But what if the work done in the new field should turn out to *be* just as innocuous as is most work in the philosophy of education and in ethics?

What we need is not so much a *new* field as a rebirth of the Socratic ethos in some of the *old* fields. What we need is some concern with practice on the part of some men who are working in such areas as ethics and political philosophy, philosophy of education and religion, and the rest. What we need is recognition of the fact that it would be a dreadful loss and dangerous for freedom if all of us tried to approximate philosophy to one of the pure sciences; for the unexamined life would flourish.

Those opposed to the scientific model usually plead either that philosophy ought to approximate theology or—as some romantics thought formerly and some existentialists do nowadays—that philosophy should aspire to the condition of literature. Plato is not a man to be agreed with, but there are few, if any philosophers from whom we can learn so much. Among the most important lessons we can learn from him is that all these alternatives are not exhaustive and leave out the paradigm of the physician.

In Plato's *Republic* no Socrates could have grown up or lived to the age of seventy. As campuses, philosophy departments, and public interest in philosophy proliferate, we, too, are creating conditions that are almost bound to stifle the Socratic spirit. We would not sentence Socrates to death; we would offer him a chairmanship, a college presidency, or perhaps a job in Washington. And if we could not lure him into logic or epistemology, like so many other promising young men, and if meta-ethics did not fully satisfy him, we might as a last resort invite him to teach a course in the philosophy of practice.

Even the post of philosopher-in-residence would be better than that. But I cannot offer you a program for developing heirs of Socrates. Only a first step can be recommended here and now. We are relatively tolerant of material heresies or what you might call deviant beliefs. But the academic community is on the whole woefully intolerant of formal heresy or unorthodox manners. This is no plea for incompetence; if anything, our standards are too *low*. We cheerfully tolerate mediocrity as long as the style is orthodox and a chap does philosophy the way philosophy is supposed to be done.

Looking back once more to the quotation with which I began,

what I find disturbing is not that philosophers nowadays lack common sense but rather that, though most talented philosophers are fortunately outside the crumbling American consensus on Vietnam, our philosophical community has developed such a strong consensus of its own. While it may be part of that consensus to question political decisions after hours, we should be more hospitable to rigorous criticism of moral and religious views, of ideologies, of political positions, of the common sense of the establishment—not only the political, religious, or literary establishment, but also the philosophical establishment. And if you are inclined to say that criticism of that sort would not be nice or comfortable, bear in mind that Socrates was neither nice nor comfortable. It is time philosophers stopped paying mere lip service to Socrates.

On this Charles Frankel and I agree, and our agreement far outweighs our differences. The question is how best to develop Socrates' heritage. To have a series of talks and discussions under the general heading of "Philosophy of Practice"—as we do now—is all to the good, and Charles Frankel deserves our gratitude for his crucial contribution. But should we recognize "Philosophy of Practice" as a new branch of philosophy? I fear that in a new subfield Socrates' heritage would be ploughed under as it has been in the old ones. My plea is that in cultivating ethics, philosophy of religion, and the other old fields we examine our traditional faith and morals.

FIRST STEPS IN THE THEORY OF PRACTICE

F. E. Sparshott

Unlike such phrases as "philosophy of history," "philosophy of practice" connotes no generally accepted philosophical discipline. We are thus free to establish our own terms of reference. I shall therefore start by distinguishing four senses of "practice" with a view to determining which if any of them might be suitable for extended philosophical consideration.

First, by "practice" one might mean the whole domain of action, of the practical; philosophy of practice would then be the same as philosophy of the practical. That is usually equated with ethics and political philosophy, but might well be taken more widely. To assume that all practical questions in philosophy are questions of ethics is to impose on our discussions a damaging flatness whose effects are already clear in Aristotle and have not diminished: it is either to make all practical issues into issues of right and wrong, good and evil, or else to ignore as philosophically irrelevant all practical issues that resist such reduction. In either event, one is reduced to a single standpoint to consider lives from, and tends to adopt unawares the intellectually crippling assumption that different choices or ways of life can be discussed only to establish which is "better," and to assume that only one of them can be "right," either absolutely or in relation to a particular agent or a particular decision. The moralization of practical thinking leaves us without any adequate way even of characterizing such questions as whether to become a doctor or a dentist, then whether to be an orthodontist or a periodontist, and so on: when they cannot be put in terms of right or wrong, they are analogously polarized into terms of more or less pleasant. More important, such questions themselves come to be treated, insofar as they cannot be made out to be moral issues, as relatively trivial; yet in real life it is less often the moral decisions than the nonmoral and even nonprudential ones that are the turning points in our lives, such as the decision to marry. Similarly, in their concentration on moral concepts or on the moral dimensions of other practical concepts philosophers tend to ignore such concepts as that of "work," which actually play crucial parts in our practical thinking.

Perhaps, then, it would be better if philosophers emphasized ethics less, and instead developed a general praxiology, or theory of practice, within which ethics might reappear as that special but logically subsidiary zone where it overlapped with general axiology or value-theory. Such a reorganization of the field, which the phenomenologists have in fact begun, would accord with the changes in the status of morality, and hence of ethics, that follow on the development of social and behavioral science. No doubt it is still true that no one can help moralizing, and that moral values must take priority over all others; but the urge to moralize sinks to the level of other psychological needs, and the priority of morality becomes a matter of logic rather than of practice or even of rhetoric. In raising children, the constant use of moral terms is necessary; in dealing with adults, it is seldom even helpful.

Meanwhile, however, most philosophers do equate practical philosophy with ethics. To redraw all the frontiers is a task beyond my powers, if only because I share the prejudice I condemn. I might plead in excuse that, idiomatically, philosophy of practice would be a strange phrase to use if one wished to refer to all that I have hinted a practical philosophy might cover. Conventionally, we restrict the word "practice" to certain more specialized applications. To some of these I now turn.

What one most commonly means by "practice" is what makes perfect, the performance of a task at leisure in order that we may be better able to perform that or a like task at need or for its own sake. But in this (our second) sense there is no evident room for a philosophy of practice. Outside of empirical psychology, all that needs to be said on the matter may well be contained in the Aristotelian treatment of "habit" as part of the theory of practical excellence, even though that inclusion itself exemplifies the very subordination of all practical considerations to moral ones of which I have just complained.

Thirdly, by "practice" one sometimes means accepted procedures, especially in the professions—that is, in those domains where what is done is organized simultaneously by technical and by institutional factors. Since the layman seldom knows on any occasion which of these two sorts of factors has determined what was done, it is not surprising that "professional practice" becomes an independent determinant which cannot be lightly challenged. The theory of such practice must be exiguous, since appeals to practice are made just when no theoretical or technical justification can be (or is going to be) given. "This is the way we do it in Toronto" is the sort of justification that amounts to an admission of unjustifiability—or rather, a refusal to consider whether justification is possible. To concede the existence of professional practice is to respect what used to be called the "mystery" of crafts and professions, that is, their right within certain areas to do things in their own way without abiding the question of outsiders and novices, to "know what they are doing" whether or not they can explain it to themselves or others. Professional practice is, as such, beyond criticism, though what is done in its name may be eminently open to criticism. Its sociology is full of interest, but its philosophical treatment may not go beyond Aristotle's remark that there are many matters in which regulations must be made or regularities observed, but in which it is a matter of indifference precisely what these regularities or regulations may be. This area of antecedent indifference is the proper province of "practice" in this third sense.

Fourthly, the term "practice" is used in a sense in which it is systematically contrasted with "theory": what holds "in theory" is distinguished from what obtains "in practice." In this context, "practice" and "theory" are almost correlative terms, a theory being what justifies or explains a body of practice and practice being the application of the relevant theory.

It might be held that the correlativeness is not strict, since practice as thus conceived is nothing but the application of theory, whereas theory has a life of its own and indeed could not properly be said to be "applied" unless it existed before its application; theory would thus always be the senior partner in the relationship. But I do not think that is so. One might equally well say that theory is always an intellectual construction which begins with the practical and must find its ultimate justification there. If theory has any priority, it is not because of the nature of the case but only because the relationship has, inevitably, been spelled out by theorists who as such have allowed their accounts of it to be infected by their theoretical bias. On balance, the implication of the contrast between theory and practice, as we commonly make it, is that theory and practice constitute distinct realms—theory a realm of mental constructs which never quite fit the real world, practice a world of endeavor which never comes up to theoretical expectations and requirements.

In all that follows I shall be concerned with practice in this fourth sense: with the applications, and failures of application, of theory in practice.

If theory and practice, in these senses, are not merely contra-distinguished, but contrasted, the very notion of a theory of practice may seem perverse and paradoxical: surely practice is precisely that of which, as such, there can be no theory. Practice of which there can be a theory is, insofar as the theory is adequate to it, merely that theory applied, and affords no room for independent theoretical consideration in its practical aspect. But this position is not merely mistaken, but self-defeating, being itself a general theoretical statement about practice. What is true is that no theory can be the theory of that practice which corresponds to it, and that the practical application of any theory must involve considerations going beyond what that theory determines. Theory, as such, deals in general terms with general types of cases, even if those types are so specified that they turn out to cover only one actual case; practice, as such, consists of (or deals with) one particular case at a time, even if that case happens to be exactly like innumerable others. We may invoke here a familiar regress: no theory can include a complete set of rules for its own interpretation and application. Of course, many theories do include (or, more precisely, have annexed to them) sets of such rules, but they are necessarily incomplete, since as rules they are general and hence in the relevant sense theoretical and themselves in need of interpretation and application; and any rules formulated for such interpretation and application will themselves need to be similarly interpreted and applied. But while practice itself comprises particular situations, the concept of practice is a general concept like any other. Consequently, nothing hinders the formation of a theory of practice in general, and of the types of relation that generally hold between practice and theory. Such a theory will attempt a general account (on which we find ourselves already embarked) of why one needs to make and emphasize a distinction between theory and practice, of the kinds of discrepancies and deficiencies in theory that practice has to make good, and of the practical value that theory can have despite these deficiencies.

The way I have now set our problem up might be objected to as implying a notion of theory that is obsolete and even archaic, according to which nature (practice) tries and fails to meet the requirements of divine law (theory). Such a notion of theory is medieval, even Platonic; ever since Galileo showed the equivalence of celestial and terrestrial mechanics we have assumed that phenomena conform with precision to correct physical laws. Observed events represent not approximation to what theory would predict but special cases which the appropriate theory precisely covers. Even a Brownian movement is in principle predictable by a Laplacian calculator, and susceptible of precise mathematical analysis. However, although what this objection urges may well be true and important, it has no bearing on our present proceedings. Although theories may be precise *in theory* they are not so *in practice*. They offer techniques whereby precise solutions might be established on the basis of data precisely ascertained. But there are limits to the accuracy with which data can actually be established, and on the complexity of the calculations that can actually be performed. Even in laboratory conditions where extraneous factors can be largely excluded and materials purified, there are limitations on the accuracy of measurement as well as on the possibility of excluding the irrelevant and incalculable from materials and circumstances. Outside the laboratory, where the environment must be taken largely as it is found, a more general consideration becomes important. Theories may yield precise solutions or call for specific actions only *insofar as* the situation at hand is covered by a description in terms of that theory; and we have seen that no theory can establish that a particular given situation answers to a given description, since the theory mentions no actual situations. Income tax laws, for example, lay down rules by which everyone can compute the tax he should pay, given that he falls into one of a set of exhaustive classifications, and rules for determining into which classification one falls. But it is still up to the courts to decide whether the new set of curtains that I bought last March for my study at home is a legitimate business expense. And beyond such determinations the individual still has to decide whether to try to apply the rules equitably, or to give himself "the benefit of the doubt," or even to cheat; and, even more important, he must decide whether to pay his taxes at all. The law that says he must is the very law he must decide whether to obey; it considers him qua citizen and taxpayer, but he must consider himself qua himself and in every capacity that he has.

Setting aside such questions as arise because more than one set of theoretical considerations may apply to a particular person or society at a particular point in time, indeterminacy arises, as we have now seen, within the scope of application of particular theories. In prudential, legal, moral, and political questions, indeterminacy enters because the relevant classifications of theory are social constructs formulated in the interests of convenience. It is thus in marginal cases indeterminate whether likeness to or difference from standard cases will be found more convenient from the relevant point of view: a court cannot discover, but must decide, whether an omission on someone's part is to count as negligence. In questions involving technology or the exact sciences, indeterminacy is introduced by the limitations on time and technique that restrict the precision with which computations can be made, the accuracy with which initial conditions can be determined, and the extent to which initial and boundary conditions can be controlled to bring them within the scope of practicable application of known and usable theories. These irremovable indeterminacies make a contrast between theory and practice unavoidable; it does not depend on any special or outmoded notions about defects in the terrestrial "world of becoming."

I have been assuming that the general and universal can be equated with the domain of theory, the particular and individual with the domain of practice. These equations seem inescapable, inasmuch as no statement could count as theoretical if it did not go beyond observed events, and one can hardly go beyond observation without having reasons of a general character, while on the other hand to act is necessarily to do something specific in a specific situation. Yet reasons could be given for wishing to qualify both equations. As against the particularity of practice, one might urge that in framing a particular law or formulating a particular policy one is legislating for, or deciding in respect of, an indefinite number of actions. But here we must distinguish. A law is (normally) general in what it prescribes, and thus falls within the scope of theory in relation to the particular actions it purports to regulate; but its formulation, as a particular enactment reached under particular pressures in particular circumstances, qualifies no less clearly as practice. The actual production of any theory is practice. The same applies to the framing of policies and the making of policy decisions, but in these cases there is something spurious in the alleged generality even of the content. A policy is a sort of generalized commitment to make an indefinite number of decisions over a period of time according to a certain rule or principle, but the commitment is provisional in a way in which that embodied in legislation is not: a policy amounts to little more than a recognized regularity of practice. An occasional act that violates the policy is no more than a departure from the regularity, while a series of such acts suffices, without need of pronouncements, to show that the policy has changed. None the less, insofar as the policy is or is acknowledged to be in force, its relation to the particular actions and decisions it covers is precisely that of theory to the relevant practice.

One could press the present line of thought further and claim that every action and decision has an element of generality. If I empty a can of dieldrin into a stream I threaten *whatever* may drink from that stream, and in deciding to do so I am in effect decreeing that whatever drinks shall die no less than if I had passed a law to that effect. One might reply to this contention that the element of generality and indeterminacy here really pertains not to my action but to what I could say about my action. My action as an action affects only those it does affect, and my decision as such is only to perform the one act of pouring, whereas a theoretical statement or pronouncement is essentially about a class or kind whose membership is, so far as the theory goes, open. That reply might be countered in turn by saying that theories likewise only apply to what they turn out to apply to, and that to act is essentially to embrace whatever the natural consequences of the action will be. I may justly be told that I have killed the fish. I do not find this counter convincing, but I know of no effective direct rejoinder; there being no time for an extended analysis, we must leave the matter there. Meanwhile, it remains true that insofar as theory and practice are correlatives, and we decided to treat them so, to think of anything as practice is always to think of it as particular, in relation to some general theory, and to think of anything as theory is to think of it as applying generally to a range of practice.

It is important not to lose sight of this correlative element, that theory is the theory of a certain practice and practice the practice of a certain theory; for contrasts between what is so "in theory" and what holds "in practice" may be made at different levels, and what is theory in one context may count as practice in another. The terms in such contrasts may be higher-order against lower-order generalizations; generalizations against particular cases; or even particular cases as conceptualized, against particular cases as experienced. Whatever the terms, what the contrast imports is the same: what is thought, expected, hoped to be so differs from what is found to be so. And what makes the shift in levels possible is the aspect of falsifiability inseparable from all judgment. What at one level of abstraction or by one criterion of verification counts as established fact may serve in another context as a falsifiable hypothesis.

Since what is said to hold "in theory" may be a particular case as conceptualized, it looks as though our second equation, that of theory with generality, may have to be given up. One can, after all, have "a theory about" a particular occurrence; but the equation fails less often than it seems to. If, for example, one says that the next bus leaves "in theory" at 10:35, what one means, although one ostensibly refers to a particular event, is that there is a general rule to the effect that the bus occupying this one's place in a series is to depart at the stated hour. And although one may have a theory about a particular occurrence, meaning a speculative as opposed to an empirically established explanation of it, what differentiates such explanations from empirical ones is that they can only rest on general notions about what tends to be the case. Experience can show what did happen, but only generalizations can show what might have happened. There is, however, one sort of case in which even this indirect element of generality is lacking. One may say that someone is "in theory" performing a certain action but actually doing something quite different, meaning only that the former is what he intends, or has been told, or is believed, to be doing, and the latter is what he is really accomplishing. Such intentions, instructions, and beliefs, are like theories properly so-called in that they represent what is thought as opposed to what is done, and that the thought was supposed to be effectual in practice but failed to be so.

II

The foregoing general considerations suggest the following program for an enquiry into the theory of practice.

Such an enquiry will formulate the general characteristics of acting, making, and deciding, insofar as they relate to but are not wholly determined by theoretical considerations; the latter being whatever can be expressly formulated as a guide for or description of such acting, making, or deciding. Thus stated the project is meaninglessly extensive, but by confining myself to a sufficiently schematic treatment on an abstract level I hope to reduce it to manageable size.

It should be possible to state what types of relation between theory and practice are in principle possible. These relations might be classified in accordance with the kinds of difficulties that people encounter in practice, and these would be of two main kinds: difficulties in determining what theory to apply, and difficulties in applying theories once determined. But for present purposes I do not want to draw up a schematic classification on these lines. I want to begin by simply enumerating and then briefly discussing seven possibilities.

(1) A theory may be straightforwardly applied to an unproblematic case which it clearly covers, it being assumed that the coverage is so complete that no further theory is relevant.

(2) A theory may be similarly applied but without the question of the adequacy of its coverage being prejudged.

(3) A situation may be confused, so that it is not clear what—if any—the relevant theoretical issues are.

(4) One may know or have decided that no relevant theory is available, and yet have to reach a decision.

(5) Different yet admittedly relevant theories may impose conflicting practical requirements, so that some compromise must be made among conflicting ideals.

(6) Theoretical requirements may be clear, but their implementation impossible for practical reasons; here again some compromise is necessary.

(7) Both these last possibilities must be distinguished from a seventh kind of situation, in which compromise is again demanded, but by

conflicting interests rather than by conflicting or impracticable theories. But these conflict-situations will presumably also belong to one of the other six kinds, depending on whether one has or lacks a theory of conflict resolution and on whether that theory is consistent and workable.

The first of these kinds of situation, the straightforward application of theory, being *ex hypothesi* unproblematic, is the simplest and for purposes of our discussion the normal case, whether or not it often occurs. The heart of its theory, and hence of the theory of practice as a whole, is the doctrine of the practical syllogism. It is in practical reasoning that the syllogism—that is, the argument which subsumes a case under a rule —finds its last resting place, if not its proper home. The theoretical syllogism is out of vogue, partly because more powerful methods in formal logic have enveloped it, partly because the positive sciences which have come to dominate the intellectual world are thought to use other, quantitative, forms of argument; but partly because of a misunderstanding that goes back through Mill to Locke. Syllogism was thought to be heuristically sterile because the major premise could not be established if the conclusion was unknown. But the original idea was that in the order of discovery one did indeed begin with the conclusion, the unexplained fact that S's were P, and arrived at the premises to explain that conclusion by discovering a middle term: S's are P because they are M and whatever is M is P. In the practical syllogism, however, where we have to reach action rather than comprehension, the premises do come first, the major premise summarizing all relevant theoretical data and the minor premise acknowledging their relevance: "And I am that kind of person and this is that kind of situation," as Aristotle put it. And the conclusion to which we then proceed is decision and action, because what made our normal case normal was precisely that all problems were supposed solved in the course of formulating the major premise. The two factors that have made the theoretical syllogism obsolete have no application here. Syllogistic form is always appropriate, because what the minor premise states is inevitable as the basis for action: that an agent finds himself in a situation which he must do something about; and any quantitative factors, or factors involving complex relations, must therefore be included within the terms of the major premise, which can only take the form, "persons of type X in situations of type Y should do Z." Unless such a syllogism is completed, full reasons for acting have not been given. Recent attempts to displace the practical syllogism as the paradigm of practical argument have not usually tried to give an alternative pattern of argument that would fully justify, but have simply reproduced the conversational, hence enthymematic and formally inadequate forms of argument used in "real life."

That first, unproblematic type of situation, as encapsuled in the practical syllogism, may afford a theoretical norm, but it is a norm that is probably never fulfilled in practice. The closest we usually come to it is our second kind of situation, in which the applicability of theory is acknowledged but its adequacy undecided. This raises one of the two main problems of practice.

The major premise of a practical syllogism may be as elaborate as we please, consisting as it does of the complete specification of a type of situation in terms of the sole or total relevant theory. But, whatever its complexity, this theoretical specification must be finite in order to be explicit. A situation can be described only insofar as it is describable. But each situation as encountered in experience is necessarily unique, if only because it is the only situation for which all preceding situations constitute its past, and because the person in that situation is what all his experience up to that moment has made him. The minor premise of the practical syllogism recognizes that the agent's present case answers to a given description, but that recognition cannot imply that the description covers all that the agent will find relevant in deciding.

Setting aside such doubts about the possible inadequacy of any major premise that can be formulated, we should note a much more straightforward limitation on the use of practical syllogisms. In recognizing that a given major premise applies, the minor premise does not require that no other major premise could be applicable. Often, one acts with a given end in view and a given set of theoretical considerations in mind—as when one is engaged in making out a tax return. One can then be confident that a given theoretical description of one's case suffers only from the necessarily excessive generality just described. But one is not always acting in a situation where the problems are thus predetermined and, if one is not, one must decide what one's problem is before one can determine what theoretical considerations are relevant. To formulate a major premise for action is then not to recognize that a body of theory is applicable but to decide that one's overall situation can be reduced to such and such theoretical terms. One could in fact go further and insist that even when acting with a limited end in view one must have reasons for deciding to limit oneself, and that these reasons really form part of the major premise of one's action. It is true that many decisions are taken and much advice given on the assumption that the framework for one's action is fixed, but the fixing of this framework actually represents the major part of one's decision even when it is a part that goes by default.

A major problem of the theory of practice then becomes whether there is any way of determining whether one situation is like another in all relevant respects, or (what comes to the same thing) whether it makes sense to speak of taking into account "all relevant considerations." If it makes sense, we can sometimes "know what to do" in a strong sense of "know," even if we then decide not to do it. But if it makes no sense, and insofar as an element of free decision enters into such determinations and especially into the bringing of deliberation to an end, theory cannot *determine* practice. One must decide what theory, how much theory, and even what sort of theory, to apply. If one carries this line of thought to the point where both the construction and the application of major premises are treated as not merely indeterminate in these ways but quite arbitrary from start to finish, one finds oneself committed to the rhetoric of existentialism.

That rhetoric agrees on one point with those it attacks as "essentialists" and with most theoretical treatments of practical questions. They all tend to assume that for a conventional person in a routine situation there is a conventional theory which could be applied in a routine way; in fact, a conventional person is one who for this very reason finds nothing problematical, and to be unconventional is to reject such fore-ordained solutions. A difficult situation is one in which different conventions conflict. But my experience has been that difficult practical situations are quite unlike anything that these writers have allowed for. Rather than being faced by a repugnant convention, or a hard choice between conventions, one simply finds one's situation confusing. One does not know what theory to apply or how to describe one's predicament at all; nothing appears definite enough to accept or reject. And this was our third type of situation, that in which one does not know what if any theory to apply.

Either/or decisions are common in restaurants, where one can choose soup or juice, but rare in the moral life. By the time one has one's problem reduced to a choice between A and B one's problem is mostly solved. What one initially confronts is the more intractable question of what to do about the situation one is in. Even that formulation of the question goes too far, for it assumes that one already has one's situation analysed and one's problem identified. More realistically, one has to make up one's mind *what to do next*: problems do not formulate themselves without our help. And even here we have assumed that there is a "next," whereas in reality one's life is not a succession of discrete occasions for action but a continuum only articulated by such imperative punctuation as sleeping and sneezing. Yet theoretical treatments of ethics and politics, as well as novels (no less symptomatic of our conventional ways of thinking about our lives, and no less susceptible to the temptation to substitute what can be verbalized for what is the case), tend to assume that lives are made up of a number of separate occasions on each of which one is confronted by one specific problem in which one has to decide between a specific number of clearly formulated alternatives. Some hidden hand, presumably, has prepared the agenda.

One can hardly suppose, however, that so widespread a way of thinking about practical life is simply mistaken. In fact the confusion of practical life as just outlined is the predicament only of individuals in their individuality. Insofar as consciousness is individual and even private, it appears as an "existential" continuum. Insofar as it is shared, consciousness is conceptualized. For men in societies and groups experience is possible only insofar as it is broken up into occasions, problems, and solutions. And this articulation extends to the life of the individual as functionary or as role-player. But it remains, at the personal level, an artificial imposition. Such institutions as the calendar, the timetable, the agenda sheet and the division lobby, whose function is precisely to break the stream of life up into occasions, problems, and solutions, represent a triumph of imagination and will whose familiarity tends to blind us to its magnitude.

Whereas our third kind of situation was that in which one did not know what theory was applicable, the fourth was that in which one knew or had decided that no theoretical considerations applied. It may now appear that that is true of all situations insofar as they belong to an individual's life considered in abstraction from its social structuring, and that no situations are such if the social dimension is taken into account. Before we adduced these considerations one might have supposed that anyone who began in a state of confusion would clarify that confusion and then discover that his situation belonged to one of three kinds. First, certain statable issues might be found to be solely relevant, and a reduction to those terms judged adequate. Second, the adequacy of the theoretical issues found relevant would remain unclear, whether because it was not clear what further specific issues might be found relevant, or because the situation overspilled its theoretical categories, or because one simply did not know how to apply the theory one had. And third, it might be found that no theoretical issues were relevant at all. But now that we have expanded our concept of the theoretical to take in whatever can be made explicit it seems that no case can ever be discovered to belong to this third kind. To establish such a negative proposition is in any case presumably possible only in a theoretically delimited situation such that one can tell that all possibilities have been checked and ruled out; and in a situation so unstructured as the one we are envisaging one could not even get so far as wondering what to do, since to wonder is already to transpose one's situation into the social terms of conceptualized action. However, if one takes "theory" in its more usual acceptance, as a restricted set of elaborated generalizations or precepts, it remains possible, for anything we have said, that one might find that no such theory was applicable to a given case.

This is perhaps the most suitable place to enter, without elaborating, a caveat against our assumption that whatever cannot be treated simply as exemplifying a *kind* of thing is for *all* practical purposes unique. If that were so, insofar as every situation is unlike any other, practice could not make perfect. But, plainly, practice does; and continued practice increases rather than diminishing flexibility of performance. Practice need not consist of a rehearsal of tasks exactly like those to be undertaken, indeed cannot do so, since reality always and necessarily turns out different from what one anticipated. The mental rehearsal of a performance is not itself a performance like that for which it rehearses so much as a sort of dramatization of beliefs about it, and a real rehearsal differs from the performance which it rehearses just in those very features which make it a rehearsal. A *fortiori*, the more generalized activity that we call "practicing" works less by anticipating actual movements to be performed than by developing a versatile skill. If then we take the essence of generality to be common applicability to many particular cases we might take the practiced adaptability of the hand to represent a kind of generality within the domain of practice which is quite different from but is in important ways analogous to the kind of generality which verbal generalization represents. Practice has its own system of likenesses that it exploits and that escape conceptualization. And the basis of this other sort of generality will be that very historicality which we said made all human situations unique. It seems clear that it would be desirable to work out an unmisleading way of describing the practical structures thus generated in relation to conceptual structures, and that this indeed forms a major topic in the theory of practice. But at present it is distracting us from our main theme, to which we now return.

Our fifth, sixth, and seventh kinds of situation I described as those in which compromise was called for. But the use of the same word "compromise" for such different cases leads to confusion. The sixth kind was that in which one fails for merely practical reasons—for lack of money or time or energy—to achieve an unquestioned ideal. What in such cases is called "compromise" is putting up with something inferior; and from such contexts the word "compromise" acquires a derogatory force which it carries over into the other kinds of situation. But these were those in which conflicting ideals had to be brought to accommodation, and those in which, all theoretical and idealistic considerations set aside, mutually incompatible interests of different parties required accommodation. These last two kinds of situation, different as they are, are alike in that they make compromise blameless and often mandatory. In most technical and many practical problems the best solution is not perfect in any one respect because other respects are equally important. In designing an aircraft for a particular task, for example, the best solution is not that which achieves the most suitable speed, or length of takeoff, or economy in operation, that technology allows. On the contrary, no solution which overemphasizes one of these at the expense of the others is acceptable. Good solutions ignore no relevant factor, and an appropriate compromise would not fail of being an optimum solution merely because it was the best that could be done "in an imperfect world." In the other kind of situation, that in which interests conflict, there is no vice in my resigning myself to not getting all I want because that would mean that you got none of what you wanted. On the contrary, such compromises are what justice demands. Yet because a refusal to compromise in our sixth kind of situation is always honorable, if sometimes foolish, one sometimes overlooks that a refusal to compromise in the fifth kind is merely silly and in the seventh kind downright vicious.

The confusion of the three quite different cases is pardonable, if not inevitable, because a given situation may well involve factors of all three kinds. One who tries strenuously to live up to one set of ideals is likely to ignore as irrelevant or invalid all rival ideals, and to deny any legitimacy to any interests that his pursuit may override. His wish to have his ideal fulfilled may seem to others to be an interest in its fulfilment, but to him it is a recognition of what the situation objectively calls for.

Confusion of our three kinds of compromise may however be more than a by-product of fanaticism. My argument here has rested on a distinction between ideals and interests which might be challenged. If all ideals are reducible to interests, all kinds of compromise are in principle defensible. The argument for such a reduction would run as follows. Any contrast between ideals and interests depends on equating ideals with sets of standards defined by a body of accepted technical or prudential theory in abstraction from all actual inclinations of individuals. But no such abstraction is valid. Ideals are really sets of interests grouped on some other principle than that of whose interests they are. They would not be formulated if they did not correspond to someone's interests, and in fact to interests widely shared. For example, one might say that opposition to atmospheric pollution is idealistic. Everyone can see that it is better to have clean air to breathe in cities, not only from the point of view of body chemistry and climatic stability, but simply because it is disgusting to befoul one's environment. And gas-burning cars pollute city air. So the clean air enthusiast may say that the way to the ideal of smog prevention is blocked by the self-interest of people who insist on driving downtown. But really all that is at stake is a choice between two sets of interests: the convenience of clean air and the convenience of the car. Why then is this represented as a conflict between interests and something else? Only because in the one case we are thinking of how what a man does immediately affects his own welfare and that of his neighbors, and in the other case we consider the remoter consequences of actions and how they affect whole groups. But if that is all the difference amounts to, the latter grouping of interests deserves no priority. On the contrary, each man knows best where his own shoes pinch, and the fact that people keep driving downtown shows that they think smog less important than automobility. What is exalted as an "ideal" is then merely a clearly articulated set of behavioral standards, formulated from a restricted point of view by people who are not necessarily going to do the behaving or to suffer from it; what is downgraded as "interests" is an all-embracing but short-range set of standards formulated by those most directly involved.

We seem now to have debunked all ideals, and the very idea of reform, by affirming that what people do shows what they really want, and whatever is, is right. But this devaluation of idealistic reform does not really follow from the reduction of ideals to interests. Given that the set of interests comprised by an ideal is long-term, indirect and widely diffused, an idealist may claim that his ideal is such that if people clearly raised the question of its desirability, which they do not, and if they realized what the effects of their actions would be, which they do not, they would either govern their conduct by the relevant standards or at least blame themselves for not doing so. Car-drivers are not really smog-preferrers; it is just that their exhaust is always behind them. The idealist can thus reinstate his ideals as *true* interests, or interests *in the long run*, or as interests with some other privileged status.

The rights and wrongs of the evaluative issue between "ideals" and "interests" may be set aside for now, to be raised later in a broader setting. Meanwhile we may ask whether the argument just outlined succeeds in reducing ideals to interests. And I think it is at least clear that if there is any reduction it is only a logical analysis. It may be that statements about ideals can all be analyzed into statements about interests; but such analysis hardly touches the initial differentiation of three kinds of situation that we described as conflicts of ideals with interests, of ideals with ideals, and of interests with interests. The only difference made is that we should need another set of terms to pose it in. As it is, we speak of an interest when someone wants something for himself, has a felt want or one that experience tells him he will feel; we speak of an ideal when someone wants to bring a situation about, not because of a want he himself feels or expects to feel, but because of what he believes and would like to see happen. The idealist's interest in his ideal lies not in enjoying the event but in knowing that something is the case, and the interests explicitly at issue are not this cognitive one but those of mankind in general, or of some other class of persons similarly abstractly conceived, in enjoying the event itself. To act for an ideal is to act on principle; to act out of interest is to act for oneself or one's group conceived in a quite concrete way. Interested action pertains to the practical as we are conceiving it, relating to the individual and specific in a concrete situation; idealistic action pertains to the theoretical, to expected consequences of kinds of action and not to actual actions themselves. This being so, we can surely hold fast to our original contention that the notion of compromise is not univocally applicable to all our last three kinds of situation. With that conclusion we complete our review of the seven kinds of situation and start afresh on a consideration of the second main problem of practice. The first problem was that of whether it was ever possible to determine that any theory was adequate to practice; our second problem is the converse, of why practice falls so short of theory.

III

Prima facie, one might have thought that there was a third problem suggested by the foregoing analysis as of equal status with the other two, that of finding nonarbitrary solutions to questions so posed as to exclude theoretical considerations. This problem has been much discussed, for example by Bertrand de Jouvenel and Wayne Leys. For Jouvenel, politics lies in the dynamic response to present situations, and its pure theory can ignore the structural and constitutional questions dear to traditional theorists; for Leys, the art of politics lies in the accommodation of interests that remain diverse within a single community. The terms of reference we have chosen, however, excuse us from considering the theory of such responses and accommodations, important as it is, since what we chose as our province was practice conceived as the correlate of theory.

Why is there such disparity between what people do and what they know how to do? Why does human practice fall so short of human ideals? Why do peoples whose agricultural and progenitive practices will certainly lead to famine in a few years continue those practices? Why do we, with all our skills in the gathering and analysis of information and in the organization of production and distribution, allow many of our own people to remain in poverty and near illiteracy? The evils are admitted, their causes often known, the means to their removal known or discoverable; yet the evils remain. In the war on poverty, who is fighting on the other side? Those troubled by such questions often speak of the wickedness of the human heart, and lament that man's ability to control his environment has not been matched by ability to control himself. But the considerations I mentioned earlier suggest that factors other than wickedness and weakness need to be taken into account.

First, the suggested reforms seem obvious and easy because we think of them as ideals in isolation, in terms of the fruition of particular branches of theory. But if they were implemented it would be as parts of actual ways of life in which other theoretical considerations might be no less important. The implementation of an ideal may prevent the implementation of others in practice, even though there is no theoretical incompatibility between them. We say "everybody could now have so-and-so" just because the technique of providing enough so-and-so for everybody has been mastered, without considering whether a life in which the steps necessary to implement the technique had been taken, and the actual social effects of implementing it realized, would as a whole be desirable. This remains true even when ideals are grouped into utopias: we consider how our lives could be rid of groups of evils, but do not, because we cannot, envisage what living in a society free of those evils would actually be like. To counter this difficulty utopians turn novelists. But even then their imaginations can only give, in the guise of a concrete presentation, a necessarily deceptive schematism. *Ars brevis, vita longa.*

Another difficulty in fitting practice to theory arises not from the multiplicity of ideals and interests but from the multiplicity of agents. Popular writing hides this difficulty by using such phrases as "man can now" or "we can now" do such and such, or simply by using the passive voice and saying that it can be done. But just who is it that can do these things? The man with the knowledge cannot do so without the help of others who lack his knowledge. Even if the results might be such as all would approve, the techniques for getting everyone to adopt the recommended practices might be unavailable. It is futile to consider technology in abstraction from institutions.

One of the problems in this area is that of joint action. Suppose for the sake of argument that everyone agreed that city centers would be cleaner and pleasanter to live in and visit if cars were kept out of them, and that a public transportation system which everyone used would be faster and more convenient than cars are now. Even so, as it is, people are driving, so that public transport is slow and inconvenient. If one person now stops driving it makes little difference to the mess downtown and is inconvenient for him. Each person chooses the better option in his actual context, but the result of these choices taken together is worse for him and for everyone else than the alternative would be.

The case here is analogous to that of the two prisoners in one version of a parable used in Games Theory. There are two partners in crime, such that neither can be convicted without the other's testimony. Each is therefore promised that if he informs he will be prosecuted on a charge carrying a lighter sentence, say three years instead of twenty. Each then reasons as follows. "If my pal peaches, I gain 17 years by telling; if he keeps silence, it makes no difference whether I tell or not." Each will therefore, if prudent, inform on the other, and each will get three years. There is no way in which by prudential reasoning each can achieve the prudentially optimum result and go free. Some of those who tell this fable treat its upshot as paradoxical, but it is not. By the terms of the problem, each is prepared to shop his mate if it suits him, and each is accordingly right not to trust the other. This being so, they do as well as they could expect. If each of them *either* trusted the other not to let him down *or* scorned the role of stool-pigeon, both would go free, and if neither condition was fulfilled they were rash to go into partnership. Uncoordinated selfishnesses are unsuited to joint action.

But while our prisoners, faced with a single problem in a tightly structured situation, could achieve an optimum solution on the basis of mutual trust or private honor, nothing like that is true of our hapless commuters. The question of public versus private transportation has never been defined for them, individually or corporately, as an isolated case for decision. And as they constitute a group of indeterminate size and membership there is no question of their trusting each other or relying on each other's actions. An optimum solution therefore cannot be reached, and practice must fall short of theory. This impossibility of integrating multiple decisions is what the popular talk of what "we" or "man" can do conceals, with its beguiling suggestion of individual or joint agency. Utopians sometimes talk as if there were a process whereby many people could simultaneously agree to make the same complex and radical change in their way of life. But there is no such process. Mastery and acceptance of a technology do not guarantee the feasibility of its actual implementation.

The difficulty of coordinating change is not the only one caused by the difference between the mythical "man" or "us" and the real individuals who do things. I have spoken as if each weighed the consequences of everyone doing A against those of everyone doing B. But this is not the choice that confronts any individual, who can only decide whether he himself will do A or B. Nor is he likely to weigh all the foreseeable results of his doing either. Rather, he will judge of his actions by his intentions. A man who drives downtown does not balance the convenience of driving against the evils of pollution and congestion. Since what he is trying to do is get downtown, that is the only effect of his action that he will consider. Since he does not mean to pollute the atmosphere he will not take into account the chance of doing so. The theories and ideals of utopians, of which our practice falls so sadly short, have to do with the public effects of many people acting in a certain way. But these mass effects are precisely those which the individual agent does not intend, but dismisses as "side effects" if he thinks of them at all. They are not the issue in the context of choice within which he operates. For example, we have been told for years that automation will increase leisure for everybody, simply because the technology of automation makes that possible. But since the introduction of automation has not faced anyone with a situation in which an immediate increase of leisure for himself or for others was a live option, it has not happened.

I have been speaking of the factors that work against spontaneous implementation of theoretically optimum practices. But the same factors inhibit their organized implementation. As a Toronto politician recently said, "You can't stop people driving their cars downtown." He did not mean that it was technically impossible to barricade roads, prohibit the sale of gasoline, forbid parking, or even refrain from building freeways; he meant that it was institutionally impracticable. The institutions that initiate, administer and enforce laws are, of necessity, practically oriented; consequently, like individuals, they are subject to routines in which only certain choices present themselves, and genuinely new possibilities can scarcely be formulated. And besides the inertia of routine, the immediate pressures on them are those of the present objectives of individuals.

So fundamental a theorem of the theory of practice as the unsuitability of institutions with an immediate practical orientation for carrying out reforms theoretically conceived is of course no novelty. It was already expounded in that pioneering study of the logic of utopianism, Plato's *Republic*. And the inevitable inference is Plato's that cultural revolutions need revolutionary institutions to bring them about. Consent may never come and can never be engineered, since no propaganda can replace evident by inevident satisfactions as the mainspring of immediate action; consent must follow on the actual reform, when its satisfactions become evident. The gap between theory and practice can be closed only by violence.

Violence, however, is no solution. Major changes in ways of living resist satisfactory enforcement. One can compel actions, but not styles, and it is easier to shatter an old routine than to establish a new one. One cannot sit on bayonets even if one makes a new chair out of them. More important, our experience of revolution suggests that violence has its own momentum, tending to engender more violence rather than to forward whatever objectives it was ostensibly employed for. There is nothing mysterious about this. New political means, being means only, can in themselves have no theoretical bias. Consequently, they are taken over by the existing practical pressures.

It is instructive to see how Plato handles this point. He begins by postulating an avowed miracle: that the revolutionary theorist should have at his command a docile force whose ultimate responsibility is to someone else, so that it can be got rid of when its work is done. Meanwhile, under its shadow, the theorist builds up a new force that is inherently indoctrinated with the relevant ideology. The new force cannot be used in the classical fashion to carry out a purge and liquidate the old force which brought the revolution about, though Plato knows of and alludes to this practice, because a force that was available for such purposes would be one whose institutional orientation was to violence as such, since its force would have to be freely disposable; and this orientation would be incompatible with the theoretical orientation which alone could make it safe for its intended purpose. Hence the original force must be withdrawn by the outside power when its initial task is over. Since this miracle is unlikely to happen, utopian revolutions are unlikely to work out.

If spontaneous consensus, political action and violence are alike unavailable for the purpose, the gap between theory and practice cannot be closed at all, and there is no way to bring about even a clearly envisioned and universally approved good except insofar as it can be brought into alignment with necessary choices made in terms of interests having no necessary connection with it. It follows that in such times as ours, times of rapidly changing technology and great advances in intercommunication and social knowledge, political practice can do little to forward, and is likely to be largely irrelevant to, the solution of what any thinking person must take to be the chief practical problems of his age.

I have been assuming that a theoretical possibility might be an unmitigated and uncontroversial good, and that whatever price might be demanded would be one that all would be glad to have paid. But perhaps this assumption is not merely seldom justified but actually non-sensical. Calculations of expected advantage must be theoretical throughout; one would not really be opting for the concrete life he was going to live, since what that would be like could only be discovered in the living of it. I made this point earlier against fanatics and utopians, but it holds more generally. Perhaps it is never true that practice falls short of theory, because theory is logically incapable of determining practice and the expression "falling short" is therefore inappropriate. Theory is one thing and practice another, and they are incommensurate. What theory offers is a practical pig in a poke; and one may reasonably refuse to give up a way of life whose inconveniences, however grave, are known to be endurable because one has endured them, in favor of one whose benefits might be offset by unforeseen evils that one would not know how to endure. Conservatives reasonably defend their felt but un-formalized goods. And yet, how can they defend them? To defend is to give reasons, but to give reasons is to invoke theory, and to invoke theory against reliance on theory seems self-defeating. The conservative is driven to take refuge in inarticulateness, in affirming his preferences and announcing his attachments, meeting all arguments in favor of re-form with the counter, "That *sounds* all right, but when you've been around here as long as I have you'll know how things are." The point I wish to make is that this stance is not an irrational one just because it abjures reasons. On the contrary, there are solid arguments in its favor.

In taking refuge in silence, the conscious conservative aligns himself with the naturally inarticulate. Mention of the latter should remind us that the presumption that if an opinion goes uncontradicted it enjoys universal support is unlikely to be legitimate: all we are entitled to say is that it has the support of the articulate. And since articulate people share their articulateness it may well be that they share values that oth-ers do not have. The day when practice at last matches up to theory may be the day when the articulate people manage to impose total frus-tration on the inarticulate. The presumption that the theoretically best measure (so-called) would be seen to be best once it was established may be falsified, not because there are aspects of the textures of actual lives that escape it (which is the conservative's case), but because the decision we call "theoretically best" may rest merely on a consensus of those sharing a particular bias. Some reformers, like J. S. Mill, speak of those outside this consensus as unenlightened fools whose condition might be remedied by education. But it may be that the consensus cov-ers only those whose IQ is 120 or more, whereas by definition half the population have IQ's of 100 or less. No doubt the opinions of slow wit-ted people are negligible, and this negligibility extends to their assessment of their own "interests" in the sense of the effect of actions on their wellbeing. But that is no reason for devaluing their likes and dislikes, or the valuation they set on what public welfare experts define as their "needs" or "best interests."

I have been suggesting that the theoretical hostility to theory may take the form either of a defence of life's richness against doctrinaire reduction, or of championing the simple man against the bullying of conceited sophisticates. But it may also be a defence of the autonomy of practical wisdom against the imposition of irrelevant forms, such as the practical syllogism, borrowed from the realm of theory. What is so wonderful about theory, after all? Consider the difficulty, pain, and inefficiency with which even such professional theorists as ourselves reach theories that even they can accept, let alone others; and then think of the ease and grace with which anyone can perform such feats as sitting down on a low sofa without spilling a cup of coffee. When we think of the achievements of science and mathematics, what we have in mind is the successful residue of a tremendous amount of bungling and guesswork: it is not the average quality, but the highest achievement, of theoretical thinking that determines the outcome. But in the world of practical affairs what counts is the average quality of thought, since it is what is thought at the time that determines what is done. And in the average quality of thought, man the theorist is a bungler, man the practical agent is deft, and his dexterity extends to the conduct of everyday life and personal relationships wherever these are guided by practical watchful responsiveness rather than the application of general rules. To make action into the practice of theory is to submit the best operations of the mind to the tyranny of the worst. Conceptualizations, and *a fortiori* rules, and *a fortissimo* doctrines, are at best mere adjuncts to the practical wisdom of the experienced man.

We are thus led once more to oppose the existentialist to the essentialist viewpoint. The latter sees life as exemplifying truths and realizing more or less perfectly patterns statically conceived; the former sees life as historical, every action being based on immediate free decision informed by the sum of previous experience but not deduced therefrom. And essentialism is quite unsuitable to practice. The essentialist who tries to do justice to life's complexities may find himself in the absurd position of equating a lifetime's experience with a monstrously extended major premise. *Praxis* is not an inadequate attempt to achieve the order of *theoria*, but has its own order, a historical order which is temporal through and through.

The existential viewpoint just expounded makes a sound point; but in asserting the autonomy of practice and cutting it off from theory altogether, its purport seems to be to reduce all science and technology, all knowledge of cause and effect, to mere conveniences, even free inventions of the mind. And that simply will not do, because what we know as science and technology is precisely the successful residue of theory winnowed by practice. In general, the uniqueness of situations and the self-transcendence of humanity do nothing to lessen the truth and importance of statements couched in general terms or based on general knowledge. A man can know, and may need to know, what will follow if he performs an action of a certain kind, and what will happen if everyone does the same. What he then knows will not be the whole truth about any situation, but will none the less be an important part of the truth.

If we are to do justice to the objections raised on behalf of the conservative, the existentialist, the inarticulate man and the vulgarian, we must admit that our initial statement of the problem of practice was tendentious. Our attempt to hold apart the three kinds of situation calling for compromise has failed us. What we called the inability of human practice to live up to human theoretical attainments may after all equally be represented as a clinging to an alternative set of standards or as a refusal to allow one's legitimate interests to be overridden. The main problem for a theory of practice then becomes not, as we called it, that of explaining a resistance, but that of exploring a tension. And this tension is not illuminatingly explained as one between the general and the particular or between thought and action. Rather, as we suggested before, it holds between two inseparable but in a sense irreconcilable aspects of human life, the private and the public: two orders, each of which has its own unassailable validity within the domain of the practical itself. Each of us has his own continuous history from birth to death, in which his life both as agent and as experient defies reduction to the describable. But each of us can only live as a member of groups with whom he communicates only in terms of what can be described, terms imposed by local conceptualizations and conditions of description. Variable as these terms themselves are, questions posed in them may admit of unequivocal and truthful answers. These considerations might tempt us to equate the personal with the incommunicable and the social with the communicated; but before doing so we should recall that each of us can represent his life *to himself* only in terms of the concepts current in his society, and that the actual lives of societies, as aggregates of the lives or shared parts of lives of their members, resist conceptualization just as those of their constituent individuals do. The task of exploring the interpenetration of these two kinds of order in human life has been among the major enterprises of the philosophy of this century, to which analysts and existentialists alike have contributed in their various ways. And it is in the direction of this complex inquiry that our first steps in the theory of practice have taken us.

IV

My remarks have been schematic and abstract, as my professional affiliation demands. Could anything so rarefied have practical relevance? Perhaps it entitles us to say that, if we revert to our earlier statement of the second major problem of practice, how practice can match up to the best theory, no sort of solution in general terms is possible. What we took for mere obstacles to the implementation of ideals turn out to camouflage a deeper disharmony. Man cannot after all make himself, but must grow; even the most urgent reforms require caution and sensitivity, and people may be expected to adjust to them in unpredicted ways. What jeremiahs have diagnosed as a social malaise of a decadent society may be a maladjustment inevitable in any age where theory and technology change steadily and fast, and simply reflects the fact that the rhythms of practice are not those of theory. This being so, I derive an admittedly irrational comfort from the fact, apparently established by carbon-14 datings, that the neolithic revolution took place some millennia earlier than was once thought. Perhaps we must expect that it will take millennia rather than decades before our own cultural revolution settles down into an order of tolerable stability and grace. We must not become disillusioned with our social engineering if it fails to bring universal happiness: its difficulties are not grave, but insuperable.

THE PHILOSOPHY OF PRACTICE AND SOME PRACTICES OF PHILOSOPHERS

(A RESPONSE)

James Gutmann

My principal difficulty in responding to Professor Sparshott's paper is a lack of specific points with which to disagree. Fortunately this is not a debate; destructive argument though not unknown among the multifarious practices of philosophers is not necessary when men meet to reason with one another, and the term *responding* gives me what has been called "much room for scope." I find myself in such substantial agreement with Mr. Sparshott's viewpoint, analyses, and program, that the most appropriate procedure might be for me to yield my allotted space to the gentleman from Toronto and ask him to add to the First Steps, specified in his title, some further advances. But, indeed, his title like his paper as a whole is all too modest and he has, I think, taken more than a few steps in developing a Theory of Practice which must do justice to the complex data which any adequate Philosophy of Practice should take into account. At one point in Professor Sparshott's essay I thought I detected an illicit reductionism, only to turn the page and find the author making the necessary correction himself. In all his first steps and his intimation of further steps which he is clearly ready to take, I believe I found only one *faux pas*. If I may mix metaphors and, so to speak, put foot in mouth, I am not even certain that Mr. Sparshott may not have had his tongue in his cheek when he wrote: "To make action into the practice of theory is to submit the best operations of the mind to the tyranny of the worst." You may recall that he had contrasted the fruitful wisdom of the practical man with the all too frequent folly of the impractical theorist and that he added to the above statement—which seems to me to carry irony (if such it be) to excess —the more moderate assertion that: "Conceptualization, and *a fortiori* rules, and *a fortissimo* doctrines, are at best mere adjuncts to the practical wisdom of the experienced man." To my hesitation about the earlier

45

sentence, I am disposed to add a query as to why conceptualizations, rules, and doctrines are *mere* adjuncts. Why must they be so belittled? To recognize them as adjuncts of practice would satisfy me and, I venture to hope, should gratify Professor Sparshott. That little word "mere" seems merely gratuitous and not quite good enough coming from the author of *An Enquiry into Goodness*.

I hope I am moving in the direction of Dr. Sparshott's admirable First Steps if I propose the assertion—which I shall in any case attempt to develop and justify briefly—that a prime test of any Theory of Practice or Philosophy of Practice should be an improved Practice of Philosophy. I do not, of course, mean that this should be the only outcome, which might imply that I am trying to revive a view of philosophy that is best symbolized by a serpent busily engaged in satisfying its hunger by swallowing its own tail. Nothing could be further from my intention or, I trust, Mr. Sparshott's. But I had hoped that someone would at long last reply to Harold Taylor's perennial *mene, mene, tekel upharsin*. My friend Taylor, and others, have been saying these things so often and so long that I really think it's time to ask whether it's all necessarily so. Modesty forbids my attempting to do the entire job myself but with the hope of using what I have learned from Professor Sparshott, I propose to take a step or two in that direction. If I falter I hope that others, better equipped, will sustain me or carry on when I fall.

Now let me say that I share many—perhaps most—of Harold Taylor's judgments and, indeed, some of his prejudices. As a student of John Dewey's I think I anticipated, not only by a number of years but in some other ways, ideas highly relevant to the topics of this conference, which were central to the interests of Taylor's great friend and teacher, Max Otto. Much in contemporary philosophy disturbs and distresses me as it does Taylor: the absorbtion in semantics and problems of language which all too often seem remote from other problems of men and at times almost become a kind of anti-philosophy. But, apparently unlike Harold Taylor, I think one can distinguish the significant use of linguistic analysis from its trivial and artificial manifestations and recognize that in the work of an Austin, for example, there is not only a skill and elegance which lesser disciples might well emulate, but a powerful tool relevant to at least some of the persistent problems of philosophy. If the therapy which philosophical analysis claims to provide leaves the body of *Philosophia Perennis* in a state and condition which might call for the application of the procedures of *habeas corpus*, it does not follow that everything which claims to be in the great tradition must be safeguarded from attack by analysts or any other group of serious critics. I learned long ago from Dewey and F. J. E. Woodbridge and Felix

Adler and, more recently, in different ways from G. E. Moore and Ernst Cassirer that not everything which claims to be *Philosophia Perennis* is, in sober fact, in the great tradition or—I would prefer to say—in any of several such lines of descent. Nor would Harold Taylor, I trust, base his accusations against the futility of much that today passes as philosophy on adherence to tradition. Moreover, the tradition of scolding even the most extreme advocates of what I have just called a kind of anti-philosophy seems to me as futile as what they are themselves doing, and I wish that Taylor and Company would stop scolding and get on with the business of philosophy. I do not mean one system of philosophy or another —not even his and mine though I think it has considerable merit—but Philosophy in all or almost all its guises. I cannot now presume to define that business as a whole but, taking my cue from Professor Sparshott, I propose to illustrate it as I see it. First, however, let me add a word about tradition in philosophy in one specific aspect.

In recent years there has been a widespread tendency to de-emphasize the study of the History of Philosophy. This I deplore (like Harold Taylor, I do my share of deploring) and greatly regret the increasing readiness on the part of teachers of philosophy to let the history of philosophy be taught as incidental to the general history of culture (while recognizing that it has a place there too) or as an aspect of a literary history of ideas. Let me repeat that I claim no monopoly for Departments of Philosophy with regard to the teaching of the History of Philosophy or, for that matter, with regard to other aspects of philosophy as well. But I think a neglect of the History of Philosophy impoverishes the study of philosophy. From Woodbridge and Adler I learned to think of past philosophers as Witnesses to be studied not as sources of Final Truth (despite Goethe's dictum: *Die Wahrheit war schon längst gefunden*) but as sources of evidence to be examined, weighed, and, as far as possible, tested to determine the nature of their power.

To test as far as possible: that, I think, is what gives priority to Professor Sparshott's "practical wisdom of the experienced man." That this "experienced man" need not be in any technical sense a philosopher is manifest, though every now and then even an academic philosopher might also be a man of experience and, indeed, a lover of practical wisdom. In saying this I may be disputing a remark by Professor Joseph Gilbert as reported in the *Times*, to the effect that "the philosopher has nothing special to say about social problems." Unless the term "special" has some special significance or unless the entire statement is a value judgment rather than a description of philosophic discourse from Plato and Aristotle, through Augustine to Hobbes and Spinoza—I skip blithely down the centuries—on to the proximate present of John

Dewey and Bertrand Russell and, indeed, Sidney Hook, I find Professor Gilbert's assertion altogether baffling. Is social philosophy not a branch of philosophy? Are philosophical scholars, whose professional concerns are primarily with social problems, no longer to be recognized as philosophers? I trust we are not to make the preposterous assumption that all philosophers are Professors of Philosophy or, alas, *vice versa*. Perhaps what is at stake, is the view that training in some philosophical methodology gives no warrant for assuming competence in the application of that method to all and every subject matter. With such a view I am, of course, heartily in agreement; and this is a principal reason for my argument—that a study of the history of philosophy as well as other disciplines is prerequisite for a Philosophy of Practice as well for the practice of philosophy in other areas associated with our discipline.

Let me briefly particularize by citing a few specific instances both from the history of philosophy and from contemporary attempts to apply philosophy to practice. My first case may seem to make Professor Sparshott's formulation, to which I initially took exception, an understatement of the contrast between theory as the worst operation of the mind, and practice—free from enfeebling theory—as the best operation. Though the traditions of western medicine go back to the Egyptians and the Greeks and no worthier expression of the ideals of medical practice has been formulated than the Hippocratic Oath, which successive generations of physicians take in transition from studious apprenticeship to full initiation into the medical fraternity, the practical control of therapy is, in many jurisdictions, relatively recent. Less than two centuries ago, at least in parts of western Europe, a philosopher holding theories of therapy was able, apparently without hindrance, to attempt treatments. One instance of this was Friedrich Schelling who, in his youth, seems to have felt confident that his speculations and experiments connected with *Naturphilosophie* qualified him to undertake the cure of patients. In at least one instance—the illness of his step-daughter—the consequences were tragic and Schelling's ministrations if they did not cause, certainly did not prevent, the young girl's death. As one part of my present argument is the salutary effect of practical experience on philosophic theory, it would be gratifying to be able to report that Schelling's latter speculations were more sober and responsible than this early misapplication of theory. I believe that there is warrant for such a claim— perhaps Schelling's turning from his youthful philosophy of medicine to his final philosophy of mythology is evidence enough; there is in any case no reason to suspect that Dr. Schelling's medical practice led to any further fatalities.

Turning from this melancholy and macabre instance of the failure of theory, let me suggest a few more fortunate instances of philosophy in the fields of practice. Less speculative than Schelling, less directly responsible for the direct application of theory to practice than numerous other philosophers, Jeremy Bentham's involvement with social reform might primarily be called observational and advisory. At least with regard to his interest in parliamentary politics, his *Principles of Morals and Legislation* and, even more clearly, his *Catechism of Parliamentary Reform* reflect the close observations of the attentive auditor of parliamentary debates. His proposals for the codification of the civil law, for revision of the criminal code, for penal reform and numerous other causes are, in large measure, the product of these experiences. Also, it may be noted, are many of the most pointed and entertaining instances of fallacies which he recorded in public debates and categorized with high comedy (would that contemporary logicians might similarly enliven their pages).

As a third and final instance of the reciprocal relations between philosophic speculation and practical experience I choose the obvious one of educational theory and practice. This may, indeed, seem more obvious in our culture than it necessarily is in others because we tend to assume the identification of philosophers with professors of philosophy, an assumption which I claim no originality for having already questioned. One need not labor the point that expertise in philosophy is far from being a guarantee of pedagogic skill. I will not expatiate but am glad to use this opportunity to call into question a frequently expressed opinion, expressed even by some who esteem and admire John Dewey's contributions to educational theory, that he was himself an inferior teacher. I would like emphatically to deny this assertion. That he was seldom if ever a pedagogic performer is true but that, as a teacher, he was above all exemplary of what Emerson defined as the scholar in the right state, *man thinking*, is the important point. Even with regard to such considerations as organization and exposition I can add my testimony, having recently had occasion to read my notebooks taken in his classes. Moreover, in the context of our present discussion, I venture to suggest that Dewey's lifelong preoccupation with actual schools and notably his early responsibilities, shared with his wife Alice Dewey, in the organization and administration of the Chicago University School, contributed mightily to his authority as a philosopher of education and as a teacher of teachers. Letters about the Chicago school in its formative years are filled with evidence of this intimate relationship.

Turning to more recent instances of the potentially fruitful relation of reciprocity between theory and practice, I am tempted to rest my case by the simple process of pointing to this program of the Interna-

tional Philosophy Year. I doubt whether I need even go beyond the list
of principal speakers on this week's program and I trust Senator
McGovern does not object to my bracketing him in this way with my
academic colleagues. We have, for better or worse, not yet reached the
ultimate of a philosopher king but those who have heard or read Senator McGovern's speeches, both in the Senate and elsewhere, might well
wish to substitute an executive for the legislative office he so admirably
fills. Perhaps Professor Frankel comes closest to being a philosopher
king. Strange as it seems, he is the first academician to occupy the post
of United States Assistant Secretary of State for Cultural Affairs since
the creation of that office. Perhaps this is an appropriate point for me to
reveal something I only recently discovered about Mr. Sparshott himself. I think it should be shouted in Gath and proclaimed in the streets
of Askalon, that Professor Sparshott is not only a subtle theorist but a
public practitioner, *a practicing poet!*

But instead of telling you what most of you already know about my
distinguished colleagues on this program, let me try to draw my thought
together in conclusion by quite immodestly revealing certain very modest efforts I have been given opportunity to make in recent years, to put
into practice some of the things I have been teaching for more than five
decades. It may be that I will be giving support and confirmation to the
one assertion in Dr. Sparshott's essay which I set out to criticize and
will demonstrate that my worst weaknesses as a theorist have suborned
my best opportunities as a practitioner.

Most of all I would like to address these concluding remarks to the
students in our audience and particularly to those who are thinking of
becoming teachers. To those of them who are, to use the current term,
"activists" let me begin by admitting that, in protest against the United
States' involvement in the First World War, I took part in the march
on Washington led by Norman Thomas in April 1917. Nor would I
have you think that I regard such activism as youthful folly; not long
ago I marched through Harlem, this time led by a phalanx of Roman
Catholic nuns in a civil rights demonstration. Yet, even though academic life is seldom quite the seclusion of the proverbial ivory tower, I
must confess that many times in campus committee meetings and elsewhere I wondered about—though I did not use the phrase—the practice
of philosophy and a philosophy of practice. I think, or at least hope,
that the teaching of philosophy gains from the teacher's involvement in
so-called outside activities. But time and opportunity are for many of us
limited and so, like other academicians, as retirement approached
(though happily no one need ever retire from philosophy!) I promised
myself to enlarge my horizons by devoting more time to causes I had al-

ready engaged in and adding some others. This is not an autobiography and I will not only be brief but limit myself to a sentence or two about three activities I have engaged in during the past five years, practicing interests which had previously been largely theoretical. My three illustrations parallel the historical instances cited above, though in the reverse order: education both academic and nonacademic; parliament watching *a la Bentham*; and medicine, I trust not *a la Schelling*.

In the American Civil Liberties Union, of which I had previously been a passive member, I have found rewarding activities more particularly in its Academic Freedom Committee. In the Encampment for Citizenship I have been fortunate to be able to join others trying to put convictions, not to say theories, to practice. An interest in Human Rights has led me with some regularity to attend sessions of the Trusteeship and Social and Economic Councils of the United Nations—I fear without attaining a Benthamite perspective though I hope I have not merely added to his collection of fallacies. Finally, though I have not emulated Schelling in attempting to practice medicine, I have taken an active part in the past five years in a Citizen's Committee for Public Health.

This last is, perhaps, the best illustration of how philosophic training can hopefully serve practical purposes of a variety of kinds. For I was asked to serve precisely because of my ignorance. This is a qualification which opens up vast perspectives of multifarious opportunities though one would, presumably, not want to build a career on it even in retirement! However little I and my fellow laymen have contributed to the councils of physicians, public health officials, nursing and medical educators, we common garden variety citizens have had opportunities to learn much and on occasion to contribute our bit of presumed wisdom. It would be impossible to measure the relation of theory and practice in any of these operations. Indeed all of this has been little more than an elaboration of John Dewey's conviction, echoed in part by Professor Sparshott, that philosophic issues derive from felt difficulties in practical situations and, as I have ventured to add, suggesting hypotheses and theories to be tested and sometimes verified by fruitful application in further practice.

DOUBTS ABOUT JUSTICE*

Walter Kaufmann

I

Reflection on justice has been close to the heart of Western philosophy at least since Plato; it has been prominent in British moral philosophy; and it attracts some of the best minds today. But most contemporary moral philosophers are as blind historically as were Plato and Kant, Hume, and Mill. Nor does it accord with current etiquette to state at the outset why one is interested in the topic one writes about.

My interest in justice is twofold. First, it is existential. I have found myself in situations—or to use less existentialist terminology, on committees—where it was my task to try to make just distributions. As we distributed coveted admissions to a small percentage of students who wished to do graduate work, or raises and promotions to younger colleagues, or Fulbright grants to colleagues all over the country, I found most philosophical discussions of justice oddly irrelevant. Many other authors must have been in comparable situations, but for the most part their writings on the subject do not show it. The point is not that they do not mention such prosaic situations, but rather that these situations point up limitations of otherwise acute analyses of justice.

* Earlier versions of this paper were presented at The University of Pennsylvania on Law Day, May 1, 1965, and as the Dr. Joseph and Rosemary Shuchart Backlar Memorial Lecture, sponsored by The University of Judaism in Los Angeles, May 16, 1966. On the former occasion, Martin Luther King, Jr., spoke after me, and the lectures were followed by a panel discussion. I now dedicate this paper to the memory of Martin Luther King, Jr., who fought injustice, embodying and teaching pride, courage, gentleness, and unconquerable freedom from resentment —"out of the mountain of despair a stone of hope."

Some of the ideas in this paper, which was read, except for a few minor additions, at the International Philosophy Year at Brockport, New York, in November, 1967, are developed further in "The Origin of Justice," *Review of Metaphysics*, December, 1969, and in "Black and White," *Survey: A Journal of Soviet and East European Studies*, Autumn 1969.

This reason might suffice, the more so because the existential interest extends far beyond the relatively trivial instances I have mentioned. The moral issues between avowedly capitalistic and avowedly socialistic countries revolve around justice—or at least injustice. So does the civil rights crisis at home. If we include so-called retributive justice, we may add that the central crisis in penology and criminal law for more than a generation now concerns the question whether we should not be better off if we abandoned the very idea of retributive justice, concentrating instead on deterrence and reform. Nothing more needs to be said to establish the importance of the subject of justice.

Even so I have another reason for dealing with it. In 1952 I laid aside a project in social philosophy for other studies, but my work during the next fifteen years has brought me again and again to the brink of justice. A single example will suffice. The relevance of Nietzsche and existentialism to ethics is a commonplace, but references to both by British and American moral philosophers are scarce and usually incredibly ill informed. The time has come to continue what Nietzsche and some of his successors have begun. Still, I shall not deal with their ideas about ethics; I shall concentrate on developing some of my own. But before attempting a detailed analysis of justice, I shall try to sketch our historical context.

II

I want to distinguish three phases of the current crisis in morality. This is not to say that there are only three, but since I merely want to suggest in broad outlines at what historic juncture we are standing now, it would be foolish to even mention more than three.

The first phase is *the growth of moral skepticism*. This is so familiar that it should suffice to enumerate a few of its elements.

1. For the majority of mankind, religion has lost its authority in moral matters. In the United States, God is still invoked occasionally to back up conflicting positions that were reached in the first place without the benefit of the clergy or the Bible. But even those who still invoke the Bible or their own religious tradition usually pick and choose what they find morally acceptable. A moral conflict between God's commands and their own conscience seems unthinkable to most of our contemporaries. They assume that if even they can see that something is wrong, God must see it too; and if the Bible or tradition do not bear this out, then somebody must have got God wrong. Thus God's name is used in vain. When it is invoked in moral matters, we are almost always confronted with a ritualistic redundancy.

2. Not only has religion lost its authority in moral matters; our

whole way of thinking has become anti-authoritarian. This is largely due to the rise of science and more important than the battles between science and religion that are commonly associated with Galileo's name and Darwin's. We have learned the habit of asking: What precisely does this mean? What speaks for it, what against it? What alternatives are available and which are to be preferred? Once these questions become instinctive enough to be directed also toward moral statements, we have moral skepticism. The development of the social sciences has done its share to make this explicit.

3. Increased social mobility has also contributed to this development. Rare is the American family in which all children live out their lives in the town in which they were born. Young people encounter many different environments and are exposed to different mores. Travel is becoming ever more widespread. All this helps to make unthinking absolutism rarer and rarer among the young, while moral skepticism is gaining ground. Had we stopped with the second point, it would stand to reason that the trend must be far more advanced among professors, and especially philosophers, than among students. In fact, this is not so: our moral philosophers tend to be more conservative than many of their students. This is due, at least in part, to the fact that many older men lived in a more stable environment when they were young, under the tutelage of parents and teachers who were still closer to absolutism, while those who are students now cannot recall stability, having been born into a world wounded by Auschwitz and Nagasaki.

Not only has war eroded moral standards, but service in armies of occupation has accelerated the growth of moral skepticism. So has the fact that more and more people live in big cities where—though not quite as much as in an army abroad—one can get away with behavior unthinkable in a small home town.

4. Both the atrocities of our time and the vast anonymity of metropolitan life have contributed to a widening sense of futility among young people. Millions have come to feel that they no longer count and that what they do or don't do will make no difference. Many have gone beyond moral skepticism into moral nihilism. From the reasonable position that whatever they do may not make any difference a million years hence, and perhaps not even 100 years hence, they infer fallaciously that therefore it makes no difference. In fact, what we do or do not do may make a tremendous difference to us and our fellow men right now.

So much for the first phase, the growth of moral skepticism. The second phase is *skepticism about law*. As for *natural law*, the collapse of any widespread belief in that is implicit in the growth of moral skepticism. The very concept of natural law is not widely familiar: philosophers, lawyers, and theologians know it; few others do. Not only is the concept mildly esoteric, but the idea that a single moral law is binding on all men, regardless of historical period or geography, no longer seems plausible to most educated people. The Roman Catholic church still clings to this notion, but few except Catholics do; and many Catholic theologians defend the Inquisition by saying that it was justified in its time but would not be justifiable today. The ferment within Catholicism today does not need stressing.

There remains *positive law*, the law actually in force in a state. The man who did most to promote skepticism about the moral authority of positive law was Hitler. Whatever one may think of the many war crimes trials from Nürnberg to Jerusalem, they did their share to convince millions that upholding and obeying the law of the state in which he lives is not always every citizen's moral duty. What a few had learned earlier from Sophocles' *Antigone*, Thoreau, Tolstoy, or Gandhi, large masses of people learned from the Nazi experience. Not only is disobedience to positive law sometimes defensible; there are times when it is a duty.

Politicians point to the loss of respect for the law to inveigh against it. One can also try to comprehend it as part of a larger development, as a second phase that takes us beyond the growth of moral skepticism. Instead of deploring it one can applaud at least some movements of civil disobedience. But the question remains in what cases civil disobedience is defensible, and when it is morally a duty.

The easy way out is to introduce natural law at this point, saying: We may, or even ought to, disobey positive law whenever it comes into conflict with natural law. By beginning my account with the growth of moral skepticism and the collapse of natural law, I meant to suggest that those who are counseling us to take this way out are advising us to return to the womb. We can no more return to such naive absolutism than "a flying bird can re-enter the egg shell from which it has emerged" —to quote Tolstoy's words from his *Reply to the Edict of Excommunication* issued against him by the Russian Orthodox church.

Another way out is more popular today: We are told that we may, or ought to, disobey unjust laws, because justice takes precedence over law. With that we come to the third phase of the crisis in morality: *doubts about justice.*

The growth of moral skepticism (phase 1) is one of the most striking features of the twentieth century. In the nineteenth century such skepticism was still rare, and few grasped its implications as clearly as Nietzsche did. Since his death in 1900, moral skepticism has gradually permeated the atmosphere in which we live. Skepticism about law (phase 2) was still rare in 1950, but the civil rights movement and the war in Vietnam are fast making it part of our climate of opinion. Doubts about justice (phase 3) are not yet widespread in any articulate form, and most of our moral philosophers have not reached them yet. At this point I cease to describe what *has* happened and attempt instead to lend a hand to what should happen.

Nietzsche's Zarathustra says: "What is falling, we should still push. Everything today falls and decays: who would check it? But I—I even want to push it" ("On Old and New Tablets," section 20).[1]

III

It is unworthy of a philosopher to invoke as an authority what he takes to be the wave of the future. It is not difficult to name trends that we ought to oppose, and it is even easier to enumerate trends that invite neither resistance nor assistance. But the concept of justice is a focal point of the confusions inherent in traditional morality. It looks preeminently objective, even absolute; it seems mathematically precise and not subject to emotion, preferences, or momentous decisions. Both the ancient Hebrews and the ancient Greeks considered justice the sum of the virtues: the just man was for both the good man. To question justice is to probe the very heart of morality, and a critical analysis of the concept of justice might be the fulfillment of the critique of morality attempted but never consummated by Nietzsche, early positivism, and existentialism.

Attempts to mount the bandwagon of history are common and contemptible. But some awareness of historical developments and of the ways in which the meanings of familiar concepts have changed is desirable, albeit rare. It is widely taken for granted that justice is a timeless idea, yet it could be shown that the meanings modern philosophers associate with justice were quite unfamiliar not only to Homer but even to Aeschylus; and Aristotle distinguished that justice which is the sum of the virtues from that justice which is a part of virtue.[2]

This is not the place for a history of the concept of justice, but at the very least we should distinguish four stages in its development. In the *first*, justice was tied to custom, and injustice meant a violation of tradition. In the *second*, justice was the sum of the virtues. This meaning still bears a close relationship to the first stage. In the *third*, justice became a particular virtue. At the cost of some oversimplification, we may associate these three stages with Homer, Plato, and Aristotle, allowing for the presence at each stage of the beginnings of the next one. Aristotle distinguished distributive and rectificatory justice and associated the latter with restitution (not with retribution);[3] he also expressly denied that justice could be reduced to reciprocity.[4] At the *fourth* stage, justice is no longer primarily, if at all, a virtue but rather a quality of laws, of arrangements, of distributions, and at one time also, though less and less so, of punishments.

My thesis can be expressed in an extremely simple way: *Punishment can be unjust but never just; and distributions can be unjust but, with the exception of simplistic cases, never just.* Many writers seem prepared to allow the first half of this thesis but proceed as if the collapse of retributive justice were irrelevant to "justice," or at least to distributive justice. *The central point of my paper is to contribute to the collapse of distributive justice.*

It is a commonplace that it is easier to preach morals than to give reasons for morals. It is also easier to praise distributive justice than to bury her. Indeed, it is easier to give reasons for clinging to the concept of distributive justice than it is to expose what is wrong with it.

Not many passages in religious literature are as moving as Isaiah's "seek justice [*mishpat*], correct oppression; defend the fatherless, plead for the widow" (1.17). Among the few that are is Amos' similar but slightly earlier outcry (5.21 ff.). The importance of the concept of justice in modern reform movements has been immense, and though great cruelty has often masked itself with the name of retributive justice, it is possible that even more good has been done in the name of distributive justice. Moreover, it seems far better to call alms *ts'dakah* (justice), as Jews have done traditionally, than to parade as charity attempts to mildly ameliorate incredible injustices.

The case for clinging to the concept of distributive justice probably rests mainly on three points. The appeal for justice is rhetorically immensely powerful. It does not hurt the self-respect of those who receive. And it *seems* to be an irreducible principle that cannot be given up without inviting distributions against which our moral sense rebels. Of course, this moral sense has a history and was influenced decisively by the Hebrew prophets; but so was mine.

If my aim were to persuade, the best strategy would be to begin with an attack on the concept of retributive justice, mobilizing your humane feelings against retribution and revenge, pointing up what seems wrong with this concept, and then to let the concept of distributive justice die of the aftereffects. But in one short paper there is not time enough to deal with both, and the case against retributive justice is much more familiar and needs less to be restated. Indeed, retributive justice is no longer a sacred cow; she may be attacked with impunity. But even some philosophers who find her utterly repugnant or "quite incredible"[5] still consider distributive justice the quintessence of morality or at least, along with benevolence, one of "the two 'cardinal' moral virtues." [6] One might suppose that the two were not that different; that both consisted in meting out to men what they deserve; and that both might die of the realization that this cannot be done.

Since I must limit myself, I shall confine my attention to the more attractive sister, in an attempt to show how confused she turns out to be on close inspection. So much for preliminaries. Let us now distinguish two conceptions of just distribution and call the first *material* and the second *formal*.[7]

IV

Material conceptions of justice tell us what should be meted out to each. One formulation, mentioned already in the first book of Plato's *Republic*, suggests that justice consists in giving each his due. In Latin: *suum cuique*, to each his own. The trouble with that definition is that it is circular and vacuous. What is due a man is indeed what justice requires to be given to him; but as long as we do not know what justice requires or what would be just, it does not help us in the least to be told *suum cuique*. The concepts of "due" and *suum* (his own) are derived from a prior conception of what is just, and as long as we do not know what is just these notions are void of content and hence of no help.

This is not the time to examine, one by one, the conceptions of justice advanced in Plato's *Republic* and in ethical and legal literature since his time. Instead of dealing very briefly with a great many suggestions, let us deal in detail with one—*that justice consists in giving each what he deserves* [8]—and then ask whether a few other, especially prominent suggestions represent improvements on this formulation.

The most suggestive comment on this definition of justice is Hamlet's: "Use every man after his desert, and who should 'scape whipping?" (II.2). These words remind us how inseparable distributive justice is from retributive justice. Like *suum cuique*, this definition covers retribution no less than the distribution of good things. And the good men deserve is as incalculable as the suffering they deserve—if indeed it makes any sense to say that a man deserves to suffer.

It is impossible to say how much income Dr. Cutter, the surgeon, deserves; or Professor Wisdom; or this carpenter; or that miner; or what kind of housing each deserves; or how much free time per day, per week, per year. Neither does it make sense to label any particular distribution of such goods among doctors, teachers, carpenters, and miners "just." Suppose a college can admit only one-fifth of the students applying for admission. It would be preposterous in almost all cases to say that 800, and only 800, deserved to be admitted, and that the decision of accepting these particular students, while turning down the rest, was just.

Instead of immediately invoking the traditional abstractions—equality, ability, need, or merit, to which we shall get around in due time—let us begin by considering a little more concretely what might conceivably be relevant to the determination of desert in a vast variety of cases. We shall distinguish eight categories, most of them with many subclasses. This can be done more easily in a chart, but it is essential here and now to communicate some idea of the complexity of the matter. The first category is

I. *What one is:*
  A. by birth:
    1. ethnic group
    2. social class.

To consider such matters conceivably relevant is not necessarily inhumane or reactionary. In India, for example, members of the so-called depressed classes are held to deserve preferred treatment in some cases, such as university admissions, partly to offset the disadvantages that have beset them from birth, partly because a society is desired in which all classes have some representation in the higher-level occupations. (Since this paper was written, the same practice has been introduced in the United States.) Other subclasses of this category are:
    3. sex (e.g., females are widely held to deserve exemption from being drafted into the armed forces)
    4. place of birth (relevant, e.g., in deciding who deserves the advantages that go with citizenship)
    5. physique
    6. citizenship
    7. relationship to the distributor.

Some of these matters may not be determined by birth, and other matters are considered according to their status, not at birth but
  B. at the time of distribution:
    1. profession
    2. rank
    3. age
    4. health
    5. intelligence
    6. other potential
    7. character
    8. residence

9. membership
10. beliefs (perhaps relevant for a bishop)
11. motivation.

So much for what one is. Next let us consider

II. *What one has:*
   A. property (land, money, shares, goods)
   B. family
   C. friends
   D. claims.

Instead of commenting on each subclass, let us proceed to

III. *What one has done:*
   A. education (1. formal, and 2. informal)
   B. military service (length, experience, exploits, decorations, highest rank attained)
   C. civilian occupations:
      1. kinds
      2. length
      3. experience
      4. achievements.

To give some idea of the complexity of determining this one small point of a man's achievements in a single civilian occupation, let us mention some of the things involved in distributing raises among professors:

   a. teaching, where we still have to distinguish
      α. levels (such as introductory, upper-class, and graduate courses) and
      β. techniques (such as lecturing, conducting discussions, supervising independent work, and laboratory sessions). Next we have
   b. publications, where we must again distinguish
      α. levels
      β. quantity
      γ. reception (e.g., reviews and comments)
      δ. impact
      ε. probable long-range importance
   c. unpublished research
   d. discussion with colleagues
   e. administrative work.

All this comes under III.C.4 and concerns no more than a man's achievements in a single civilian occupation. He may have achieved a great deal in other civilian and military occupations before becoming a professor, or he may be competing with others who have. Depending on what is being distributed, his rank and age and several of the other points already mentioned, or still to be mentioned, may be relevant too. For example,

  D. other accomplishments:
    1. public service, including offices held
    2. private service (e.g., lives saved)
    3. extracurricular activities, publications, lectures, etc. And in some contexts one might also take into account
  E. sufferings (one may deserve compensation)
  F. crimes (which may end "what one has done").

IV. *What one is doing:*
Here one might distinguish, for example,
  A. professional work (not to be confused with I.B.1. profession; for a man may be doing his boss's work)
  B. public life
  C. in one's family
  D. on one's own.
Now we are ready to consider needs. Let us distinguish

V. *What one needs for oneself:*
  A. for subsistence
  B. for comfort
  C. for some project
  D. for optimal development, and

VI. *What one needs for one's dependents:*
  with the same four subclasses, on whose vagueness we shall soon have to say something further.

VII. *What one desires:*
  Although this is ignored in most discussions, it is relevant in many cases unless we assume that a man often deserves something as a reward that in fact he does not desire at all. Finally, there is still

VIII. *What one has contracted:*

  There is no need for subheads here or for further categories; the eight suggested here with their subclasses suffice to show how impossible it is to measure what men deserve. With that, the material conception of justice breaks down. But before we turn to consider what might be called a formal conception of justice, let us consider *some objections to our analysis.*

V

It might seem that our analysis, for all its complexity, is still not nearly complex enough. For we have assumed for the sake of the argument that justice consists in giving each what he deserves, and "desert," as Joel Feinberg has shown, "represents only a part, and not necessarily the most important part, of the domain of justice." [9] Thus a man may "deserve" an honor or office but not qualify for it, and in that case justice does not require that he receive it.

Even as Aristotle distinguished that justice which is the sum of the virtues from that justice which is a part of virtue, we should distinguish that "giving each what he 'deserves' " which represents the material conception of justice as a whole from that "desert" which is merely one consideration among others. Feinberg's point concerns "desert" in the narrow sense, while we have been considering "desert" in the other sense, which is so generous and inclusive that his point is easily taken care of in my chart, under claims one has (II.D) or what one has contracted (VIII). If neither heading did suffice, one could easily expand the chart. So far from damaging my case, that would actually be grist to my mill.

My thesis that distributions can be unjust but hardly ever just is not reducible to the claim that merits and needs conflict, and that any attempt to do justice according to one is bound to violate the other. Let us consider *merit* first.

Some writers suppose [10] that if only we were willing to take our stand on merit alone, our system, though morally objectionable, could be made to work. In our present system, it has been said, the right to vote is quite independent of merit; but—and here I quote—"This kind of arrangement would look like whimsy or worse, like sheer immoralism, if the only values recognized in our political community were those of merit." [11] In fact there is such a *crisscross of merits* that it makes excellent sense to say: People's merits are not equal but nevertheless cannot be arranged in any single scale; hence a merit system, while workable in some very limited contexts where criteria can be clearly specified, is unworkable in other contexts. When it comes to the right to vote, it may be *the least evil* to give every adult one vote, provided he is, say, over eighteen and able to read the ballot.

To consider merit relevant in this and many other contexts is not unjust, nor does justice demand that people who know nothing about the issues be allowed to vote. To deprive people of the vote on grounds of size, weight, hair color, or skin color *is* unjust, but no particular system can claim to be just. One might call the least unjust "just," but in practice one cannot be sure of any system that it *is* the least unjust.

It is one of the aims of my complex chart to show vividly that there *is* a crisscross of merits and that the popular notion that conflicts arise only when we heed both merits and needs is false.

VI

It might seem that our analysis is needlessly complex and could easily be reduced to a simpler model. Instead of distinguishing eight categories, one might distinguish merely three: merits, abilities, and needs. But this model is too simple and has to be supplemented in two ways.

First, much of what we have included under what one is, has, is doing, desires, and has contracted is relevant to just distribution but has no place in the tripartite model. Place of birth, citizenship, and residence are almost universally considered relevant to the distribution of offices and of the right to vote, and it is far from evident that this is unjust. Relation to the distributor is almost universally considered relevant to the distribution of goods in a will, and again it is not evident that this is unjust. But none of these considerations are reducible to merits, abilities, and needs.

Secondly, these three categories are not as simple and unambiguous as the fact that there is one word for each makes them sound. In the case of merit, we have shown this. In the case of *need*, we obtained two categories by distinguishing what one needs for oneself and what one needs for one's dependents, and then divided each into four more subcategories: for subsistence, for comfort, for some project, and for optimal development. On reflection, these four are still utterly unclear. What is literally needed for *subsistence* is so pitifully little that it is generally understood that this is *not* what is meant; but what *is* meant is *not* understood.

Comfort is equally unclear and obviously involves a crucial subjective component. Once one is used to certain things—cigarettes, television, so many meals a day, such and such furniture, a car, or perhaps several cars in the family, a W.C., or perhaps three full bathrooms, two-day weekends, a month in Florida every winter, a three-month summer vacation, a forty-hour work week or perhaps no more than six hours teaching a week—one is apt to be uncomfortable without these things. It is thus possible to make every member of a group comfortable while the distribution of goods is strikingly unequal, and it is even possible for the person with fewer needs and goods to be more comfortable than some who have far more goods but "needs" that outstrip their possessions. Needs are not fixed data but can be created, cultivated, and—though this is much more difficult—diminished and even eliminated.

What is "needed" for a *project* is often far from clear: foundations are frequently persuaded that extremely questionable needs are authentic; and more often than not, they assume that the significance of a project is proportionate to the claimed need for money. This widespread assumption is obviously silly and vicious. Moreover, does not justice require a weighing of the needs for the completion of various projects and a comparative ranking of how much each project is needed?

If we want to give each enough for his *optimal development,* how do we determine what a man needs for that? To answer the last two questions, we require a decision about goals—an idea or vision of man and society as we should like them to be.

Ultimately, every attempt to spell out a material conception of justice involves a decision about the kind of society we want. It is an abiding testimony to Plato's genius that, although he was the first philosopher to deal with justice at book length, he recognized this crucial fact. It is a central fault of many discussions of justice since his time that this point is overlooked.

VII

It may seem as if one material conception of justice did not involve any ultimate value judgments. For there are some who would disregard differences in merit and need, taking their stand on *absolute equality.* Again, the meaning of equality is not as simple as one might suppose. Is it considered just to give each the same, regardless not only of his needs and desires, his merits and his ability to make use of what he is given, but also of what he already has (E.1)? If food is distributed, for example, is it just to give equal amounts to those who have plenty and those who have nothing? If this suggestion were rejected as palpably unjust, need would be reintroduced. But it might still be argued that absolute equality really means that all should be equal *after* the distribution has been made, or at least as nearly equal as the distribution can make them. In that case, those who *have* would receive nothing till all have-nots had received as much as *they* have (E.2).

Although this system is not followed in any civilized country anywhere, it has some plausibility when the goods at stake are food, but hardly any when the goods are books, violins, canvas boards, offices, or honors. Different criteria are appropriate for different kinds of goods. Some things may reasonably be distributed in accordance with men's merits, others with men's abilities, still others with men's needs, without being open to the charge that the distribution has been unjust in principle.

To sum up: E.1 is so absurd that one can understand it only as a counsel of despair, a way of saying that no better system can be made to work. E.2 is also absurd if it is applied to *all* things that are to be distributed. To mention only one further objection to E.2: in that case no incentives would remain.

It is arguable that if food, lodging, and money were to be distributed in accordance with this plan, sufficient non-material incentives would remain. Thus one can easily imagine a faculty on which all teachers received the same material benefits, while there were not only instructors, assistant professors, associate professors, and full professors but, say, eight ranks, and promotions would be based on a merit system. We have shown earlier how impossible it is to rank professors according to merit. This is not to deny, however, that rank can be a more powerful incentive than money; even now some young teachers, given the choice between a raise and a promotion, would choose the higher rank. It would not be too difficult to imbue a society with an ethos in which rank and honors would provide enough incentives for performance, while material goods were distributed relatively equally. Whether those publicly branded as inferior would be happier than those are whose salaries, which are not publicly known, have not had the benefit of any merit raises is another question. It is highly probable, I think, that non-material inequalities in a highly merit-conscious society would be felt more deeply and would therefore make for more unhappiness than most material inequalities in our society.

Inequalities in the distribution of *some* goods, material or otherwise, is necessary as an incentive. Without it, some jobs will not get done, unless we abolish a great deal of personal freedom, empower a central authority to draft people to do whatever jobs are thought to be needed to be done, and then introduce some system of random selection. It might be held that such a society would be more just than any society in which exertion is rewarded, but anyone who abhorred the required loss of freedom would not be in the least likely to feel that it was more just, and he might argue—as I would—that *injustice meted out at random remains injustice.*

In sum, it is only in a situation in which, *ex hypothesi*, no conceivably relevant differences exist among the individuals concerned that any distribution could be reasonably called just. Dividing eight apples among eight children at the end of a party at which all have had plenty to eat might be a case in point. But the moment we suppose that some of them are much too full by now to eat the apple right away and will take it home to a house in which apples and other kinds of food are plentiful, while other children at the party are about to return to homes in which hungry brothers and sisters are plentiful, even this apparently so simple and trivial case may be seen to support the dictum that distributions can be unjust but hardly ever just.[12]

VIII

At this point one might wish to fall back on *a formal conception of justice* and say *that justice consists in treating like cases alike*. Alas, no two cases are alike. No two students applying for admission are alike any more than two young men up for promotion or a raise in salary. It was one function of my chart, with all its detail about conceivably relevant considerations, to show this.

The man who wants to avoid being unjust must ignore *irrelevant* unlikenesses and base his decision on *relevant* likenesses and unlikenesses. But often it is exceedingly difficult to judge what is and what is not relevant. In some cases it is easy to say that the basis for a decision was blatantly irrelevant and that heinous injustice has been done, but our thesis still stands: It is hardly ever possible to claim that justice has been done. The point is not that we know what is just but lack the strength to do it. Rather, injustice is often palpable, but we could not say in most cases what would be just.

The obvious rejoinder, mentioned previously, is that we are just when we minimize injustice, and that a rule is just when it is not unjust. What does this mean in practice? The demand for justice is the demand to give reasons for unequal treatment—to show relevant inequalities, or, in other words, to be rational, or, in a legitimate sense of that word, honest.

What outrages us in cases of palpable injustice is usually rank dishonesty; for example, in the Scottsboro trial and in the techniques that have been used to keep Negroes from voting. Justice does not require that illiterate people should be allowed to vote. But the claims that have been made again and again in this connection, like the testimony accepted by the court in the Scottsboro trial, have been dishonest with a vengeance.

Still, it is possible to be honest but unjust. In such cases we confront either brutality (a lack of love) or low standards of honesty, or both. Honesty, in the sense germane here, should not be mistaken for the easy sincerity of those who have never bothered to develop their intellectual conscience. Men who sincerely claim what only a few minutes earlier they knew to be false, or what they would find to be false if they took even elementary pains to investigate the matter, have low standards of honesty. High standards of honesty involve scrupulous attention to evidence and to meanings, to pros and cons, and to alternatives. And what I mean by love is, above all, the habit, which can be cultivated, of thinking about how others feel and sharing their problems and sufferings.

Justice is not an irreducible principle that is required to guard against distributions that would outrage the moral sense of most philosophers who think we must rely on the concept of justice. In *The Faith of a Heretic* (1961) I proposed four cardinal virtues (section 83) and then (84) tried to show how various situations in which most philosophers would invoke justice could be dealt with by relying on these four. It would be tedious to quote or paraphrase at length what has been published elsewhere, but since these pages may be unfamiliar, it may after all be best, or the least evil, to repeat here a single example, desegregation.

The first cardinal virtue, humbition, is a fusion of humility and ambition. The man who acknowledges this ideal and cultivates this habit would admit his ignorance of many pertinent considerations without resigning himself to ignorance. He would neither assume at the outset that he was right and his opponents wrong, nor would he take for granted that those of his own color are superior to those of another. He would engage in open-minded discussion and be willing to learn.

The second virtue, love, involves seeing and sharing the hurt and grief of other human beings and assuming some responsibility and being willing to make sacrifices to help. "Without believing all things and hoping all things, without expecting the millennium from a piece of legislation and without giving up because there will be no millennium, love persists."

Thirdly, "courage does not shrink from danger, does not hide from risks in sloth and resignation, even if they are concealed behind the name of prudence. If lack of humbition, lack of love, and lack of courage do not fully account for the injustice inflicted on the Negro, dishonesty remains."

Honesty is the fourth cardinal virtue, and any attempt to show in detail how heavily racial prejudice and discrimination depend on its violation would extend this paper beyond reason.

An analysis of several such examples would show that the collapse of distributive justice does not entail the collapse of decency and humanity, and that the work that "justice" could not do can be done in other ways. This may be the best place to suggest one more example that shows how justice cannot do the job it is supposed to do.

Let us turn back to the view that "benevolence and justice are the two 'cardinal' moral virtues" and that "all other moral virtues can be derived from or shown to be forms of them." [13] In the first place, I do not see how humility and ambition, courage, and honesty can be derived from these two. In the second place, it is clear that justice, defined as the disposition to treat people equally, is invoked lest benevolence alone —that is, the disposition to maximize the balance of good over evil— should inspire distributions in which a slight excess of good over evil is purchased at the price of immense inequalities. But this attempt to work improvements on utilitarianism is open to several objections.

Suppose we could choose between two states. In one there would be only 100,000 people, all of them extremely happy, wise, and creative. The balance of good over evil—waiving for the moment the absurdity of all attempts to measure that—might be said to be, say, 100,000. In the other state there would be a billion people, none of them very happy, wise, or creative, but all of them a little more happy than unhappy. While in the first state, each man had achieved a balance of good over evil that amounted to one full point, in this state the balance for each came to, say, .01. Even so, the total balance in the first state would be only 100,000; but in the second one, ten million—a hundred times greater. Equality would be present in the second state, too; hence those who add justice to benevolence as a second cardinal virtue would be at one with the utilitarians in being compelled to choose the second state. But I should opt for the first, and I trust you would, too.

What has gone wrong? Most of our moral philosophers fail to see that the most interesting moral questions are what sort of society we want and—we come to this as soon as we try to give reasons for our answer—what we would like to become of man. Our answers to these two questions are decisive when questions of justice arise in practice.

IX

Let us return to the problem of selecting a few hundred students from thousands applying for admission. The counsel to admit those who deserve admission is empty if we do not know how to compute desert. The demand that we treat all applicants equally is equally unhelpful. Should we be guided solely by achievement so far? (What kinds of achievement? Scores in multiple choice tests? Examination essays? Course grades? Extracurricular achievements, and if so, which?) Or should we be guided more by promise? (Of what?) If it is our desire to maximize the impact of our limited resources and it is a fact that the rate of attrition among women students is so high that hardly any go on to obtain the doctorate and even fewer then go on into professional careers, is it "unjust," whatever else it may be, to give preference to men? And if we want to have more Negro leaders with a first-rate education and more Negro lawyers, surgeons, and professors, is it "unjust" to admit some Negro students who, but for their so-called race, would not have been admitted?

What *is* unjust is to announce one set of criteria for admission—or for fellowships, raises in salary, promotions, leaves of absence, and other rewards—and then to invoke different standards in practice. But such injustice comes down to dishonesty. If we announce our criteria and then do our best to stick with them in practice, can we still be said to be unjust? Can the *criteria* be unjust? They can be, in two ways. First, they may be arbitrary and irrelevant to our stated goals. In that case we may be convicted of low standards of honesty or a lack of love. Or our standards may be relevant and well designed to implement our social goals, but the society that we desire may be open to severe objections.

What sort of objections? The most telling criticism would be that the society did not promote humbition, courage, love, and high standards of honesty. In practice, those who call a society unjust often mean all or part of that. But it is neither necessary nor possible to summarize briefly near the end of this paper possible objections to societies. What is important is rather to insist that many questions about justice resolve into a dispute about different visions of man and society.

Our moral philosophers generally avoid such disputes and give— and probably have—the impression that at that point we are dealing with irrational preferences. But it is one of the most important tasks of philosophy to consider the pros and cons of different visions of man and society, weighing critically what can be said in favor of each, and to try to arrive at a reasoned conclusion.

X

In the end, let us relate this approach to justice to a very different one. Polemics have no place here, since space does not permit me to deal adequately with the views of those with whom I differ. My reason for nevertheless referring to the writings of some colleagues is to define my own position more clearly, and to indicate what seems to me to be at stake. While I am naturally making every effort to be fair, my central purpose here is not to refute anyone but to articulate my own doubts about justice.

There is a tradition in ethics that considers it the main problem of justice to neutralize what I shall call "grabbiness." Thus a recent writer on the subject says: "Questions of justice arise when conflicting claims are made upon the design of a practice and where it is taken for granted that each person will insist, as far as possible, on what he considers his rights. It is typical of cases of justice to involve persons who are pressing on one another their claims, between which a fair balance or equilibrium must be found." [14] But in the examples I have given—admissions, promotions, and raises—grabbiness may be totally out of the picture. Nobody need press any claim, each of the young men concerned may go out of his way to suggest his own unworthiness, and the decision may be up to senior professors who have nothing to gain whatever. The question before them may ultimately be a question of goals, of the kind of society to be desired.

The writer I have quoted says: "Amongst an association of saints . . . the disputes about justice could hardly occur; for they would all work selflessly together for one end, the glory of God as defined by their common religion . . ." [15] But selfless men can and often do disagree about the best distribution. The reference to the common religion is gratuitous; it introduces a point that has nothing to do with selflessness; and it ignores how much disagreement there has been among saints and, for that matter, among rabbis.

The crux of the view I reject is that justice consists in impartiality and transcends preferences. It is supposed to be a matter of rationality, which is associated with calculation and objective findings. Thus we are asked to imagine a society of rational men, and part of the very meaning of their being rational is that "they know their own interests more or less accurately," [16] as if one's own interests were always and entirely something knowable and not—as in fact they often are—matters of more or less informed and responsible choices.

The most crucial question about distributive justice is whether *any* distribution, outside of simplistic cases, should be called just. I have given reasons for saying No. The view I am now considering says: Yes, a distribution is just if it fulfills various conditions that can be enumerated. Among these conditions are at least two that are, I think, open to very serious objections. The first is that grabbiness is neutralized.[17] This does not strike me as so difficult to achieve, at least in a large number of interesting cases; but problems of justice persist even when grabbiness is out of the picture. The second condition is that "inequalities as defined by the institutional structure or fostered by it are arbitrary unless it is reasonable to expect that they will work out to everyone's advantage." [18] This I consider a utopian condition that crystallizes the unwarranted faith that we need not make tragic choices.

Any attempt to keep the discussion of justice this side of preferences and choices seems hopeless to me. Even men who are, or try to be, rational and selfless are not alike. Even if the intelligent did not push the claims of intelligence, and the artistically gifted the importance of fostering artistic talent, some who are not themselves brilliant might urge us to weight intelligence, and others, though quite lacking in artistic genius, might argue that a society is ultimately to be judged by its accomplishments in art.

Indeed, right now the rules about college admissions and advancement of young college teachers are not designed or adopted by those who are most affected but by older men who have come through the system, and grabbiness is thus largely eliminated. But if this setup were changed and the rules were up to the people most affected, would *any* feasible arrangement be to the advantage of *all?* Surely not. This utopian notion is part of the false assumption that one system is rational and true without involving any choice or argument about goals.

In concrete cases, I would not necessarily differ with any of the writers I have singled out for criticism. This is not merely because I have selected only men who happen to be my friends, on the assumption—not biased, I hope—that they are among the very best living writers on the subject. Even as Protestants, Catholics, Jews, and unbelievers can work together for civil rights, philosophers who disagree about the best analysis of justice may agree in practical decisions. From this, however, it does not follow that nothing of practical importance is at stake, nor even that philosophy "leaves everything as it is." [19]

Even when the decision about distribution is the same, it makes a difference whether we tell those who are affected by it—say, those who are not admitted or promoted—that our decisions and our rules are just, or rather that we realize that no such absolute claim is defensible. In the latter case, we might say: "These were our rules or criteria, which neither *are* perfect nor *could* be. We may yet be convinced to revise them. Meanwhile we have done our best to stick by them and not to be swayed by points whose relevance is tenuous. We know from experience that even at that level mistakes are made, but we did try hard to preclude them." To speak that way instead of invoking the chimaera of absolute justice is more honest and loving, more humane, and more mindful of the self-respect of those we disappoint.

We can point to examples of love and honesty, humbition and courage. We do not know in the same way what justice is, and we cannot point to examples of just distribution without becoming highly abstract and deliberately excluding a great deal of relevant data, as I have tried to show in the case of distributing apples among children after a party. Once we realize and admit this, and also that our rules and criteria are linked to our vision of a good society, we should become more humane, less sure of ourselves, and more inclined to argue the pros and cons of different visions of a good society. This would make philosophy more humane, too.

XI

Perhaps my attack on distributive justice would seem more acceptable if I said—but I am not going to—that distributions, always excepting simplistic cases, can never be unjust any more than just. As it stands, my position may appear paradoxical.

It may help to note that the situation of distributive justice is not unique in this respect. Scientific theories, as well as interpretations of works of art and literature, can be proved false, but it is arguable that they can never be proved true. Many mutually incompatible theories may be tenable, but we should not call several mutually incompatible theories true. Yet there is no good reason why some untenable theories should not be called false.

The closest parallel to distributive justice is furnished by retributive justice. If a defendant is guilty and his punishment is neither cruel and unusual nor arbitrary, we still should not call it just or say that "justice has been done." Punishments never have the quality that Kant and other retributivists have associated with them, and that many retributivists still associate with capital punishment for murder. There is no one punishment that is the right one, any more than there is one distribution that is the right one. To call all tenable or defensible punishments or distributions just, bestowing this epithet on an indefinite number of mutually incompatible solutions, is sufficiently out of keeping with the traditional and still widely accepted meaning of justice to make it preferable and reasonable to suggest that neither punishments nor distributions should be called just. Yet both punishments and distributions often have the very qualities generally associated with injustice, and there is no good reason for never saying that an injustice has been done. If an innocent man is framed, or unequal punishments or shares are meted out for no relevant reason, we need not hesitate to call the punishment or distribution unjust.

Many distributions and punishments we should call neither just nor unjust. Anyone reluctant to accept this conclusion has three options. (1) He can call unjust all solutions except the one he considers the best, or (2) he can call just all tenable solutions, or (3) he can suggest that in fact only one punishment or distribution *is* just, although we are generally unable to tell which one is. All three alternatives seem to me to involve such significant departures from the usual meaning of "just" and "unjust" that my solution is better.

It is neither desirable nor possible to "use every man after his desert." However we treat men, we cannot claim, excepting simplistic cases, that they got what they deserved. But not all ways of treating men are equally undeserved. When unequal treatment is not based on relevant inequalities, or when one set of criteria has been announced and another is invoked in practice, we may say that an injustice has been done.

Thus men who do not agree on what would be best can still work together to minimize injustices, even as men with different theories may agree that *some* theories are demonstrably false. This is not paradoxical but glad tidings. While philosophers should argue more about rival visions of man and society, not all practical efforts and cooperation have to wait until they have come to agree.

It may seem that justice, unlike love, can be demanded. But this is wrong, as I have tried to show. What can be demanded is less injustice. If this should be demanded or offered as "simple justice," it may yet turn out to be tomorrow's "injustice."

Martin Luther realized that conscience can always ask whether we could not have done better. But because justice could not be found in the pursuit of good works, Luther concluded that man could be made just by faith alone—faith in Christ's redemptive sacrifice, faith that Christ had died for our sins. At that point Luther reverted to an archaic notion of justice: the magical sacrifice of the innocent scapegoat. Here our ways part.

After using their reason and examining the evidence, physicians and surgeons often do not know what is the best course. But if they therefore throw reason and evidence to the winds, they act irresponsibly. We expect them to use both in order to exclude a great many alternatives, even if in the end they cannot be sure that their course was the best.

Am I guilty of the old heresy that man knows the devil but not God? My heresy is worse. We know neither God nor the devil; we are beset by an endless number of devils—"No worst, there is none." [20] To fight evil without the illusion that it is the greatest ever, to choose the lesser evil without the faith that it is surely the least evil, to endure darkness without the boast that none could be blacker, and to create more light without the comfort of excessive hopes—that is humbition, courage, love, and honesty.

NOTES

1. The student rebellions of 1968 should be seen in this perspective. Many of the rebels had not only lived through skepticism about morality and law but

were close to nihilism and despair. Few had reached conscious doubts about justice. But their often alarming self-righteousness did not depend on having seen the face of justice. Sure of the injustice of existing arrangements, they were eager to fight, if not destroy, "the establishment." *Their* application of Zarathustra's dictum was marred by the impatience of youth. They need to be reminded how important it is to evaluate alternatives—and how those who helped to topple the wretched Weimar Republic cleared the way for Hitler.

2. *Nicomachean Ethics,* Book V. 1 and 2.

3. *Ibid.,* 2–4.

4. *Ibid.,* 5.

5. William Frankena, *Ethics* (1963), 59.

6. *Ibid.,* 50.

7. We shall get to the formal conception in section VIII.

8. Because I accept this definition and have some notion of what justice is, I can say that punishment can be unjust but never just, etc.

9. "Justice and Personal Desert" in *Nomos VI: Justice* (1963), 70.

10. E.g., Gregory Vlastos in "Justice and Equality," in *Social Justice,* ed. Richard B. Brandt (1962), 46.

11. *Ibid.,* 45.

12. The example of the children and the apples does not depend on some prior social injustice. All that is required is some relevant inequality; say, that some children need to eat more than others, or that some are allergic to apples, or that some are allergic to other foods but not to apples. I am indebted to Gilbert Harman for his comments on this paper, which have led me to clarify this point as well as several in section X below.

13. Frankena, *op. cit.,* 50.

14. John Rawls, "Justice as Fairness" (1958), revised version in *Justice and Social Policy,* ed. Frederick Olafson (1961), 87. For a critique of Hume's close association of justice with the restraint of selfishness see my article "The Origin of Justice," pp. 221–23.

15. *Ibid.,* 90 f.

16. *Ibid.,* 85.

17. To arrive at justice, the most important step is, in this view, to devise a situation in which "there is no way for anyone to win social advantages for himself" (*ibid.,* 87). In a more recent essay, "Distributive Justice," Rawls says similarly: "Consider the simplest problem of fair division. A number of men are to divide a cake: *assuming that a fair division is an equal one,* which procedure will give this outcome? The obvious solution is to have the man who divides the cake take the last piece. He will divide it equally, *since in this way he assures for himself as large a share as he can. . . .* We can design a procedure *guaranteed* to lead to [the outcome that is just]" (*Philosophy, Politics and Society: Third Series,* ed. Peter Laslett and W. G. Runciman, 1967, 77; all italics mine).

The italicized assumption is more problematic than meets the eye: see our example of the apples. Moreover, the "just" outcome is *not* guaranteed unless we assume that everybody is as grabby as the man dividing the cake is explicitly assumed to be. If he were not that grabby and assumed that other people weren't either, he might cut pieces of different sizes to accommodate different tastes and appetites; and if he *is* as grabby as the "since" clause suggests but knows that his friends are not, he may make one piece much bigger than all the rest, confident that it will be left to the last.

18. "Distributive Justice," 61. The same point is central in "Justice as Fairness."

19. Ludwig Wittgenstein, *Philosophical Investigations,* Section 124.

20. Gerard Manley Hopkins, poem #65. The question about the old heresy was raised by Abraham Edel in his prepared comments when I read this paper November 5, 1967, at Columbia University to the Conference on Jewish Philosophy.

IN DEFENSE OF "JUSTICE"

(A RESPONSE)

Sidney Hook

One faces some formidable obstacles in commenting on Professor Kaufmann's paper. It is eloquent, colorful and moving. To dissect it seems irrelevant and almost irreverent. The obstacles are multiplied by the fact that the final section of Professor Kaufmann's paper, handed me when I arrived yesterday, seems to take back or qualify some of the extreme and startling statements made in the preceding sections in which he developed his position.

My difficulties with Kaufmann's position are many. I'll mention some peripheral matters at the outset. First of all, I fail to see the relevance of his discussion to the philosophy of practice, either in the sense in which Professor Frankel understood it, or to the concrete, practical concerns in social life today, to e.g., the question of the justice of open housing or the justice of student draft deferments. Indeed, I shall argue that some of his apparent doubts about justice stem from a misconceived theoretical approach to some of the illustrative instances he does mention. His enumeration of the eight or more categories of consideration that bear on questions of justice, have only a hypothetical significance for any specific case. They function as so many variables. But in a concrete, historical context, when we delineate the problem as it is actually faced, most of them do not apply. The question of what is just in this or that specific case is complex enough, and our answers are only probable. If we have to consider the complete range of hypothetical considerations, the answer to all questions of justice (or for that matter to any question about anything) would be indeterminate. This would remain true no matter what criteria are employed for settling conflicts about questions of just distribution or punishment.

I am not even sure that Professor Kaufmann would disagree with this. Consider the following statement:

75

Thus men who do not agree on what would be best can still work together to minimize injustices, even as men with different theories may agree that *some* theories are demonstrably false. This is not paradoxical but glad tidings. While philosophers should argue more about rival visions of man and society, not all practical efforts and cooperation have to wait until they come to agree.

But the point is precisely how to establish and further this agreement, and to establish and further it in such a way as to maximize the justice or minimize the injustice in the specific case that confronts us. To do this by Kaufmann's own admission does *not* require agreement about rival visions of man and society (the contrary of which he stressed in the course of his paper) but some shared interests and shared values in terms of which we can work out a just solution here and now. The reference which analogizes between actions deemed just and theories deemed true seems to me to confuse types of situations—one in which we look for "demonstrations" or better, confirmations, where theories are concerned, and situations in which we offer justification for actions. To draw this parallelism, as Kaufmann does, would open the door to just as grave doubts about truth and falsity as about justice and injustice.

A second peripheral and relatively minor point is that I read the contemporary situation rather differently from Kaufmann. For me the current crisis in morality, especially among the young, is defined not so much by the growth of moral skepticism or even of moral nihilism but by the resurgence of absolutism, the conviction that certain things are absolutely right and wrong, just or unjust, to a point that the liberal virtues of open inquiry, hearing both sides, assessing evidence, qualifying conclusions in the light of other valid conclusions, is denounced as pussy-footing, moral cowardice, or what not. "Natural law" may be out but "absolute human rights" are in. "Revolution" has become the password, "reform," a byword. The demonstrators on our college campuses and their faculty sympathizers have no doubts about justice at all! A reckless and intransigent fanaticism of "virtue" has emerged which proudly proclaims that any and all means are justified, no matter how violent, to achieve what it regards as the ends of justice. The end result of this position is totalitarianism.

I return to my basic difficulties with Professor Kaufmann's discussion. These are aggravated by the fact that in certain places he seems to be perfectly aware of them but dismisses them as if his recognition of these difficulties exonerates him from the necessity of resolving them. Before such assurance, the conscientious critic must ask himself whether he has missed the obvious point. I therefore would like my criticisms to be construed as questions.

The main thesis of Professor Kaufmann's paper is that "Punishment can be unjust but never just; and distributions can be unjust but, with the exception of simplistic cases, never just." He adds: "The central point of my paper is to contribute to the collapse of distributive justice." In the final section, as if to forestall criticism, he says that "distributions, always excepting simplistic cases, can never be unjust any more than just. As it stands my position may appear paradoxical."

This position seems to me to be not so much paradoxical as unintelligible—a clear case of trying to eat one's semantic cake and have it too. If Kaufmann has valid grounds for denying that the term "justice" can be intelligibly applied in any situation, then these grounds would be sufficient for denying that the term "unjust" can be intelligibly applied in that situation. In any particular case, if a certain mode of treatment is declared unjust, it can only be on the basis of *some* conception of what is required by a just mode of treatment. The logic of significant usage with respect to justice is no different from that which obtains with respect to some of the expressions Kaufmann would substitute, mistakenly it seems to me, for justice, for example, "honesty." If anyone were to say: "A man can be dishonest but he can never, except in simplistic cases, be honest," we would all be bewildered, including I dare say, Professor Kaufmann. Charge a man with dishonesty in a specific situation and, if you are intellectually responsible, you must have some conception of what honest behavior would be in that situation. Otherwise you would have *no* guide as to what kind of behavior to forbid or condemn.

There are some ways of stating Kaufmann's position which are not equivalent to the statement he calls his thesis. For example, he says "injustice is often palpable but we could not say in most cases what would be just." This is innocuous enough. It is not equivalent in meaning to what he calls his thesis. And it could very well be true provided "often" hasn't got the sweep or force of "most." In that case there would be some situations of which one can say that they are palpably unjust and yet be unable to say what would make them just—which seems to me semantically absurd.

Some ambiguities in Kaufmann's discussion may account for his denial of the apparently obvious. In one sense, we can know that something is the wrong answer to a problem or question without knowing *the* specifically right answer. But in such a case we must have some conception of what would constitute *a* right answer, i.e., the requirements any right answer must meet. If we are bereft of any notion of what would constitute *a* right answer, we have no conception of what would constitute a wrong one. If there are no right answers or if there cannot be a right answer, there cannot be a wrong answer. ·

Sometimes Kaufmann seems to be objecting not to the quest for justice but to the quest for "the chimaera of absolute justice" or complete justice. Here indeed is a profound and fruitful theme, highly relevant to our times, but alas! left unexplored. There is a sense in which one can say that the quest for absolute justice is self-defeating because it is unrealizable. Its unremitting pursuit tends to lead to a disregard or violation of other values in the moral economy that are as important and possibly more important than justice. Hegel reminds us that *summa jus, summa injuria.* History and ordinary life best point up the moral of futility in seeking an absolutely just solution. Revolutions revenge themselves against contemporary individuals who are not responsible for the conditions out of which present oppression develops. Wars and feuds by seeking to even up the score of past injustices invariably generate others.

What is true for the fate of empires holds for individual life too. Smith loses his vision in an accident for which Brown is adjudged at fault. Smith receives fair compensation, but no matter how much money he receives he still cries out for his sight. Even in a primitive society where Brown would have to pay for Smith's injury with the loss of his own sight, Smith's vision would not be restored. He cannot get absolute justice even if some day he learns to see again, for nothing can erase the memory of the pain and fear. On the other hand, the damages Brown must pay, which bankrupts him and causes great hardship to his family, are altogether disproportionate to the gravity of his offense, failure to check on his brake fluid, a piece of carelessness of which tens of thousands are guilty. Even if we adopt a system that socializes all risks as the most just way of distributing the burdens and compensations for injuries, absolute justice cannot be achieved. We must settle for less.

One would have expected Kaufmann to develop this theme in conjunction with the presence of the tragic in human experience. Instead, he speaks of "absolute justice" as if it were something else again: an action reached by a train of infallible thought after envisaging all conceivable relevant circumstances in any situation that calls for a just distribution. Granted that we cannot achieve such a goal. If it is impermissible to call a mode of distribution just because we cannot know it to be absolutely just, then by the same logic we cannot call any mode of distribution unjust because we cannot know it to be absolutely unjust.

Take Kaufmann's paradigm illustration of his dictum that distributions can be unjust but not just—dividing eight apples among eight children at a party. It may be unjust to deny an apple to one of the children, who needs and wants one, while we give one to each of his play-mates. But this is not *absolutely* unjust. We would be treating him even more unjustly if we taunted and baited him with our refusal and in addition deprived him of all food as well as the apple. Does this mean that we have no right to call the first mode of treatment unjust? Obviously not, says Kaufmann. Then why can't we call a mode of treatment *just* even if there *may* be other modes of treatment (were there other relevant circumstances and were we to know about them) that would be more just?

If I understand Kaufmann's answer, it is not hard to put the finger on his error. He tells us: "In sum, it is only in a situation in which, *ex hypothesi, no conceivably relevant differences* exist among the individuals concerned that any distribution could be reasonably called just." (my italics) But such a demand is itself unreasonable! There are always *conceivably* relevant differences. But the question is whether there are any existing or likely relevant differences. *Conceivable* differences are not empirically given. They may also be imaginary. Kaufmann's standard is *a priori* and inapplicable to different situations, because it holds in advance of experience for *all* situations. It seems to me more valid to say that *an equal distribution can be reasonably called just when, after intelligent inquiry, no apparently relevant differences exist among those who are the recipients of distribution.* Here is a fourth option open to us in the use of the term "just" whose validity is unaffected by Kaufmann's critique.

The cry for justice, heard throughout the ages, when clear, has always been a cry for the elimination of specific inequalities in specific historical contexts. It is a demand for equality of treatment or consideration or opportunity in some specific respect in which it is currently being denied. It never dreams of contending or establishing that "no conceivably relevant differences" are present that would affect the justice of its demand. A position like Kaufmann's lends itself to mischievous uses and abuses that he himself would firmly condemn. One can imagine a segregationist saying: To be sure I grant you that to deprive anyone of the right to vote on grounds of size or color is unjust but no system by which it is replaced can claim to be altogether just. Why bother then to replace one unjust system by another unjust system? Of course, "One might call the least unjust 'just,' but in practice one cannot be *sure* [my italics] of any system that it *is* the least unjust."

But why must we be *sure*, in order to call a system just and to fight for it, that it is the least unjust? Sufficient unto the day is the evidence thereof! There may be eight or eighty-eight different categories of consideration that bear on a man's deserts. But the burden of proof that they are sufficiently relevant to justify inequality of treatment in the specific historical context in which the question arises, rests on those who defend the inequalities, not on those who demand equality of treatment.

Professor Kaufmann is aware of this rejoinder, i.e., the less unjust a rule is the more just it is. But he tries to turn it aside by collapsing justice into other virtues. He says: "What does this [rejoinder] mean in practice? The demand for justice is the demand to give reasons for unequal treatment—to show relevant inequalities, or, in other words, to be rational, or, in a legitimate sense of that word, honest."

Even if this reduction were valid, it would not make less true the view that the less unjust a rule is, the more just it is, and that in any specific case, if we have eliminated all the relevantly known possibilities of injustice, we have done all we humanly can to achieve justice. This is all that can be reasonably expected of us. (We can draw analogies here that show how commonsensical the position is—the less ignorant we are of a subject, the more knowledge we have of it, even if we can't claim perfect or complete or certain knowledge: the less unhealthy in certain respects the organism is, the healthier it is in those respects, etc.) But Professor Kaufmann's reduction is not valid. To be just may depend upon being rational, but it is not merely being rational; to be rational may depend upon being intellectually honest to ourselves, but it does not mean being merely intellectually honest. At best these are necessary conditions of justice that cannot be reduced simply to either one or both of them. There are many situations in which it would be absurd to say that a charge of injustice is reducible to a charge of dishonesty in any customary sense. When I say it is unjust to visit the sins of the fathers upon the heads of the children, no less the children unto the third and fourth generations, I am not saying it is dishonest to do so in any sense of "dishonesty" that is recognized in normal English usage. Or if I say to someone, "It is unjust for you to be both plaintiff and judge in your own case," I am not saying that it is dishonest for him to be both. (He may even rejoin, "Don't worry. You can trust me. I am an honest man." Honest or not, it would still be unjust for him to play both roles.) It is unjust for someone who knows that I am faint from hunger to exact an onerous wage agreement from me. It is not dishonest.

I find puzzling the fact that Professor Kaufmann sometimes says that outside of "simplistic cases" (p. 57) no just distribution is possible, and sometimes that justice is "hardly ever possible." (p. 66) I assume that "a simplistic case" is at least a simple case, and that "hardly ever" is separated by a semantic if not ontological gulf from "never." The question I put to Professor Kaufmann is: Does it not follow from this that the determination of justice in cases that are not simple is *difficult* rather than impossible? If so, we do not need a Solomon come to judgment to tell us this.

II

Professor Kaufmann is convinced that we can dispense with the notion of justice and just distribution, and that any useful functions these expressions serve can be performed as well by the invocation and application of the four cardinal virtues of humbition, courage, honesty, and love. My doubts about this are stronger than Kaufmann's about justice. In most cases I can think of, it appears to be easier to resolve questions concerning distribution in a morally satisfactory manner by operating with the principles of justice—impartially administered equality of treatment except where valid grounds for inequality exist—than with these four cardinal virtues. My reasons are many but I shall state only a few.

First, strange and extended meanings must be read into these terms in order to bring them into line with our ordinary judgments of justice and injustice. Take the institution of slavery. It can be condemned as clearly unjust because it crassly violates the principle of equality of human rights to which even slaveholders give lip allegiance. It is not at all clear that slavery must be condemned from the standpoint of humbition—a curious virtue whose unlovely name suggests a cross between Uriah Heep and Horatio Alger—or courage, or honesty, or love. The subject is vast and cannot properly be pursued here. As far as the abolition of slavery is concerned, the most widespread and historically effective ground has been its injustice. Love, sacred or profane, had very little to do with abolition. Kaufmann defines love "as the habit of thinking how others feel and sharing their problems and sufferings," which is more like sympathy. Even so, it is not clear how and why love necessarily leads to equal or just treatment. The emotion of love is usually discriminatory. We cannot love all of mankind as we do our friends and members of our family, and we delude ourselves if we think we can.

Secondly, the expression of these virtues must itself be limited by the principle of justice. With regard to love this is obvious. Justice is blind only to what is irrelevant. It is all-seeing with respect to what is relevant. Love's blindness is total, because the distinction between what is relevant and irrelevant is irrelevant to love. Where only two persons are involved in love, "the cautious and jealous" (Hume) virtue of justice, and its emphasis on reciprocity and fairness, is otiose if not odious. But where love or any other emotion involves more than one other person, e.g., parents, and children, teachers and small nursery children, the question whether love is being justly bestowed or exercised may be both meaningful and highly relevant. Children often imagine they suffer from partiality shown by parents to their siblings. Unfortunately, this partiality is sometimes present even when children do not imagine it.

Professor Kaufmann's own illustrations of how the virtue of honesty enables us to dispense with the virtue of justice in our moral judgments shows that he lapses into the very principle of distributive justice that he seeks to collapse. In one of his writings that he cites to support his position, he refers to the example of a teacher grading his students.

Must we not [he asks] introduce justice as a virtue in this case? Surely, he ought to treat like cases alike. But in this situation honesty suffices. To call excellent a paper that is not excellent, or to rank in the bottom quarter a student who *deserves* better is dishonest. (*Faith of a Heretic*, p. 329, my italics)

To refer to a student who *deserves* better is to make a judgment of justice, not of honesty; "desert" here does not depend on any one or all of Kaufmann's cardinal virtues. Indeed, I think it could be shown that, once we extrude the notion of justice from our vocabulary, we would have to declare vacuous or supererogatory an entire family of related concepts like guilt, innocence, and responsibility. They are not reducible to humbition, courage, honesty, or love.

Thirdly, these cardinal virtues often conflict in specific situations. If they are all integral to the concept of justice, we would be unable to reach any judgment. For example, a teacher may rate papers of equal quality differently in order to encourage one student to do better or to penalize another for not doing as well as he can. This may be pedagogically unwise but it is not dishonest. It may be unjust. But the right or moral thing to do in some situations may be the kind thing to do, not the just thing to do, just as it may be morally better to forgive a debt than to insist on collecting it.

Finally, although I agree that the demand for justice in most situations ultimately presupposes some conception or vision of a good or desirable society, it is also true that it makes sense to ask whether that good society is also a just society, meaning by a just society one in which all its citizens are regarded as possessing equal rights with respect to the distribution of the goods and services and whatever else are considered as criteria of the good society. That is why I cannot accept the position of those who, having described or postulated a good society, simply define a just action as one that tends to preserve such a society and an unjust action as one that tends to subvert it. This impoverishes the notion of justice.

III

Although justice in any situation has an irreducible connotation of impartiality and equality, these are not sufficient to establish the presence of justice. This can be established very simply. We say that "justice consists in treating human beings in the same or similar relevant circumstances equally." We would never dream of saying that "justice consists in *mistreating* people equally in the same or similar relevant circumstances." Yet with respect to equality both sentences are on all fours. A macabre illustration of this is provided by a tale of the occupation. A commandant warns a village that he will take stern reprisals if any of his men are ambushed by the underground. They are ambushed. Whereupon he commands the male inhabitants to line up and count off by tens. He then orders every tenth man shot. To the screams of protest by one of the women whose husband is a tenth man, he replies that it would unfair to make exceptions and spare her husband, that justice requires his execution. In her desperation she retorts that the commandant is being unjust to the class of tenth men. They should be treated in the same way as the other classes from the first to ninth. Whereupon the commandant reflects for a moment, turns to her and says: "You are right. We must show no partiality or discrimination!" He then orders: "Shoot them all!"

It seems to me that in examining the situations in which we cite relevant circumstances as making a difference to the respect in which justice is being done, the equalitarian rule is coupled with the ideal of reducing human suffering. We find ourselves committed to a variant of negative utilitarianism in judging which type of action among all the known possibilities of equal treatment is just. Some years ago a movement was launched with great fanfare by feminists calling for the adoption of an equal rights amendment to forbid all legislative measures discriminating against sex in employment. It never got off the ground because it was widely felt that, although it was manifestly unjust to discriminate against persons who applied for the rough and dangerous work of mining on the ground of their color or religion or nationality, it was not unjust to refuse to employ women because of the harm it would do them and their offspring. This would be considered discrimination in favor of women not against them. The guiding consideration determining what similarities and differences are relevant to discriminatory policies flow from our commitment to reduce inequalities of human suffering. We assume that human beings are more alike in the kind and degree of pain they can endure than in the pleasure or happiness they can enjoy. When we surrender our seat to a crippled person or allow him privileges that we deny able-bodied individuals we feel we are not bestowing charity but dispensing justice. All nations in times of crisis when it is necessary to ration goods and services in short supply follow the rule of equality in distribution subject to special modification of need and function. Everyone is entitled to so much bread and gas but for obvious reasons nursing mothers get more bread and physicians get more gas—and justly so. For we thereby equalize or at least equitably diminish human suffering.

This goal can only be approximated. When we reflect on the alternative modes of treatment open to us, we find that the moral sensibility that underlies our commitment to justice deems it more worthy of man to prefer equality of human suffering, where men must suffer, than the sacrifice of some human beings and the imposition of suffering upon them as the price for others' escape from it.

THE SPIRIT OF PHILOSOPHY AND
THE PRACTICE OF POLITICS

George McGovern

Charles Frankel has reminded us that the relationship of intellectuals to public affairs remains a vexatious problem. That observation, I take it, embraces the relationship of the philosopher to the practicing politician. I share what I believe to be Mr. Frankel's view that philosophers and politicians, though frequently resentful and uncomplimentary toward the other, nonetheless cling to a guarded mutual admiration based on a recognition of their interdependence.

H. L. Mencken, "the Sage of Baltimore," threw many a caustic barb into the hides of politicians. Of those who direct our government, Mencken observed:

On the lower levels one encounters men so dreadful that it would be painful to describe them realistically. Nonetheless, the government goes on. There is some disorder, but not enough to be uncomfortable. A certain amount of money is wasted, but not enough to bankrupt us. The laws are dishonest and idiotic, but it is easy to imagine worse. How are we to account for this? I can conjure up but two plausible theories. One is to the effect that the country is actually under the special protection of God, as many clergymen allege every Fourth of July. The other is that the hated and reviled bureaucracy must be a great deal more competent than it looks.[1]

Mencken never lost hope that our government is more practical than it appears; he was fascinated by the world of public affairs. In spite of the uncertain mixture of contempt and respect between political practitioners and philosophers, which Mencken illustrates in exaggerated fashion, the two disciplines interract in a number of important ways which help to determine our political life.

Such diverse politicians as the two Roosevelts, John Kennedy, and Lyndon Johnson have sought the approval and frequently the counsel of scholars. "There is no substitute for brains," Kennedy said, as he raided the faculties of Harvard, Yale, MIT, and other centers of philosophical enterprise. And for their part, growing numbers of intellectuals have responded either with a hitch in government or service to a compatible politican as speech writer, counselor, idea man, or critic.

The most fitting example in my acquaintance of the philosopher turned practitioner is Professor of Philosophy Charles Frankel, now Assistant Secretary of State for Educational and Cultural Affairs. He lends support to my conviction that a good man with proper intellectual and moral equipment can move between the worlds of philosophy and public affairs without grave difficulty, and will, indeed, enrich both worlds as well as himself in the process.

Mr. Frankel has defined the philosophy of practice as "a critical and evaluative activity, not a science in pursuit of special truths." He has suggested that contemporary philosophers can play an important role, especially in illuminating the interrelationships that exist between the various fields of practitioners—reminding us that the practitioner becomes an amateur when confronted with fields other than his own.

In introducing their great study of American civilization, the Beards long ago observed that "as long as the various divisions of history are kept separate, each must be incomplete and distorted; for, as Buckle says, the philosophy of any subject (that is, the truth of it) is not at its center but on the periphery where it impinges on all other sciences." [2]

Mr. Frankel calls not for a single system to embrace all human knowledge, but rather for thoughtful analysis of practical judgments by disciplined outsiders. Such an effort, he believes, will help "to sift values and clarify human choices" and might also shed "significant new light on philosophical issues that have long been debated within other contexts."

The new Random House Dictionary of the English Language suggests that philosophy is "the rational investigation of the truths and principles of being, knowledge, or conduct . . . [or] a system of principles for guidance in practical affairs . . . [or, again,] a philosophical attitude, as one of composure and calm in the presence of trouble or annoyances." A philosopher is defined as "a person who regulates his life, actions, judgments, utterances, etc., by the light of . . . reason [or, again, as] a person who is philosophical, especially under trying circumstances."

But, alas, after defining politics as "the science or art of political government" the same dictionary suggests that politics may also be the "use of intrigue or strategy in obtaining any position of power or control, as in a business, university, etc." And "policy" is defined as "a definite course of action adopted for the sake of expediency, facility, etc."

Without any intention of being overly generous to philosophers or unappreciative of my fellow practitioners, I generally accept these definitions. And I confess to a special admiration for that philosophical attitude defined "as one of composure and calm in the presence of trouble or annoyances."

As an American politician, I have come to an almost desperate conviction of our need, in Mr. Frankel's words, "to sift values and clarify human choices." Nowhere is the need for such a philosophy of practice more evident than in today's world of politics and diplomacy. I believe that we are in grave danger of losing our way as a nation if we cannot find methods of applying a greater measure of practical wisdom to the formation of national policies and priorities at home and abroad.

More than a decade ago, Walter Lippmann observed that "there is a deep disorder in our society which comes not from the machinations of our enemies . . . but from within ourselves." [3] Lippmann's concern with the disorder from within has deepened sharply in recent years, as indeed it should. Without minimizing the real difficulties that confront us in a turbulent world and in our own borders, I am more and more convinced that we are chiefly afflicted by the results of our own irrational policies and priorities.

I do not know how it can be done, but I am sure that we must find ways of giving new force in policy determination to philosophy's concern with truth and values. And who would challenge the mounting need for "composure and calm in the presence of trouble or annoyances"?

I believe it is important that the spirit of philosophy and the practice of politics reinforce each other in several areas. First, it is a matter of urgent importance that more rigorous standards of truth be applied to the formulation and enunciation of public policy. There can be no doubt that "the credibility gap" is a painful fact of contemporary political life. Large numbers of Americans no longer trust their government either to seek the truth or to tell the truth. Much of this problem stems from the desperate efforts of policy-makers to interpret our tragic involvement in Southeast Asia as a glorious struggle for freedom instead of a costly blunder which we should seek to limit and hopefully resolve.

Our policy-makers have told us, for example, that we are in Vietnam to strengthen the process of self-determination there. Whether we should or should not be on our present course in Vietnam, it would seem that any reasonable concern with the truth would make it clear that our intervention has hampered rather than advanced self-determination for the Vietnamese. If one accepts President Eisenhower's considered judgment that in 1954 Ho Chi Minh had the support of at least

80% of the people of Vietnam, North and South, how can it be seriously argued that our efforts since 1954 were designed to encourage Vietnamese self-determination?

I am convinced that the military forecasts, both French and American, relating to Vietnam in the last two decades have proved consistently wrong because those forecasts have ignored such simple political truths as the unpopularity of the political regimes we have backed in Saigon and, conversely, the grass-roots appeal of the NLF and Ho Chi Minh.

It was much the same kind of oblivion to truth that led the Kennedy Administration into the Bay of Pigs. The thoughtful warning to President Kennedy delivered orally and in writing by a philosophical politician, William Fulbright, could have saved us from that Cuban debacle, but expediency prevailed over truth at the moment of policy determination. It is true that the Bay of Pigs and our more serious involvement in Vietnam both occurred at a time when scholars and philosophers abounded in various government posts. But many of these men abandoned their professional objectivity for the claims of expediency or "practicality," while others were overruled by practitioners from the Pentagon, the CIA, the State Department, and the White House.

Today, increasing numbers of philosophically inclined individuals are speaking out against the horror of Vietnam. Representatives of our academic and religious communities are expressing dismay on an almost unprecedented scale. It is my own bias that this articulate, sensitive outcry must become more even, more widespread, and more effective if we are to find our way out of the Southeast Asian morass.

What disturbs me most about the interaction between scholars and policy-makers, with reference to Vietnam, is the facility with which some scholars in government have forced disturbing facts to conform with a stubbornly held theory. In a perceptive article on Walt Whitman Rostow, the presidential assistant who has played a key role first in persuading President Kennedy to send American ground forces into combat in Vietnam and then in rationalizing the bombing of North Vietnam as ordered by President Johnson, Alex Campbell concludes: "Rostow's rash attempts to make his high and hasty abstractions illuminate stubborn bodies of complex facts have proved wholly disastrous to American foreign policy. What he himself has called his 'dangerous essays in generalization' have merely afforded other men a handy philosophical framework for their own gut reactions." [4]

The trouble with this approach is that it abandons both objectivity and humility in dealing with changing conditions that might counter one's assumptions. Instead, it provides new rationalizations to justify ill-conceived policies that no longer conform to reality. In this sense the philosophy of practice is at the service of both bad theory and bad practice; the philosopher in government becomes the apologist of the credibility gap and no longer illuminates the untruths which gave rise to the gap between truth and policy.

I believe there is frequently a tendency on the part of scholars in government to abandon the intellectual and moral claims of their own disciplines in order to avoid the suspicion of politicians who might regard them as "impractical" or excessively "idealistic" or even "soft." It is usually safer to be "hard" than "soft" and this normally means a preference for more military action as against diplomatic accommodation, or watchful waiting. It means, too, a tendency to prefer bold unilateral intervention as against the slow and often frustrating processes of the United Nations.

And so the scholar-philosopher in politics is tempted to "go along" rather than to hold to the best habits of mind and spirit of which his special discipline is capable. But this temptation only points up the need for a tougher, more carefully nurtured philosophy of practice based on a consistent effort to apply the test of truth to public policy as best we can.

A worthwhile philosophy of practice is one that also insists on keeping open the channels of discussion, inquiry, and dissent. Walter Bagehot's reflections on history and politics led him to the conclusion that discussion is the chief instrument of both freedom and progress. History's answer to why some societies stagnate and others progress is revealed, Bagehot wrote, in "that the change from the age of status to the age of choice was first made in states where the government was to a great and a growing extent a government by discussion, and where the subjects of that discussion were in some degree abstract, or, as we should say, matters of principle." [5]

If I may refer again to the Vietnam imbroglio, I find the most deplorable aspect of the entire matter to be the efforts of those who would silence dissent by equating it with assistance to the enemy and rising American casualties. One easily recognizes that there can be and are strongly held differences of opinion as to the wisdom of our course in Asia. But there is no room in the proper formation or execution of policy in a free society for silencing discussion and dissent. There can be no valid reason for fighting so blindly to secure freedom in Saigon that we sacrifice it in Washington. To suggest that Senators, clergymen, teachers, students, journalists, and others should swallow their doubts to avoid misleading Hanoi as to our national resolve, is to suggest that we should abandon freedom of inquiry and speech because those essentials of democracy are not understood by those who have not experienced them.

The most enduring sources of our national strength are those wise principles of individual freedom and dignity which Jefferson, Madison, Adams, and other philosopher-statesmen wrote into the Declaration of Independence and the Constitution. Our whole history as a nation has been an experiment. It began with those who had the courage to break from all they knew and make the perilous journey to the New World. We became a nation in violent revolution against established order and authority. We grew and prospered because daring men crossed into the uncharted and terrifying West and explored the unknown ranges of science and invention.

It is this which tells us what is most important about the American nation: America is not an established or completed institution; it is not a particular piece of geography or a collection of people. It is not even a government or a Constitution. It is a process. It is a method of liberating the skill and energy of individual men so that they may contribute to the freedom and well-being of our people. Therefore, the highest faithfulness to country does not lie in blindly accepting the ideas of the past or the policies of the present, but rather in the willingness to question and challenge all that we are and all we do, so that we may bring the reality of America closer to the ideal.

The right to propose new ideas and challenge old ones, to express the conclusions of mind and the commands of conscience, is often spoken of as a freedom or a privilege. It is much more than this. It is the most imperative necessity. It is not simply something we allow, but something a free society demands. It is not just something we can live with; it is something we cannot live without. It is not only consistent with patriotism; it is the highest patriotism.

To remain silent in the face of policies that one believes to be hurting the nation is not patriotism, but moral cowardice. Backing our soldiers in Vietnam does not mean cheering them on to their deaths in acquiescence to what one regards as a dangerously ill-conceived course. Criticism of public policy does not weaken the nation; rather, it serves to refine, correct, or strengthen our national course. If the policy is sound, it will become better understood and therefore more effective under the searchlight of analysis and debate; if not sound, it can best be remedied by constructive examination and frank discussion.

The philosopher and the practitioner should form an unswerving alliance to insist *not* that they have embraced all truth, but that all channels to the examination and discussion of truth and error must be kept open.

Finally, a philosophy of practice will seek some order of priorities and values in public policy. Instead of frantic makeshift responses to each crisis, real or imagined, we need to cultivate the kind of composure that makes possible greater discrimination in determining what is worthy of our major energies and resources, and what is not.

There is a disturbing American tendency to overreact to certain ideological and military factors while overlooking issues of vastly greater relevance to our safety and well-being. A civil insurrection in Santo Domingo or Cuba is dramatic, but what is its significance compared with such quiet challenges as the proliferation of nuclear weapons, the surging of nationalism and social upheavals in the developing world, or the mounting crisis of hunger and population? What, too, is the relationship of the quality and strength of our own society to our position in the world? How will the world see us if we succeed in pacifying Saigon but fail to pacify Newark and Detroit?

Many Americans, having grown impatient with the frustrations of the cold war, see each international tension as an urgent crisis calling for a direct and decisive attack on the enemy. Moreover, there must be no halfway measures: "Either get in or get out!" Those who suggest that there may be a proper limit to American power are branded as "neo-isolationists."

Having agreed for years on basic foreign policy assumptions—and especially the containment of Communism—our political party leaders have found it necessary to devise other areas of combat. Each side knows that it must capitalize quickly on even inconsequential events lest the opposition do so first with telling political results. Politicians out of power have found it expedient to interpret each international incident as a mortal danger to the republic. Politicians in power must demonstrate that they are taking swift and forceful steps to save the nation from disaster.

The meagerness of genuine discussion about fundamental issues and our tendency to magnify minor incidents have caused us to miss many opportunities for constructive new initiatives both at home and abroad. We have, for example, concentrated too heavily and too long on an all-out military response to the international challenge, while neglecting the economic, political, and moral sources of our strength. In a thoughtful book recently published, Dr. Frankel cites American educational and cultural policy abroad as "The Neglected Aspect of Foreign Affairs." Frequently, we have confused means with ends and then argued about those means with all the passion ordinarily reserved for sacred principles. The crisis mentality and the emphasis on means usually call for more and bigger weapons. The crisis addict becomes impatient when it is suggested that a nation's strength is measured as much by the quality of its schools, the health of its citizens, the vigor of its culture, and the treatment of minorities as by the size of its weapons. He lacks the perspective to realize that the steady, peaceful development of Asia, Africa, and Latin America is of far greater significance to American security than the political color of future regimes in Southeast Asia or the Caribbean.

America has achieved a position of power and influence in the world that is unprecedented. We have often used that power generously and courageously, perhaps more than any other nation of our age. I have no doubt of our capacity to respond effectively to a genuine crisis that calls for vigorous and decisive action. I should like to believe that we will also develop a talent for discovering and responding rationally to the underlying forces at work in our time. But to those innumerable tensions, struggles, and incidents of the future that we neither can nor should control, I hope we will manifest a measure of Ralph Waldo Emerson's wisdom: "Let him not quit his belief that a popgun is a popgun, though the ancient and honorable of the earth affirm it to be the crack of doom."

I stress again the fact that the practicing politician needs to be disciplined by that philosophical attitude defined as "one of composure and calm in the presence of troubles or annoyances."

I doubt that I have shed any significant new light on the problems involved in building a philosophy of practice. Perhaps, I have simply been restating for my own satisfaction what Plato said long ago: "Until philosophers are kings, or the kings and princes of this world have the spirit and power of philosophy, and political greatness and wisdom meet in one . . . cities will never have rest from their evils—no, nor the human race . . . have a possibility of life and behold the light of day." [6]

NOTES

1. H. L. Mencken, On Politics (New York, Vintage Books, 1960), p. viii.
2. Charles A. and Mary R. Beard, The Rise of American Civilization (New York, Appleton & Co., 1873), p. vii.
3. Walter Lippmann, The Public Philosophy (Boston, Little, Brown, 1955), p. 5.
4. Alex Campbell, "Walt Whitman Rostow" in The New Republic, November 4, 1967.
5. Walter Bagehot, Physics and Politics (New York, The Macmillan Co., 1930), p. 158.
6. Plato, Dialogues, V.2. The Republic, trans. by B. Jowett (Oxford, Clarendon Press, 1953), p. 5.

VALUE AND FACT

Kurt Baier

It is generally agreed that among the most important and difficult problems facing mankind are problems of value: problems whose solutions hinge on knowing the true value of things, experiences, motives, goals, actions, lives, and institutions. Yet it is also a very widely held view, perhaps the dominant view, that answers to such value questions must be formulated in so-called value judgments and that these are neither themselves empirical factual statements, capable of being true or false, verified or falsified, confirmed or disconfirmed, nor deducible from such factual statements. It is a corollary of this view that the empirical sciences cannot hope to answer value questions and should therefore not only refrain from raising such questions but should meticulously avoid making any value claims. And since there are no other methods for answering such value questions, there must remain, at the very heart of some of the most important human concerns, questions that cannot be authoritatively answered. Concerning these important matters, therefore, the best we can hope for is that we can train ourselves to stop asking them or disagreeing about them. My main aim here is to argue against this widely held theory. In my view, value judgments are a species of empirical, factual statement, capable of being true or false.

I

Before I can begin to argue for my contention that value judgments are factual statements, I must say something about the method for singling out, from the mass of remarks, those which are value judgments. It had better not be an arbitrary stipulative definition, for any theory with such a basis would be about value judgments only by good fortune, namely, if the arbitrary stipulation happened to single out value judgments and nothing else—which would be unlikely.

How, then, can we single out value judgments without prejudging the question of their nature? I think we can safely say that in calling a remark a value judgment, we ordinarily make two claims about it: that *it is a judgment* and that *it ascribes value to something*. A judgment is a certain sort of claim, namely, one made by a person with the necessary qualifications (blind men cannot judge paintings) and made with the necessary care (one look is usually not enough for judging a painting). Unless otherwise stated, any value claim purports to be a value judgment, just as observational claims purport to be based on observation, or claims about impending political moves on adequate information. For our purposes the difference between judgments and other kinds of claim can be ignored. For us, the important question is, what is it to *ascribe value* to something? What follows purports to be an accurate account of how we ordinarily use and what we ordinarily mean by the word 'value.' My later remarks about the nature of value judgments are based on that account.

The first thing we notice is that value judgments are of many different types and that for clarity's sake we need to put them in some sort of order. I shall distinguish three levels of *complexity*, and the corresponding types of value claims: *basic*, *comparative*, and *quantitative*. Thus value judgments will be either basic, comparative, or quantitative. And I shall also distinguish an indefinite number of degrees of *abstractness*, from the fully concrete to the fully abstract, depending on the degree to which the dimensions of a value judgment are specified in the judgment in question. I shall begin my account with a brief characterization of this classificatory system, then dwell at some length on basic concrete value judgments, and finally explain by what transformations we arrive at value judgments of the other types. By thus displaying the anatomy of value judgments I hope to make clear how they can all be complex empirical statements, capable of being true or false.

To begin with complexity, we may distinguish three main types of value claims:

(1) *Basic:* 'O has (no) value,' e.g., 'Exercise after forty has (no) value.' Basic value claims are either-or claims, not involving comparisons, in respect of value, with other things.

(2) *Comparative:* 'O has more (less) value than P,' e.g., 'Up to forty exercise has more (less) value than after forty.'

(3) *Quantitative:* 'The value of O is M,' e.g., 'The value of exercise is great (little, nil).' Claims of this type differ from basic value claims in that they involve *standards* of comparison.

These three types of value claims of different levels of complexity may be formulated in more or less fully concrete form. The examples so far given are in fairly abstract form. They abstract from the identity of the beneficiary, the kind of benefit conferred on him, and the conditions under which the benefit accrues to him. A fully concrete claim of the basic type has this form:

(4) 'O is, at time t, under the benefit conditions, C, of assistance to the beneficiary, BY, in attaining an end, E, from which BY derives a benefit, BT,' e.g., 'Your compass was of value to us; without it we would have spent the whole night in that forest.' Fully concrete claims quite clearly exhibit the characteristic content of value claims. They display all their dimensions. They mention, or at least strongly suggest, how each of these dimensions is to be filled in. In our example the value object is the compass; the benefit is that derived from not having to stay in the forest all night; the beneficiaries are we; and the suggested benefit conditions are having and using the compass.

An understanding of abstract value claims presupposes an understanding of concrete ones, and an understanding of comparative and quantitative ones presupposes an understanding of basic ones. I therefore turn to an examination of the central value claim, the basic concrete value claim. Such an examination brings to light three distinct components:

(5) BY does a in C in order to attain E at t or thereafter.

(6) O is, at t, in C, of assistance to BY in doing a.

(7) Doing a with the aid of O, in order to attain E at t or thereafter constitutes a benefit for BY.[1]

(5) does not require attention here. Whatever difficulties attach to claims of this form cannot be, and to my knowledge have never been, attributed to (5)'s being a value judgment. However, (6) and (7) do call for scrutiny. Let us begin with (7), the problem of whether a change in a person's life constitutes a benefit to him. I shall argue that this depends on whether the change is a favorable, an unfavorable, or a neutral change, and this depends on whether it brings that person's life closer to the optimal life for him, takes it farther away from it, or leaves it at the same distance.

The idea of the optimal life for a person may be explained by analogy with the idea of the healthy state of his body. Since we (physicians) know what the healthy state of his body is, and what are sick states of it, we can in principle tell of any change in his body whether, from the point of view of health, it is a favorable, an unfavorable, or an indifferent change, depending simply on the distance from the state of health at which this change left that person's body.

Does the analogy hold? Of course, much more is known about health than about the optimal life for a person. But then reliable medical knowledge is comparatively recent, and even today our knowledge is often insufficient to determine whether a given change in someone's body is, health-wise, a favorable change. Despite this ignorance and the difficulty of remedying it, the importance of health, at all stages of our knowledge about it, justified continued efforts to make the idea clearer and to expand our knowledge relevant to it. All this seems to me true also of the idea of an optimal life.

Again, it might be said that whereas health is the same for everybody, the optimal life for a person is incurably relative to personal tastes. But the plausibility of this objection rests on a confusion of two ways of characterizing health, which we may call "functional" and "descriptive," respectively. Suppose we think of health as a state of the body; then we characterize health in a functional way if we set out the requirements a healthy body must satisfy in terms of its power to ensure a certain desideratum: positive well-being and the full possession of physical powers, or at least the absence of discomforts and the full possession of physical powers. In the functional sense, health is not person-relative, but is the same for everybody. We characterize health in the descriptive way if we spell out in a terminology that implies nothing about health or ill-health, the condition the body must be in if it is to be *called* healthy. Thus the functional way of characterizing health lays down conditions that any descriptive account must satisfy. In the descriptive sense, health is person-relative, for that condition depends on personal, nonuniversal factors, e.g., sex, age, blood group, height, and so forth.

If this distinction between the descriptive and functional way of characterizing something is borne in mind, then it becomes clear that the optimal life for a person is no more person-relative than health. Of course, when descriptively characterized, the optimal life for a person is determined by the peculiarities of that person, including his tastes. But when functionally characterized, the optimal life is the best life permitted by an individual's position in life (largely determined by his birth).

How could we determine the optimal life (or lives, for there may be indefinitely many apparently equally good) for a person? Philosophers can at best give an account in functional language. An applied science, analogous to medicine, would have to fill in the descriptive details. Even this modest philosophical undertaking is difficult, and I am quite likely to make serious mistakes. There are, at any rate, two separate lines of investigation. One line involves a survey of the paths open to a particular person, the other the comparison in respect of excellence of the lives resulting from following these paths. I shall begin with the second of these.

Comparison of lives in respect of excellence are made from one or another or all of three points of view, which we may call (without being unduly misleading) *worthwhileness, worth,* and *worthiness.* Only those changes which affect the worthwhileness of a life are *directly* relevant to the question of whether they constitute a benefit. But those that affect a life's worth or worthiness may be *indirectly* relevant. This point will become clear shortly.

The worthwhileness of a life is judged on the basis of three possibly conflicting criteria: satisfyingness, richness, and cultivatedness. The satisfyingness of a life (to the person leading it) is judged on the basis of the extent to which that life contains what its owner *finds* (or if it were part of his life, *would* find) worthwhile, rewarding, or satisfying, regardless of how this affects others about whom he does not care. We can say of A's actual life, L_1, that it is more satisfying than some possible alternative life, L_2 *if* L_1 caters *more fully to* A's tastes than L_2 would. Given that if A led L_2 he would have the same tastes as he now has in L_1, L_1 is more satisfying than L_2 provided L_1 contains more than L_2 would, of the things A finds worthwhile.

However, L_2 may contain experiences (training) as a result of which A would come to appreciate things present in both L_1 and L_2 which in the absence of this training he does not appreciate. Such training develops his tastes, makes him a more cultured person, and so extends the range of satisfactions of which he is capable. Thus, education may make a life better by opening up the appreciation of things which could well be part of someone's life but which, for lack of that appreciation, he sees no reason to make part of it. The broadening of one's tastes is thus a change in one's life which increases one's *capacity* for leading a *more* worthwhile life. But, as is well known, it is not necessarily a favorable change, for one's life may not contain any or many of the things that would cater to more cultivated tastes. Lastly, A's life L_1 may be more worthwhile than an alternative possible life L_2 *if* L_1 is a *richer* life than L_2; if it contains what caters equally fully to *a broader range* of his tastes than L_2.

In the ideal case, the cultivating and broadening of a person's tastes by his educational progress would go hand in hand with an increase in his resources, so that he is in a position to cater more fully to his more cultivated and broadened tastes. To say this is not to deny, of course, that there often will be difficult choices to make between allocating scarce resources to the task of cultivating or broadening someone's tastes and allocating them to the task of catering more fully to the relatively uncultivated and narrow tastes he already has, and that no clear guidelines are available about which allocation makes a more favorable difference to his life. But even if these questions can never be answered, (which I do not believe), we can hope that with our increasing resources the allocation of some to each of these tasks will at any rate produce continuous improvements in our lives, though perhaps not the unquestionably optimal ones.

I have spoken only of comparisons between a person's actual and some alternative possible lives, perhaps one day producible at will by some deliberate intervention at a given point. I have said nothing about such comparisons between the lives of different people. Fortunately, for our purposes of determining the optimal life of a person, such interpersonal comparisons are not necessary.

We compare lives in respect of *worthiness* if we compare them in respect of the extent to which their owners have met the legitimate demands that others may make on them. Worthiness implies desert, the reward due to a person who, in the face of difficulties, has met these legitimate demands, or the penalty due to one who has failed to meet them in the absence of excuses. We compare lives in respect of *worth* if we compare them in respect of the extent to which their owners have contributed to the excellence of the lives of others. Worthiness assesses a person's performance in cases of conflicts between his own good and the legitimate demands of others. Worth assesses a person's accomplishments in the cause of human welfare. "The widow's mite" adds greatly to her worthiness, little to her worth. Instead of 'a life of great worth' we could also speak of 'a life of great value,' a 'valuable life.'

The worthiness and worth of a life are not directly relevant to its worthwhileness: The greater worthiness and worth of a life may well detract from its worthwhileness. Neither favorable nor unfavorable changes in a person's life *ipso facto* affect its (or his) worthiness or worth. However, worthiness and worth may be indirectly relevant to the worthwhileness of a person's life, for that person may derive satisfaction from the thought that he is leading a life of great worth or worthiness, and so may want to lead such a life. If so, then the things that give his life worthiness or worth have indirectly become worthwhile for him.

The second line of investigation required for the determination of an optimal life for a person involves a survey of *the paths* open to him. What are these paths? Their main outlines are mapped out by the society into which he is born. In caste societies, the only path open to him is fixed by his birth. In open societies, his position in society (and the accompanying role) is determined not solely by birth, but also by the many permissible choices open to members of that society, particularly those of his calling, occupation, or career. Of course, a person's position, whether rigidly fixed as in a caste society or at least partly a matter of the individual's choice as in open societies, determines only his primary role, that is, the tasks he is socially required to perform and the rewards he is to obtain for the performance of these tasks. Within the limits fixed by one's position there is usually still ample room for choices of secondary roles, such as those determined by marriage, political activity, various forms of association in churches, clubs, and societies, and the pursuit of leisure activities. However, even there one's station will seriously delimit the range of the choices open to one in these secondary matters.

Having surveyed the various life paths available in a given society, we must eliminate those which are legally closed to the person in question and those which, though legally open, are practically closed because of social, racial, geographical, or other barriers. Lastly, we must add those that might become open, and subtract those that might become closed, either as the result of probable social changes or of his entering another society.

However, even if empirical investigation along these two lines has enabled us to answer both what sorts of things would make Jones's life more or less worthwhile and what are the various life paths open to him, we still cannot determine the *optimal* life path for him. For a given life path does not wholly determine the degree of worthwhileness of the life of the person moving along that path. In most (perhaps all) of the roles determining a particular life path, there is room for different rates of progress or advance. The word 'career' most clearly implies this idea of rate of progress. But the worthwhileness of a given life depends to some extent on the rate of progress, for the rewards a given life path offers vary with the progress made. Hence in order to know which of the life paths open to Jones (if more than one) is the optimal life path for him, we must ask first to what extent progress along these life paths would cater to his tastes, i.e., would secure for him the things he finds worthwhile and the opposite; we must ask secondly how well his own resources (physical, intellectual, artistic) qualify him for progress along each of these paths. The life path which for him is probably optimal, is then the one in which the progress he is likely to make, given his resources, offers the highest likelihood of the most worthwhile life. And the optimal life for him is that life along this optimal life path that makes the greatest possible progress in all the roles he is playing. Once a person has entered on a given life path with its various roles, events in the world around him, the doings of others, and his own doings, can be looked at *from the point of view of his interest*: they either are or are not in his interest, depending on whether they do or do not promote progress along his path.

Once we know the optimal life for someone, then we can consider any change in that person's life, from the point of view of that optimal life. We can compare the life before and as a result of any given change in respect to its "distance" from the optimal life for that person. If the change has produced a state that is closer to the optimal life for him, then it is a favorable change; if the distance has remained the same, then it is neutral; if it has become greater, it is unfavorable.

It might be objected that this account of 'favorable change' must be false, for we often know that a change in a person's life is a favorable change, e.g., when he wins a lottery or lands a good job, although we have no idea of the optimal life for him. Moreover, this is just as well, for determining the optimal life for a person is not going to be an easy matter. This objection is well taken: we do know quite well that certain changes in a person's life are favorable changes without knowing the optimal life for that person. But the reason is not that these changes are favorable even though they do not bring that person's life closer to the optimal life, but because certain changes do so whatever the optimal life of the particular person may be. This point will become clearer below.

Does a change in a person's life constitute a benefit for him if and only if it is a favorable change? Not quite. Some unfavorable changes also may constitute benefits. The loss of a leg is normally an unfavorable change. But, if to prevent gangrene a surgeon amputates a soldier's leg, then, because the amputation *prevents* a worse unfavorable change, it constitutes a benefit to the soldier. Considered merely as a change, the loss of a leg is an unfavorable change in one's life. But considered as what is involved in a necessary amputation, it is a benefit. The difference between these two judgments is not due to different criteria or standards, for in both cases, we are considering the distance from the optimal life for the same person. Rather, the difference lies in how we select the relevant states for comparison. In the first case, we are comparing the actual life *before and after* the loss of the leg, a clear case of moving further away from the optimal life. In the second case, we are comparing the actual life as a result of the amputation with the life *as it would be* if the amputation had not occurred. In the first case, we are comparing two actual states, an earlier and a later one. In the second case, we are comparing two simultaneous states, an actual and a possible alternative one.

Two questions arise: What is the appropriate hypothetical alternative to consider, and how must this hypothetical alternative compare with the actual change under consideration for a change to count as a benefit? In answer to the second question, the actual change must be a lesser deterioration in the agent's life than the hypothetical change would have been. The loss of a leg is less of a deterioration than gangrene leading to death.

In answer to the first question, the hypothetical change to consider would seem to be the change that would have come about if the actual change under consideration had not prevented it. Suppose that if Jones had not lost his leg, he would have died of blood poisoning; then the loss of the leg, by saving his life, *constitutes* a benefit to Jones. Anyone saving Jones's life by amputating his leg *confers* a benefit. If, Walter Mitty-fashion, he amputates his own leg, he confers a benefit on himself. If an unforeseeable or unlikely event in nature (famine in China) brings about changes (rise in wheat prices) that are better than the justifiably anticipated or most likely changes that it prevents (bankruptcy for farmer Jones) then we can think of this event as conferring a benefit, and the changes as constituting one.

I have argued that a benefit to a person is constituted either by some improvement in his life or even by a deterioration, provided it is not as great as the deterioration it prevented would have been. It should be noted that, on my view, a change may be a benefit even if it is a lesser benefit than some that Jones himself could have brought about by some other intervention he did not in fact make,[2] or a greater deterioration than some that someone else could have brought about (but did not) by some other intervention. To deny this would be to deny that anything other than the greatest favorable change practically possible for that person is a benefit to him. But this is not how we do or should conceive of a benefit.

Benefits thus include more than actual improvements in a person's life. They include also all those changes that are practical alternatives to worse deteriorations. Furthermore, they include all those changes in the person himself and in his environment that increase his power to improve his life or to prevent or reduce deteriorations in it, such as increases in his theoretical and practical knowledge, his health, or his income; and those that increase the range and depth of his enjoyments and appreciations, such as a broadening of his education, activities, and experiences. They also include all those public amenities that provide increased opportunities for an individual to improve his life, such as theatres, museums, parks, and those social measures which protect, and maintain the level of these opportunities, such as defense, medical care, public education, and communications.

This point is of social and political importance, for it shows us that we can know that a given change in a person's life is a favorable one, even if we do not know the optimal life for him. We can know this because some changes, such as increases in his practical and theoretical knowledge or improvements in his health will be favorable changes, *whatever the optimal life for him*. Thus in introducing welfare measures, a government can know that it benefits everyone, although it cannot consider everyone's optimal life.

The second component of a basic concrete value claim (proposition 6 above) is also to the effect that something constitutes a benefit. That something is of value to someone means either that it is an *indispensable means* to, or that it is *an aid*, is *helpful* in the attainment of the end through which the benefit accrues. In the first case, the value lies simply in the benefit accruing through the attainment of the end. This case explains our inclination to say that the value of means is derivative. In the second case, however, another characteristic benefit is conferred: Aid, assistance, help may consist in enabling the person aided to attain his end with *greater ease* than he would have been able to without the aid. He thus attains his end at reduced cost in time, energy, concentration, skill, and risk, thereby freeing these resources for other purposes. The characteristic benefit is economy—a saving of resources. This sort of benefit is not derivative.

This completes my account of basic concrete value claims. They involve three essentially different assertions: one to the effect that someone tried to attain an end, the second to the effect that something was an aid to him in trying to attain that end, and the third to the effect that the attempt to attain that end with the aid of that thing constituted a benefit. To attribute value to a thing which has played such a role in such a context is thus to contend that through playing that role it conferred benefits on a person. That a thing (actually) is at a certain time of value to someone thus means that this thing has at that time realized its capacity to confer benefits. By isolating and specifying the conditions under which things realize this capacity, we can separate the capacity from the conditions under which it is realized. We then make possible the transition from concrete to abstract value claims, that is, claims in which we attribute to things *the potentiality* to be of value to someone, without saying anything about its realization.

The second kind of transformation is that from basic value judgments, whether concrete or abstract, to more complex ones. That transformation is made when we do not ascribe value to one single object, but compare several objects in respect of their value, as in 'up to forty, exercise has greater value than after forty,' or 'your compass was of greater value to us than your guide book.' A special and highly sophisticated case of such a comparison is the quantitative value judgment. We make quantitative value judgments when we compare objects to be assessed in value with a standard object whose value serves as our basis of comparison, somewhat as the average man serves as the basis of our judgments of tallness, stoutness, intelligence, and so on.

These complex value judgments allow considerable refinement in respect to specificity and precision. We can, for instance, specify the benefit conferred by spelling out wherein the ascribed value consists. One way of doing this is by qualifying the word 'value,' as in survival value, surprise, shock, preventive, prophylactic, explanatory, curative, nutritive, political, pedagogic, commercial, snob, news, documentary, artistic, aesthetic, literary or entertainment value. Not all such qualifying expressions are used to specify the benefit. When we speak of sentimental, market, dollar, exchange, or intrinsic value, we are pointing to sorts of value sorted on grounds other than kinds of benefit conferred by the things claimed to have these sorts of value. We could add other ways of specification, as in various forms of economic value.

Information concerning the capacity of things to confer benefits is itself valuable, for it enables a person in the appropriate circumstances to secure for himself the benefits these things can confer. It is also of value to a person to have information about the comparative value of several things of one and the same sort. It is not really surprising, then, that such information is made available where alternative aids to the same ends are available to us. We tend to confine the title 'appraisal' to those value claims which, unlike the basic either-or claims, involve such comparisons of two or more aids to the same ends.

What, then, are appraisals and how do they differ from other kinds of orderings? Appraisals are comparisons (explicit or implicit) of things in respect of those properties that enable them to satisfy a given *desideratum*, i.e., something generally acknowledged to be found worthwhile by a significant number of people, and not objectionable. Suppose the desideratum is success at basketball or at riding race horses. Then being a certain height is one such property. We appraise candidates on the basis of a *criterion*, which tells us which property (or combination of properties) is relevant and how it is relevant—in both our cases height is relevant but in opposite ways. The order established by an appraisal is a hierarchical or preferential order, an order with a top and a bottom. Things are placed *higher* in the order if they are capable of satisfying the desideratum to a greater degree. Experts know what properties a thing must possess to be so capable. They are therefore in a position to place things in such an hierarchical order prior to putting them to the test. However, in many cases, it requires expertise to tell even after the test which things have satisfied the desideratum to a greater degree.

Appraisals are of two forms, ranking and grading. In the former we compare at least two entries with one another. In the latter we compare one or more entries with a known and fixed standard. Standardization enables us indirectly to compare entries which have never been directly compared with one another. It should be noted that whereas criteria necessarily are determined by the desideratum, standards may well be selected on the basis of convenience.

II

We can now turn to our main question, the relation of value and fact. What then are questions of fact? Even a cursory survey reveals that this expression is used to mark one pole of many different contrasts. Questions of fact contrast with questions of opinion, questions of taste, questions of convention, questions of interpretation, questions of calculation. Some of these contrasts refer to the *method* of establishing answers to questions. Thus we may contrast questions of fact, i.e., *empirical fact* (e.g., 'Are there any more chairs in the hall?') with questions of *calculation*, or derivation (e.g., 'The 20th is a Thursday, so the 25th will be . . . ?'), questions of fact, i.e., *brute fact* (e.g., 'What did he say?') with questions of *interpretation* (e.g., 'What did he mean?'); questions of fact, i.e., *natural fact* (e.g., 'How much did he give her?') with questions of *convention* (or usage) (e.g., 'What is it customary to tip here?'). A word should perhaps be said about questions of convention, or usage. They include questions of law, etiquette, custom, the morality of the group, religious rules, rules of games. With regard to all of these matters we can ask questions of convention, namely, what the appropriate rules say, what the done thing is. The question whether Jones used a knife to sever a certain part of someone's body is a question of natural fact, but the question of what the appropriate rules say is not a question of natural fact but a question of convention. However, whether Jones (in using a knife to sever this part) did the legally, customarily, morally, religiously *proper* thing are complex questions that require answers *both* to questions of natural fact *and* to questions of convention.[3]

Another pair of contrasts refers not to how answers *can be*, but to how well they *have been* established. Thus we contrast questions of fact, i.e., *established fact* (e.g., 'When was the battle of Waterloo?') with questions of *opinion* (e.g., 'When will the Chinese have ICBM's?').

Lastly, some refer to the reach or scope of the remark. Thus we may contrast questions of fact, i.e., *objective fact* (e.g., 'Is this dress too small for Mary to get into?') with questions of *taste* (e.g., 'Is this dress too close-fitting for Mary?').

This gives us five pairs of distinctions between factual and nonfactual statements; statements of:

1) empirical fact – calculation (derivation)
2) brute fact – interpretation
3) natural fact – convention (usage)
4) established fact – opinion
5) objective fact – taste

It is clear that these distinctions do not cut along the same line. Hence, a factual statement in one sense need not be factual in any, let alone every other sense. 'Liverwurst is delicious' is a statement of natural, but not of objective fact. 'President Johnson will be reelected in 1968' is a statement of objective, but not of established fact. Hence, from the fact that judgments of taste are not statements of objective fact, it does not follow that they are not statements of empirical, natural, brute, or established fact. That a given remark is not a statement of fact in one of these senses, does not entail that it is not a statement of fact unless we so use 'statement of fact' that it means 'statement of fact in *every one* of these five senses.' But then a significant proportion of ordinary factual statements will not be statements of fact either: no statements of calculation, interpretation, conjecture, and convention will be. If we want to preserve the ordinary denotation of 'factual statement,' we shall have to loosen the requirements. We shall have to say that anything is a factual statement in one or other, or in a combination of these five senses.

But with this looser requirement, it is clear that most or perhaps all value judgments will be factual statements in one or another of these senses. It is true, however, that few if any are statements of brute (uninterpreted) fact, and very few are statements of established fact. Few are statements of brute fact because many value claims require the balancing of conflicting criteria, which is a matter of judgment. Few are statements of established fact because many of them are based on predictions of highly complex future developments that must remain matters of opinion. Lastly, of course, those many value claims that are based on matters of taste are not statements of objective fact. But as we have seen, this does not *ipso facto* make them nonfactual in any of the other senses.

There remains one more contrast to consider, that between so-called descriptive fact and norm. Value judgments are often said to be essentially *normative*. And this usually means that in making a value judgment one *ipso facto* gives an answer to some question of what to do. But if value judgments are answers to such practical questions, then, it is thought, they cannot be factual statements. For, it is thought, only commands, imperatives, or prescriptions can answer practical questions. (See, for example, R. M. Hare, *The Language of Morals*, pp. 46 f.) This view, in other words, contrasts questions of fact with practical questions.

I believe that if it is true at all that value judgments imply answers to practical questions, it is true only in a very loose sense of 'imply.' If someone says that a certain piece of information would be of value to him, that it would be useful or good for him to have this piece of information, does anything follow with regard to what anyone should or should not do; or even anything with regard to what he thinks anyone, including himself, should do? It seems not. But let us sidestep this question. Let us agree, for argument's sake, that value judgments do imply answers to practical questions. Does this show that value judgments cannot be factual statements?

The view that it does, seems to me to rest on a misconception of practical questions. When I ask someone what to do, what I should do, or what I ought to do, I ask for help with a practical problem; I ask for a solution to it. I am not asking to be commanded, ordered about, or told to do something or other. Solutions to my practical problems are lines of action, namely, those which I can, must, or should follow to solve my problem. An answer to a practical question purports to be at least a solution, possibly a good solution, perhaps the best solution to the practical problem involved. It can be a sound or an unsound answer, since it may or may not be a solution. The fact that such answers can be in the form of imperatives is unimportant. What matters is what these imperatives are used to say. If my account is correct, then answers to practical questions are appraisals of alternative lines of action as solutions to practical problems and therefore as capable of being factual statements as are the value claims previously discussed.

I conclude that value judgments are highly complex claims to the effect that under certain conditions things confer benefits on people and that such claims are often, perhaps mostly, factual statements, in one or other or several of the most important senses of this expression.

III

It may be helpful to conclude with a few words about how my account of value judgments differs from a few currently fashionable theories. One way in which my account differs from all others is that it takes very seriously a requirement which I think should be but often is not taken seriously, namely, that such an account should be an empirically verifiable characterization of what can properly be called value judgments. An account of value judgments should therefore involve two distinguishable steps: the selection on the basis of the appropriate criteria of what are properly called value judgments, and their examination to determine their important characteristics. In going through the literature, one does not find a separation of these two steps. Instead, one finds philosophers producing a few examples of what they would be prepared to call value judgments and mentioning a few characteristics of these, such as their being expressions of feelings, attitudes, tastes, preferences; their prescribing, dictating, commending, recommending, proposing something; or their being regulative, performative, ceremonial, and so on; and then a declaration to the effect that it is the possession of one or other of these features that *makes* judgments evaluative.

One could, of course, interpret this procedure as a rather swift way of doing what I try to do. In that case, one has to say that philosophers have simply failed to single out the proper object for examination. Instead of studying value judgments, they have studied other things such as expressions of feelings, commands, advice, and so on. Very few have studied the same thing. Agreement and disagreement among them therefore depends largely on whether they happened to pick the same subject for study. Disagreement among them is largely due to their being at cross purposes, one talking about one thing, another about another thing, both thinking it is the same thing.

One can, however, interpret this procedure in another way. One can take it to be a recommendation of a certain use of the term 'value judgment.' So interpreted, the currently fashionable accounts are not, of course, open to the objection that they misrepresent value judgments, for then such accounts do not set out to represent them correctly, but rather to recommend a new use of the term. However, there are three objections to this interpretation. The first is that to my knowledge no one has offered his account unambiguously as a mere recommendation. Indeed the currently prevalent theories are causing a great deal of confusion and consternation since they are usually taken as characterization of what ordinarily goes by the name of value judgment. As such they are disappointing and disheartening, because they represent value judgments as epistemologically rather inferior. The second objection is that no reasons whatever are offered for these divergent recommendations. The third and most important objection, however, is that in recommending a new meaning, these philosophers would simply deprive us of a well-established name for an important type of judgment, and would shirk the task of analyzing and characterizing it.

A second respect in which my own differs from the currently prevalent accounts is this. On my account, value judgments are a very special type of highly complex judgment to the effect that certain things to which value is ascribed do or can play a certain sort of causal role in making a favorable difference to people's lives. Both elements in this judgment, the playing of the causal role, and the making of a favorable difference to people's lives, though highly complex and often difficult to confirm, are nevertheless capable of confirmation, at least in principle. The facts relevant to such judgments are, roughly speaking, of two kinds: facts about what various types of people find worthwhile, and facts about what would help them to shape their lives in such ways as would make them worthwhile lives.

My account therefore differs from these currently fashionable in that it treats as merely superficial, nonessential, and unimportant those characteristics which these other accounts regard as central, e.g., being commendatory, expressive, hortative, dynamic, prescriptive. At the same time, my account, if correct, would explain why philosophers, in examining what are genuine value judgments, discover these characteristics. For in ascribing value to things, value judgments assert that these things are or can be causal factors in favorably affecting people's lives. It is not then surprising to find that in giving such information the speaker also commends, expresses a favorable attitude, and so on. On my account, value judgments essentially give a certain kind of complex information that is the basis and ground for all these other things a person may but need not also be doing when making a value judgment.

My account, as I said, treats value judgments as judgments of a very special type. It may therefore be objected that this account has selected *too narrow* a type of judgment; that the term 'value judgment' should be allowed to cover a much wider range of judgments than I admit. It may be granted that my way of selecting value judgments is the most natural, given our current use of words but it may be claimed not to be the most useful. It may be argued that what is interesting and important about value judgment is not that they ascribe value to things, but something quite different, something that value judgments in my sense share with certain other judgments, and which importantly distinguishes them as well as these other judgments from scientific, fact-stating, or descriptive statements. It is this something, the objection continues, on account of which many judgments, among them those I call value judgments, have been and are rightly called *evaluative*. Thus, if by 'value judgment' we mean a judgment which has what it takes to make it evaluative, then we must reject my account as too narrow and furthermore as not having picked on the important peculiarity of evaluation.

I think several of the currently popular theorists would wish to raise this objection, but they would differ from each other in respect of that peculiar property on account of which a judgment should be called evaluative.[4] We may mention four such properties: being appraisals, being about matters of taste, being expressions of feelings, etc., and being prescriptive.

Let us begin with appraisals. On this theory, what I have called value judgments would be only one of several types of evaluative claims, for not all appraisals are concerned, at least directly, with the conferment of benefits. Thus, we make assessments of the *quality* of substances used by man (wood, steel, honey); assessments of the *worth* (in terms of time, effort, money) of things, activities, or experiences;[5] and assessments of various forms of *excellence* of persons, such as expertise, strength of character, or desert. On this view, what I call value judgments are evaluative, not because they ascribe value to something, but because they are or at least involve appraisals. We should note that what I call value judgments are *not necessarily* appraisals; the basic ones, e.g., "the compass was of value to us," are not, for they are not comparisons of things in respect of value, as comparative and quantitative value judgments are. But all value judgments, including the basic ones, *involve* appraisals, for they involve claims to the effect that a certain change was a favorable one. But that means that this change is to be ranked above some other comparable change, on the basis of their relative proximity to the optimal life for that person. Such a comparison of two changes in a life is a ranking, and thus an appraisal, because the respect in which they are compared, proximity to the optimal life, is plainly a desideratum.

The second theory of what makes judgments evaluative holds that it is their being answers to questions of taste or their being judgments based on the speaker's personal tastes. Now, it is clear that what I have called value judgments often are of this sort. Thus, the question of whether a person's life is worthwhile depends on whether what life brings him caters to his tastes. Of course, we need not accept as hard data the tastes with which a person is born, or even the various modifications his tastes undergo in the course of the experiences to which he happens to become exposed during his life. Should one then deliberately modify other people's tastes? And if so, who should and in what direction? On this difficult question, I can do no more than offer tentatively a general principle: They should be modified, if at all, in such a way that, in the light of the paths open to an agent (or the class of agents to which he belongs), and of the resources available to him, the optimal life path for him will make possible a life of the greatest worthwhileness. This leaves open for further investigation the question of whether and to what extent a person's tastes should be modified so that he will in fact find worthwhile what is inevitable, and will not desire what is not attainable, or whether and to what extent a person should be left with aspirations beyond the possibility of fulfilment.

Thus, what I call value judgments do indeed involve answers to questions of personal taste. But we must note that not all value judgments depend on such answers. Some, such as the value of certain medicines, a sound education, or adequate life insurance, are independent of the particular tastes of given individuals. Similarly for other appraisals: The quality of technical articles such as lawn mowers or machine guns, or excellence in certain skills such as mathematics or long-distance running, does not involve matters of taste at all. Conversely, many judgments of taste, such as the claim that one had found someone's behavior disgusting or a ride in a ferris wheel exhilarating, are not themselves what I have called value judgments nor appraisals nor based on appraisals, for they do not ascribe value or involve comparisons with other things in respect of disgustingness or exhilaratingness. Hence, if we accepted this use of the term 'value judgment,' we would be including some judgments that would be excluded and excluding others that would be included if we accepted my theory that what makes judgments evaluative is that they ascribe value, or the theory earlier discussed, that what makes them evaluative is their being appraisals.

However, even if we accept this second alternative account of value judgments, we need not fear that we have to accept the usual skeptical or noncognitivist accounts of value judgments. Take such taste-dependent claims as that the creation of certain amenities had improved the quality of life in certain parts of the country and thereby conferred certain benefits on those who lived there. Clearly, the building of stadiums, state parks, museums, theatres, concert halls, casinos, zoos, and the like, are benefits (directly) for those and only those who have a taste for these things. Benefit claims of this kind are therefore true if and only if the provision of such amenities caters to someone's tastes, and they are true only for those to whose tastes they cater. We therefore can know that such claims are true or false if and only if we can know whether a given change does or does not cater to the tastes of the persons concerned, and so only if we know what their tastes are. One way of finding out would be simply to ask them, provided of course they themselves can know what their tastes are. Another way would be to make certain observations of them which might enable us to tell their tastes even better than they can themselves, or at any rate without having to rely on their willingness to answer and answer truthfully. It would seem, then, that if we can know our own tastes and perhaps also find out other people's tastes, we can confirm and disconfirm benefit-claims and other appraisals that are taste-dependent.

Can one know one's own tastes? It certainly seems so, for one can often answer the question whether one likes, enjoys, finds worthwhile, a certain experience or activity, on a particular occasion or in general, and one can be mistaken in some of these answers and discover one's mistake. One may, for instance, come to believe that one enjoys gardening, but later discover that what one enjoys is not gardening as such but, rather, gardening in one's own garden. Such a discovery is made if one finds that one does not enjoy gardening in other people's gardens. Or one may find that one no longer feels like gardening when one has the services of a gardener. In that case one takes pleasure in and likes to have a well tended garden, but takes no pleasure in gardening itself. The mistake concerning one's tastes consists, in other words, in a mischaracterization of what it is one likes, enjoys, or derives pleasure from. Such a mistake is not one about whether one is at a given time deriving pleasure from something or other, but rather about exactly what it is the pleasure is derived from. It is not necessary for our purposes to explore the difficult problem of the exact nature and range of this mistake. It is enough to be clear that this sort of mistake is possible. For our ability to answer questions concerning what we enjoy, like, and find worthwhile, the possibility of making but also uncovering mistakes in such answers, fully justifies us in speaking of our knowing, discovering, being ignorant of, and mistaken about our own tastes.

How, then, do we know our own tastes? Do we know from experience? Surely, the answer must be in the affirmative. We know what we like and dislike, enjoy and suffer through, find worthwhile and repugnant or at any rate boring, from and only from an experience of these things. What other people tell us about gardening and the like may give us reason to think that we would feel what they feel about it. However, experience alone can prove it, for it is notorious that people differ in tastes. But if we know from experience, do we know *by observation?* Surely not if by 'observation' we mean a use of the senses by which anyone could answer this question. Of course, I can't find out whether I like a painting by Francis Bacon without *looking* at it, or whether I like turtle soup without *tasting* it. But looking at the *painting* or tasting the *soup* will not help *others* to tell whether *I* like them. Conversely, while others often can, by observing *me*, tell whether I find something enjoyable or unpleasant, I myself need not, indeed, cannot in this way answer the same question. If knowledge 'by observation' is knowledge of some particular fact that anyone can acquire by observation, then my knowledge of my tastes is not knowledge by observation. It is another kind of "empirical finding," one which is not intersubjectively valid, but person-relative.

Can one come to know another person's tastes? Again, the answer is surely in the affirmative. Of course, my tastes are not to be identified with my tendencies to react in certain characteristic ways (enjoyment-behavior, pain-behavior) to certain things I live through or undergo, for if they were, I could and presumably would come to know my tastes by observation. Nevertheless, my having certain tastes is the *explanation* of my reacting in these ways and my engaging in certain pursuits and avoidances, namely, those which cater to my tastes or at any rate succeed in avoiding offences to them. With the aid of this conceptual point about the role of tastes in the determination of one's behavior others can come to know my tastes, because they can often know that my behavior, on a particular occasion is due to my tastes, and so can infer what my tastes must be.

I see no fatal objection to widening the term 'value judgment' so as to include all appraisals or all judgments of taste or both. No skeptical views about value judgments can be derived from such a widening. For, as we have seen, both appraisals and judgments of taste can be performed badly or well. They themselves can therefore be appraised, just as can other linguistic performances, e.g., reporting, describing, explaining, arguing, and giving reasons. Admittedly, the criteria on the basis of which we appraise such linguistic performances vary from case to case, and so do even the terms by means of which we formulate such appraisals, e.g., valid-invalid, sound-unsound, accurate-inaccurate, true-false. But there can be no doubt that for each such type of linguistic performance there are appropriate appraisals. And so, even if value judgments are not appraised in terms of truth and falsity, some other comparable pair of terms, e.g., sound-unsound, will be available.

At the same time, I can see no *good* reason for so extending the term 'value judgment,' and some good reasons against doing so. We still need to distinguish the important class of judgments that I call value judgments from appraisals and from judgments of taste. Clearly, no term for that important class is more suitable than 'value judgments' and no other class of judgments is more accurately characterized by this term than that class. For the sake of clarity, it therefore seems to me best to adhere to the terminology I am advocating.

By contrast, the third account of value judgments, which I call the *Expressive Theory*, is open to really serious objections. In essence, that theory says that what makes judgments evaluative is the fact that they are expressions, or what the theory treats as much the same thing, exclamations, ventings, reactions, responses or manifestations, and that for this reason, value judgments cannot be factual, cannot make statements, give information, be true or false. The Expressive Theory has often been refuted only to be restated in a less vulnerable form. If I understand him correctly, G. H. von Wright, in his recent Gifford Lectures, propounds yet another and highly sophisticated version of it. In what follows, I offer with some diffidence, my criticism of this latest version of that theory. I am doubly diffident because von Wright does not address himself explicitly to my question, "What makes judgments evaluative?" though he does write as if he were giving an answer to it. Hence my criticism is not always of his explicitly stated position but merely of what he seems plainly committed to. Even if my criticisms are not applicable to von Wright, they seem to me to bring to light some of the important confusions that make the Expressive Theory plausible.

Von Wright begins by drawing a distinction between three types of concepts—value-concepts, normative concepts, and anthropological concepts. The most important value-concept, he says, is the concept *good*. (*Varieties of Goodness*, The Humanities Press, New York, 1963, p. 6.) However, von Wright apparently does not think that what makes judgments evaluative *is that value-concepts are used in them*, for he discusses judgments of various types which, although value-concepts are always used in them, are sometimes not evaluative. The three types of judgment I have in mind are hedonic, eudaimonic, and intrinsic value judgments, in which the value-concepts, *good, happy*, and *in itself wanted* are used. It is no exaggeration to say that these are in his system the most basic value judgments. If it were not for them, the other types would presumably not exist. The truth about these types of value judgments should throw the sharpest light on the nature of valuation.

Since much the same considerations apply to all three of these types of value judgment, I can confine myself to the discussion of hedonic value judgments, which are the least complicated. Von Wright distinguishes two main types, primary hedonic judgments (e.g., 'the taste of this apple is good') "the logical subjects of which are sensations or other states of consciousness" (*op. cit.*, p. 71), and secondary hedonic judgments (e.g., 'This is a good apple'), "the logical subjects of which are events or things in the physical world" (*ibid.*). Since secondary ones can be analyzed in terms of primary ones and causal statements (e.g.: " 'this apple is good' means 'this apple produces pleasant gustatory sensations' "), we can ignore secondary ones. However, not all primary hedonic judgments are value judgments, for some are merely reports of value judgments and so are not themselves evaluations. According to von Wright, only the sub-class he calls "first person" hedonic judgments are value judgments. The other subclass, "third person" hedonic judgments, are merely reports of such "first person" ones and so not value judgments, but they can be true or false (*op. cit.*, pp. 72–5). He says hedonic judgments cannot be *both* value judgments and capable of being true or false. Why should this be so?

His answer is this. "First person" hedonic judgments are those in which "the subject is judging of a sensation, which he is himself now experiencing or having, that it is agreeable or pleasant, that he likes experiencing or having it" (*op. cit.*, pp. 72–3). "Third person" hedonic judgments are those in which "the subject is judging of the past, present, or future sensations of another subject that this other subject found or finds or will find them pleasant. Also the case, when a subject judges of the hedonic quality of his own past or future sensations, will here count as third person judgments. The subject is then, as it were, speaking of himself from the outside, in the perspective of time" (*ibid.*). Thus when von Wright speaks (rather infelicitously) of "third person" judgments, he includes all those cases in the first person that are in tenses other than the present tense.

Von Wright thinks that "third person" judgments clearly are true or false, and that "first person" judgments provide the best evidence for them. But he thinks that in "first person" judgments "no statements are made at all, and that the judgments therefore cannot properly be called true or false. When the words 'the taste of this apple is good' are used as a first person judgment, they *express* ('give vent to') my pleasure at the taste and do not *state* that I am pleased or *describe* myself as a being, who approves of the taste" (*op. cit.*, pp. 74–5).

Von Wright then draws a parallel between his account of hedonic judgments and the emotive theory of moral judgments. He distinguishes between two versions of that theory, which he calls *naturalistic subjectivism* and *non-cognitivist subjectivism*, respectively. The former holds that moral judgments can be true or false, the latter that they are merely "verbalized expressions of emotion and therefore lack truth-value." (*Op. cit.*, p. 72.) He suggests one might think that both these theories have their due share in the truth: the first because of the "propositional character" of "third person" hedonic judgments, the second because of the "interjectional character" of "first person" hedonic judgments. But, in his opinion, this would obscure the important point

that the third person judgments, just because of the feature of theirs which makes them true or false, viz., that they are about the valuations of other subjects (or about the judging subject's own valuations viewed in the perspective of time), *are no genuine value-judgments at all*. They are no value-judgments, since they do not value, but report or conjecture about human reactions, i.e., such reactions which we call valuations. The only genuine value-judgments in the context are the first person judgments. In them the judging subject values his sensations. They are not true or false, and therefore, in a sense of the word, no "judgments" even. For this reason it seems to me fair to say that non-cognitivist subjectivism represents the correct view of hedonic value-judgments, whereas naturalistic subjectivism is not a theory of value-judgments at all (*op. cit.*, p. 74).

Von Wright thus makes the following claims:

1) Nothing can be both a "first person" and a "third person" hedonic judgment because "third person" hedonic judgments are reports of "first person" ones, and (presumably) because nothing can be a report of itself.

2) "First person" hedonic judgments are reactions, ventings, interjections, expressions, or manifestations, and therefore cannot be true or false.

3) "First person" hedonic judgments are value judgments because they are the sort of human reactions that we call valuations; "third person" hedonic judgments are not value judgments because they are not themselves such reactions but merely reports or conjectures about such reactions.

These premises support von Wright's conclusion that unlike other types of value judgments, e.g., instrumental, technical, and utilitarian ones (*op. cit.*, 74), hedonic value judgments cannot be true or false. I believe that the premises and the conclusion are false.

Ad 1) It is simply not true that no remark can be both a "first person" and a "third person" judgment. If I say 'This flavor is good,' meaning something like 'I like this flavor' (*op. cit.* 76) what I say can be correctly characterized as both stating that I like this flavor which I now taste and as expressing my liking for (or my attitude towards) this flavor that I now taste.

It is, of course, true that first person judgments in the past or future tense cannot be both "third person" and "first person" judgments, in von Wright's sense, but not because "third person" judgments are mere conjectures or reports about someone's reactions vented or expressed in "first person" judgments nor because *therefore nothing* can be both a "third person" and a "first person" judgment. The reason is rather that one cannot *vent* or *manifest* what at some time was or will be in one's mind, but only what is there now. (It is not true even that one cannot *express* the content of one's own, or, for that matter, other people's past or future feelings, thoughts, attitudes, opinions; e.g., 'He —his speech—beautifully expresses what we all felt at the time'.) There is, therefore, no reason to think that nothing *can* be both a "third person" and a "first person" judgment.

It is simply a mistake to think that there is some sort of incompatibility between being a statement and being an expression of something. The truth is that stating is a species of the genus expressing. Whatever can be stated, can be expressed, but not everything that can be expressed can be stated; and every statement of something is an expression of something (not necessarily the same thing), but not every expression of something is a statement of something. As far as feelings, attitudes, emotions, pleasure, opinions, beliefs, are concerned, both expressing them, and stating that one has them, are ways of conveying to others *what* one's feelings, etc., are, where conveying includes misconveying. However, one can express things in nonverbal ways (e.g., by a shrug or a song) or in verbal forms that do not amount to a statement (e.g., 'Oh, how delicious'). Conversely, however, a statement to the effect that one has a feeling or attitude does normally qualify as an expression of it. The main difference between these two ways of conveying to others one's feelings, etc., is this. The expression of a feeling may convey what the feeling is without spelling out what it is: The statement that one has a feeling cannot convey what that feeling is without spelling out what it is. Expression thus is a *possibly nonexplicit*, statement, a *necessarily explicit* form of conveying something about oneself.

Thus it is true that sometimes when we express our feelings we are not stating that we have these feelings. But from this it does not follow, and it is in fact not true, that when we state that we have certain feelings we are necessarily not expressing them. This would follow if it were also true (as von Wright claims, *op. cit.*, p. 74) that stating that someone has certain feelings, etc., is reporting that he is expressing them. But this is not true. The Expressive Theory (and also its cousin, the Emotive Theory) is therefore mistaken in one of its central claims, namely, that no remark can be both a "first person" and a "third person" judgment. Hence, even if it is true that hedonic value judgments are "first person" judgments, it does not follow that they cannot *also* be "third person" judgments and so capable of being true-false. Thus, even if saying 'I like this taste' "expresses ('gives vent to') my pleasure at the taste" (*op. cit.*, p. 74), it can (and typically does) at the same time state that I like this taste, that this taste is giving me pleasure, and so on.

Ad 2) It must be granted, however, that there are "first person" hedonic judgments that express pleasure without stating that a certain sensation which one is having is giving one pleasure. The question arises whether these can be true or false. And here the answer is indeed that they plainly cannot. But this is not the whole of the story. Let us distinguish between *acts of communication*, i.e., cases in which the person's behavior constitutes a deliberate act of conveying something, and *expressive signs*, i.e., cases of mere reflexes or reactions to some stimulus, which, however, enable an observer to draw conclusions about the person's feelings, attitudes, etc.

Consider first, acts of communication. Then, whether we deal with a groan, a cynical shrug, a cheerful song, nonchalant whistling, a facial expression, or a verbal exclamation, none of which can be true or false, such acts of communication can, nevertheless, deliberately misconvey the speaker's feelings, attitudes, states of mind, and so on. They can be ways in which the speaker spontaneously, or with deliberation, cleverly or clumsily conveys to another how he feels, etc., or in which he is trying to deceive another about how he feels. Because these are *nonexplicit* ways of communication—because nothing is asserted, perhaps no words used even—they involve nothing that can be true or false. Yet they contain what involves something quite similar, namely, candor or concealment, simulation or dissimulation, honesty or deception. Thus, insofar as acts of communication are concerned, they are, of course, subject to the same types of appraisal to which all forms of interpersonal dealings, including statements, are subject, namely, those having to do with honesty and deception. The inapplicability of truth or falsity to such acts of communication is not therefore a very important difference between such expressions and statements, for such expressions can be used, just like statements, for the purpose of inducing true or false beliefs in others. Others may or may not be taken in by such expressions in the same way as they may or may not be taken in by the corresponding statements. As von Wright says, N. N. may be a very polite man, and so his 'yes, I like it very much' and equally his 'ah, delicious' may be a polite deception (cf. *op. cit.*, p. 73) which does not convey his real attitude towards the taste of the apple.

And now consider the cases of mere reflexes or reactions, as when a person involuntarily grimaces after biting into a lemon or cutting his finger, or when he exclaims 'damn' after hearing he has lost at the races or realizing that he has left his umbrella in the taxi. These are not ways of conveying something, but reactions to sensations or to other mental events, a venting of his feelings or emotions. Another person may read off from these signs how he feels, but there is no question here of honesty or deception. Similarly, there is no question of error or self-deception.

If, by "first person" hedonic judgments von Wright means expressive signs, then "first person" hedonic judgments are indeed ventings and reactions. They can neither be true or false, nor even honest or dishonest, misleading or not misleading. If, however, he means acts of communication, then "first person" hedonic judgments, though they cannot be true or false, can be honest or dishonest, misleading or not misleading, and therefore the persons making such judgments can be called truthful or untruthful, honest or dishonest, on the basis of these acts. In this case, "first person" judgments are not reactions to sensations, nor can they be said to vent them, for such acts of communication may express feelings, emotions, attitudes, etc., that the person expressing them does not have. But one cannot vent feelings, etc., one does not have. Presumably, the expression 'how delicious' of the polite N. N. cannot be said to *be* the reaction to the sensation: it is surely the opposite of that reaction. If, as von Wright's actual examples suggest, he means neither acts of communication nor expressive signs, but expressions couched in a grammatical form that makes them first person assertions, then they are at the same time statements to the effect that the speaker has a certain favorable attitude towards the sensation he is then experiencing, and so both expressions and statements, are both "first person" and "third person" judgments and therefore, capable of being true or false.

Ad 3) It now remains to ask in which of these interpretations of "first person" judgment, it is most plausible to say that such judgments are value judgments. The answer is that it is implausible in all interpretations, but least plausible in the interpretation in which von Wright's claims about hedonic value judgments are true, and most plausible in the interpretation in which these claims are false.

Von Wright claims, it will be recalled, that "third person" hedonic judgments are not genuine value judgments because they do not value, but report or conjecture about human reactions, i.e., such reactions which we call valuations, and that "first person" judgments are value judgments because they are such reactions, because in them we value our own sensations. A brief look at the use of 'valuing', and 'valuation' will show that this is simply not so.

The verb 'to value' has three main uses, as in 'sorry, Charles is out, he *is valuing* the Jones estate.' 'Charles *valued* the diamond ring at $3,000,' and 'I have always *valued* your friendship, Charles'. In the first use the verb refers to the skilled activity of assessing the (monetary) value of something. In the second, it refers to the result of that activity. In the third it refers to a certain sort of behavioral disposition, namely, being prepared to expend some of one's resources on maintaining possession of something one has, in the belief that such maintenance will benefit one.[6] It is simply not true that when I say 'I find this taste good' or 'I like this taste,' I am valuing my sensation or that I have valued it or that I value it.

Turning now to the noun 'valuation,' this is most naturally used in connection with the first and second uses of the verb, e.g., 'His valuation is taking a long time' or 'His valuation (at $3,000) is rather high.' As these words are most naturally used, they refer either to an appraisal of great sophistication or to the verbal formulation of its results. Valuation therefore involves comparisons with other comparable things in respect of some desideratum, and therefore criteria and possibly standards for valuation. It is quite clear that something as unsophisticated as what I have called "expressive signs," which are indeed reactions and ventings, would not qualify as a valuation. Indeed, it is obvious that 'valuation' applies to an activity the more naturally, the further away it is from a mere reaction or venting and the closer it is to something which has the characteristics von Wright attributes to what he calls "third person" hedonic judgments. But in saying this we must remember that, contrary to von Wright's opinion, hedonic judgments in any person, first, second, or third, and in any tense, past, future, or *present*, can have these characteristics!

Of course (unlike von Wright?) one may not be concerned to render the natural meaning of the words 'valuing,' 'valuation,' or 'value judgment.' One is then presumably recommending some improvement of current usage. This involves pointing out some shortcomings of the natural, and some merits of the recommended use. But what could these be? I know of no discussion of the shortcomings of the ordinary use of these words. In fact, I do not think their ordinary use has ever been set out clearly before. And the only advantage I can think of which von Wright's use would have is that in this use, hedonic, eudaimonic, and intrinsic value judgments could be sharply and simply distinguished from reports, conjectures, predictions, descriptions, and the other "respectable" types of remark that philosophers use as their main models. But, unless one is already persuaded by some false account of what we mean by 'value judgment' that they are thus different and inferior, one would hardly regard the introduction of a new usage to fit such a false account as an advantage of it. For, as I pointed out before, the new usage does not get rid of the important judgments we now refer to by these words. Therefore, if the new usage is adopted, one would have to look for a new term to refer to those important judgments that had previously been called value judgments. Moreover, this new terminology really is rather awkward, since it would compel us to call value judgments remarks that are not even judgments, as von Wright points out (*op. cit.*, p. 74). I cannot then see that there is anything to be said for von Wright's third premise.

But if 1), 2), and 3) are false, we have no ground for the conclusion that hedonic value judgments cannot be true or false. Therefore even von Wright's highly sophisticated version of the Expressive Theory must be rejected. I hope I have said enough to indicate that other versions are unlikely to fare better.

There remains the fourth theory, that what makes judgments evaluative, is that they are prescriptive. That theory suffers from two major flaws. It misleadingly conflates value judgments and normative judgments, and it gives an untenable account of the conceptual relation between normative judgments, such as 'Jones ought to do A,' and the corresponding report, 'Jones is doing A.' but since I discuss this theory in some detail elsewhere, I shall not go into it here. Here it must suffice to say dogmatically that to maintain that what makes a judgment evaluative if its being commendatory or prescriptive is to pick, arbitrarily, a not very important characteristic as the defining criterion of value judgments. The most important thing about a value judgment is the benefit-related information conveyed in it and the empirical method (outlined in section I of this paper) for supporting the claim that something or other confers a benefit or has the capacity to do so. The presence of the commendatory factor adds nothing of importance. It would add nothing even if it were true that in giving such benefit-related information one *ipso facto* commended something. It is not the commendation, but rather that properly grounded judgment which conveys highly important (because benefit-related) information and which can and should be adduced in support of any commendation, which is, if I am right, properly called a value judgment.

NOTES

1. O may be of value to BY even if BY does not *succeed* in attaining E. For he may derive benefits of economy (saving resources) from having and using O, when doing a. For details, see below.

2. Unless the other person's intervention prevented Jones from making that other intervention, as when Jones persuades Smith to exchange lottery tickets with him and Smith's wins first prize, whereas Jones wins only a consolation prize.

3. I am not, of course, maintaining that in all these matters, correct statements of natural fact and correct statements of convention together suffice to yield correct answers to these questions. On the contrary, I hold that in moral matters, for instance, answers to questions of convention are themselves subject to further tests.

4. Cf. C. L. Stevenson, *Ethics and Language* (Yale University Press, 1944), pp. 83–4; *Facts and Values* (Yale University Press, 1966), pp. 205–7. R. M. Hare, *The Language of Morals* (Oxford University Press, 1952), pp. 168–9.

5. Ascertaining the *worth of things* is a much more complex matter than determining their *worthwhileness*. The latter is detected in the course of an appropriate experience by whether one finds the thing worthwhile or not. The

former involves comparing the worthwhileness of having the thing with the worthwhileness of other things which could have been acquired at the same cost.

6. For additional details, cf., my article, "What is Value: The Analysis of the Concept," in *Values and the Future*, ed. Kurt Baier and Nicholas Rescher (The Free Press of Glencoe, 1969).

THE BOUNDS OF MORALITY

Anthony Quinton

I

A rather curious feature of the teaching and study of philosophy, in the English-speaking world at any rate, is a certain asymmetry or lopsidedness in the treatment given to the theory of knowledge on the one hand and to moral philosophy on the other. These two disciplines—epistemology and ethics—are generally regarded as the indispensable foundation stones of philosophical study. Any course in philosophy which is at all specialized in character, which goes beyond treating philosophy as an element in the general history of culture, must include both. No amount of work in the field of logic and methodology in one direction, or in aesthetics or philosophical theology in the other, can compensate for them in anything that claims to be a rounded philosophical education.

It is not at all unreasonable that they should be accorded such a central position. If philosophy is conceived, academically, as a critical inquiry into thinking, rather than, popularly, as the development of a general conception of and attitude to life and the world, it is natural that it should be divided into two parts, just as thinking is itself. Some of our thinking is practical, undertaken with a view towards choice between alternative possible actions. Some of it is theoretical, undertaken with an immediate view, at any rate, to the acquisition of true beliefs, without direct pressure from the exigencies of practical choice. It is, then, the task of ethics to study practical thinking, and of epistemology to study its theoretical counterpart.

The curious fact I mentioned is that by and large epistemology does address itself to the whole range of our theoretical thinking, but that ethics, at least as it has been pursued in the last few centuries, does not. The most elementary introduction to the theory of knowledge will cover the sense-perception that gives us knowledge of our immediate physical environment, the awareness that we have of our own mental states, the general knowledge we have of natural laws and regularities, the knowledge we have of the past by way of memory or historical investigation, and our knowledge of the necessary truths of logic and mathematics. But ethics, on the other hand, as it is and has for a long time been pursued, restricts itself almost exclusively to a single form of practical thinking, that which issues in the judgements and principles of morality. In effectively identifying the whole of practice with morality it is, I should contend, acting in the same way as an epistemology which would identify theoretical knowledge as a whole with perception or memory or science or mathematics.

I am not suggesting that the other forms of practice are ignored absolutely. But to the extent that they are mentioned at all by writers on ethics it is usually by way of more or less parenthetical contrast. They are almost never seen as deserving of philosophical attention in their own right. But even Kant, the most doggedly moralistic of all ethical philosophers, feels obliged to distinguish the obligations of morality from the counsels of prudence and the rules of technical skill.

There can be no uncontroversial answer to the question "how many kinds of practice are there?" any more than there can be to the corresponding question about kinds of knowledge. But it should be possible to draw up some sort of provisional list, without any implication that all the elements in it are fundamentally distinct, or again that there are not further kinds of practice which have been left out. A useful clue here is provided by the fact that, in general, practical action, and by this I mean action proper, rational, and controllable, even if not always explicitly deliberated, action, is the pursuit of value. If this is correct there will be as many significantly distinguishable kinds of practice as there are significantly distinguishable kinds of value.

For old times' sake we may put morality at the head of the list. The type of value it pursues is indeed a matter of controversy; there is a well-established school of thought which denies that moral activity is, insofar as it is moral, aimed at any valued end at all and maintains that it derives its value from being what it is or from the motives from which it is undertaken. Secondly, there is prudent or self-interested or self-regarding activity whose end is the overall advantage or welfare of the agent in the long run. Just as we praise a moral agent by calling him virtuous, we praise a conspicuously prudent man by calling him sensible or wise, perhaps worldly-wise. Thirdly, there is the field of action directed towards the attainment of given ends with the minimum expenditure of effort, time and costly material, the field of technique. Technically good conduct we praise as efficient, a technically competent man as skilled or skillful.

So much for Kant's trinity of kinds of action or practice. But we can go further. There is, fourthly, the medical or hygienic domain of health. The valued end here is a healthy condition of the body, to be achieved by the adoption of healthy personal habits in eating, sleeping, dress, accommodation, exercise and so on. Fifthly, there is the domain, bordering on and continuous with that of morality, of customs, manners, and etiquette, in which action is recommended as proper or polite, in virtue of its being conventionally expected by and acceptable to those affected by it. The list could be extended further by considering the pursuit of aesthetic satisfaction and of less elevated immediate enjoyments; but enough has been done to show the range and variety of nonmoral action or practice.

One qualification must be inserted here. To say that the moral, the prudential, the technical and so forth are different kinds of practice is not to say that if a particular action is of one kind it cannot be of another as well. What we have here is rather different kinds of evaluation or appraisal of actions in the light of the different kinds of value they may realize. A single action can be appraised in several different ways. Prudence may advise one to serve gently when playing tennis with one's employer, a course that technique would reject and about which morality might be indifferent, perhaps in equilibrium between the competing demands of charity and honesty. A single action, in other words, may have effects on the values proprietary to several different kinds of practice.

What substantiates the idea that these varieties of practice are different but coordinate kinds of the same fundamental type is that there is a set of very familiar concepts which occur in the evaluation of activities of each kind. These are the concepts of what is good, what is right, of what ought to be done. The words that express them, commonly miscalled moral words, are just as much at home, in a wholly nonfigurative employment, in discourse about nonmoral practice as they are in moral utterance. If it is right to tell the truth, it is also, and quite as literally, right to take some salt in one's diet, to make financial provision for retirement or to leave the brake on in a parked car. If the goodness of a good man is, primarily and generally, moral, that of a good colour TV set or a good sculptor or a good place to live is not.

It would certainly be an exaggeration to say that the moral philosophers of the present and comparatively recent past are wholly unaware of these rather obvious considerations about the promiscuity of the words *good, right,* and *ought.* But it is surprising how little they let their occasional explicit admissions of the fact influence what they say about morality. One piece of evidence for this claim is the readiness with which philosophical theories about the nature of moral convictions are generalized into theories about judgements of value in general. It is at least not utterly implausible to say that moral judgements are expressions of feelings or universal imperatives, though I do not think it is true. But it is surely absurd to say that the evaluative injunctions, "you ought to take more exercise," "it is unhealthy to take as little exercise as you do" are not really statements of fact but emotive ejaculations or the consequences of impersonally directed commands such as "let everyone take more exercise than you do." Pathology, after all, makes a universally accepted claim to be a science and the writers of textbooks on the subject do not feel it incumbent upon them to preface their books with some kind of autonomous *prise de position* on the empirical criteria of health and disease. Similar considerations apply to anyone who would take what G. E. Moore has to say about the concept of goodness to cover the non-moral uses of that concept.

In the sort of case just mentioned we have an ethical philosopher advancing a theory about values in general almost by inadvertence, through the agency of an unreflective generalization. But matters are not much improved when moral philosophers turn explicitly to nonmoral valuation. It is sometimes said that to judge something to be good in a nonmoral way is merely subjective, is a way of saying that one likes it. This can be explained only as another instance of that well-known deficiency disease of philosophers which is brought about by too one-sided a diet of examples. What may at a pinch be true of the satisfied diner, pushing himself away from the table with the words "that was a good dinner," does not even begin to look true about such nonmoral observations as "that is a good electron microscope" or "he is a very good dentist" or "it is good to eat one's meals at regular times."

The effective identification by ethical theorists of morality with practice as a whole has unfortunate effects. It prevents ethical theorists from securing the illumination they might get about the nature of morality from comparing it with other forms of practice, from seeing how the concepts with which they are concerned work in the nonmoral applications they unquestionably possess. Let me mention just one example. G. E. Moore's *Principia Ethica* comes eventually to the conclusion that the supreme ends to which moral activity should be directed are affectionate personal relations and the contemplation of beauty. These are, of course, good things but only someone who either had no understanding of the nature of morality at all or who had never seriously reflected upon it could give them the place Moore does. Is it because they are hostile to affectionate personal relations that we are morally bound to control our aggressive and selfish inclinations? Is it because it will foster elevated friendships and discriminating aesthetic enjoyment among them that we believe it is morally right to give something out of our abundance to help feed the hungry of the world? Moore's conception of morality, as well as betraying the emotional limitations of an Edwardian maiden aunt of cultivated tastes, reveals an extraordinary intellectual blindness to the problem I shall discuss here.

In this respect Moore's successors have done better than he. They have seen that morality is distinct from other kinds of action and value and they have tried to show how. For the most part the distinguishing criteria they have proposed are formalistic, in that they do not mention the concrete, empirical character of the ends typically pursued by moral activity. It is the main part of my purpose here to argue that no criterion of this formalistic variety succeeds in making the required distinction.

II

Before I begin to consider formalistic accounts of the distinguishing feature of morality I must say a few words about the specific object and methods of the undertaking. I shall assume without argument that there is a distinction between the moral, on the one hand, and the prudential, the technically efficient, the healthy, and so forth on the other, the items on either side of the distinction being linked together as different kinds of action or evaluation. In order to test the correctness of the formalistic criteria I examine I shall aim to show that to adopt them would require the admission that what is indisputably nonmoral is moral or that what is indisputably moral is nonmoral. But where am I to find the indisputable instances of the moral and the nonmoral that I need?

What I have to presume here, it might seem, is that even if there is difficulty about arriving at an explicit criterion of the moral, there is still a reasonable coincidence about *particular applications* and refusals of the concept of morality as between different people with perhaps very different sets of moral convictions. Such a presumption would not be questionable about the concept of knowledge, which it is the epistemologist's first task to define, or about the concept of a person or the concept of a cause. But with concepts like art, morality, and the state it may be questioned whether the same degree of coincidence can be taken for granted. All I can do is to record my awareness of this difficulty and to resolve to select instances of as central and obvious kinds as I can find.

I shall treat the four formalistic criteria in what I take to be the reverse order to that of their interest and importance.

The first, and thus, in my view, least interesting and important, is that which contrasts the moral as categorical, absolute, and unconditional, with the nonmoral as hypothetical, relative, and conditional. Moral evaluations alone, say Kant and his modern followers, are fully expressed in categorical imperatives. Non-moral evaluations, if categorically formulated, are always incomplete and elliptical; for full expression they require the addition of a hitherto suppressed if-clause. The moral injunction "you ought not to treat him like that" is complete as it stands: the non-moral injunction expressed in the same words must carry with it the unexpressed supplement "if you don't want him to give you a lot of trouble."

How are we to tell in the case of a categorically formulated injunction that it is, in the sense of this criterion, really elliptical and hypothetical? If someone says to me "you ought to do X," how am I to find out whether it carries with it an elided if-clause or not? A natural answer would be that a categorical injunction is shown to be really hypothetical if the person who makes it recognizes the appropriateness and relevance of the challenge "why should I?" But consider the remark "you ought to spend more time with your great-aunt." In doubt as to what sort of injunction this was, I might ask why. "It would please her very much" is one possible answer; "she might alter her will in your favour" is another. It seems fairly clear to me that if the first answer were given it would show that the original injunction was moral; if the second, that it was prudential. But in each case the question, the request for supplementation, is relevant and appropriate. It could be replied that this is only because the answer "because it will please her very much," although compatible with a moral reading of the original injunction, does not conclusively establish that it is moral. My adviser may be interested only in ensuring that my great-aunt is less depressing and doleful during the period of her annual Christmas visit. To get clear about this I should presumably have to repeat my inquiry: "Why should I seek to give her pleasure?" The suggestion here would be that if this is intended morally the only possible reply to it is "you just ought, it is a good thing that she should be less miserable," whereas if it is not so intended the reply would be "because her visit next Christmas will be as depressing as this if you don't."

It is true enough that the answer to the second challenge which clearly shows the injunction to be moral is pretty obvious. But then so is the only answer that could be a given to the question "why should I?" if this were put to someone who said "you ought to seek an alteration of her will in your favour." For what could he reply but "it would be a good thing for you to have more money than you do" which is equally obvious? What I am suggesting is that, whether an injunction is moral or not, a request for completion with justifying considerations can usually be satisfied even if in some cases it is hard to imagine that they could be at all useful or informative to the inquirer.

It might be argued, however, that there is still a residual difference between the moral case and the prudential ones. The final justification in the moral case included the words "you just ought," an admission of terminality which did not occur in the other cases. But suppose there is someone whom I believe to manage his life in a very muddled and irrational and foolishly impulsive fashion. I might say to him "you ought to pay more attention to your long-run advantage than you do, you ought to be more prudent." If he replies "why should I?" the only direct answer I can give is in effect to repeat myself by saying "well, you'll be better off all round in the long run." What I would be more likely to do is to talk in detail about the advantages he has missed by behaving in the way he does, backing up the implied claim that he could do better for himself than he does. What I suggest is that just as there are some irreducibly categorical moral injunctions so there are some irreducibly categorical nonmoral ones. If this is right, being really categorical, when fully expressed, is no more a sufficient condition of the moral status of an injunction than it is a necessary condition. In this respect there is a complete parallel between the moral and the nonmoral. Injunctions of both sorts can be usefully and informatively expressed in a hypothetical way. Sometimes hypothetical expression is significant but practically otiose. Sometimes hypothetical expression is merely repetitious.

If, as I believe, there is an essential connection between morality and the general welfare, in particular the avoidance or minimization of suffering, the admittedly somewhat more categorical *appearance* of moral judgments can perhaps be explained. When I recommend a course of action to someone as necessary to his good health, I leave open the question of whether he really should pursue this particular end, perhaps at the expense of other things of value. This might partly be because in most circumstances what he does about his health is really none of my business. So I guard against an accusation of intrusiveness by hedging my recommendations. "You ought to take more exercise if you want to be in better health," I will say. But when I reprove someone for spreading malicious falsehoods I do not add "if you want to diminish suffering," because, as I am one of the potential sufferers I have a direct interest in the end in question.

A further reason for the qualification in this sort of case is the limitedness of the end involved. If health alone were the only possibly relevant consideration I might not speak in this way. But in fact health is only one of a large number of approximately coordinate particular ends that we pursue in the general management of life and is one, further-more, whose demands are often in conflict with those of social pleasure, professional achievement and simple comfort, to take only a few exam-ples. To make clear that it is reasons of health on which one is basing one's recommendation is a way of showing that one has not taken into consideration possible counter-claims of the same general order.

This is confirmed by the fact that there is, after all, something rather odd about the clause "if you want to be healthy." For what after all is health but a condition of the body that is either itself satisfactory or is a necessary condition of future bodily satisfaction, by which I mean absence of pain and the ability to perform standard functions. Now to want something at least implies that one expects satisfaction from it, so it would seem to be a necessary truth that one wants to be in that con-dition of the body that one believes to be healthy in the sense defined. Yet there is no contradiction in the statement "I wish I were ill." But it is only intelligible if there is something which one wants more than health in the circumstances, such as to avoid military service or an unat-tractive social obligation. The man who wishes he were ill in such a situ-ation would still like to be well, just as the driver would still like to park his car in a convenient place even though he wants still more that his car should not be towed away by the police. What this implies is that the condition "if you want to be healthy" shows that the recommenda-tion to which it is attached is based on the assumption that health is the sole relevant consideration or that the desire for it is the preponder-ating desire in the circumstances, an assumption which may not be cor-rect.

The defender of the criterion of categoricalness is now put in a po-sition to say that this kind of qualifying proviso is never appropriate in the moral case. But this is by no means self-evident. The claims of mo-rality often conflict with those of prudence so that it is often not the sole relevant consideration and equally a man's preponderating desire is often for something other than what is morally indicated. But, it may be objected, morality ought to be the sole relevant consideration and the desire to act in accordance with its requirements ought to prepon-derate. At this point the view that morality is categorical in a proprie-tary way becomes identical with the claim that it is somehow overriding or supreme, the fourth of the formalistic criteria I shall examine, so that I shall defer further discussion of it until later.

III

The second formalistic criterion which has had some currency is that of autonomy. In the ethics of Kant the idea that morality is autonomous while other forms of practice are heteronomous is first presented in such a way as to make it hard to distinguish from the criterion of categoricalness that I have just been talking about. A decision is heteronomous if it is dictated by some outside end, it is autonomous if it is somehow self-justifying. By distinguishing the essential nature of man as a rational being from his desires, Kant is led to the conclusion that the imperatives of morality, which, as uniquely categorical, are the only imperatives unrelated to further ends, are self-legislated, while the other imperatives of prudence, technique and so forth are forced on the agent by his inclinations. These are conceived as something external to him, as is shown by the literal interpretation Kant gives to the apparently metaphorical phrase "dictated by an outside end."

More recent proponents of the criterion of autonomy have taken the idea of morality as essentially self-legislated in a more straightforward way. For them the contrast is not between two kinds of motivation, internal reason and external inclination, but between two kinds of moral authority, that of the agent himself and that of people or institutions other than the agent. They contend that for a conviction about right conduct to be moral it must be one that is freely adopted or chosen by the agent himself and not imposed by or passively accepted from others.

This is not a doctrine that it is easy to state clearly. But there do seem to be two quite different ways in which it can be understood. A rule of conduct could be held to be autonomous if the agent actually endorses or accepts it and does not merely act in accordance with it from some motive that is irrelevant to its substantiation, as a man might be induced by fear to obey a law of which he disapproves or employ a technique which he regards as inferior in order to placate a teacher. On the other hand something quite different might be intended. A rule of conduct might be held to be autonomous to the extent that the person who accepts it has worked it out for himself and has not accepted it on the authority of someone else.

I do not think that autonomy, in either of these senses, is either a necessary or a sufficient condition of the moral character of a rule or decision. It is not necessary in the first sense since we sometimes do what others think morally right, but that we do not, in order to placate them. It may be that we think that the act required is morally wrong or it may be that we are morally indifferent to it. The unbeliever who has his child baptised to please his believing parents may fit either case, depending on how he views the morality of his submission to their wishes. It can very well be objected that such a decision can hardly be called a moral decision by the agent. But in that case the requirement is trivial for it is equally true of the parallel case in which technique is substituted for morality. Someone who employs what he regards as an inferior technique in order to please his employer can no more properly be said to be acting on a technical decision than the unbeliever mentioned above can be said to be acting on a moral one. The nature of the rule or decision on which a man is acting is determined in moral and nonmoral cases alike by the nature of the reason for action which is in fact operative for him. In other words, all decisions, properly so called, whether moral or not, are autonomous in this sense.

If this is so it follows, of course, that autonomy is not a sufficient condition of the morality of a rule or decision. This is anyway obvious on its own account. We clearly do act on prudential, technical, and medical rules that we endorse and have freely accepted. And if, as would seem reasonable, we define the practical character of a decision or action in terms of the operative reason for it, it follows that in every type of case, decisions and actions must be autonomous in this sense.

We may turn, then, to the other sense which the requirement of autonomy may be given, that in which a rule of conduct is autonomous to the extent that someone who accepts it has worked it out for himself and has not accepted it on the authority of someone else. Since it is obvious that some people work out their own cooking recipes, health regimens, technical procedures, and prudential principles, it is also obvious that this kind of autonomy is not a sufficient condition of morality. It is equally clear that people rely to a very large extent in all these practical domains on the authority of others, on cookery books and classes, on health manuals, on technical primers, and on the personal advice columns of newspapers. They may seek to rationalize their selection between competing authorities in a given sphere by comparing the satisfactoriness in practice of the competing advice they give but they do not have to do so. If the performance in application of the recommendations of the first cookbook a woman ever opens turn out to match the promise of the illustrations she may come to rely on it exclusively and never think of opening another.

The crucial question, then, is whether morality is distinguished from the other forms of practice in that autonomy in this sense is necessary to it as it is to none of the others. I do not see that there is any justification for this belief whatever. A man might have acquired his moral convictions from parents and teachers who were in close moral agreement with each other and have become so set in his ways by the time he becomes aware that there are conflicting ideas about what is morally right that he never gives them serious consideration. Someone who lives contentedly by the rules inculcated by his moral teachers or the authorities of his church, who endeavours to conform his conduct to the rules that they enjoin and he professes, who feels guilty when he fails to conform and feels more or less indignant about the nonconformity of others, accepts the rules that guide his conduct just as genuinely as someone who has arrived at his rules only after a long critical and reflective process of a morally innovative or originative kind.

It is, I suppose, a rather uninteresting logical necessity that not everyone can be morally heteronomous in this way if an infinite regress of dependence on external moral authorities is to be avoided. It is uninteresting because the regress-terminating moral innovator could well be located in the remote past. But the same is true of the other forms of practice. It is also reasonable to maintain that since there can be no rational progress in the field of moral convictions unless there are some moral innovators from time to time then, as there is reason to think that the critical revision of moral beliefs is a good thing, is genuinely progressive, it is a good thing that there should be some moral innovators of a critical turn of mind. But, once again, exactly the same is true of the other forms of practice. If a fixed stability of rules can be objected to as ossification in the moral domain, so can it in the domains of technique, health, prudence and so on. (I should add that I introduced the qualification "rational" when I spoke a moment ago of the development of moral convictions, to rule out unintended and unnoticed deviations from authoritative tradition brought about by forgetfulness, misunderstanding, unconscious reinterpretations of terms and other such possible non-rational causes of change, for these could only fortuitously bring about real moral progress and are perhaps more likely to bring about its opposite.)

It has sometimes been said that the requirement of autonomy I have been discussing is not a neutral, logical characterization of the essence of morality but is rather the expression of a particular moral demand. I fully agree with the negative side of this statement but the view that the requirement of autonomy is a moral one is more questionable. Is an attitude of moral conformity really a moral offence, even if it is supposed that it is, generally, a bad thing? One who does make this supposition will regret conformity when he encounters it, he will be sorry that it exists and wonder what should be done educationally to diminish it. But, speaking as someone who does make this supposition, I do not find myself disposed to *blame* moral conformists, even when their particular moral convictions are different from my own.

IV

The third formalistic criterion of morality I shall examine is universalizability and since it has been the subject of a good deal of discussion

I shall try to be fairly brief about it. Here, even more than in the two preceding cases, the initial problem of precise formulation presents difficulty. One reasonably clear way in which it has been expressed is that "A (a given person) ought to do X (a kind of action)" is a moral judgment if and only if "A ought to do X" entails that everyone in A's circumstances ought to do X. The requirement about the same circumstances, or circumstances, as it is sometimes put, that are similar to A's in the relevant respects, is a soft point in this formula. It may be enough to say that "A ought to do X" is moral if and only if "A ought to do X" entails "there is some description F, which is true of A, such that everyone who is F ought to do X."

Now I should agree that every moral judgment must satisfy this condition but only for the trivializing reason that every rational judgment of any kind whatever has to be universalizable in this way. Suppose I am watching an incompetent person hammering a nail into a wall to hang a picture on. I say to him "you ought to hammer that nail in with small blows to start with." In saying this I pretty obviously take him to fall under the description "man who wants to put a nail in a wall in a minimally destructive way" and I believe that everyone of whom that description is true should take small strokes first because I know from experience that this is a fairly reliable guarantee against causing noticeable damage. I may, of course, be wrong about the hammerer. He may be animated by a malicious intention to damage the wall. In that case my judgment does not apply to him in the sense in which I intended it. But I could express a different judgment in the same words on grounds of prudence, realising that the wall's owner will detect the malice and take his revenge for it. This too would be universalizable: anyone hammering nails into the walls of perceptive and vengeful people ought to take care to do it non-destructively. I could, again, make a moral judgment with the original words, one whose universalization would be "everyone hammering nails into other people's walls should do it in such a way as not to cause distress."

The reason for this, in the non-moral cases at any rate, is that what ought, nonmorally, to be done is determined by what can be rationally expected to yield some valued result. But rational expectations about the consequences of action are inevitably based on general, inductive knowledge. It is only because this, as yet unexecuted, act is of a certain general kind, which past experience has shown to have a certain sort of result, that it can now be rationally recommended. Thus the only reason one could have for recommending a particular act must also be a reason for recommending anyone in the same relevant circumstances—namely those features of the situation which are invoked in the prediction of valuable consequences—to act in the same way.

Unlike most defenders of formalistic criteria of morality from Kant onwards I should not wish to restrict the relevance of consequences to nonmoral cases. Anyone who takes a broadly consequentialist view about the justification of all kinds of action, moral and nonmoral, can take their common dependence on consequences as an explanation for their common universalizability. But anyone who denies the moral relevance of the consequences of action while admitting that consequences are relevant to nonmoral evaluation is committed to the conclusion that nonmoral injunctions can be universalized while he has no explanation for the universalizability of just those moral injunctions to which he claims that it is peculiar.

I am not wanting to suggest that the universalization criterion is simply a gratuitous mistake. I believe, indeed, that there is a sense in which moral judgments are at least *universal* in a proprietary way. But this universality is not a formal feature of moral judgments. It is, rather, a feature of what I should regard as the characteristically moral end; namely, the general welfare. On this view an act is morally recommended if the value it is expected to realize is the welfare of everyone, or of everyone likely to be at all significantly affected by it. An inarticulate recognition of this material factor would seem to be part of what lies behind the formal criterion of universalizability.

But there is also another consideration that should be mentioned. The requirement of the universalizability of moral judgements is often defended as necessary to guard against a common failing. There is something, it is felt, seriously wrong with a purportedly moral injunction which a man addresses to others while not being prepared to apply it to himself. This failing can be construed in formal terms as a kind of converse of universalizability as I have defined it. "A ought to do X" is universalizable, I said, if it entails that there is some description F, which is true of A, and such that everyone who is F should do X. What often happens is that people apply rules to other people which they do not apply to themselves. To exclude this we might lay down a requirement of self-applicability: if everyone who is F ought to do X then if I am F I ought to do X.

There are two possibilities to consider here. Failure of self-application may take the form of denying that I ought to do whatever it is that the rule recommends or it may be that I admit that I ought to act in the way recommended but simply fail to do so. In the first case I am just being inconsistent, if I really have committed myself to the position that everyone who is F should do X and if I am in fact F myself. But, of course, in practice it may be hard to establish conclusively that I have committed myself to that principle. I may take refuge behind the excuse that my statement of it was elliptical and did not mention a differentiating property which excludes me from the scope of the principle while leaving all the other people to whom I have applied it within its scope. In such a practical case one just has to see what the differentiating excuse is. A material criterion is of considerable use here since we can appeal to it to determine whether the differentiation is morally relevant.

The crucial point for my argument is that there is an exactly parallel situation in the field of prudential advice. Suppose I say to someone "you ought to put some money aside for your retirement" but deny that I ought to do this myself while unable to point to any relevant difference in our circumstances (I can speak of relevance here since its determination is uncontroversial). If we are much the same in age, expectation of life, present wealth, earning power, testamentary expectations and so forth then I am plainly inconsistent and my advice is not to be taken seriously. Thus far, then, self-applicability is no more peculiar to moral judgements than universalizability. It may be that the relevant factors are even more indeterminate in the prudential case than they are in the moral one. Perhaps I believe that saving would be more painful for me or that I will mind a destitute retirement less than he will. But I suspect that a parallel indeterminacy could be found in the moral case without much ingenuity.

Let us turn to the other possibility of failure of self-application, that in which I admit that I ought to do what I recommend to others but in fact do not do it. The doubt that is raised here concerns rather the sincerity of my profession of principle than my ability to apply it consistently. Of course failure of performance can take many forms. I may fail to do what I say I ought to do with regret, after an inward struggle, and so on. On the other hand I might fail without a qualm. If the failure is agonized then, unless the agony comes to be of a very mechanical and repetitive sort, unless it turns into a placatory ritual, we should probably accept the sincerity of the profession *both in the moral and in the prudential cases.* But if the failure is blithe it might seem that there is a difference. Blithe failure to do what one says one morally ought proves insincerity; blithe failure to do what one says one prudentially ought does not.

I do not think this is so. Blithe failure to conform with one's prudential professions is just as insincere, in the sense of establishing that the professed principle is not really held, as is the parallel failure in the moral case. Where they differ is that moral insincerity is morally offensive, since it is a common device for taking advantage of other people, whereas prudential insincerity is merely rather silly. It should be noticed that in making some insincere prudential profession I may in fact be giving perfectly good advice, by accident, just as by answering a question with the first thing that comes into my head or with something I believe to be false but which is actually true I may, by accident, convey true information.

V

I come now to the fourth and last of the formal criteria of morality, that which says that where there is a conflict of considerations, moral considerations are always overriding or supreme. This idea has been familiar to students of moral philosophy since Bishop Butler wrote of the authority of conscience, but only in recent times, with the revival of some of his concern with the relations between morality and other forms of practice, has it been given much attention.

In what way is this supremacy of moral considerations to be understood? Is it a matter of power or authority? Is it claimed that they always do override others or, rather, that they always should? There are difficulties about each conception. At first sight it seems obvious that there are frequent occasions on which moral considerations do not override others. People in a situation where they are in no doubt as to what they are morally required to do may nevertheless, under the influence of immediate self-interest or passionate desire, do something else. I know that I ought not to pass on this delightfully scandalous piece of information which has been given to me in strict confidence, but I succumb to the temptation to entertain or give an impression of being in the know. In terms of our intuitive distinction between the moral and the nonmoral it appears indubitable that moral considerations, accepted by the agent, are commonly overridden by considerations of a nonmoral kind.

Yet this has been denied by philosophers, by all those who, identifying virtue and knowledge, contend that a man cannot knowingly do what he thinks to be wrong. On such a view the final and authoritative test of what a man's real convictions are, as contrasted with the convictions he verbally professes, is what he does. There is something to this idea. If a man professes to condemn a certain kind of conduct morally and yet acts in that way himself without a qualm before or after, whenever there is an attractive opportunity for doing so, we should regard his moral professions of the general principle as hypocritical and insincere. But it is to exaggerate this truth out of recognition to maintain that an agent's moral professions cannot be sincere unless his own conduct conforms to them without exception.

Very peculiar consequences follow if the full rigour of this doctrine is accepted. What sense can be made of yielding to temptation? It has to be understood in an extraordinary retrospective way; it must be to have done something which one now thinks wrong but did not think wrong at the time, as is proved by the fact that one did it. Remorse, again, cannot be regret for acting wrongly, but can only be regret for not having thought something wrong which one now believes to be so. In general, the fact that total and emotionally unobstructed failure to conform with a principle of conduct one professes proves the insincerity of the profession does not entail that sincerity requires the diametrical contrary opposite situation of exceptionless conformity.

But if the supremacy of moral considerations does not mean that they always do override nonmoral ones, how are we to take the only relevant alternative, that they always ought to override nonmoral considerations? Does this mean that they morally ought to be supreme? This can hardly be doubted, but simply because it is so very insubstantial. Where morality says I ought to do one thing and prudence another, I morally ought to do what morality says I ought to do. Of course. To say that there is a moral consideration in favour of doing something is to say that I morally ought to do it. This version of the supremacy criterion simply affirms that I morally ought to do what I morally ought to do.

Before attempting another account of this normative version of the supremacy criterion there is a further difficulty to be considered. The standard situation of practical choice which those who speak of morality as overridding have in mind is that in which there is a conflict between moral and nonmoral considerations. But other forms of conflict of choice can be envisaged. On the one hand there are situations in which different moral considerations come into conflict with each other; on the other hand there are situations in which no moral consideration has a bearing on the case at all, let us call them situations of purely moral and purely nonmoral conflict respectively.

If there are purely moral conflicts it follows that if they *are* resolved then some moral consideration must in fact be overridden, and if there is any way in which they *ought* to be resolved then some moral considerations ought to be overridden. It follows that, however the criterion of moral supremacy is interpreted, it is not a necessary condition of the moral status of a consideration. It must be the case that some moral considerations are not and should not be overriding.

The possibility of purely nonmoral conflict is equally fatal to the claim that supremacy is a sufficient condition of the moral character of a consideration. When prudence and appetite come into conflict, as they seem so often to do, one of them *will* triumph and it is natural to assume that one of them *ought* to triumph. It follows that nonmoral considerations will often override others and that some nonmoral considerations ought to triumph.

It is only in the mixed cases, where moral and nonmoral considerations are both involved, that the principle of moral supremacy can apply. But this shows that, whatever else may be true of it, the statement that moral considerations are supreme cannot be used as a means of identifying which of the considerations recognised as relevant to a situation of practical choice is moral. For, before the principle is applied, the case has to be identified as one in which a moral consideration is in conflict with a non-moral one.

Allowing, then, that supremacy cannot be a criterion of the moral and that the supremacy of the moral is a normative and not a factual matter, an assertion about what ought to prevail and not about what always in fact will, we may still ask whether there is not a sense in which moral considerations, independently identified as such, ought to override others. I am inclined to think that we could envisage a kind of resultant or consummatory sense of *ought* in which it means something like "ought in the end, all particular considerations having been taken into account." What I call here "particular considerations" would be statements to the effect that something ought to be done which would if correct each be a sufficient reason for doing it in the absence of any countervailing considerations. If there are conflicts between such particular considerations, as there plainly appear to be, we need a rational procedure for arbitrating between them. Now a possible solution to this problem, which has an attractive simplicity at any rate, is to say that if one of the considerations involved is moral then it ought, in this consummatory sense, to prevail over the rest. (This proposal does not, of course, deal with the case of purely moral conflict, but the existence of this type of case is perhaps controversial.)

Although this is a possible solution I do not think it is the correct one. To make this clear let me draw attention to what might be called the inadvertent moral totalitarianism of certain kinds of ethical theory. According to G. E. Moore, and in this respect he is at one with most teleological ethical theorists, to say that A morally ought to do X is to say that of all the things it is at this moment possible for A to do X would have the morally best results on the whole. This definition has the most surprising implications. One is that at every moment there is one morally required thing that we ought to be doing (and only one unless two possibilities have equally good results) and that most of the time it is very likely indeed that we are not doing it. When I am in the bath or lingering over a meal or flattering somebody else's wife at a party I could perfectly well be doing something positive to reduce the general load of major human misery instead. I should be a more morally admirable person if I were to do it. But is it really sensible to say that I am committing a moral offence by taking the easier path? There is an argument which would justify these mildly enjoyable nonmoral activities as causally necessary to effective moral action, as a kind of recreation indispensable to prodigies of effective moral effort. Advanced on behalf of anyone but a saint I should regard this argument as absurd. But this morally totalitarian attitude requires us to be saints or nothing.

Compare the situation I have just described, where private pleasure is pursued at the expense of a morally good possibility, with one in which I linger over my meal when I ought to be watching some young children in a swimming pool as I have promised to do. Here the neglected moral possibility is not just something which it would be good if it were realized, but a definite moral obligation. If we can distinguish between the morally obligatory and the morally desirable we can formulate the principle of moral supremacy in a reasonable way. Where there is a conflict between moral obligation and other considerations, morality is supreme, in the sense that it ought, in a resultant or consummatory way, to prevail. The fulfillment of moral obligations is the indispensable minimum condition of a good life in general for men as social beings. But this is not true of the supererogatory activities of those for whom morality is an individual vocation. Whether or not this attempt to give some useful residual interpretation to the principle of moral supremacy is accepted, it remains true that supremacy cannot serve as a criterion of the moral.

VI

Since I do not know how to show that there are no other plausible formal criteria of morality—criteria, that is to say, which do not mention the *empirical kind* of actions that moral assertions enjoin or the *empirical kind* of ends whose pursuit they recommend—I cannot claim to have shown that the criterion of morality is material. I should, however, claim that a material criterion, which accounted a recommendation moral to the extent that it was justified by reference to the capacity of the kind of action recommended to diminish suffering in general, would be found to draw much the same line between the moral and the nonmoral as our unreflective discrimination in this field.

But such a claim would need to be defended against an array of familiar objections. One of these is that we should hardly question the moral nature of a rule of life which required complete obedience to the commands of God, whatever the content of these rules might be, and however much their adoption might increase suffering. Here I can do no more than point out that even the most authoritarian and self-sacrificial of religious moralities is usually associated with the belief that self-sacrifice is amply compensated for by avoidance of suffering after death. A more fundamental point, perhaps, arises from the question whether the moral perfection of God is definitive of him or not. If God is by definition morally perfect we should, no doubt, be morally obliged to obey his commands, provided we could find out what they were. But then, in order to decide whether some powerful supernatural being was actually God, we should have to be able to tell, on independent grounds, whether he was morally perfect. If God is not morally perfect by definition then we have to settle the moral problem of whether or not we ought to obey him. (In either case, of course, if he is omnipotent, it might well be prudent to obey him.)

Another objection considers the case of a man who devotes himself, and calls for the devotion of others, to self-sacrificial service on behalf of some ideal excellence, such as the augmentation of knowledge or the creation of beauty. Such a rule of service to an impersonal ideal could, it is argued, play the same part in a man's life that concern for the suffering of others plays in the life of men whom the objector would regard as holding a more ordinary and conventional morality. I should agree that such a rule of life might have something of the same emotional significance as ordinary morality. One who adopted it would look on his own failures with remorse and those of others with indignation. But it would have one serious deficiency by comparison. Rather little of what most people do has any noticeable bearing on the protection and increase of knowledge or beauty, but a great deal has an influence on the suffering of others. In consequence such an ideal would simply fail to provide a substitute, other than common prudence, for great areas of possible conduct which are covered by ordinary morality.

This example suggests that a criterion could be developed, I am not sure whether to call it a material one or not, in terms of the psychological attitude of the agent, rather than in terms of the empirically discoverable effects of action. Westermarck's moral anthropology defines as moral those rules of conduct whose breach by others excites what he calls "impersonal resentment," in other words indignation, as contrasted with the personal resentment or simple annoyance that is excited by the merely inconvenient or disadvantaging conduct of other people.

One way of arguing against this proposal would be to ask how an emotional response to the conduct of others is to be identified as a case of indignation, rather than mere annoyance, without some independent standard for the morality of the rule infringed. It will not do to say that resentment is impersonal and thus moral if its natural expression contains such typically moral terms of condemnation as "evil," "wicked," "sinful," "disgraceful." For this inevitably raises the question why these, as compared with other terms of reprobation, should be picked out as moral. What this criterion now adds up to is that a rule is moral if its infringement by another excites a response whose natural expression uses terms of moral reprobation. In other words, the criterion is too good to be very useful: indignation *is* simply strong moral disapproval.

But I should also argue that a psychological criterion like Westermarck's does in fact point in the right direction. For resentment is the proper response to an action which is thought to be responsible for suffering, dissatisfaction or displeasure. Impersonal resentment, then, will have as its proper object action thought to cause suffering to anyone. In view of this close connection between this psychological criterion and the material criterion I should favour, it perhaps should be classified as material as well. At any rate it owes its plausibility, I should maintain, to the material criterion that underlies it.

UNIVERSALIZABILITY AND JUSTICE

Paul W. Taylor

I

A traditional objection to Kant's ethical theory is that no moral prescriptions can be made to follow from a purely formal principle alone. Although I shall not here be defending Kant's own views from this attack, I intend to set forth an argument showing that, by a special application of a purely formal principle to a certain class of cases, the rational ground for a universal, cross-cultural standard of social justice can be established. I shall also try to show that if this argument is sound, it provides a justification for anyone's adopting the basic norm of "justice as fairness," developed by Professor John Rawls in his article of that name.[1]

The purely formal principle to be used in my argument is the principle of universalizability, understood as a logical property of all normative (evaluative and prescriptive) assertions.[2] If an object X is judged to be good, then any other object similar to X in the relevant respects must be judged to be good. The reason for this is that the grounds on which the goodness of an object is determined are standards of evaluation and to claim that the object is good is to claim, among other things, that it fulfills the standards to a certain degree. A person would be inconsistent if he then judged another object *by the same standards* not to be good, if that other object was similar in relevant respects. For the relevant respects are those properties of any object in virtue of which it fulfills the standards. The same holds true when we evaluate something as being good in some respects and bad in others. This happens when it has certain properties in virtue of which it fulfills some of the standards we apply to it and other properties in virtue of which it fails to fulfill other standards we apply to it. The object in this case has both good-making and bad-making characteristics. But the condition of universalizability is still satisfied: Any similar object must also be judged to be good in some respects and bad in others when the same set of standards are applied. For a "similar" object, by definition, is one which has the same relevant properties, that is, the same good-making and bad-making characteristics.

When we turn to prescriptive statements and rules of conduct, the principle of universalizability is again seen to be embodied in the very logic of the normative words we use. What is right for one person to do in a given situation must be right for any similar person to do in a similar situation. The reason is the same as that given above. The ground for judging an act to be right, that is, the reason a person would give to justify his prescribing it as something that ought to be done, is the fact that the act conforms to a rule (or set of rules) or that it fulfills a standard (or set of standards) which that person has adopted as guides to choice and conduct. The word "similar," whether applied to the agent, the act, or the circumstances, refers to those properties held to be relevant by the one who prescribes the act. What makes the properties relevant is the fact that they are the "right-making" properties of the given kind of act—the properties the person himself would cite as reasons why he believes an act of that kind to be right. Given these reasons, it necessarily follows that any similar act must be prescribed as right for a similar agent to do in similar circumstances.

To sum up this argument concerning universalizability: Whenever an evaluation or prescription is made, the justifying reasons given as its grounds will specify what the evaluator or prescriber takes to be the good-making or right-making characteristics of the object or act. All characteristics are universal properties and as such can be exemplified by more than one instance. If their exemplification in one case is accepted as a reason for saying that an object is good or that an act ought to be done, then consistency requires that the same be said of any other object or act that exemplifies those properties.

What is right (or wrong) for one person, then, must be right (or wrong) for every similar person in similar circumstances. But this does not tell us what is right or wrong for anyone to do. To know this we must also be told what it is about the act that makes it right or wrong for a person to do in the given set of circumstances. We must know, in other words, what rules and standards are being applied to the act. It is for this reason that universalizability is a purely formal principle. It is true of all normative statements, regardless of what is asserted in such statements. It has sometimes been called the principle of "formal justice," [3] but it is only a necessary, not a sufficient condition for justice. A person would indeed be unjust—in fact, inconsistent—if he said it was right to treat one individual in a certain way and wrong to treat another *similar* individual in the same way. But as far as universalizability goes, *any* difference between two individuals can be cited as a characteristic that justifies difference of treatment. It is precisely because universalizability allows differences of treatment on any grounds anyone might wish to consider relevant that an additional condition must be satisfied for a rule to determine just treatment of persons. This additional condition is a principle governing the treatment of different persons that *rules out* certain kinds of treatment as unjust. Universalizability, however, does not rule out any kind of treatment; it only demands that we be consistent. Someone who set up a social practice (or participated in one) in which all persons with blue eyes were burnt alive at the age of thirty would be just as consistent as someone who discriminated among persons, not on the basis of age and eye color, but on the basis of acceptance of religious dogma, and who burnt alive those who rejected such dogma. And a third person who refused to burn anyone alive for any reason would be no more consistent than either of the other two. In each case, then, whether justice is done depends on something more than consistency.

What is this something more? The answer I wish to consider in this paper is that the something more is *impartiality*, understood as the principle that everyone has an equal right to the fulfillment of his interests. I shall take "fulfillment of a person's interests" to mean providing for him something he desires or giving him the opportunity and ability to obtain for himself something he desires. The contrary would be the frustration of a person's interests, understood as either directly depriving him of something he desires or interfering with his ability and opportunity to obtain for himself something he desires. The "protection" of a person's interests can then be defined as bringing about and maintaining those conditions that prevent the frustration of his interests. Though what a person desires, he *may* judge to be bad, he will frequently desire something insofar as he judges it to be good. Thus a person's interests will include the fulfillment of all the value-standards he has adopted.

A rule of conduct is impartial in the sense I am here concerned with if and only if the conduct it prescribes conforms to the principle that all men have an equal right to the fulfillment of their interests (a principle that entails an equal right to the protection of their interests). This statement of the condition of impartiality, however, contains a concept that is as problematical as that of impartiality itself, namely, the concept of equality of rights. Just how problematical it is may be brought out by seeing what happens when it is analyzed in terms of similarity and difference of treatment of different persons.

We notice straight off that equality of rights requires something more than the rule: Similar cases are to be treated similarly and different cases differently. For this is merely a new way of putting the purely formal principle of universalizability. What is needed to supplement it is some test for deciding when difference of treatment is just, or in other words, when such treatment does not violate the condition of impartiality.

Let us suppose the following is suggested as the necessary test: A rule of conduct is impartial if and only if it prohibits anyone from so acting as to fulfill or protect one person's interests to a greater or lesser degree than another's, unless there is a relevant difference between them. It can immediately be seen that we are once more merely being given the principle of universalizability. For, as I pointed out above, a relevant difference between persons is any difference determined by the standards or rules adopted by anyone with regard to the conduct in question. Therefore, no kinds of (consistent) behavior are being ruled out by this condition. But we are now in a position to recognize the crux of the matter. It is necessary to specify some *criteria of relevance* by which the grounds for a just difference of treatment, that is, impartiality of treatment, can be determined.

Before stating my own view of how such criteria can be arrived at, I want to examine an argument that has been given to show that such criteria can, after all, be derived from the principle of universalizability itself. This argument is presented by Professor R. M. Hare in Chapters 6 and 7 of his book, *Freedom and Reason*.

Hare's argument begins thus. Suppose we say that in certain circumstances it is right for one person, A, to do a certain act to another, B. Then the principle of universalizability requires us to say that it is right for anyone similar to A in those circumstances to do the same kind of act to anyone similar to B. Let us further suppose that the act is such that it affects B's interests negatively and A's interests positively. That is, B's interests are to some degree frustrated by the act while A's interests are to some degree fulfilled. It follows from universalizability that if it is right for A to do the given act to B, it must also be right for B to do the same act to A if the *only* difference in the circumstances of the two cases is the reversal of roles held by A and B. By "reversal of roles" is meant that B becomes the agent (the one who does the act) and A the patient (the one to whom the act is done). Therefore, unless A can show some relevant difference between himself and B, he must admit, if he is sincere in his normative statement, that it is right for B to treat him in the way he thinks it is right for him to treat B.

Hare does not give a clear reason why the reversal of roles itself cannot constitute a relevant difference between persons. Since this is essential not only to his argument but also to the general argument of this paper, I propose the following as a way of establishing the point. A relevant difference between any two acts must be a property or set of properties, the presence of which in one act is cited as a prima facie ground for judging it to be right (or wrong) and the absence of which is cited as a prima facie ground for judging an *otherwise similar* act to be wrong (or right). The property or set of properties, in other words, must make a normative difference. This is a consequence of the fact that it is a property or set of properties in virtue of which the act in question fulfills or fails to fulfill a norm (a standard or rule) adopted by the person who is evaluating or prescribing the act. Given his adoption of a norm, consistency requires that he consider whatever fulfills the norm to be, to that extent and in that respect, good or right, and whatever fails to fulfill it to be, to that extent and in that respect, bad or wrong.

The property of being-an-agent (that is, being in the role of a person who intends to do an act and does what he intends) cannot by itself be a relevant difference. A relevant difference must be a property that it is possible for an agent of an act to possess and another agent of an exactly similar act in exactly similar circumstances to fail to possess. If there were no such property the two acts in question would have to be judged equally right or equally wrong. Suppose, for example, that we have the following two cases, where a reversal of roles is the *only* difference between them:

Case I: A does act X to B in circumstances C.
Case II: B does act X to A in circumstances C.

If act X is judged to be right in case I and wrong in case II, there must be some property present in the one case and not in the other. Since *ex hypothesi* the two token-acts designated X and the two sets of circumstances designated C are exactly alike, the property must be a characteristic of person A but not of person B (or vice versa). Such a property, however, cannot consist in the mere fact about A that in one case he does an act which he does not do in the other case, for the *same* fact is true of B. There must be some difference between A and B to account for the difference in the value of the acts performed in the two cases. Being an agent in one case but not in the other is not such a difference. Therefore the property of being an agent cannot serve the logical function required of a relevant difference. It cannot by itself constitute a right-making or wrong-making characteristic.

Let us now return to Hare's argument for the derivation of impartiality of treatment from universalizability. Hare reasons as follows. Suppose someone is contemplating doing an act (or laying down a rule, or supporting a social policy, or participating in a practice) which he knows will involve the frustration of the interests of others. He must then ask himself: Can I honestly prescribe that this act (rule, policy, practice) be carried out universally? Or, to put it in a Kantian way: Can I will that this act (rule, policy, practice) become a universal law? In deciding the answer to this question, the person must not only consider *all* the interests that will be affected if such a prescription were followed (disregarding whose interests they may be), but he must give *equal weight* to the interests of others as he does to his own. That is, he must acknowledge that the interests of all those being affected by the prescription have the same claim to fulfillment he makes in behalf of his own interests, which he wants to fulfill by means of the prescription. For if he were to give greater weight to his own interests, he would be asserting in effect that it is right for his interests to be fulfilled at the cost of preventing or hindering the fulfillment of someone else's interests and, by the principle of universalizability, he cannot consistently assert this unless he can specify some reason that would justify the difference of treatment. Assuming for the moment that he admits there are no relevant differences among persons or circumstances in the given situation, he cannot honestly give his assent to the judgment that it is right for him to do an act unless he can also honestly give his assent to the judgment that it is right for others to do the same kind of act, even if it were he whose interests were being frustrated by their doing the act.

Under these conditions he (logically) cannot give his sincere assent to the latter judgment. In admitting that there are no relevant differences between himself and others, he has ruled out any ground that would justify the satisfying of others' interests at the cost of frustrating his own. And in the fact that his own interests would be frustrated if others were to do the act, he has a reason for prescribing that the act ought not to be done. Therefore he must assert that he ought not to do an exactly similar act. Hare sums up this argument as follows:

The principle often accepted by utilitarians, "Everybody to count for one, nobody for more than one" can . . . be justified by the appeal to the demand for universalizability. . . . For what this principle means is that everyone is entitled to equal consideration, and that if it is said that two people ought to be treated differently, some difference must be cited as the ground for these different moral judgments. And this is a corollary of the requirement of universalizability.[4]

To illustrate this, Hare offers the following case:

Suppose that three people are dividing a bar of chocolate between them, and suppose that they all have an equal liking for chocolate. And let us suppose that no other considerations such as age, sex, ownership of the choco-late, etc., are thought to be relevant. It seems to us obvious that the just way to divide the chocolate is equally. And the principle of universalizability gives us the logic of this conclusion. For if it be maintained that one of the three ought to have more than an equal share, there must be something about his case to make this difference—for otherwise we are making differ-ent moral judgments about similar cases. But there is *ex hypothesi* no rele-vant difference, and so the conclusion follows.[5]

In order to consider the case in which there *is* a relevant difference, Hare adds the following:

Suppose, on the other hand, that one of the three does not like chocolate. Then they can all happily prescribe universally that those who do not like chocolate should not be given any (leaving out of consideration the possibil-ity that they might be given it to trade with, or given other things in lieu). And so they can all agree that the chocolate ought to be divided in the ratio of 1 : 1 : 0.[6]

This last case is not really an example of a justifiable frustration of someone's interests on the ground of a relevant difference. For no one's interests are being frustrated. The one who gets no chocolate does not want any, and hence he has no interest which makes a claim to fulfill-ment. What Hare should have considered is a case where all three want to have the bar of chocolate, and yet all can "happily" (willingly and honestly) prescribe that one shall get less than the others or shall get none at all. An example, I suppose, would be that the one who gets less has just been given a greater share in something else that was desired by all three. Or perhaps he gets none at all because he has done something which, according to the rules accepted by all three, deserves punishment and his punishment in this case is "no chocolate." Or else he has not worked as long or as hard as the other two in producing the bar of choc-olate. The important thing, of course, is that the difference of treatment be justified on the ground of some *relevant* difference, and for reasons given earlier I think Hare is perfectly correct in claiming that this is an implication or corollary of universalizability.

But we must remember that what Hare has so far shown is only that universalizability can yield the principle of impartiality if some cri-teria of relevant differences be already assumed. All he has proven is that, unless there is *some* reason why the interests of one person should be fulfilled or frustrated to a greater or lesser degree than those of oth-ers, everyone's interests have an equal claim to fulfillment. He has not told us what kind of reason would qualify as a "justicizing ground" for difference of treatment. So we remain with the crucial problem: What criteria of relevant differences between persons are required if differences of treatment among such persons are nevertheless correctly claimed to be just? Hare tries to derive such criteria from universalizability itself, and here I think his reasoning goes astray. Let us look at his argument.[7]

A relevant difference between persons must be a property or set of properties, the possession of which constitutes a prima facie reason for his interests to have a greater or lesser claim to fulfillment than those of someone who lacks the property or set of properties. Hare points out, rightly I think, that any such property must be a universal characteristic that may be thought to be exemplified by anyone in a hypothetical situation. So let us reconsider the case where one person, A, believes it is right to treat another person, B, in a way in which A claims it would be wrong for B to treat him. A can defend his claim by citing some difference between himself and B as a relevant one—one that not only gives *him* a justification for doing the act to B, but gives anyone in his position a justification for doing an act of the same sort to anyone in B's position. Let us designate by the letter P the property cited as relevant and let us suppose it is a property possessed by B and not by A. (The logic of the situation would remain the same, be it noted, if the property were possessed by A and not by B, that is, if its absence rather than its presence were held to justify difference of treatment.) Since P is a universal characteristic it would be possible for A to possess it and B not to possess it, in a hypothetical situation where the roles of A and B were reversed. Then, by the principle of universalizability, we get the following result: If A claims it is right for him to frustrate B because B possesses P, then he commits himself to the claim that it is right for anyone to treat anyone else who has P in the same way, and this implies that it would be right for B to frustrate him, A, in the hypothetical situation where P is present in A and absent from B and their roles are reversed. But in cases where A has chosen properties like race or religion as the basis of difference of treatment, he is unwilling so to commit himself. Therefore, if he is to be consistent, he is forced to withdraw his original claim. As Hare puts it:

Either the property of his own case, which he claims to be morally relevant, is a properly universal property (i.e., one describable without reference to individuals), or it is not. If it is a universal property, then, because of the meaning of the word "universal," it is a property which might be possessed by another case in which he played a different role . . . ; and we can therefore ask him to ignore the fact that it is he himself who plays the role which he does in this case. This will force him to count as morally relevant only those properties which he is prepared to allow to be relevant even when other people have them. And this rules out all the attractive kinds of special pleading.[8]

But does it? I don't think it would bother the thoroughgoing racist at all. He would say that if his skin was black then it would indeed be right for others to prevent him from eating in certain restaurants, going to certain schools, living in certain areas, or having certain jobs. The racist is quite willing to be consistent about this; indeed, he would insist on it. Hare has two further moves to make with regard to this kind of person. Neither of these, it seems to me, are arguments which have any bearing on the principle of impartiality or justice.

The first move is to ask such a consistent racist to imagine himself in the situation where the roles are reversed. Hare believes that very few people will continue sincerely to claim that it is right for their interests to be frustrated when they have vividly imagined themselves in the other person's shoes. Well, perhaps some would change their minds, but some would not. In fact, those who would change their minds can rightly be accused of what Hare calls "backsliding." 9 What can Hare then say to the consistent racist?

At this point he makes his second move. This is to show that the person who does not change his mind is a certain kind of man, whom Hare calls a "fanatic." The definition of a "fanatic" is anyone who believes it is right, or even that it is his duty, to frustrate the interests of others in order to further or maintain an ideal of his own. In particular, the fanatic is willing to have other people prevented from living in accordance with their ideals, while he is permitted to live in accordance with his own. And his own ideal might well demand that he stamp out the ideals of others.

Is the fanatic inconsistent? Hare would have to admit that he is not, so long as he cites some relevant difference to justify such difference of treatment. We are then brought back to the question with which we began: How can we determine what properties constitute relevant differences? What criteria of relevance are acceptable? It is important to realize that this is not merely an academic question. The people who are most vehement in their racism are just those who, being deeply committed to their ideals, are completely consistent on such matters. To call them names like "fanatic" is of course not to touch the logic of their position. They could just as easily retort: "You egalitarians are the real fanatics, since you are willing to prevent those of us who are striving to preserve the purity of the Caucasian race from working toward our goals. You are even willing to use legal coercion to frustrate us. But you cannot claim to be right in doing this unless you can show why we are wrong in our conviction that race is a relevant difference. You say that race is not a relevant difference, we say it is. Perhaps we cannot establish the truth of our position, but you have as yet failed to establish the truth of yours."

I conclude that, as far as Hare's argument goes, we are still without a defense of the principle of impartiality. For we have not been able to rule out such properties as race or religion—or indeed any property of persons at all—as legitimate grounds for difference of treatment.

II

I shall now argue that, by means of a particular type of appeal to universalizability, the principle of impartiality (that all men have an equal right to the fulfillment of their interests) can be justified as a valid social norm. I also hope to make clear how this argument gives us the logical grounds for the principle of mutual acknowledgment or consent, which Professor John Rawls has developed in his essay on "justice as fairness." [10]

We have seen that the principle of universalizability entails that no one's interests may be frustrated or fulfilled to a greater or lesser extent than anyone else's unless there is a relevant difference between the two persons that justifies (or "justicizes") this difference of treatment. Thus a relevant difference must be cited if one is to have a reason that can make it permissible for anyone's interests to be frustrated to a greater degree than someone else's. Furthermore, the fact that an act will frustrate a person's interests to *any* degree is a prima facie reason, on the part of that person, against doing the act or against allowing it to be done. This is simply one of the "rules of practical reason" that guide our decision-making when we are confronted with alternative courses of action.[11] In general, with reference to any act that brings about or involves the frustration of anyone's interests, there is a prima facie reason for its not being done. This is either a reason on the part of the agent for not doing it (if he is the one who will be frustrated by it), or it is a reason on the part of the patient for not permitting it to be done to him, or for trying to prevent someone doing it to him (if he is the one who will be frustrated).

What kind of reason could outweigh this prima facie reason against an act's being done? Our foregoing considerations about universalizability yield the following answer. The only kind of reason that can outweigh the prima facie reason is one that satisfies three conditions: (1) The reason correctly asserts that at least one person's interests will be protected or fulfilled to some degree by the act's being done in the given circumstances. (2) The reason cites a difference between the person who is frustrated and the one who benefits. (3) *This difference is accepted by both parties as a relevant and universalizable one*, that is, as a property or set of properties whose presence or absence justicizes a difference of treatment not only in the given case but in all similar cases (where "similarity" is defined in terms of other properties that are accepted by all parties to be relevant and universalizable).

The first condition is necessary because an act that did not in the least benefit someone by protecting or fulfilling any of his interests would be supported by no reason on the part of anyone. No one could have a reason either for doing the act or for having it done to him, and hence there would not even be a prima facie reason, on anyone's part, to justify the doing of the act. And if, as we are assuming here, the act frustrates, even to the slightest degree, someone's interests, then there is a prima facie reason for its not being done. There would be, then, at least one reason against the act and no reason for it. Therefore no act would be justified unless this first condition was satisfied.

The second condition is necessary because difference of treatment requires that some ground be given on the basis of which one person is allowed to benefit and the other to be frustrated. Whatever this ground may be, if it is to serve as a reason for treating two or more persons differently it must consist of the citing of some property, the presence or absence of which will provide a prima facie justification for frustrating the interests of a person who has (or lacks) it and for fulfilling the interests of a person who lacks (or has) it. Otherwise the difference of treatment is groundless and arbitrary. As such, it would be incapable of counting against, to say nothing of outweighing, the prima facie reason we already have against the act in that it frustrates someone's interests. Every property is universal, so that if the presence of the property in one case justifies the frustration of a person's interests, it justifies such frustration for everyone who has the property, other things being equal.

The third condition is the one that brings in a new consideration, and one that is essential for justice. This condition is that the property or set of properties stated in the second condition be freely and knowingly acknowledged by all affected parties to be relevant criteria for difference of treatment. The reasoning behind this condition is as follows. Suppose a difference between A and B is cited as a justicizing ground for treating them differently, and suppose A accepts this difference as such a ground but B does not. Let us further suppose that A benefits by the treatment and that B is frustrated by it. By the principle of universalizability A cannot sincerely say it is right for the difference of treatment to occur when these conditions hold unless he also can sincerely say it would be right for it to occur under these conditions whenever any two persons were differentiated in the same way, even if he were in B's position and someone else were in his. But this he cannot sincerely say, since one of the conditions is that the person who is frustrated does not acknowledge the difference to be a justicizing ground for difference of treatment. In other words, A (logically) could not judge the act to be right if the roles were reversed and he were similar to B in respect of *not* recognizing the difference in question as a relevant one. For in that case he would not have a reason for doing the act or letting it be done, but quite the reverse (since he would then be frustrated by it). Because A can claim it is right to have the act done only when he accepts the difference as relevant, the same must be true for everyone in similar circumstances, and hence true for anyone in B's position. For otherwise the principle of universalizability would be violated.

It does not matter whether there is agent-patient inequality (the agent being the one who will have his interests fulfilled and the patient being the one who will be frustrated) or the difference of treatment is between one patient and another. What matters is that the one who benefits cannot sincerely assent to the act's being done unless he can assent to its being done even if he were in the position of the other person involved. And this he can do only if, being in the position of the other person, he can freely acknowledge that the property or set of properties used as the basis for the difference of treatment are relevant grounds.

We thus arrive at the principle that, in order for any ground of difference of treatment to be a justicizing or "just-making" ground, it must consist in the appeal to a difference the relevance of which is freely acknowledged by all whose interests are affected by the treatment in question. I shall call this *the principle of mutual acknowledgment*. Since it provides the justification for adopting criteria of relevant differences, it lies at the heart of social justice. And if my foregoing argument holds, the principle is seen to be a necessary consequence of the very logic of our normative discourse, in particular, that aspect of its logic that has been designated by the term "universalizability."

The above argument for the principle of mutual acknowledgment is absolutely fundamental to our understanding the precise conceptual relation between universalizability and justice. In order to make it unmistakably clear, I shall now restate it in a slightly different form.

The proof rests on the point that no one can give his sincere assent to the following principle: It is right for a person's interests to be frustrated by the operation of a criterion of relevant difference which he does not freely and knowingly acknowledge to be a good reason for his being treated in the given way in the given circumstances. The "can" in the phrase "no one can give his sincere assent" is a logical "can." The phrase is equivalent to: "It is inconsistent for someone to give his sincere assent. . . ." The reason is this. If someone were to give his assent to the principle, then his assent would entail, by universalizability, that he give his assent to any particular value judgment that is an instance of it. One such judgment is: It is right for me to be treated in such a way that my interests are frustrated when I do not acknowledge that the criterion being used to discriminate between myself and others is a good reason for being treated in that way. This is a self-contradiction. The last clause entails: ". . . when I do not judge that it is right to be treated in that way," and this contradicts the first clause: "It is right for me to be treated in such a way. . . ."

To avoid this contradiction the following move might be made. A wishes to discriminate against B, knowing that B does not accept the difference cited by A as a relevant one. A may then argue that B's not acknowledging the criterion is to be *disregarded* because B's interests, which are being frustrated, just do not count as making a claim to fulfillment which A is obliged to recognize. Thus the fact that B does not accept the difference as a relevant one is, for A, no reason to refrain from frustrating him. A holds this view on the ground that B *is* different from A in a relevant respect, namely, in just that respect which B does not consider relevant. A would argue that if he had the property that B has, his interests would not make a legitimate claim to fulfillment, either. So A appears to be perfectly consistent.

The contradiction, however, has not been successfully avoided. In this argument A is tacitly assuming the very point in question. Hence he is not really giving a reason—to say nothing of a good reason—in defense of his discrimination against B. A realizes that universalizability requires that he give a reason for disregarding the fact that B does not acknowledge the property in question as a relevant difference, since he, A, would not judge it right for someone else to disregard the same thing if he were in B's position and hence did not accept the difference to be relevant. And the reason he gives is that B's interests do not make a claim that he has an obligation to recognize, and consequently B's frustration need not be considered in deciding what he, A, ought or ought not to do. But universalizability again requires that A give a reason for not counting B's interests as having a legitimate claim to fulfillment (since A is certainly making such a claim on behalf of his own interests). A's reply, we have seen, is to point out that B is different in the given respect from A. This is simply to *assume* that the difference is a relevant one, an assumption which B denies. It is not to give a *reason in justification* of A's original position that it is permissible for him to disregard B's denial. B could just as well use the same "reason" to "justify" his claim that the difference is not a relevant one. No argument is being provided on either side. So A has not escaped the contradiction, and the validity of the principle of mutual acknowledgment has not been brought into question.

III

I shall now examine the logical role of the principle of mutual acknowledgment in Professor Rawls' analysis of the concept of "justice as fairness." Rawls sets forth two principles of justice as valid criteria or standards for judging social practices:

First, each person participating in a practice, or affected by it, has an equal right to the most extensive liberty compatible with a like liberty for all; and second, inequalities are arbitrary unless it is reasonable to expect that they will work out for everyone's advantage, and provided the positions and offices to which they attach, or from which they may be gained, are open to all.[12]

The relation between the two principles, according to Rawls, is that the first states a *presumption of equality* on behalf of each person to pursue the fulfillment of his interests without interference from others, while the second specifies those *inequalities* of fulfillment and frustration of different persons' interests that can defeat or put aside the presumption laid down in the first principle. In terms of similarity and difference of treatment, the two principles together amount to the assertion that, unless there are relevant or "just-making" differences among any group of persons, each is to be treated in the same way as far as their freedom to further their interests is concerned. Such an assertion, as we have seen, can be deduced from the principle of universalizability plus the value judgment (which each person would make) that it would be wrong for anyone to interfere with or otherwise restrict his freedom to pursue his interests. It should be noted that, in stating the second principle, Rawls makes two additional points. The first is that the only legitimate ground for difference of treatment is that such difference will in the long run "work out for everyone's advantage." The second is that the various positions or roles of a social practice be "open to all."

With regard to the first point, Rawls makes it appear that each individual is acting from self-interest and that consequently he will agree to limitations on his freedom only if such limitations are ultimately to his personal benefit. Indeed, Rawls seems to imply this when he sums up his view of justice in this manner: "The conception at which we have arrived, then, is that the principles of justice may be thought of as arising once the constraints of having a morality are imposed upon rational and mutually self-interested parties. . . ."[13] It is not necessary, however, to think of a person's seeking to fulfill his interests by means of participation in a practice as a pursuit of his *self-interest*. If the term "interest" is taken in its broadest sense to cover anything a person desires, either as an end in itself or as a means to an end, then the pursuit of one's interests will include the striving to do that which one believes to be right and to bring about that which one believes to be good. At least some of the interests a person has may therefore be altruistic.

The altruistic interests of one person may come into conflict with the interests (altruistic or prudential) of another, either when the other is not the specific individual whose welfare is the object of the first person's altruistic concern, or when the other's view of what will further his own interests is at odds with the altruist's view of the same matter. Thus the possibility of competing claims arising from conflicts of interests does not require an assumption of egoism on the part of the individuals whose interests conflict. And the problem of justice is with us whenever these conditions hold. For questions of just differences of treatment demand resolution precisely in circumstances where one person's or group's [14] pursuit of its interests (of any kind: moral, religious, aesthetic, prudential, or other) conflicts with another's pursuit of *its* interests (which again may be of any kind). Living in accordance with the standards, rules, or principles to which a person or group has committed itself will be one sort of interest, in this broad sense of "interest." And the fact that the different value systems of individuals or groups conflict is sufficient for a situation of competing claims to arise where a question of justice must be decided. Rawls' basic notion of a just social practice, then, can be generalized so that the second principle reads: "Inequalities (differences of treatment) are arbitrary unless it is reasonable to expect that they will operate in such a way as to promote or protect the interests of everyone."

When expanded in this way, it will more easily be seen how this second principle of justice does provide the ground for a successful rebuttal to the presumption of equality set forth in the first principle. The argument rests on the more fundamental principle of mutual acknowledgment. It is the latter that Rawls appeals to when he takes up the question: What kind of reasoning would lead us to adopt these two criteria of a just social practice? He points out that if all parties involved in a situation of conflict of interests were freely to acknowledge a set of general rules for distributing fulfillment and frustration of interests among any individuals in a situation relevantly similar to theirs, they would accept those limitations on their freedom that are necessitated by the application of the general rules to their own case. They would consequently judge such limitations as not being wrong. Their sense of justice would not be violated and they would not conceive of themselves as being compelled to act against their will. They would recognize the fairness of the distribution which, in the given case, required their own frustration.

Similar considerations may be seen to hold for the second aspect of Rawls' second criterion of justice: that each individual be regarded as having the right to (try to) qualify himself for—that is, to be in competition for—any of the offices or positions of the social practice. This is a corollary of the principle of mutual acknowledgment. For when a practice conforms to that principle no one will be excluded from any office or position unless he freely consents to the rules that specify the conditions of exclusion (which will be equally applicable to everyone in the same circumstances). Different offices and positions will be just only if they are such as to involve difference of treatment for different persons on relevant grounds, and relevant grounds are those which all can freely and knowingly acknowledge even when they operate to exclude some from the advantages or benefits of certain positions.

The principle of mutual acknowledgment is thus used by Rawls as the ground for his two criteria of a just social practice. In typical situations of competing claims where questions of justice arise, Rawls argues, rationally self-interested persons (or groups) would propose to each other, for their mutual acceptance, rules that would determine their respective benefits and burdens, rights and obligations, in the carrying on of social practices in which they were engaged. The two principles of justice are the fundamental conditions such persons would demand that their practices meet if those practices are to be considered by them to be just. It is in the context of this kind of social relationship that the concept of fairness enters, according to Rawls. For a practice to be fair, it must satisfy "the principles which those who participate in it could propose to one another for mutual acceptance," and when a practice does satisfy such principles it is fair.[15] Thus fairness is both a necessary and a sufficient condition for just social practices.

Furthermore, since each individual must freely give his assent to all the rules of the practice, no one can claim to have legitimate authority over another at this level. Who has authority over whom and with regard to what range of cases are matters to be defined by the rules themselves. They are consequences of the decision to adopt a set of rules, not determinants of that decision. Accordingly, each individual, as a chooser and as a critic of the rules of the practice, has an initial status of equality in relation to every other individual.

This idea of everyone's having an *equal right* in the choosing and evaluating of the rules of a practice lies at the foundation of social justice. Let us try to be as clear about it as we can. We have seen that fairness, according to Rawls, is the condition that holds when any differences of enjoying benefits and suffering burdens (or, in my terms, of having one's interests fulfilled or frustrated) resulting from people's participation in a social practice are acceptable to all, when all are given an equal chance to determine what the grounds for the differences shall be. What does "being given an equal chance" mean here? The answer lies in the conditions under which the mutual acknowledgment of rules must take place. There are four such conditions:

(1) The acknowledgment must be freely given by each person.

(2) Each person must be allowed ". . . to propose the principles upon which he wishes his complaints to be tried with the understanding that, if acknowledged, the complaints of others will be similarly tried." [16]

(3) They should each understand that no complaints will be heard at all until everyone is agreed on the principles to be used.

(4) They each understand ". . . that the principles proposed and acknowledged on this occasion are binding on future occasions." [17]

Rawls sums up the general effect of these conditions thus:

The idea is that everyone should be required to make in advance a firm commitment, which others also may reasonably be expected to make, and that no one be given the opportunity to tailor the canons of a legitimate complaint [I should say: to tailor the criteria of a relevant difference] to fit his own special condition, and then to discard them when they no longer suit his purpose. . . . These principles will express the conditions in accordance with which each is the least unwilling to have his interests limited in the design of practices, given the competing interests of the others, on the supposition that the interests of others will be limited likewise.[18]

If a social practice fulfills these conditions it meets the requirement of fairness. It may then correctly be considered just, even if the particular rules or principles agreed upon by everyone are not explicitly referred to.

It is this notion of the possibility of mutual acknowledgment of principles by free persons who have no authority over one another which makes the concept of fairness fundamental to justice. . . . One activity in which one can always engage is that of proposing and acknowledging principles to one another supposing each to be similarly circumstanced; and to judge practices by the principles so arrived at is to apply the standard of fairness to them.[19]

Suppose we grant this view that a practice is just when the rules governing it are freely accepted by all participants. There would then be no need to specify the particular kinds of consideration that, in a just practice, can legitimately rebut the initial presumption of equal liberty. The only condition needed is that set by the principle of mutual acknowledgment itself. For whatever rules of a practice are acknowledged to be fair by all participants will be such as to satisfy each person's sense of a valid claim being recognized by himself and by others in relevantly similar circumstances. Each will propose principles that determine criteria of relevant differences. These principles, on being proposed, will be open to the reflective consideration of all. When all freely give their consent to the adoption of a principle as part of the practice, then, whatever their motives (reasons) may be for proposing or acknowledging the principle, the practice will, to this extent and in this respect, satisfy the criterion of justice. It will, indeed, be judged by its participants to be fair to this extent and in this respect. And if a practice embodies a principle that has not been freely acknowledged by someone whose interests are affected by the practice, he will, as Rawls points out, think of himself as being coerced by others; he will see the demands placed upon him by the rules of the practice as being imposed against his will. That he is unable to further his self-interest or even to fulfill the standards of his own value system is not to the point. The unfairness lies not in any personal frustration or restriction, but in the fact that an individual has been given a status not equal to that of others in so far as his consent has not been recognized as being of equal weight with the consent of others in the adoption of rules that affect him as much as others.

When the principle of mutual acknowledgment is violated, we have seen that a basic element in the logic of our normative language—namely, universalizability—is being disregarded. For as I have argued in Section II, no one can sincerely say it is right that a person be treated differently from others unless he knows that the person in question would freely acknowledge that the difference in his case was a relevant one. And this is precisely what the concept of fairness amounts to, when the difference of treatment is stipulated by a rule of a social practice. Therefore universalizability, as the ground for mutual acknowledgment, also serves as the logical basis for "justice as fairness."

IV

We have one challenge still to be met. Suppose someone argues that he can *consistently* reject the principle of mutual acknowledgment as follows. He denies that criteria of relevant differences must be acceptable to all who are affected by their use on the ground that some who are so affected *ought* not to be given a voice in choosing the criteria. When it is pointed out to him that his use of "ought" in this instance shows that he is *presupposing* some criterion of relevant differences in discriminating between those who are to have a choice and those who are not, he replies that he is indeed using such a criterion and that he has a good reason for doing so. He then cites as his reason that the criterion is required by a "true social ideal." For example, a White Suprema-

cist uses race as a relevant difference, denying Negroes an equal right
with Caucasians in the choice of criteria of relevant differences. He then
defends such discrimination on the ground, first, that it is entailed by
the ideal of a society in which Caucasians maintain a position of superi-
ority over Negroes, and second, that this ideal is a true one.

Let us look at this argument more closely. Two reasons are being
given for denying everyone an equal right in the choosing of criteria of
relevant differences: (1) That such denial is entailed by a certain social
ideal; and (2) that this ideal is a true one. It is necessary to add the second reason to the first, for if the first alone were given the following
objection could be raised. Suppose the Racist were to argue that it is his
ideal of White Supremacy that demands that Negroes not be given a
voice in deciding whether race is to be used as a ground for difference of
treatment in matters of jobs, housing, education, and the like. This position immediately can be countered by pointing out that the social ideals
of those who are being excluded from the choice of criteria demand that
they be given this right. Consequently, by the principle of universalizability, if it is right for the White Supremacist to do what is demanded
by his social ideal, it is right for the Egalitarian to do what is demanded
by his, unless there is a relevant difference between them. If the White
Supremacist now claims that there *is* a relevant difference, namely race,
and supports this claim by appeal to his ideal, he is reasoning in a circle.
For he began by defending the use of race as a relevant difference on
the ground of his ideal. He is now saying that his ideal (but not that of
someone else) is a legitimate ground to appeal to because there is a relevant difference between himself and the other. This is a circular argument. As such, it is not a genuine argument at all. Using the same
"logic," the other person can reply simply by making a similar assertion
on behalf of his own ideal, saying that *it* is a legitimate ground while
the racist's ideal is not, because there is a relevant difference between
them. Since both can use the same reasoning, no argument is actually
being given to justify the appeal to one ideal rather than another. In
short, a claim is being made without a ground on which a contrary
claim can be rejected.

In order to escape this circle the Racist must add a second reason
in his defense. He must show that the social ideal which demands the
exclusion of Negroes from the choice of criteria of relevant differences is
a *true* social ideal, an ideal that sets a *valid* standard for everyone to live
by (including Negroes themselves). For as we have just seen, unless this
claim is made and established, any social ideal can be appealed to by
anyone in support of his method for deciding who shall be given the
right to choose such criteria.

This additional claim must be established by some process of sound reasoning. Whatever may be meant by the words "true" and "valid" as applied to an ideal or a standard, anyone who uses these terms must be prepared at least to show that there are good reasons for the adoption of such an ideal or standard as a guide to life. And whatever may constitute good reasons in this context, they must not be such as to involve one in an inconsistency in accepting them. I shall now try to show that an inconsistency is in fact always involved and that therefore no social ideal of the kind in question can ever be justified.

In Section II it was argued that the principle of universalizability, which is built into our normative language, compels a person to give his assent to the following general principle: If it is wrong for another to discriminate against him on the ground of a difference he does not acknowledge to be relevant, it must also be wrong for him to discriminate against another on the ground of a difference the other does not accept as relevant. It would be inconsistent for someone to say it was wrong in the first case but right in the second. Now it is this inconsistency that is involved in the argument we are considering. For whatever differences among persons are made relevant by a social ideal, if it is known that a certain class of persons, C, do not freely and knowingly accept that ideal and consequently do not acknowledge the given criteria of relevant differences, one is compelled by the principle of universalizability to judge it wrong to use such criteria in discriminating against the class of persons, C. The reason is that the individual himself would judge it wrong for others to use their social ideal as a ground for adopting criteria of relevant differences that he did not freely and knowingly acknowledge. It would not matter that the others believed their social ideal to be a true one. Their belief could not, in his view, be rationally justified. He could not consider their social ideal to be "true," even if they claimed to have good reasons in support of it. For suppose he acknowledges that they do have good reasons and that their ideal is a true one. He then will accept the criteria of relevant differences entailed by that ideal and hence will not think of himself as being discriminated against on irrelevant or unjustifiable grounds. And in that case the principle of universalizability would not be violated. However, this is not the sort of case we are considering.

The hypothesis of the case we are considering is that there is a class of persons, C, who do not freely and knowingly accept the criteria being used to deny them an equal right in the choice of criteria of relevant differences. This implies that good reasons do *not* exist, in their view, for adopting the social ideal in question. So even if a Racist, for example, honestly believes he has good reasons to justify his ideal, he must admit that these reasons may not be accepted by Negroes. Under the condition that they are not accepted by them he cannot consistently argue that their rejection of race as a relevant difference should be ignored, simply because they *are* Negroes. For universalizability requires that he say that his own rejection of a criterion should be ignored when he does not acknowledge the criterion being used against him as a legitimate one, and this would be inconsistent for him to say.

In light of this we may formulate a general principle that has the logical power to invalidate or falsify any social ideal imposed upon a class of persons against their own consent, whatever reasons may be given by others to support the claim that the social ideal in question is a true one. The general principle is: Criteria of relevant differences, not acceptable to all whose interests are affectd by them, cannot be used as grounds for excluding anyone from having an equal right in deciding what criteria are to govern those social practices that affect his interests. A particular instance of this principle is that a social ideal, which is not accepted as a justifiable or true one by a class of persons, cannot provide a valid ground for the exclusion of those persons, regardless of the reasons alleged by others to establish the truth of that ideal. Thus the Racist's argument given at the outset of this section is invalid.

If my reasoning in this last section is correct, then no denial of the principle of mutual acknowledgment is warranted on any grounds. And if this conclusion holds, the *principle of impartiality* has been established in what is undoubtedly its most important context of application. That principle states that all men have an equal right to the fulfillment of their interests. This right does not imply that each person's interests are to be fulfilled to the same extent as every other's. For differences among persons and their circumstances may be relevant and thus constitute good grounds for differences of treatment among them. But the *relevance* of any difference cited as such a ground must be established. It is at this more basic level, where the adoption of criteria of relevance takes place, that impartiality must be maintained if any set of social practices are to meet the requirements of justice. And it is at this level that everyone must be granted an equal right in deciding upon criteria of relevant differences that affect his interests.

I have tried to show that equality of rights at this level follows from a special application of the principle of universalizability, and that this argument cannot be successfully rebutted by appeal to any particular social ideal as a "true" one. If my reasoning is sound, the claim that "justice as fairness" is a universally valid standard for social practices is capable of a strict proof.

NOTES

1. John Rawls, "Justice As Fairness," *Philosophical Review*, LXVII, 2, 1958, pp. 164–194.

2. In recent philosophical literature a number of different concepts have been labeled "universalizability." I shall be using the term in accordance with the way it is analyzed in Charles E. Caton, "In What Sense and Why 'Ought'-Judgements Are Universalizable," *Philosophical Quarterly*, XIII, 50, 1963, pp. 48–55; and in R. M. Hare, *Freedom and Reason* (Oxford, Oxford University Press, 1963), Ch. 3 and 6.

3. See Ch. Perelman, *The Idea of Justice and the Problem of Argument* (London, Routledge and Kegan Paul, 1963), pp. 11–29.

4. R. M. Hare, *Freedom and Reason*, p. 118.

5. *Ibid.*, pp. 118–119.

6. *Ibid.*, p. 119.

7. The main passages in *Freedom and Reason* concerned with this problem are to be found on pages 106–7, 170–2, 216–19, and 221–2.

8. *Op. cit.*, p. 107.

9. This point is argued by Professor Alan Donagan in his article, "Mr. Hare and the Conscientious Nazi," *Philosophical Studies*, XVI, 1–2, January–February, 1965, pp. 8–11.

10. Like Rawls, I consider justice as being logically independent of utility, and my argument is one way to demonstrate this independence. That utility and justice are not only independent but may yield contradictory normative judgments has recently been shown very clearly in David Lyons' brilliant book, *Forms and Limits of Utilitarianism* (Oxford, 1965). A different sort of argument regarding the mutual independence of justice and utility is to be found in Nicholas Rescher, *Distributive Justice: A Constructive Critique of the Utilitarian Theory of Distribution* (Bobbs-Merrill, 1966).

11. See Kurt Baier, *The Moral Point of View* (Ithaca, N.Y., Cornell University Press, 1958), Ch. 3 and 12.

12. John Rawls, *op. cit.*, p. 165.

13. *Ibid.*, p. 183.

14. Rawls does allow groups (including families, organizations, and other types of associations) to count as "persons" in the formulae of the principles of justice. But even here he seems to conceive of the goals and interests of each group as a matter of its "advantage" or "self-interest," rather than as a matter of the promotion and protection of all of its values and ideals.

15. J. Rawls, *op. cit.*, p. 178.

16. *Ibid.*, p. 171.

17. *Ibid.*, p. 171.

18. *Ibid.*, pp. 171–2.

19. *Ibid.*, p. 179.

INTERESTS, ROLE REVERSAL, UNIVERSALIZABILITY AND THE PRINCIPLE OF MUTUAL ACKNOWLEDGEMENT

(A RESPONSE)

Joseph Gilbert

Professor Taylor argues that "a relevant difference must be cited if one is to have a reason that can make it permissible for anyone's interests to be frustrated to a greater degree than someone else's . . . the fact that an act will frustrate a person's interest to *any* degree is a prima facie reason, on the part of that person, against doing the act or against allowing it to be done. [And] in general, with reference to any act that brings about or involves the frustration of anyone's interests, there is a prima facie reason for its not being done."

Taylor states three conditions that must be satisfied to outweigh this prima facie reason against an act being done. The first condition requires, if an act is to be supported by reasons, that at least one person's interests are protected or fulfilled. To satisfy the second condition it is necessary to cite some property in terms of which difference of treatment may be justified. The first condition, which appears to be true by definition, and the second condition, which is compatible with an appeal to any privilege whatever, I shall not consider.

The most important is the third condition, for it provides Taylor with the *principle of mutual acknowledgement*, which, he claims, lies at the heart of social justice, since it provides the justification for adopting criteria of relevant differences.

Taylor states the third condition thusly: "*This difference is accepted by both parties as a relevant and universalizable one,* that is, as a property or set of properties whose presence or absence justicizes a difference of treatment not only in the given case but in all similar cases (where 'similarity' is defined in terms of other properties that are accepted by all parties to be relevant and universalizable)."

We then arrive at the principle of mutual acknowledgement: "In order for any ground of difference of treatment to be a justicizing or just-making ground, *it must consist in the appeal to all whose interests are affected by the treatment in question.*" Taylor argues that *no denial of the principle of mutual acknowledgement is warranted on any grounds.* For Taylor, then, no one can give his sincere consent to the following principle: "It is right for a person's interest to be frustrated by the operation of a criterion of relevant differences which he does not freely and knowingly acknowledge to be a good reason for his being treated in the given circumstances." I shall apply Taylor's reasoning to the following cases.

The judge, who is about to pass sentence on the criminal, realizes that the consistency-requirement commits him to give a reason for disregarding the fact that the criminal does not acknowledge the property in question as a relevant difference. For he, the judge, would not judge it right for someone else to disregard the same thing if he were in the criminal's position and hence did not accept the difference to be relevant. In other words, the judge (logically) could not judge the act to be right—to sentence the criminal—if the roles were reversed and he were similar to the criminal in respect of *not* recognizing the difference in question as a relevant one. Because the judge can claim it is right to have the act done *only when he accepts the difference as relevant,* the same must be true for everyone in similar circumstances, and hence true for anyone in the criminal's position. Otherwise the consistency-requirement would be violated.

What matters, Taylor tells us, "is that one who benefits cannot sincerely assent to the act being done unless he can assent to its being done even if he were in the position of the other person involved." But since the criminal's interests are being violated, i.e., he has an interest in not being sentenced, in not having his freedom or life removed, it follows (logically) that the judge would have such an interest if he were in the situation of the criminal.

On the conditions of Taylor's argument we would never be able to justify punishing anyone no matter how horrendous the crime. We can justify punishment for crime if the reasons used for the difference of treatment are relevant. Taylor's mistake is in thinking that the appeal to a relevant difference consists in the difference being freely acknowledged by *all* whose interests are affected by the treatment in question. The principle of mutual acknowledgement is too broad in scope. Taylor should have indicated when this principle is in order and when it is not. As stated, it does not provide for justifying relevant differences, and though it may lie at the heart of social justice, it does not uncover the "precise conceptual relation between universalizability and justice." In fact, on Taylor's grounds, it would be inconsistent or immoral or both to take legal action against anyone who argued that his interests are being violated. The murderer, thief, vandal, etc., could argue that: "No denial of the principle of mutual acknowledgement is warranted on any grounds."

Another example will indicate that "reversal roles" have little or no moral import, and far less rational import than Taylor maintains.

The racist does not believe that his treatment of others on the basis of color is immoral. He believes that color is a relevant property justifying difference in treatment. Appeal to the consistency-requirement will not convince him otherwise—what is required in this context is appeal to humanity, not consistency. The racist who denies Negroes entrance to his restaurant may realize that the consistency-requirement commits him to give a reason for disregarding the fact that Negroes do not acknowledge the property in question as a relevant difference. But, the racist would not judge it right for someone else to disregard the same thing if he (the racist) were in the Negro's position and hence did not acknowledge the difference to be relevant.

The racist could argue that the Negro (logically) could not judge the act—to deny Negroes entrance to restaurants—to be wrong if the roles were reversed and he were similar to the racist in respect of *recognizing* the difference in question to be a relevant one. Because the racist can claim it is right to have the act done *only when he accepts the difference as relevant*, the same must be true for everyone in similar circumstances, and hence it follows (logically) that the Negro would have such an interest if he were in the situation of the racist. Otherwise the consistency-requirement would be violated. Since both parties can use the same reasoning, no argument is actually being given to justify the absence or presence of color as a relevant difference.

The racist might say: if I am expected to play the 'reversal of roles game' it is not unreasonable to expect the other party to play the same game. In this context, reasoning by analogy is quite suspect. If similarity *is* identity, the role reversal would either be impossible, or unnecessary, since there would not be *two* distinct roles. Even if we do not take "similarity of person" to mean "identity of persons" reasoning by analogy becomes more troublesome the more the "bliks" of the parties concerned, differ.

If my argument is correct, then Taylor is mistaken in claiming that "one is compelled by the principle of universalizability to judge it wrong to use such criteria in discriminating against" the class of persons in question. Taylor's account of what it is to accept a moral principle is also mistaken. I agree that we cannot make different moral judgements about two cases when we cannot justify any differences between the cases which serve as the ground for the difference in moral judgement. This is one way of stating the requirement of universalizability. But I disagree with Taylor's claim that the principle of mutual acknowledgement is required to justify different treatment. That principle implies that we would never accept any maxim of obligation which would permit us to do something disagreeable to other people. But we cannot accept the fact that someone would not like it or that it would violate his interests to be the subject of legal proceedings (or whatever), as a good reason for justifying difference in treatment.

The racist *qua* Negro will not accept color as a criterion of relevant difference and will think of himself as being discriminated against on irrelevant or unjustifiable grounds. In that case the consistency-requirement would be violated. The Negro *qua* racist will accept color as a criterion of relevant difference and will not think of himself as being discriminated against on irrelevant or unjustifiable grounds. And the consistency-requirement will not be violated.

In short, we would not consider the criminal's rejection of his sentence legitimate simply because of a violation of his interests; nor would we accept the racist's argument concerning the 'reversal of roles game' as justification of his treatment of the Negro. Accordingly, Taylor has not shown that interests, reversals of roles, universalizability and the principle of mutal acknowledgement will provide the justification for adopting certain social norms. If my reasoning is correct, Taylor has not established the claim that "justice as fairness as a universally valid standard for social practice is capable of a strict proof." In fact, the principle of mutual acknowledgement is no solution, but is just another way of presenting the problem.

Taylor argues that "by means of a particular type of appeal to universalizability, the principle of impartiality (that all men have an equal right to the fulfillment of their interests) can be justified as a valid social norm." This argument is to give us the logical grounds for the principle of mutual acknowledgement or consent which John Rawls has developed in his essay on *Justice as Fairness*.

The principle of mutual acknowledgement is certainly not without its difficulties in application. What precisely though, is the connection between universalizability and impartiality?

Taylor argues that we can deduce "two principles of justice as valid criteria or standards for judging social practices . . . [and] . . . in terms of similarity and difference of treatment, the two principles together amount to the assertion, that unless there are relevant or 'just-making' differences among any group or persons, each is to be treated in the same way as far as their freedom to further their interests are concerned." This assertion Taylor tells us, "can be deduced from the principle of universalizability plus the value-judgement (which each person would make) that it would be wrong for anyone to interfere with or otherwise restrict his freedom to pursue his interests."

Taylor has shown that R. M. Hare has not successfully established the principle of impartiality, for the appeal to universalizability alone is perfectly compatible with any privilege whatever. But what has Taylor established? He is not, it seems to me, very clear on the connection between formal and moral considerations. We can certainly deduce valid criteria or standards for judging social practices and show that there are certain logical problems involved in violating these standards, if we appeal to universalizability and *also* require that each person make a value judgement in order to show that to violate the standard is either to be immoral or inconsistent, or perhaps both. But if this is what Taylor has done (and I think it is), his criticism of Hare is misguided, in certain respects. For Hare claims that "It is very important not to confuse the thesis of universalizability with the substantial moral principles to which, according to it, a person who makes a moral judgement commits himself." [*Freedom and Reason*, 30.]

It is not easy to reach a decision as to just how far Taylor is making a purely logical point and how far he is revealing his own equalitarian preferences. I agree with Taylor that Hare's central problem involves specification of just those features we are to appeal to as constitutive properties. If these are moral properties, then we must assume some moral principle. If not, we again raise the question of justification of appeal to any moral principles, i.e., these principles cannot be justified if the ethicist maintains that his meta-ethical analysis presupposes no antecedent moral principles. It is clear that Hare wants to avoid the issue of deriving a moral judgement, or the negation of a moral judgement, from a statement of fact about people's interests, etc., and, as such, he hopes to avoid violating Hume's law: "no 'ought' from an 'is.' "

Hare has argued that a formal analysis (at least *his* formal analysis) of morality does not presuppose any antecedent moral principles of any particular morality; so if universalizability is put forward as a necessary condition of normative discourse, it must be so interpreted that no moral principle, even one requiring impartiality, can be deduced from it. It is not at all clear to me just how Taylor has justified connecting a purely formal consideration, universalizability, with a moral principle, i.e., the principle of impartiality. Is the principle of mutual acknowledgement a moral or a formal criterion of relevant differences? Is it morally neutral or does it enjoin a particular line of conduct? Is Taylor saying that his appeal to universalizability will do the job (while Hare's appeal fails), because he appeals to universalizability in the relevant sense? That is, that his appeal is not merely a formal one, but depends on such concepts as equality, fairness, or impartiality? In this sense does universalizability become a moral requirement?

What work does the word 'relevant' do here? If one points to some real or fancied difference which he *claims* is morally relevant, how can we show that it is not a relevant difference? Taylor is not clear as to whether *relevant difference* is to be made on moral or logical grounds. If he appeals to the latter, he cannot exclude any sort of privilege—as he consistently admits. But if he appeals to the former, he is engaging in moral discourse and not offering us a formal analysis of universalizability and justice. If Taylor is offering a formal analysis of the connection between universalizability and justice, i.e., one which presupposes no antecedent moral principles, then he can distinguish between moral and nonmoral considerations. But he cannot distinguish, on the basis of the analysis alone, between moral and immoral considerations. How could he, if he presupposes no antecedent moral principles?

I agree that the issue concerning what are moral and what are logical considerations is a tenuous one, indeed. Few writers on the subject appear to avoid oscillating between logical analysis and moral recommendation. There are those who hold that the principle of universalizability is a moral one and those who hold that it is purely formal. Much disagreement and confusion exists regarding what is intelligible and what is morally permissible. Taylor himself seems to conflate the logical thesis with a moral thesis. The varieties of universalizability, so clearly mapped-out by D. H. Monro in his *Empiricism and Ethics*, are all consequences of the consistency—requirement. The principle of impartiality, which, in Taylor's view seems to become confused with universalizability, is itself a moral principle and accordingly, not morally neutral.

As Monro and others have shown, the difference between moral and nonmoral considerations can't be a moral difference, because moral differences are all to be found within the moral domain. And if they are correct, then we cannot consistently stigmatize as immoral, at the level of moral discourse, what has been defined out of the moral category at the level of meta-ethics. This is not to deny those who are fond of the 'moral point of view' argument. For if a man refuses to acknowledge any moral considerations at all and yet understands moral considerations, his behavior, which is out of the moral category altogether may still be correctly said to be immoral. Of course, any man who simply disregards or flaunts all moral considerations whatsoever, and yet understands moral considerations, is indeed, immoral. But I cannot call him immoral if I do not appeal to any moral principles at all, i.e., if I claim that my analysis does not presuppose any moral principles. Given the latter, I am not prepared to make any moral judgments, but simply to establish the scope of moral and nonmoral considerations.

Is universalizability a necessary condition of a principle being a moral principle? Does this imply, or is it meant to imply, that nonmoral principles are not universalizable? Or is the expression 'universalizable principle' a pleonasm? I want to maintain, along with Monro, that universalizability is a necessary feature of reason or principles as such, whether moral or nonmoral. The distinction that the principle of universalizability points to, is not primarily a distinction between the moral and the nonmoral, but rather between the deliberate and arbitrary (or whimsical and random). To make the principle of universalizability applicable to moral considerations, it is necessary to appeal to moral reasons or moral differences. Here we must abandon the "neutrality thesis," map out moral distinctions, and make moral decisions.

KELSEN'S DOCTRINE OF THE UNITY OF LAW

H. L. A. Hart

Introduction

In this lecture I propose to examine one of the most striking doctrines expounded by Kelsen in his *General Theory of Law and State* and his more recent *Pure Theory of Law*.[1] Its central positive contention is that all valid laws necessarily form a single system [2] and its central negative contention is that valid laws cannot conflict.[3] This is the strongest form of Kelsen's Doctrine of the Unity of Law; but arguments are also to be found in Kelsen's books which support a weaker form of this doctrine, namely, that though it is not necessarily true that all valid laws form a single system and cannot conflict, it just is the case that they do form a single system and do not conflict. For Kelsen, this doctrine of the unity of law yields certain conclusions concerning the possible or actual relationships between international law and all systems of municipal law.[4] On the strong version of his theory international law and systems of municipal law necessarily form one single system,[5] and there can be no conflicts between the laws of international law and municipal law.[6] On the weaker version it just is the case that all these laws form a single system and there are in fact no conflicts between them.[7] Kelsen develops similar, though not identical, views concerning the relationships between law and morals. He does not however contend that valid legal and moral norms either necessarily or in fact form a single system. Instead he argues that from one point of view there are only legal norms and from another point of view there are only moral norms; that these two points of view are exclusive of each other; and they are exhaustive, so there is no third point of view from which there are both valid legal and valid moral norms.[8]

I believe, and shall attempt to show, that Kelsen's doctrine of the unity of all valid laws and his conclusions concerning the possible and

171

actual relationships between international law and municipal laws, are mistaken. But I think for a number of different reasons that much is to be learned from examining his doctrine. The effort of criticism of these difficult doctrines is, I think, rewarding because it brings to light at least two things. First, it shows that there is a good deal of unfinished business for analytical jurisprudence still to tackle, and this unfinished business includes a still much needed clarification of the meaning of the common assertion that laws belong to or constitute a *system* of laws, and an account of the criteria for determining the system to which given laws belong, and of what individuates one system from another. Secondly, the examination of certain features of Kelsen's doctrine takes us to the frontiers at least of the logic of norms and their inter-relationships, and perhaps points beyond the frontiers to the need for something more comprehensive than the present familiar forms of deontic logic.

I shall discuss the main issues which I have mentioned in the following order. In Section I, I shall consider Kelsen's theory of the unity of international law and municipal law, dealing first with the weaker version and then with the stronger version. In Section II, I shall consider the 'no conflict' theory of International Law and Municipal Law, dealing first with the stronger version (pp. 702–72) and then with the weaker version. In Section III, I shall attempt to draw some morals from these criticisms of Kelsen's theories that may help in the construction of a more satisfactory analysis of the notion of a legal system and of the nature of the criteria determining its membership and of the principles of individuation of legal systems.

I shall not, in this paper, discuss Kelsen's doctrine concerning the possibility of simultaneously valid legal and moral norms, and of their conflict. I omit this topic not only because I have discussed some aspects of it elsewhere,[9] but also because, though Kelsen repeats this doctrine in his latest book, he neither repeats his previous arguments for it nor adduces new ones.

I

The Unity of International Law and Municipal Law

(A) *Monistic and Pluralistic Theory*

Kelsen calls his own theory that international law and municipal law form one system a 'monistic' theory and contrasts it with the traditional view that they are independent systems and terms this view a 'pluralistic' theory.[10] It is however a complication of Kelsen's doctrine that there are two possible forms of monistic theory:[11] 'two different ways of comprehending all legal phenomena as parts of a single system'.[12] For according to Kelsen it is possible to structure or arrange the components of the single system which comprehends both international law and all systems of municipal law in either of two ways. One of these ways ('primacy of international law') treats international law (or, more accurately, the basic norm of international law) as the foundation of a single unified system and all the rest, including all systems of municipal law, as subordinate parts of the system ultimately deriving their validity from this foundation. The other way ('primacy of municipal law') treats one (any one) system of municipal law (or, more accurately, its basic norm) as the foundation of a single unified system, and all the rest, including international law and all other systems of municipal law, as subordinate parts of the single system deriving their validity from its foundation. The choice between these two alternative points of view (primacy of international law or primacy of municipal law) is, according to Kelsen, a matter of political ideology, not law, and is guided by ethical and political considerations.[13] However, the contents of both international law and municipal law are totally unaffected by this choice: the legal rights and obligations of states and individuals remain the same whichever of the two alternative systems is adopted.[14] I shall not in this paper question this complication of Kelsen's theory (though in fact I think it eminently questionable), for it is in fact not relevant to the main monistic doctrine of the necessary unity of all law, and Kelsen's arguments for the monistic theory of the relations of international law and municipal law are unaffected by his view that there is a choice between according primacy to international law or to a system of municipal law.

Kelsen claims that an analysis of the actual systems of international law and municipal law shows that they form a single system. But this claim rests on a special interpretation of the legal phenomena which seems to me, for the reasons I give below, profoundly mistaken. But before I examine this interpretation it may be helpful to characterize in general terms, with the aid of a simple example, the kind of error which in my view infects Kelsen's interpretation. The example is the following. Suppose the question arose whether I, Hart, wrote this paper in obedience to someone's order that I should write it. Let us assume that evidence is forthcoming that just before I sat down to write this paper the Vice-Chancellor of Oxford University despatched to me a document purporting to order me to write a paper on Kelsen's Doctrine of the Unity of Law. It is plain that whether or not I wrote this paper in obedience to that order could not be settled by comparing the contents of the order ('Hart: write a paper on Kelsen's Doctrine of the Unity of Law') with a true description of my later conduct ('Hart wrote a paper on Kelsen's Doctrine of the Unity of Law'). This comparison would indeed show correspondence between the content of the order and the description of my conduct, in that the action-description contained in the order is applicable to my subsequent conduct. But though in order to establish that I did write this paper in obedience to this order it would be *necessary* to show this correspondence between the content of the order and the description of my conduct, plainly this would not be *sufficient*. It would also be necessary to establish certain facts that have to do not with the content of the order, but with the circumstances surrounding the issue and reception of the order, involving consideration of such questions as the following. Did Hart receive the Vice-Chancellor's missive? Did he recognize it as an order? Did he write the paper in order to comply with this order? Did anyone else give such an order? If so, whose order did Hart intend to obey? A "pure theory" of imperatives that ignored such facts and circumstances surrounding the issue and reception of orders, and restricted itself to the characterization of the relationships between the contents of orders and the description of actions, would necessarily be incompetent to settle the question whether any person had obeyed a particular order. However, since the correspondence relationship between content and action-description is a necessary condition of obedience, the theory would be competent to identify cases where orders had not been obeyed; though it is important to remember that 'not obeyed' is not the same as 'disobeyed.'

I will try to show that in somewhat the same way, though not precisely the same way, the pure theory of law suffers from the defects of my imaginary pure theory of imperatives, for it concentrates too exclusively on the contents of laws and pays too little attention to circumstances that concern the making or origin of laws (rather than what laws say) and whether they are recognized as authoritative and by whom. When we have laws that explicitly or implicitly refer to other laws, or their existence or validity, we cannot determine from these relationships alone whether they belong to the same or different systems. This depends on facts concerning the making and recognition of laws. The pure theory of law is too pure to attend to such facts; and, as I shall attempt to show, that by treating what are at best necessary conditions as if they were sufficient conditions of laws belonging to the same system, the pure theory reaches false conclusions as to the unity of international or municipal law. With this general characterization of the type of error which I think is inherent in the content-obsessed pure theory of law, let me turn to the examination of Kelsen's interpretation of the legal phenomena.

(B) The Completion Relationship between Laws

Kelsen attacks with some force a crude and misleading dichotomy between international law and municipal law. International law, it is sometimes said, imposes obligations and confers rights on states, whereas municipal law imposes obligations and confers rights on individuals. This distinction is often used to support the pluralistic theory. It is said that international law and municipal law are independent legal systems because they regulate different subject matters: international law regulates the behavior of states and municipal law regulates the behavior of individuals. Kelsen criticizes this argument for pluralism in two ways.[15] He shows that there are rules of international law, no doubt exceptional, that apply directly to individuals in the same way as the rules of municipal law. Examples of these are the laws against piracy, and the rules of international law making punishable acts of illegitimate warfare, i.e., hostile acts on the part of individuals not belonging to the armed forces of the country. But quite apart from these exceptional cases, Kelsen maintains that if we understand the logical structure of such expressions as 'the state' as a technique or method of referring indirectly to individuals identified by certain legal rules and lay aside the misconception of a state as an entity over and above the individuals that compose it, it is apparent that laws which purport to apply directly to states in fact apply to individuals, though the manner of their application is indirect. Hence the description of the rules of international law as 'applying to states' should not be construed as contrasting with 'applying to individuals': it is to be contrasted with applying *directly* to individuals, i.e., without the aid of, or supplementation by, other rules identifying the individuals to whom the first rules are applicable.[16] The rules of international law, according to Kelsen, when they purport to apply to states are "incomplete": they specify themselves only *what* is to be done or not to be done, but they leave or, as Kelsen says, 'delegate' the identification of the individuals who are or are not to do these things to the rules of municipal law,[17] and the latter rules, identifying the individuals, 'complete' the rules of international law.

Kelsen illustrates this completion of international law by the rules of municipal law by the following simple example.

There is a time-honoured rule of common international law to the effect that war must not be begun without previous, formal declaration of war. The third Hague Convention of 1907 codified this rule in the stipulation (art. 1) that hostilities "must not commence without a previous and unequivocal warning, which shall take the form either of a declaration of war giving reasons, or of an ultimatum with a conditional declaration of war." This norm states only that a declaration of war has to be delivered, not by whom,—that is to say, by which individual as organ of the State—it has to be done. Most constitutions empower the head of the state to declare war. The constitution of the United States (art. 1 s.8) says that "the Congress shall have the power to declare war." By thus determining the personal element, the American constitution completes the norm of international law just mentioned. The characteristic of international law that it "obligates States only" consists merely in the fact that its norms generally determine only the material element, leaving the determination of the personal element to national law.[18]

Let us call the relationship between a set of rules one of which leaves to the other or others the identification of the individuals to whom the first applies, the 'completion relationship', and let us call the set of rules so related 'a completing set'. Kelsen's insistence that many rules of international law and municipal law are related by the completion relationship is in many ways illuminating, and I shall not quarrel with his use of this idea in attacking the crude and confused theory that international law and municipal law are independent or different systems because international law applies to states and municipal law to individuals. It is however very important to appreciate that the fact that the completion relationship holds between certain rules is not itself sufficient to show that the rules between which it holds belong to one and the same system: for unless it can be independently shown that the very idea of the existence of different systems of law rules is illusory, and that there is only *one* system of rules, it seems quite clear that the completion relationship may hold either between the rules of the same system or between rules of different systems. It is necessary to stress this fact because it may be obscured by Kelsen's frequent (and, again, often illuminating) insistence on the similarity between the relationships holding on the one hand between the rules of international law and municipal law, and the other hand between a statute of municipal law and the bye-laws or regulations of a corporation.[19] This similarity, obscured by the personifying or reifying terminology of 'state' and 'corporation,' resides in the following facts. When a rule of international law purports to impose some duty directly on a state it is in fact indirectly imposing those duties on the individuals identified by the state's municipal system, and those individuals' actions and obligations are imputed to the state. Similarly, when a statute of a municipal legal system imposes some duty on a corporation it indirectly imposes that duty on the individuals (officers or members of the corporation) identified by the internal bye-laws or regulations of the corporation. Both cases thus exemplify the completion relationship.

The relation between the total legal order constituting the state, the so-called law of the state or national legal order, and the juristic person of a corporation is the relation between two legal orders, a total and a partial legal order, between the law of the state and the by-laws of the corporation. To be more specific it is a case of delegation.[20]

In considering this interesting parallel between the relationships of municipal statutes to corporation bye-laws on the one hand and international law to municipal law on the other, it is important not to lose sight of the fact that when a rule of municipal law e.g., an English statute, imposes obligations on a corporation incorporated under English law, the regulations or bye-laws of the corporation which identify the individuals who, as officers or members of the corporation are to execute this duty, derive their validity from other English statutes determining the manner in which corporation regulations may be made and limiting their content. As Kelsen says, the bye-laws constituting the corporation are created by a legal transaction determined by the national legal order. Hence, the statute imposing the obligation on the corporation, and the earlier statutes under which the company regulations were made belong to the same legal system quite independently of the completion relationship holding between the statute imposing the obligation on the corporation and its regulations. These statutes and bye-laws all belong to the same system because they satisfy the criteria recognized by English courts as identifying the laws which they are to enforce. Of course, an English statute might impose obligations on a foreign corporation e.g., a Swedish corporation. Here too, the completion relationship would hold between the English statute and the regulations of the Swedish corporation, for the latter would identify those individuals who as officers or members of the corporation were bound to execute the duty. But the regulations of the Swedish corporation which would thus complete the English statute derive their validity from a statute of the Swedish legislature determining the manner in which Swedish corporation regulations are to be made. This Swedish statute exists as part not of English law but of Swedish law, and so existed before the enactment of the English statute imposing obligations on the Swedish corporation, whereas in the case where the English statute imposes obligations on the English corporation the regulations of the corporation existed as part of English law.

It is perhaps worth observing that completion relationships between laws of the same or different systems are not confined to cases where we speak of abstract juristic entities such as state or corporation. Thus an English statute might confer certain rights, e.g., the right to vote, on individuals whom it might define only as persons liable to pay certain rates and taxes under some other English statute, or it might exempt from taxation certain foreigners if they are liable under the law of their own country to certain similar taxes. In the first case the completion relationship would hold between laws of the same system; in the second case it holds between laws of a different system.

(C) The Relationship of Validating Purport

In spite of some ambiguity of language,[21] Kelsen does not, I think, conceive of the completion relationship between laws as in itself sufficient to show that they belong to the same system for he writes: 'Since the international legal order not only requires the national legal orders as a necessary complementation, but also determines their spheres of validity in all respects, international and national law form one inseparable whole.' [22] The words which I have quoted introduce Kelsen's central argument for the monistic theory and, as I believe, his central mistake. The argument, reduced to its essentials, is this. International law contains among its rules one that Kelsen terms the 'principle of effectiveness' which 'determines' or 'is the reason for' the validity of the national legal order and their territorial and temporal sphere of validity. The contents of this principle of effectiveness are spelt out by Kelsen in his latest formulation of it, as follows:

A norm of general international law authorises an individual or a group of individuals on the basis of an effective constitution, to create and apply as a legitimate government a normative coercive order. That norm thus legitimises this coercive order for the territory of its actual effectiveness as a valid legal order and the community constituted by this coercive order as a "state" in the sense of international law.[23]

Because the principle of effectiveness thus legitimizes or validates the separate coercive orders effective in different territories, international law, to which the principle of effectiveness belongs, forms a single system together with the various systems of municipal law, which it legitimizes or validates. It forms with them, Kelsen says, 'one inseparable whole.' [24] In considering this argument it is important to understand precisely what in Kelsen's view is the relationship between the principle of effectiveness and the various municipal legal systems which it is said to legitimate, or the validity of which it is said to determine. The principle of effectiveness says that other rules of a certain description (i.e., roughly, coercive rules effective in certain territories) are valid; and it is a fact that there are certain rules (the actual systems of municipal law) that satisfy this description. Let us call this relationship the relationship of validating purport. I shall argue that what was said above about the completion relationship applies also to the relationship of validating purport: it is not sufficient in order to establish that two rules form part of a single system to show that one of them provides that rules of a certain description satisfied by the other are valid. I shall also argue that when such a relationship holds between two rules it is dangerously misleading to express this fact by stating, *without stressing a very important qualification*, that one rule 'determines the validity' of the other or is 'the reason for its validity.'

Kelsen's argument depends on the use he makes of the fact that the relationship of validating purport holds between the principle of effectiveness considered as a rule of international law and the rules of municipal legal systems. The inadequacy of this argument and also the character of the important qualification I have just mentioned can be seen from the following wild hypothetical example. Suppose the British Parliament (or *mutatis mutandis*, Congress) passes an Act (the Soviet Laws Validity Act, 1970) which purports to validate the law of the Soviet Union by providing that the laws currently effective in Soviet territory, including those relating to the competence of legislative and judicial authorities, shall be valid. The enactment of this Act by Parliament or Congress would not be a reason for saying that English (or American) law together with Soviet law formed one legal system, or for using *sans phrase* any of the Kelsenian expressions such as that Soviet law 'derives its validity' from English law or that English law was 'the reason for the validity' of Soviet law. The reason for refusing to assent to these propositions is surely clear and compelling: it is that the courts and other law enforcing agencies in Soviet territory do not, save in certain special circumstances,[25] recognize the operations of the British (or American) legislature as criteria for identifying the laws that they are to enforce, and so they do not recognize the Soviet Laws Validity Act, though a valid English (or American) statute, as in any way determining or otherwise affecting the validity of Soviet law in Soviet territory. It is true indeed that the relationship of validating purport holds between that Act and the laws made by the Soviet legislature, which the Soviet courts do recognize; but the division of laws into distinct legal systems cuts across the relationship of validating purport, for that relationship, like the completion relationship examined above, may hold either between laws of different systems or between laws of the same system.

The important qualification that should be made in drawing any conclusion from the existence of the relationship of validating purport between rules is perhaps obvious. On the passing of the Soviet Laws Validity Act it would be right to say that *for the purposes* of English law, or according to English law, Soviet laws were validated by or derive their validity from an English statute, and the effect of this would be that English courts would apply Soviet law in adjudicating upon any transaction or conduct to which the Soviet authorities would apply Soviet law. The Soviet Laws Validity Act would make Soviet law part of English law for such purposes. But the two pairs of questions

> A 1. Do English law and Soviet law form part of a single system of law?
> A 2. Does Soviet law derive its validity from English law?

and

> B 1. Does English law treat Soviet law as forming part of a single system with itself?
> B 2. Is Soviet law valid according to English law?

are questions of different kinds. The first pair are not questions that concern merely the content of laws and so are to be settled by considering what laws say; whereas the second pair are questions concerning the content of laws and are settled in that way.

There is the same difference in kind between the pairs of questions

> C 1. Do international law and municipal law form a single system?
> C 2. Does municipal law derive its validity from international law?

and

> D 1. Does international law treat (e.g., by its principle of effectiveness) municipal law as forming part of a single system with itself?
> D 2. Is municipal law valid according to the international law (e.g., through its principle of effectiveness)?

The pure theory blurs the distinctions between these very different types of question; it does so because it concentrates too much on what laws of validating purport *say* about other laws, and pays too little attention to matters that do not concern the content of laws but their mode of recognition. The pure theory, therefore, has a juristic Midas touch, which transmutes all questions about laws and their relationship into questions of the content of law or questions concerning what laws say; but the touch is perverse for not all questions are of this kind.

I conclude that the arguments in support of the weaker version of Kelsen's version of the doctrine of the unity of international law and municipal law fail. This is not to say that arguments different from Kelsen's might not succeed in establishing the weaker version of his thesis —at least up to a point. For whether or not international law and the law of a state form one system depends on the manner in which and extent to which a given state recognizes international law. If in cases where international law conflicts with the law of the state the courts of that state treat the state law as invalid or overridden by international law, this would be a good reason for saying that international law and the law of that state form parts of a single system of law—or at any rate it would resemble the reason for saying that the law of a state of the United States and federal law form part of a single system. But Kelsen's arguments fail because the fact that the relationship of validating purport exists between the principle of effectiveness treated as a rule of international law (or any other rules of international law purporting to determine the validity of municipal law), and the rules of municipal law, does not show that the latter derive their validity from the former, and does not show that "pluralists" are wrong in denying that international law and municipal law form a single system.[26]

I now turn to the examination of the stronger form of Kelsen's thesis that international law and municipal law necessarily form one system.

(D) The Necessary Unity of all Valid Law

Very little by way of argument is to be found in support of Kelsen's stronger thesis that all valid law *necessarily* forms a single system with its corollary that international law and municipal law necessarily constitute such a system. Kelsen asserts that this is a 'postulate of legal theory.'[27] 'The unity of national law and international law is an epistemological postulate. A jurist who accepts both sets of valid norms must try to comprehend them as parts of one harmonious system.'[28] This postulate is frequently referred to in the terminology of logical necessity. 'It is logically not possible to assume that simultaneously valid norms belong to different, mutually independent systems.'[29]

For these assertions I have identified only two arguments. Neither need occupy us long. The first argument reduces to the contention that all that is law forms a single system because there is a form of knowledge ('jurisprudence'[30] or 'connaissance juridique'[31]) or a science of law which studies both international law and municipal law as falling under the single description 'valid laws' and thus represents 'its object' as a unity. Kelsen expresses this argument in the following words:

[The] pluralistic construction is untenable if both the norms of international law and those of the national legal orders are to be considered as simultaneously valid legal norms. This view implies already the epistemological postulate: to understand all law in one system . . . as one closed whole. Jurisprudence subsumes the norms regulating the relations between states, called international law, as well as the national legal orders under one and the same category of law. In so doing it tries to present its object as a unity.[32]

Surely we might as well attempt to deduce from the existence of the history of warfare or the science of strategy that all wars are one or all armies are one.

The second argument really shows that Kelsen's argument for the necessary unity of valid law is dependent on his thesis that there can be no conflicts between valid laws for he says:

If there should be two actually different systems of norms, mutually independent in their validity . . . both of which are related to the same object (in having the same sphere of validity), insoluble logical contradiction between them could not be excluded. The norm of one system may prescribe conduct A for a certain person, under a certain condition, at certain time and place. The norm of the other system may prescribe, under the same conditions and for the same person, conduct non-A. This situation is impossible for the cognition of norms.[33]

Of course this does not deal with the possibility that there might be two legal systems simultaneously effective in different territories in which the possibility of conflicts is excluded because the constitution of each system secured that what Kelsen calls 'the sphere of validity' of the laws of each system should be different. The laws of the two systems might, for example, according to their constitutions apply to conduct in different territories. Kelsen asserts [34] that such a limitation would have to be imposed by a single superior law to which both systems with limited scope would be subordinate and with which they would form a single system. But he does not support this assertion with any arguments, and it is difficult to see why it should not just be the case that two communities chose independently to adopt constitutions limiting the scope of the laws in this way. However, the argument from the alleged impossibility of conflict though it does not cover this case, remains Kelsen's only remaining argument for the necessary unity of all valid law.[35] I examine the thesis that conflict between valid laws is impossible in the next section.

II

The 'No Conflicts' Theory [36]

Kelsen claims that in spite of appearances there really are no conflicts between international law and municipal law. He admits that if there were such conflicts the monistic theory that international law and municipal law form one system could not be sustained: indeed he says the absence of conflict is the 'negative criterion' [37] of the unity of international law and municipal law in a single system. If, however, there were such conflicts the result would be, according to Kelsen, not that international law and municipal law would constitute separate systems of valid laws as the conventional "pluralist" holds; instead we would have a choice between treating international law as valid while ignoring any conflicting rules of municipal law, or treating a system of municipal law as valid while ignoring any conflicting rules of international law. This is, according to Kelsen, actually the position with regard to laws and morality: when their norms conflict we have a choice between treating the legal rules as valid, ignoring conflicting moral norms, or treating moral norms as valid, ignoring any conflicting laws.[38]

Before we can evaluate these somewhat surprising doctrines it is plainly necessary to canvass some preliminary questions. What is it for laws or systems of laws to conflict? How is a conflict between laws related to logical inconsistency or contradiction? Unfortunately, Kelsen's own analysis in his books of the notion of conflicts between laws and norms consists only of a few scattered observations, though what he has to say touches upon some important and indeed controversial logical issues. This is not the place for full investigation of these issues, but in my statement and criticism of Kelsen's doctrines I will use, as undogmatically as I can, some relatively simple distinctions which have been drawn by writers on deontic logic and the logic of imperatives, who have concerned themselves with similar questions about conflicts.

(A) Conflict as the Logical Impossibility of Joint Conformity

Many writers favor the idea (which seems intuitively acceptable) that conflict between two rules requiring or prohibiting actions is to be understood in terms of the logical possibility of joint obedience to them. Two such rules conflict if and only if obedience to them both ('joint obedience') is logically impossible. The crudest [39] case of such a conflict are rules which respectively require and forbid the same action on the part of the same person at the same time or times. The logical impossibility of joint obedience may be exhibited in the following way.[40] For any rule requiring or prohibiting action, we can form a statement (an 'obedience statement') asserting that the action that is required by the rule is done, or the action prohibited by the rule is not done. Two such rules conflict if their respective obedience statements are logically inconsistent and so cannot both be true. Thus (to take one of Kelsen's examples) suppose one rule requires certain persons to kill certain other human beings, and another rule prohibits the

same persons from killing the same other human beings, the obedience statements corresponding to those rules would be of the general
form, 'killing is done,' and 'killing is not done.' Of course, before we can
determine whether two statements of this general form are logically inconsistent or not, they would have to be filled out with specifications of
the agents and victims and times to which the rules, explicitly or implicitly, related. If the same agents are required by one rule to do, and by
another rule to abstain from, the same action at the same times this will
be reflected in the corresponding obedience statements which would be
logically inconsistent. Joint obedience to the rules would be logically impossible.

It is to be observed that this definition of conflict between rules
leaves entirely open the question whether or not it is logically possible
for two conflicting rules to coexist as valid rules either of the same or
different systems. To most people it would certainly seem possible for a
law of one legal system made by one set of legislators to conflict with
the law of another legal system made by another set of legislators; and it
would perhaps seem equally obvious that one such law could conflict
with some moral rule or principle. Joint obedience to these rules would
be logically impossible, but their coexistence as valid rules would be logically possible. Further, though it would certainly be deplorable on every
practical score if laws of a single legal system conflicted and the system
provided no way of resolving such conflicts, it is still far from obvious
that even this is a logical impossibility. So far as the nature and logical
possibilities of conflict are concerned, there seems little difference between rules requiring and prohibiting action and simple second person
orders and commands addressed by one person to another. Two such orders ('kill' and 'do not kill') conflict if joint obedience to them is logically impossible and this can be shown in the form of logically inconsistent obedience statements. But it is certainly logically possible for
conflicting orders to be given by different persons to the same person,
and though we might think a person who gave inconsistent orders at
short intervals to the same person, mad or split-minded or lacking a co-
herent will and perhaps in need of clinical attention, such situations do
not seem logically impossible. In the end no doubt, if he insisted on
producing streams of inconsistent orders and these could not be explained, e.g., by lapse of memory, we should conclude that he did not
understand what he was saying, and might well refuse to classify what
he said as constituting orders at all.

In one important respect, however, which is relevant to Kelsen's
theory, conflict between laws and other rules is more complicated than
conflict between such simple orders. Laws and rules, as Kelsen

acknowledges [41] instead of requiring or forbidding action may either expressly permit action, or by not forbidding them, tacitly permit them; and it is clear that there may be conflicts between laws that forbid and laws or legal systems that expressly or tacitly permit. To meet such cases, we should have to use not only the notion of obedience, which is appropriate to rules requiring or forbidding action, but the notion of acting on or availing oneself of a permission. We might adopt the generic term 'conformity' to comprehend both obedience to rules that require or prohibit and acting on or availing oneself of permission, and we could adopt the expression 'conformity statements' to cover both kinds of corresponding statement. In fact, the conformity statement showing that a permissive rule (e.g., permitting though not requiring killing) had been acted on will be of the same form as the obedience statement for a rule requiring the same action (killing is done.) So if one rule prohibits and another rule permits the same action by the same person at the same time, joint conformity will be logically impossible and the two rules will conflict.[42]

(B) Conflict and Logical Inconsistency

Kelsen would I think accept such a definition of conflict between rules in terms of the logical impossibility of joint conformity. Certainly his few examples of conflicting rules and of what he sometimes terms 'opposite' or 'incompatible' behavior are consistent with this, and he makes at least one passing though informal reference to what is in substance the joint conformity test of conflict.[43] But Kelsen's account of the connection between conflict between norms and logical inconsistencies is different and more controversial. For his doctrine as expounded in his books is that the statement that two valid norms conflict is or entails a contradiction: for Kelsen it is a logical impossibility that there should coexist valid but conflicting norms either of the same or different systems. And it is not merely the case for him that joint conformity to them is logically impossible.[44]

Kelsen's arguments for these conclusions depend on the use which he makes of a distinction (itself important and illuminating) between laws made or applied by legal authorities, e.g., statutes of a legislature, which cannot be either true or false, and a class of statements describing the content of laws, which Kelsen called 'legal rules in a descriptive sense' and which can be either true or false. These rules in a descriptive sense are of the following general form: 'According to a certain positive legal order a certain consequence ought to take place' or 'according to a certain legal norm something ought to be done or ought not to be done.' In such statements 'ought' according to Kelsen is used in a descriptive sense, and I shall refer to such statements as 'descriptive-ought statements.' [45]

A simple illustration of this doctrine is as follows. If there exists a legal order, e.g., the English legal system, and among its duly enacted laws there is a statute requiring under certain penalties men on attaining the age of 21 to report for military service, these facts constitute part of the truth grounds for the descriptive-ought statement 'according to English law the following persons . . . ought to report for military service . . .' If there is such a law the descriptive-ought statement is true; if there is not, it is false. Three things however should be borne in mind when considering Kelsen's descriptive-ought statements.

1. 'Ought' is used by Kelsen in a special, wide sense, so that 'ought' statements include not only descriptions of laws that forbid or require action but also those that describe laws or legal systems which expressly or tacitly permit actions. 'Ought' in Kelsen's usage is a kind of deontic variable ranging over what he terms prescriptions (or commands), permissions, and authorizations.[46]

2. Descriptive-ought statements are not confined to the law. Similar statements, similarly capable of truth or falsity may be made concerning non-legal, e.g., moral norms;

L'ethique décrit les normes d'une morale determinée, elle nous enseigne comment nous devons nous conduire selon cette morale, mais, en tant que science, elle ne nous préscrit pas de nous conduire de telle ou telle façon. Le moraliste n'est pas l'autorité morale qui pose les normes qu'il décrit en propositions normatives.[47]

3. The words which appear at the beginning of the formulation of descriptive-ought statements in the above quotations ('according to a certain positive legal order') and the words 'selon cette morale [déterminée,]' are important for the following reasons. Kelsen has been sometimes accused of holding a metaphysical belief that there is a realm of 'ought' (including the 'ought' of legal rules) which is not man-made, but awaits man's cognition or discovery, and of believing that it is this realm of ought, over and above the world of facts, that true descriptive-ought statements describe. As against such critics, Kelsen insists that for him all norms are made and not merely discovered by human beings and although, given the existence of positive legal orders or systems, true descriptive statements can be made about their content in the form of ought statements, the truth of such statements is not "absolute" but relative [48] to the particular legal system or order concerned. Indeed it could be argued in support of Kelsen that so long as we bear in mind this essential relativity to a given system his account of descriptive-ought statements clarifies a certain kind of discourse frequent among lawyers.

Lawyers often ask such questions as 'What is the legal position with regard to military service?' and tender in answer to such questions, such statements as 'Men on attaining the age of 21 must report for military service' and regard the answers as true or false. There is frequent occasion for lawyers to describe what they might call 'legal position' in relation to some subject without referring to the particular enactments or regulations or other sources of the relevant law, though of course it would be always understood that the 'legal position' thus described is that arising under the laws of a particular system, and a more accurate formulation would make this explicit by including such words as 'according to English law . . .'

The immediate relevance of Kelsen's descriptive-ought statements to the question of conflicts between laws can be seen from the following quotations:

Since legal norms, being prescriptions (that is commands, permissions, authorisations), can neither be true nor false the question arises: How can logical principles especially the Principle of the Exclusion of Contradiction and the rules of inference be applied to the relation between legal norms if, according to traditional views, these principles are applicable only to assertions that can be true or false? The answer is: Logical principles are applicable indirectly to legal norms to the extent that they are applicable to rules of law which describe the legal norms and which can be true or false. Two legal norms are contradictory and can therefore not both be valid at the same time if the two rules of law that describe them are contradictory: . . .[49]

Kelsen explains several times that descriptive-ought statements describing two legal rules requiring what he terms 'opposite' behavior would be of the form 'A ought to be' and 'A ought not to be' and statements of this form referring to actions to be done by the same agents at the same time are said by Kelsen to 'contradict each other,'[50] and their joint assertion is said to be meaningless: 'to say that A ought to be and at the same time ought not to be is just as meaningless as to say that A is and at the same time that it is not.'[51] Accordingly, it is a logical impossibility for two such rules to be valid: only one of them can be regarded as valid. Kelsen thus speaks throughout his books as if conflicts between laws were a form of logical inconsistency, so that it is logically impossible that conflicting rules should coexist and not merely that joint conformity with them is logically impossible.

Kelsen's arguments raise a host of difficulties;[52] fortunately not all of them need detailed consideration here. We may waive for the moment (while noting for later use) the objections that if 'A ought to be' and 'A ought not to be' are logically inconsistent they are not, as Kelsen says, contradictory but contraries. The contradictory of 'A ought not to be done' is 'it is not the case that A ought not to be done,' and two ought-statements of this form would describe not two rules that required and prohibited the same action, but two rules, one of which prohibited and the other which permitted the same action. But apart from this, it is not a self-evident truth of logic that 'A ought to be done' and 'A ought not to be done,' even if they describe rules of the *same* system, are logically inconsistent at all. Certainly some argument is required to show that they are. No doubt, if we assume certain premises (viz. 1. 'ought' implies can, and 2. 'A ought to be done and A ought not to be done' entails 'A ought both to be done and not to be done') it would then follow that 'A ought to be done' and 'A ought not to be done' cannot logically both be true. [53] It is also of course possible to define 'ought' in such a way that 'A ought to be done' entails 'it is not the case that A ought not to be done'; but it is worth noting that logicians of repute in constructing systems of deontic logic have allowed for the possibility of conflicting obligations ('one ought to do A' and 'one ought not to do A'). There seems no formal inconsistency in such a notion, and a logical calculus which is out to catch the logical properties of actual human codes of behavior should not rule out such possibilities of conflict in advance by taking it as an axiom that 'one ought to do A' entails that it is not the case that one ought not to do. A.[54]

It is not necessary, however, in order to assess Kelsen's thesis that international law and municipal law cannot conflict, to press the point that conflict even between laws of the same system is not a logical impossibility. For Kelsen's arguments that there can be no such conflicts between international law and municipal law are intended by him to be independent of the thesis that they form one system.[55] Kelsen's arguments for the impossibility of conflicts turn entirely on his view of the logical relations between the descriptive-ought statements describing conflicting laws, and his arguments seem to be vitiated by a simple error. He disregards the important fact that, as he had previously himself observed descriptive-ought statements when true are true only relatively to the systems that they describe, and, accurately formulated, should be pre-fixed with such words as 'according to English law.' [56] Hence if we were to concede for the sake of argument that 'A ought to be' and 'A ought not to be' are, as Kelsen claims, logically inconsistent, or that laws of the same system could not conflict, it would not follow, nor is it the case, that descriptive-ought statements of the form 'according to international law A ought to be' and 'according to English law A ought not to be' are logically inconsistent. Indeed there seems no reason at all, once the relativity of descriptive-ought statements is borne in mind, for thinking that two statements of this form cannot both be true. Since Kelsen therefore has given no satisfactory reason for saying that international law and municipal law form one system, there seems nothing to support the thesis that their rules cannot conflict.

(C) The Weaker Version of the 'No Conflict' Theory

With these rather top-heavy but necessary preliminaries we may turn to the evaluation of Kelsen's claim that there are in fact no conflicts between valid rules of international law and municipal law. Kelsen's proof that there are no conflicts between international law and municipal law takes the following form.[57] According to a conventional 'pluralist' theory, a conflict between international law and municipal law arises if a state enacts a statute which is incompatible with a provision of a treaty to which it is a party, and which is valid according to international law. He cites as an example the case of a treaty between two states, which I shall call A and B. The treaty provides that the members of a minority group in the population of a State B should have the same political right as the majority. If in State B a law is enacted depriving the minority of all political rights notwithstanding the treaty, conventional pluralist theory would claim that here the statute, valid according to the law of State B, and the treaty, valid according to international law, conflicted: it would be impossible to comply both with the treaty and with the statute, for this would be both to allow and not to allow the minority to exercise certain rights.

Kelsen argues that to regard such cases in this way is to misinterpret the rules of international law according to which such treaties are binding on states. Such rules make the enactment by a state of statutes, which are incompatible with the terms of a valid treaty to which it is a party, an offence or delict under international law, exposing the state to the sanctions of international law. But though the *enactment* of such a statute is forbidden by international law, once enacted it is nonetheless valid even according to international law (though illegally enacted), and does not conflict with the rules of international law relating to treaties; for their true force is exhausted in making the enactment by the state of such a statute illegal,[58] i.e., a delict or offence against international law. In other words, the rule of international law does not seek to determine directly the content of state statutes, but only the legality or illegality of their enactment. There is therefore no conflict between the rule of international law, so interpreted, and the statute, though the latter's enactment violates the rule. Kelsen cites, as a parallel, one interpretation of constitutional provisions protecting fundamental rights in those systems of municipal law which contain no provision for judicial review or for the nullification of statutes which are unconstitutional because they violate the fundamental rights which the constitution purports to protect. Instead of judicial review the constitution, in such cases, is interpreted as making officials or legislators liable to punishment for their part in the enactment of such unconstitutional statutes. In such cases the constitution does not directly determine the content of statutes, but only the legality of their enactment; and there is no conflict between the constitution so interpreted and the statute which remains valid though its enactment constitutes a punishable offence under the constitution.

This argument is ingenious, but even if we concede the suggested interpretation of the rules of international law relating to treaties it does not, in fact, banish conflict between international and municipal law; it merely locates such conflict at a different point and shows it to be a conflict not between rules requiring and prohibiting the same action (the treaty and the statute) but between rules prohibiting and *permitting* the same action, i.e., the enactment of the statute. It is a conflict of this latter form that arises when a state enacts a statute in violation of its treaty obligations, if its enactment is an offence according to international law, but is not so according to municipal law. There are certainly many systems of municipal law, among them the English, according to which it is not an offence to enact or procure the enactment of any statute and so this is permitted. It is logically impossible to conform (in the wider sense of this expression noted above) both to the permissive rule of municipal law permitting the enactment of any statute and the rule of international law relating to treaties which (if we accept Kelsen's interpretation of them) prohibits such an enactment and makes it an offence or delict. This being the case, even if we accept Kelsen's interpretation of the rules of international law, this does not establish that they do not conflict with municipal law.[59]

III

Membership of a Legal System

In this concluding section I shall try to distill from the above criticisms of Kelsen some more constructive points that may help our understanding of the concept of a legal system and of the criteria of the membership of different laws in a single system. I certainly am not able to advance a comprehensive analysis of these difficult notions. Such an analysis is, as I have said, part of the still unfinished business of analytical jurisprudence and I am not yet competent to finish it. Yet the general form or direction of such an analysis may perhaps be at least glimpsed from what follows.

(A) Recognition and Validating Purport

Let us reconsider that relationship between laws, which I called the relationship of validating purport, and recall the Soviet Laws Validity Act, which I dreamed up in order to exhibit the absurdity of the view, which Kelsen seems to share, that this relationship is sufficient to make the laws between which it holds members of the same legal system. I argued that this view is absurd because the Soviet Laws Validity Act, though it purports to validate the law-making operations of Soviet legislators, would not be recognized by the Soviet law-identifying and law-enforcing agencies as having any bearing on the validity of Soviet Law. Without such recognition, we can only say the Soviet Laws Validity Act purports to validate the laws of the U.S.S.R., or that according to English law, or for the purposes of English law, Soviet law is a subordinate part of the English legal system; we cannot, unless there is such recognition, say that the validity of the laws of the U.S.S.R. is derived from the Soviet Laws Validity Act, or that the law of the U.S.S.R. and the U.K. form parts of a single system. Perhaps some qualification is needed of this last point. No doubt we could collect together all laws between which the relationship of validating purport holds, irrespective of the legal system from which they come, and call the group of laws so collected "a single legal system." This would be to introduce a new meaning for the expression "legal system"; for a group of laws linked together solely by the relationship of validating purport would not correspond to the concept of a legal system that lawyers and political theorists or any serious thinkers about law and politics actually use. The new definition would have very little utility and would be retrograde if it displaced the existing sense of a legal system, and so barred us from saying that the laws of the U.K. and the U.S.S.R. belong to different systems, notwithstanding the existence of the Soviet Laws Validity Act. "Systems" of laws constructed solely out of the relationship of validating purport would ignore the dividing line introduced by the idea that recognition by the law-identifying and law-enforcing agencies effective in a given territory is of crucial importance, in determining the system to which laws belong. It is surely obvious that these dividing lines could not be ignored by any fruitful legal or political theory. To deny their importance would be tantamount to denying the importance to lawyers and political theorists of the division between nation states.

(B) The Individuation of Laws

When we turn our attention away from the relationship of validating purport to consider how the idea of recognition by courts or other identifying agencies effective in different territories is used to distinguish between legal systems, and as a criterion of membership of laws in a single system, some important points thrust themselves upon us. For example, an important contrast now emerges between two different ways of individuating or distinguishing between different laws. On the one hand, we may individuate or distinguish a law simply by referring to its content (e.g., as "the law making the possession of LSD a criminal offence"). However, since the idea of two different laws with the same content is perfectly intelligible we may, and sometimes actually need to, individuate or distinguish laws not only by their content (i.e., by what the laws say or provide) but also by reference to their authors, mode of enactment, and date (e.g., as 'the law making possession of LSD a criminal offence enacted by the British Parliament on 30 December 1967').

The relevance of this to our present problem is as follows. The relationship of validating purport is a relationship between the content of those laws that purport to validate other laws or lawmaking operations and those other laws or operations. The most important examples of this relationship are laws that confer powers to legislate upon persons or bodies of persons. The simplest example of such power-conferring laws is a law conferring power upon an individual X (a monarch or a minister) to make laws or regulations. The law conferring such power in effect says 'the laws X enacts are to be obeyed.' In Kelsen's terminology, such a law conferring legislative power 'authorizes' X to create new laws, and X's enactment is 'a law creating act or event,' while the laws created by X are said to "derive their validity" from the law conferring the legislative power which is "the reason for their validity." Clearly in such cases if a law conferring legislative power is to be a reason for the validity of other laws it is necessary that the description of those other laws (in this case 'enacted by X') should correspond to the description used in the law conferring the legislative power (e.g., "laws enacted by X are to be obeyed"). In order that the relationship of validating purport should hold between the law conferring the power and the enacted laws, this correspondence is not merely necessary but is sufficient. But, as I have argued above, though this is necessary, it is not sufficient to show that the laws made by X actually do derive their validity from the law purporting to confer upon X to make laws. What is needed in order that we may move from 'This law purports to validate laws enacted by X' to 'The laws enacted by X actually derive their validity from this law' is that the courts or law identifying agencies of the territory concerned should recognize a particular law purporting to confer powers on X and treat it as a reason for recognizing also the laws it purports to validate. But in answering the question whether this law is so recognized, we must identify it not by its content alone as we did when we were concerned only with the relationship of validating purport, but by its authors or mode of creation or date or all of these. We must, in other words, shift our attention from the content to these other individuating elements. That this shift in attention is necessary is evident from the following considerations. The actual constitution of the U.S.S.R. and the Soviet Laws Validity Act may have precisely the same content, and both have the relationship of validating purport to the law-making operations of the Soviet legislature. But the Soviet courts would distinguish between them; and in recognizing, not the Soviet Laws Validity Act, but only the Soviet constitution as relevant to the validity of Soviet laws and belonging to the same system as those laws, they distinguish between them by such individuating factors as I have described above, notwithstanding the identity of content.

(C) Derivations of Validity and Criterion of Membership

These considerations show that in considering whether two laws belong to the same system or different systems we cannot use as our criterion of belonging to the same system the fact that one of them derives its validity from the other. This is so because until the question of membership is settled by the independent test of recognition we cannot discover whether one of the laws does derive its validity from the other. We can only know that one purports to validate the other. The criterion of membership of laws in a single system is therefore independent of and indeed presupposed when we apply the notion of one law deriving validity from another. Only when we know that the Soviet constitution is recognized by the Soviet courts as a reason for recognizing laws enacted in accordance with its provisions, and so belongs to the same system as those laws, are we in a position to state that the latter derive their validity from the former. Until we know that the constitution is so recognized we can all say that this constitution, like the Soviet Laws Validity Act, purports to validate such laws.

(D) The Basic Norm as a Criterion of Membership

Readers of Kelsen will recall that in all the versions of his theory he adheres to the view that what unites different laws in a single system is the basic norm,[60] and it does so because all the positive laws of the system, according to him, derive their validity directly or indirectly from the basic norm. The basic norm, according to Kelsen, unlike all other norms of a system, is not a positive or created norm: [61] unlike all the other laws of a system (positive laws) it does not derive its validity from any other laws. It is a "presupposed" norm, which is 'the reason for the

validity' of the constitution; it may be formulated as "one ought to behave as the constitution prescribes," [62] and is presupposed by anyone
who regards the constitution as a valid norm.[63]

Since the basic norm is the reason for the validity of the constitution that derives its validity directly from it, all the other laws of the system that derive their validity directly or indirectly from the constitution,
derive it indirectly and ultimately from the basic norm. Kelsen's view is
that laws form one system because their validity is thus to be traced
back and derived from one basic norm. If, however, as I have argued
above, we can only trace back the validity of laws to other laws (as distinct from the relationship of validating purport), if we already know by
the test of recognition to what system the laws belong, it cannot be
traceability back to the basic norm that tells us to what system laws belong or accounts for their unity in a single system. Again, our hypothetical example makes this clear. The basic norm of the American constitution is (roughly) that the constitution is valid; but unless we have some
independent criterion of what it is for laws to belong to one system we
cannot trace the validity of laws back to the constitution and thence to
its basic norm; we can only trace relationships of validating purport, and
these, as we have seen, will cut across different legal systems. They will
link together with the American constitution not only the Soviet Laws
Validity Act (supposing it to be enacted by Congress) but all the Soviet legislation that it purports to validate. If our sole criterion for membership of the system is the traceability of validating purport we cannot
break off at the dividing line at which we would wish to break off. We
cannot, as the Soviet courts do, stop at the Soviet constitution, and ignore the Soviet Laws Validity Act as belonging to a different system, although it purports to validate Soviet law; we have to go on from the
laws enacted by the Soviet legislator to the Soviet Laws Validity Act
and thence to the American constitution, and thence to its basic norm,
beyond which by definition no further relationship of validating purport
is to be traced. But the journey is fruitless, because it shows neither that
these laws derive their validity from the basic norm nor that they belong
to a single legal system.

IV

Problems of Recognition

The previous section, as I have said, constitutes no more than a
tentative account of the appropriate criterion for determining the membership of a legal system and for the individuation of different legal systems. It is plain that the notion of recognition that I have stressed will

need refinement in different directions, and I shall end by explaining very shortly some of the considerations that have caused me to express myself thus tentatively.

1. I have spoken of recognition by the law identifying and law-enforcing agencies effective in different territories. This obviously envisages arrangements of modern municipal legal systems where there are courts and special agencies for the enforcement of law. But we cannot leave out of sight more primitive arrangements: there may be no courts and no specialized enforcement agencies, and the application of sanctions for breach of the rules may be left to injured parties or their relatives, or to the community at large. International law, at least according to Kelsen, is itself such a decentralized system. Presumably, in such cases we shall have to use as our test of membership the notion of recognition by the society or the community, and certain problems in defining what constitutes sufficient recognition will have to be faced.

2. Even in the case of modern municipal legal systems the notion of recognition by a court is not without ambiguities. On a narrow interpretation, recognition by a court as a criterion of membership could mean that a rule could not be said to belong to a legal system until it had been actually applied by a court disposing of a case. This interpretation would come nearer to Gray's [64] theory and to the doctrine ascribed to some later American legal realists; but it is surely very unrealistic, for there seems little reason to deny that a statute enacted by the legislature of a normally functioning legal system is a law of the system even before it is applied by the courts in actual cases. However, the precise formulation of a wider interpretation of the idea of recognition which would include rules that courts would apply as well as those actually applied would not be uncontroversial.

3. All civilized legal systems contain special rules for dealing with cases containing a foreign element (e.g., contracts or marriages made abroad). These special rules determine both when courts have jurisdiction to try cases with such foreign elements and which legal systems should guide the courts in the exercise of this jurisdiction. These are the rules known as private international law or conflicts of law, and if we are to take account of them the notion of recognition by courts will have to be refined in further different directions. If a man and his wife whose marriage is valid according to the laws of the country where it was celebrated travel through many different countries, they can be confident that the courts of most of these countries will treat their marriage as valid, at least as far as the formalities of its celebration are concerned. This is only one very simple example of cases where courts of one country would be said to recognize and apply the laws of another country.

Unless the notion of recognition advanced above as a criterion of mem-bership is in some way qualified we should have to draw the conclusion that laws of one country that are recognized and applied by the courts of another country belong to the legal system of the latter country as well as of the former. It is possible to object to the language I have used in describing such cases since it may be said that when, for example, an English court treats a marriage solemnized in say, the Soviet Union, as valid because the formalities were those required by Soviet law, though they differ from those of English law, it does not really apply Soviet law, but applies to the parties before it, a rule similar in content to that which a Soviet court would apply to the parties if they appeared before it in a similar case but of purely domestic character.[65] This would avoid the awkwardness and possibly misleading character of the assertion that one and the same rule was applied by courts of different systems; but it still leaves us without any satisfactory distinction between the kind of recognition that courts give to foreign laws in such cases involving for-eign elements, and the recognition that is to be used as a criterion of membership. We need such a distinction, for it seems plain that in some sense of recognition courts do *recognize* foreign laws in cases rais-ing questions of private international law even if, in deference to the ar-gument cited above, we do not say they *apply* the foreign law, but apply a law of their own with a similar content to that of the foreign law that they recognize.

Perhaps this difficulty may be met by distinguishing two different sorts of recognition that might be called 'original' and 'derivative' recog-nition. In an ordinary case where there is no foreign element, for exam-ple, where an English court simply applies an English statute, the court does not base its recognition and application of the statute on the fact that courts of some other country have recognized or would recognize it; this is original recognition. But where as in cases raising questions of pri-vate international law, part of the court's reasons for recognizing a law is that it has been or would be originally recognized by the courts of an-other country this is derivative recognition of the foreign law. Whether in such cases we should say the court applies the law that is thus deriva-tively recognized or only that it applies a law with similar content does not, I think, affect this distinction, though I have no doubt it needs fur-ther elaboration.

NOTES

1. I refer to the *General Theory of Law and State* (Harvard, 1949) as *GT* and to the *Pure Théory of Law* (University of California, 1967) as *PTL*. I refer to the fuller and generally more accurate French version of the original of the latter work, *Theorie Pure de Droit* (Dalloz, 1962) as *TP*.

2. *GT*, 363. "It is logically not possible to assume that simultaneously valid norms belong to different mutually independent systems" of *PTL*, 328.

3. Kelsen in *GT* and *PTL* regards conflicting norms as "contradictory" (see *infra*, section II) and so expresses his doctrine that valid laws cannot conflict by saying "two norms which by their significance contradict and hence logically exclude one another cannot be simultaneously assumed to be valid," *GT*, 375, cf. *PTL*, 74. Note that from *PTL*, 18 (end of second paragraph) the translator has omitted the crucial words which appear in *TP*, 25, "on peut considerer comme valable soit l'une, soit l'autre norme; il est par contre impossible de les considerer comme valable et l'une et l'autre à la fois."

4. The unity of International Law and Municipal Law in one system is called by Kelsen an "epistemological postulate," *GT*, 373, and to comprehend them as such is "inevitable." *PTL*, 332–3, and cf. *PTL*, 328.

5. *PTL*, 329, and *supra* 1 n.3.

6. *PTL*, 328.

7. *PTL*, 330–1. The same doctrine in a different terminology in *GT*, 371–2.

8. *GT*, 374 ff.; *PTL*, 329.

9. *Kelsen Visited* in *U.C.L.A. Law Review*, Vol. 16 (1963), 722 ff.

10. *GT*, 363–4; *PTL*, 328–9.

11. *GT*, 376–83; *PTL*, 333–9.

12. *GT*, 387.

13. *GT*, 387–8.

14. *GT*, 387–8; *PTL*, 340–2.

15. *GT*, 342–8; *PTL*, 324–8.

16. *GT*, 342; *PTL*, 325, 327.

17. *GT*, 348–9; *PTL*, 325.

18. *GT*, 343.

19. *GT*, 349; *PTL*, 325; cf. *PTL*, 179.

20. *GT*, 100.

21. Notably *GT*, 349; and *PTL*, 325.

22. *GT*, 351.

23. *PTL*, 215; cf. *PTL*, 336–40, and *GT* 121.

24. *GT*, 351.

25. Cases involving a 'foreign element' see *infra*., pp. 742–75.

26. I consider later the possibility of *introducing* a meaning for "legal system" such that the mere existence of the relationship of validating purport between laws is sufficient to constitute the laws of a single system. This would not of course refute the conventional pluralist for it is not in this sense of "system" that he asserts that international law and municipal law are separate systems.

27. *GT*, 373.

28. *Ibid.*

29. *GT*, 363.

30. *PTL*, 328.

31. *TP*, 430.

32. *PTL*, 328. Professor J. L. Mackie has pointed out to me that Kelsen's

claim that there can only be one system of valid laws resembles Kant's claim that there is only one space. "For . . . we can represent to ourselves only one space; and if we speak of diverse spaces, we mean only parts of one and the same unique space" (*Critique of Pure Reason* A25). I have the impression that underlying Kelsen's theory of law there is the *assumption* that there is a single "normative space" which must be describable by a consistent set of rules in a descriptive sense" (See *infra*).

33. *GT*, 408.

34. *GT*, 407–8.

35. Quite apart from its failure to cover the case mentioned, this argument for the necessary unity of all valid law in one system is incomplete, even if conflict between valid laws is (contrary to the argument of the next section) admitted to be logically impossible. To complete the argument it would have to be shown that what Kelsen calls "insoluble logical contradictions," which he thinks might arise in the case of two independent systems, could not arise in the case of one system.

36. This section is concerned with Kelsen's views on conflicts as expounded in his books *GT* and *PTL*. In a later essay on *Derogation* in *Essays in Honour of Roscoe Pound* (New York, 1962) Kelsen admits the logical possibility of conflicting valid norms. He does not however explain why he has abandoned his previous views or refer to the exposition of them in *GT* and *PTL*. Nor does he withdraw or modify the monistic theory of international law and municipal law expounded in these books. See, for an examination of this latest phase of Kelsen's thought, A. G. Conte, '*In Margine All'Ultimo Kelsen*' in Studi Giuridici (Studia Ghisleriana, Pavia, 1967), p. 113.

37. *PTL*, 328.

38. *GT*, 410; *PTL* 329.

39. Crude, since most cases of conflict between two rules arise because some contingent fact makes it impossible only on a particular occasion to obey them both, and not because the rules by explicitly forbidding and requiring the same action are such that on no occasion could they both be obeyed.

40. See B. A. O. Williams, *Consistency and Realism*, Proceedings of the Aristotelian Society, 1961, p. 1. I am much indebted to this lucid account of the logical issues involved.

41. *PTL*, 16. Kelsen describes such permissive rules (express or tacit) as 'negative regulation' of conduct and distinguishes a positive sense of permission when rules prohibit interference with another's conduct.

42. *PTL*, 18, but note text of *TP* (n. 3 *supra*); *PTL*, 25, 205.

43. The 'joint-conformity' test of conflict is applicable only to rules all or all but one of which require or prohibit action. Permissive rules cannot conflict, but joint conformity with two permissive rules may be logically impossible (e.g. "Opening the window is permitted," "Shutting the window is permitted") I am indebted to Professor J. L. Mackie for this point.

44. *GT*, 409; *PTL*, 18, 205–8, 329.

45. *PTL* 73, 78. The corresponding term in *TP* is 'proposition de droit' as distinguished from 'norme juridique'; and in the original German is 'Rechtsatz' as distinguished from 'Rechtsnorm'. In the long note to *TP*, 99 (omitted by the translator in *PTL*) Kelsen cites Sigwart in support of the notion of 'ought' in a descriptive sense' cf. the similar views of von Wright on normative statements in *Norm and Action* 78 ff.; cf. Castaneda on "Deontic Assertables" in (1967) Proceedings of the Aristotelian Society, *Actions, Imperatives and Obligations*, p. 25.

46. *PTL*, 5.

47. *TP*, 99, note (omitted from PTL).

48. *PTL*, 18.

49. *PTL*, 74.

50. *PTL*, 206.

51. *Ibid.*

52. Among these difficulties, much in need of exploration, is the determination of the meaning for Kelsen of "valid." *Sometimes* he writes as if to say that a norm is "valid," is to say that it is a final and uniquely correct standard of conduct and so excludes the validity of conflicting norms, e.g., *GT*, p. 410.

53. See Williams, *loc. cit.*

54. See for a clear discussion of this point E. J. Lemmon 'Deontic Logic and the Logic of Imperatives,' *Logique et Analyse*, 1965, esp. pp. 45–51.

55. His position is that if there were such conflicts we could not regard international law and municipal law as one system, and absence of conflict is the negative criterion of unity of system. See p. 20. *supra.*

56. E.g., *PTL*, 73, 205.

57. *PTL*, 330.

58. *PTL*, 331; cf. *PTL*, 274.

59. It is to be observed that throughout this section I have ignored as Kelsen himself does, an argument in favour of the weaker form of the 'no conflict' theory which would be available if his own controversial interpretation of all laws as 'sanction-stipulating norms' addressed to organs or officials determining the condition under which sanctions 'ought' to be applied were taken seriously. According to this interpretation "only the coercive act functioning as a sanction ought to be" (*PTL*, 119), i.e., the only persons who 'ought' to do anything according to law are the 'organs' or officials, and what they 'ought' to do is to apply sanctions if the conditions stated in the law are fulfilled. Since in different states these organs or officials are different persons, no conflict would ever arise between the laws of different states: joint conformity to the laws would always be possible. Thus, even if laws of State A stipulated that sanctions ought to be applied by its officials to certain persons in the event of their doing certain specified actions, and the laws of State B forbade the application by its officials of sanctions under those same conditions, no conflict would arise since the officials of the two states would be different persons. Similarly, since the sanction-applying agencies in international law are (according to Kelsen) the representatives of the states against whom a delict or offence has been committed, whereas the sanction-applying agencies of a state are its own officials, no conflict could arise. There is nothing in Kelsen's accounts of what it is for laws to conflict which excludes this argument. I do not myself accept Kelsen's interpretation of law as sanction-stipulating norms and so would not regard this argument as sound. Kelsen might also have used as an argument in support of the 'no conflicts' theory his own (in my view erroneous) doctrine that the legal 'ought' must (to avoid a vicious regress) have the sense of 'permitted' or 'authorized' rather than 'commanded' (*PTL*, 25).

60. *GT*, 110, 367; *PTL*, 195, 201.

61. *PTL*, 199.

62. *PTL*, 201: its formulation will be different if municipal law is regarded as a subordinate part of international law.

63. *PTL*, 204, n. 72.

64. See his *Nature and Sources of Law.*

65. See W. W. Cook, *The Logical and Legal Bases of the Conflict of Laws,* Chapt. 1.

COMMENTS ON THE UNITY OF LAW DOCTRINE
(A RESPONSE)

Ronald Dworkin

I shall start by discussing Hart's arguments against Kelsen's view that if international and municipal law conflict, one cannot regard them both as valid. Hart uses Kelsen's own positions to refute this proposition. Kelsen said that the validity of a norm is relative to a particular legal system. It follows that if international law and municipal law are separate legal systems, the statement that in municipal law a certain norm is valid (e.g., that all men must wage war if ordered) cannot be inconsistent with the statement that in international law another norm is valid (e.g., that no man may wage war even if ordered). Since Kelsen's test of the inconsistency of norms depends on the inconsistency of the statements that they are valid, these norms are not inconsistent, and may both be valid.

But this argument overlooks a complexity in Kelsen's writings. Kelsen devotes much space, throughout his work, to two problems, and though he uses the word "validity" in connection with both of these, he uses it with different implications.

He is concerned, first, to identify the science of law, or of legal exposition, and to distinguish that science from sociology. He describes the science of law as making statements about norms, and he calls these "descriptive-ought statements" to show that they are concerned with the question of whether norms are valid as distinguished from the question of whether they are effective or what their effects are.[1] In this connection, the statement that a law is valid asserts that it has been created in accordance with a basic norm which structures some legal order, and is therefore a statement relative to that legal order. Kelsen clearly had this concept of validity in mind in the passage Hart quoted: ". . . the science of law cannot formulate the rule of law otherwise than by saying: 'According to a certain positive legal order and under certain conditions a certain consequence ought to take place.' " [2] He also had this concept in mind, though he was speaking of ethics, or moral science, when he said that, "The validity of a norm according to which a certain behavior ought to be . . . does not exclude the possibility of the validity of a norm according to which the opposite behavior ought to be . . ." [3]

Kelsen's second concern is with the dynamics of legal reasoning, and in particular with the structure of an argument that ends in the decision that some man or some official ought to do something, meaning not that he has good reasons for doing it, but that it is, on balance, what he must do. The statement that some norm is valid figures in this sort of argument, but in this context Kelsen is anxious to point out that such a statement presupposes the validity of one particular basic norm, that is, that it presupposes that one basic norm "is binding" on the particular officials and persons concerned. It is this conclusory notion of validity that Kelsen uses when, speaking of possible conflicts between law and morals, he says that "an individual who regards the law as a system of valid norms has to disregard morals as such a system . . . no viewpoint exists from which both morals and law may simultaneously be regarded as valid normative orders. No one can serve two masters." [4] The key words here are "viewpoint" and "simultaneously"; Kelsen's view is that one person cannot regard both norms as valid in the sense of deciding the issue of what he ought to do on some occasion.

Hart's argument, I think, confuses these two contexts, by applying an analysis of validity Kelsen gives in one context to a problem he raises in another. When Kelsen says that if international and municipal law conflicted, we could not speak of them both as valid at the same time, he means that someone who had to decide what he ought to do—a judge for instance—could not treat them both as valid in the conclusory sense, could not, in Kelsen's phrase, serve two masters. This is consistent with Kelsen's test for contradiction between norms, mentioned earlier, because the appropriate statements to use in that test are not the statements Hart used, e.g., "according to international law one must not wage war," and "according to American law one must wage war," which are clearly consistent, but rather statements like "because international law so provides, you are forbidden to fight," and "because American law so provides, you are required to fight," which are not clearly consistent. The juxtaposition of these last two statements seem to me to present the essence of Kelsen's point.

I

Are these two statements consistent? That question brings us to a point Hart made in passing. He raised the question whether two rules that cannot both be satisfied may not still be valid, even within the same system. It is true that deontic logics can be constructed so that this is the case, just as indicative logics can be constructed in which "p and not-p" is not a contradiction. The issue for legal philosophy, however, is whether such a deontic logic would illuminate the ground rules of legal reasoning. Professor Bernard Williams, in an article Hart cites,[5] points out that a club might have house rules that collide on some occasion ("What is laid down for Catholics is incompatible with what is laid down for Socialists," and a rare Catholic Socialist visits the club), and manage these occasions not by deciding which rule prevails, nor by enacting a new rule, but simply by keeping silent and letting the chips fall where they may. In that case we might want to say that both rules continue valid as before, in spite of the conflict. This is an illuminating point, precisely because "keeping silent" is not a permissible move in adjudication. If such a case comes before an Anglo-American court, the court cannot ignore the conflict, but must subordinate one rule, or fashion a new one. It cannot, that is, take the position that the rules collide and are both valid. Kelsen's view, therefore, seems better to record our practices of adjudication than does a deontic logic that would permit such a solution. (I should add that I am speaking, as do Kelsen and Hart, of legal rules, not legal principles and policies, which follow a rather different logic.)

There is one dramatic consequence of these ground rules in the field of private international law. Suppose an accident takes place in New York, and a Connecticut driver kills a New York resident. New York law imposes a $25,000 ceiling on damages, but under Connecticut law the actual damages of $75,000 are recoverable in full. Why should a court not consider splitting the difference, and awarding damages of $50,000? No court, to my knowledge, has done this, and I believe the reason to lie not so much in concerns of federalism or other policies, as in the assumption that since the two rules about damages conflict, only one can "apply" to a particular case. There are conflict cases, however, in which ingenious judges have managed a less visible compromise, reaching a different decision than they would if the facts were wholly domestic to either of the two jurisdictions involved (e.g., Holmes' decision in Polson v. Stewart) [6] and many private international law scholars now argue for this "transnational" approach. This is different, of course, from the club stewards who remain silent. The transnational approach differs from the orthodox, not in rejecting Kelsen's stricture that valid rules cannot conflict, but in allowing both conflicting rules to play a part in shaping the new rule that dissolves the conflict. We cannot follow the stewards, and let a case go with no implications for the future, because the doctrine of precedent automatically attaches such implications to judicial decisions.

All this raises the question, important for the connection of logic and legal philosophy, of how we should use the modalities in describing our legal practices. Should we say that it is *impossible* for two conflicting laws of the same system to be valid? After all, even our most secure practices may change, and perhaps one day our courts will decide cases by just "remaining silent" in the face of conflicts, taking the position that both are valid. Perhaps this is what Hart means when he says that a "logical calculus . . . should not rule out such possibilities of conflict in advance."

But if we abstain from modalities, on the ground that our deep-seated practices may change, then we lose some effective language for making important distinctions. We do want to distinguish the fact that in New York law two conflicting rules are not both valid, from the fact that in New York law an endorsement of a blank check carries certain consequences. We could, of course, make the distinction in terms of degree of likelihood of change, but this would miss the point that the first fact seems conceptual in a way that the second does not.

It would also rob us of the useful notion that a social practice may have a logic, in the sense of ground rules of reasoning so basic that they are taken for granted, and that the logic of a practice may be explored by logicians and compared with the logic of other practices that may be different. I should prefer to use the modalities in this way, keeping some place in mind the fact that even these basic ground rules are social creations. I should add, somewhat dogmatically, that this reservation must be borne in mind whenever the modalities are used. (I have in mind the now enormous literature on the foundations of mathematics, and on the distinction between "analytic" and "synthetic" statements.)

II

Hart also argues against Kelsen's view that, in fact, international and municipal law do not conflict. Here Hart is fully justified in turning Kelsen's own definitions against him. Kelsen defines "norm" and "ought" in such a way that the norm, "A is forbidden," conflicts with the norm, "A is permitted." Two norms conflict if one cannot comply with both, and one cannot comply with a permissive norm except by doing what it permits. Under these definitions Kelsen is vulnerable to Hart's point that international and municipal law conflict if international law forbids an official act that municipal law permits.

Kelsen's mistake, however, lies in his definition of conflict, and I shall pursue this point, because Hart seems to agree with Kelsen that the definition is a useful one. It is often unrealistic to describe two norms as conflicting if one forbids what another permits. Consider this hypothetical case. The New York legislature has passed a statute prohibiting the use of someone's photograph on advertising copy without permission, but Connecticut has no such law. A, a Connecticut resident whose store is near the border, uses a photograph of B in his window without B's permission; B suffers embarrassment and sues in Connecticut asking that the New York statute be applied. Under the Kelsen-Hart test, Connecticut and New York law conflict on this issue, and the Connecticut court would have to choose which to apply. If the court followed either the decrepit *lex-loci* rule, or the hyper-modern "interest theory" analysis of Professor Currie, it would decide for A.

It is hard, however, to see where the conflict lies. If A had not used B's photograph, he would have been in full compliance with the laws of both states. He would not have taken full advantage of Connecticut law, to be sure, but each of us spends his days not taking advantage of permissive laws, and it is bizarre to say that in so doing we are failing to comply with the law.

There would be some minimal case for saying that A, by abstaining, was not complying with Connecticut law, if Connecticut's failure to adopt a law like New York's represented a policy of encouraging businessmen to use photographs in advertising and so perk up Connecticut business. That, in any event, would be a reason for a Connecticut court's refusal to apply the New York statute. It would also be a reason for that decision if Connecticut's failure to forbid the practice represented an institutional judgment, evidenced by legislative consideration and rejection of the statute, that imposing liability for such acts is morally wrong. In that event, the court might use the Connecticut determination to shield A from New York liability, on the ground that its institutions believed such liability unfair. But it does not follow from the fact that Connecticut law permits the practice that it follows the policy of encouraging the practice or that it has judged and found that liability would be unfair. More evidence is needed; in the absence of other evidence we may conclude only that Connecticut has not imposed the liability that New York has.

It happens that New York levies an income tax on Connecticut residents who work in New York. Connecticut has no income tax, but it would not occur to us to say that New York and Connecticut law are in conflict on the issue of whether the tax should be paid. Perhaps we should treat my hypothetical case in the same way, and say that New York has imposed, on Connecticut residents whose activities affect New Yorkers, a burden additional to those that Connecticut has imposed. In that event, we should decide the case for B, assuming, as we do in the tax case, that A has sufficient contact with New York and sufficient notice to make that fair.

The question of whether New York and Connecticut law conflict, forcing a "choice-of-law," or whether they cumulate, like the two positions on taxation, cannot be settled by a definition of "compliance" that makes a law forbidding and a law permitting the same act necessarily conflict. It can be settled only by a careful analysis of the principles and policies that in fact support the rules in question. We must resist applying a deontic logic that turns cases of cumulation into false conflicts.

III

In the last section of his lecture, Professor Hart raises some questions about the concept of a legal system. I shall separate these into two basic questions: (a) How do we tell whether a given legal system exists, and the extent of its sway? (b) How do we tell whether a particular rule belongs to a given legal system?

We might well describe the first of these as a sociological question, because, as Hart points out, it is essentially a question about the social behavior of groups. We use rough criteria and make rough judgments in deciding whether a legal system exists. There are some obvious cases, like the English and the Russian systems, and some close cases, like the primitive communities Hart mentions. The crucial tests we use, I suppose, are standards of complexity and independence. A legal system must have some institutional structure, and a range of independent force. We would find it odd to speak of the Brockport legal system, even though Brockport has separate legal institutions and tax rates, traffic laws, and no doubt other ordinances.

Hart raises some logical questions about the grounds we must have for the judgment that a particular legal system exists. He points out that we cannot infer that a set of institutions and rules make up a legal system simply from the fact that some of these purport to authorize the others. We must know, independently of this purported authorization, that the institutions and enactments in question are part of the same system, and we can discover this only by attending to the behavior of the pertinent officials and citizens.

That is true, though I might add that Hart does not mean to deny that the fact that particular people and groups are purporting to enact and authorize is generally an important part of the evidence that a system exists. The behavior of purporting to govern is part of the behavior we must look to, though it is not, as Hart reminds us, all of it. The Soviet Law Validating Act would be evidence that America and Russia should be regarded as one legal system, though the contrary evidence would be overwhelming. If there were some remote area of Siberia, however, whose citizens were generally disobedient to the Kremlin, we would take the fact that Russian statutes purported to apply as strong evidence that the area should nevertheless be regarded as part of that legal system. We might say that the system was not being enforced in that area, but that is a different judgment.

The second question—how do we decide whether a given rule belongs to a given legal system—seems to me less worth asking than the first, at least in that form. I understand the queston, "is the rule that cousins cannot marry part of the Russian legal system," to be only another way of asking, "under Russian legal practice, are cousins permitted to marry?" I prefer the second way of putting the question, because it does not make use of an assumption I find troublesome, namely that the law of a community is usefully regarded as an independent system of rules. This concept of a legal system—an organized set of rules—is, of course, different from the sociological concept of a legal system—a set of institutions and practices—used in the first question.

NOTES

1. I set aside, as not directly in point, the various difficulties others have found in Kelsen's concept of the "descriptive-ought" statement.
2. PTL, p. 78.
3. PTL, p. 18.
4. PTL, p. 329.
5. Cf. the passage omitted from PTL cited by Hart in his footnote 3. Since this passage followed what I cited at note 3 above, it is no wonder the translator was confused.
6. 167 Mass. 211; 45 N.E. 737.

CIVIL DISOBEDIENCE AND THE
POLITICAL-QUESTION DOCTRINE

Graham Hughes

Stemming from the civil rights movement and the war in Vietnam, civil disobedience has in recent years attracted a great deal of popular and intellectual interest in the United States. Professional philosophers have revived a longstanding debate in western thought about the nature of the moral obligation to obey the law, while sociologists and psychologists have explored the social origins and repercussions of disobedience. It is important to notice that the disobedience to law which has of late taken place is of two kinds, though the division is rough and there is certainly overlapping. Firstly, there is the simple refusal by an individual to comply with a demand that the law makes upon him which he conceives to be unjust or which he feels would make him an accomplice in doing injustice. Refusal of induction into the armed forces because of moral objection to the war in Vietnam is of this kind. Secondly, there is participation in organized campaigns of law violation that are mounted in order to persuade government or private institutions to change policies or practices that are felt to be wrong. In this second case the disobedience may be directed at laws which are themselves quite unexceptionable, but which are broken in order to apply pressure and to bring about a change of mind in the party whose practices are found to be offensive. An example of this type of disobedience directed at social change would be sit-ins on the premises of firms which, it is alleged, have discriminatory hiring policies.

In any discussion of either kind of civil disobedience lawyers must inevitably find themselves in a peculiarly delicate stance. They are professionally very familiar with the notion that participation in crime is rarely if ever excused by purity of motive. But in recent experience, as with the Nazi regime, the legal system itself could be viewed in some aspects as a deliberate and deadly attack on values cherished in our morality, and our applause was reserved for those who took the awful risk of disobeying. The enormity of evil expressed in modern tyrannies has undermined any simple faith in the central importance of fidelity to law. At the same time there has been ample evidence that skilfully organized campaigns of civil disobedience can be very effective in securing desirable changes in the law. Those who have occupied the office of Solicitor General of the United States are not prominent advocates of illegal behavior, but Professor Archibald Cox, a former holder of that office, has written recently:

Social protest and even civil disobedience serve the law's need for growth. Ideally, reform would come according to reason and justice without self-help and disturbing, almost violent, forms of protest. . . . Still, candor compels one here again to acknowledge the gap between the ideal and the reality. Short of the millennium, sharp changes in the law depend partly upon the stimulus of protest.[1]

But whatever emotional conflicts the lawyer may experience about civil disobedience, it is not readily apparent what assistance his professional expertise can bring to any discussion of the topic. The question of whether it can ever be morally justifiable not to obey the law is manifestly not a legal question, and it may indeed be exactly this sense of extra-legality that causes a lawyerly recoil from confrontation with the problem. I want, though, to suggest that in some situations civil disobedience does raise important questions about a proper judicial response within a legal system. These are sometimes questions that entail a more or less technical debate about legal doctrine; they are always questions of legal philosophy.

I want to concentrate on a doctrine of American constitutional law that I think has profound implications for any discussion of civil disobedience in the American system, but, before coming to that, let me first refer briefly to some more obvious connections between civil disobedience and the role of the judiciary.

Breaches of the law will normally result in criminal prosecution, and, if conviction ensues, the judge must exercise his discretion in assessing a punishment within the legally prescribed maximum. The motivation of the accused is certainly a proper factor to be considered at this point, even though it may not generally be relevant to guilt. But what significance we should attach to the circumstance that the defendant deliberately engaged in violation of the law as a response to what seemed to him to be pressing moral demands is not at all clear. In one aspect such a person seems clearly less deserving of reprobation than one who breaks the law for personal profit and who would not even pretend to offer a moral defense of his behavior. For if we are satisfied that the defendant was indeed moved by moral conviction to disobey the law, we can surely sufficiently vindicate the ideal of fidelity to law by the denunciatory impact of conviction, coupled perhaps with nominal or light punishment. The infliction of a severe penalty on a person who, while not being insane or sociopathic, has been morally impelled to do what he has done is only cruelty. Such a notion has been apparent for a long time even in such an area as murder in circumstances of euthanasia where a variety of devices has been employed to secure a light sentence for the accused.

But in another light it is possible to regard civil disobedience stemming from moral conviction as especially dangerous to society. Those who have deep moral objections to the law's demands are likely to proselytize others to join them in their disobedience. They make a public appeal to the conscience of their fellow citizens, quite unlike the man who breaks the law for greed or in violence. They may be stubborn in their convictions and unlikely to yield to a threat of only mild punishment. If the demand made by the law and rejected by the disobedient is one felt to be vital to the security or well being of society, then it may be thought that harsh punishment is necessary to reduce the number of disobedients to those with unshakable certitude and unconquerable courage. This may explain the traditionally severe punishments meted out to those who in time of war refuse to serve in the armed forces for conscientious reasons that are not accommodated by the statutory scheme for conscientious objection, and, no doubt, the substantial sentences imposed recently on draft card burners.

The treatment of civil disobedients by judges in the business of sentencing thus almost inevitably reflects a tension between retributive and deterrent aspects of punishment. It is indeed a dilemma for judges of an acute kind. To treat these defendants with great lenity runs the risk of making defiance of legislative judgments too easy. To treat them severely runs the risk of brutalizing the institution of punishment and undermining respect for the legal system generally, for few of us can be happy about the imposition of severe sanctions on a man whose motives we agree are honorable though we may question his judgment. The wiser course is surely to persist in lenient treatment until the social dangers of the disobedience are indubitably obtrusive. If there is a suspicion that moral positions are being advanced only as camouflage by those who wish to avoid the burdens of complying with the law, or if there is a belief that those who are disobeying have, because of the lightness of previous penalties, not reflected long and soberly enough, then this can be expressed by a gradual escalation of sanctions. Even when we are convinced of the honesty and reflective nature of the defendant's stand but believe his rejection of the law's demands to be very dangerous because of the vital nature of the duty involved, a slow hardening of penalties is still to be preferred. To assert that the most dangerous man in our society is the one of strong moral conviction and courage is an unhappy admission about the nature of our society. It is one that we should not be in a hurry to make.

II

In a legal system such as that of the United States, which includes judicial power to review and quash legislation on the ground of violation of constitutionally entrenched guaranties, it is necessary to isolate a situation that is only marginally, if at all, one of civil disobedience. This situation arises when the protestor deliberately violates a statute or executive ruling or ordinance that he believes will be declared unconstitutional by the courts and when his predominant motive is to engineer a test case for review of the constitutionality of the rule. If the statute or ruling violated is unconstitutional in the opinion of the court, no difficulty presents itself; but the situation is more complicated when the court disagrees with the legal judgment of the protestor and holds the statute violated to be valid and constitutional.

Lawyers could begin to think of such a situation in terms of a mistake of law on the part of the defendant which, traditionally, has been said not to be a defense at all to a criminal prosecution. But, even as the law now stands, mistake of law is occasionally recognized as a defense. It has been admitted as a defense in cases where the defendant's mistake proceeded from bad advice by an official concerned with the administration of that branch of the law.[2] A few years ago, the Supreme Court of the United States opened up new doctrine in this area in the case of *Lambert v. California*[3] by holding that ignorance of the existence of a criminal prohibition could be a defense when the statute required a positive act on the part of the defendant and government had failed to take adequate steps to bring the law's requirements to the notice of persons to whom it applied. Nothing in the existing cases, however, would warrant the argument that the mere presence of a belief in the defendant that the violated law was unconstitutional should be a defense, even if that belief were based on the opinion of attorneys. I would like to suggest that the development of such a doctrine is well within the power of the courts and might be salutary if confined within careful limits. The restrictions on such a defense would have to include at least the following:

(1) that the defendant had the purpose not of disobeying the law but of demonstrating its unconstitutional character;

(2) that there was legitimate doubt about the constitutionality of the law as perhaps evidenced by expert testimony about the state of professional opinion;

(3) that there was no way short of disobedience by which the defendant could have obtained a determination of the validity of the law;

(4) that the disobedience was non-violent.

The contention here is that a declaration of the validity of the law is not quite the same as a determination that the defendant should be convicted and punished. Other factors are relevant to guilt, and it would be quite a proper decision to say that, although the law is now found to be constitutional, the defendant shall not be convicted because of the exculpating circumstance of his honest and reasonable doubt as to its validity. Such a doctrine and such a holding would, of course, preclude the successful raising of such a defense in the future once a judicial determination had been made of the validity of the statute, since no assertion of its unconstitutionality could afterwards be regarded as reasonable for purposes of excuse.

III

The special features of a legal system with judicial review of the constitutionality of acts of the legislature and executive have given rise to a much more difficult and delicate question which at present intimately connects in the United States the civil disobedience directed against the war in Vietnam with the activity of the courts. Those who contest the conduct of the government with respect to the war in Vietnam sometimes contend that the acts of government are illegal and unconstitutional. This argument rests chiefly on two grounds: that the military action in Vietnam is a war and therefore orders to participate in it are unconstitutional since war has not been declared by Congress, and that the military action in Vietnam is in violation of the treaty obligations of the United States which form part of the law of the United States. Efforts to raise these arguments before the federal courts have so far not been fruitful. In *Mitchell v. United States* [4] where the petitioner had attempted to challenge his induction into the armed forces on the ground that this might involve him in participation in an illegal war, it was held that his claim was premature in that the power to levy an armed force was independent of the question of the constitutionality of orders given to an individual once inducted. The Supreme Court refused certiorari, though with a dissent from Mr. Justice Douglas. In *Mora v. McNamara* [5] the petitioners were already in the armed forces and were ordered to report to a center for shipment to Vietnam. They brought a suit to prevent this order from being carried out and asked for a declaratory judgment that the military operations in Vietnam were illegal. The lower federal courts refused a declaratory judgment and the Supreme Court denied certiorari, with dissents by Mr. Justice Stewart and Mr. Justice Douglas. It is apparent from the dissents in *Mora v. McNamara* that the fundamental preliminary question in that case and in similar cases is whether the suit involves a political question that the court cannot or will not rule on.

The political-question doctrine in American constitutional law is a smoldering volcano that may now be about to fulfill its long promise of erupting into flaming controversy. It is essentially an expression of the classical idea of a separation of powers—that some authoritative determinations are to be made by the legislature, some by the executive, and some by the courts. It is commonplace to observe that the very notion of judicial review of legislative and executive action is an important qualification on the idea of separation of powers. The legislature is the proper authoritative body for enacting general laws in the form of statutes, but in our system a court has a power to decide that the norms enacted by the legislature fail in their law-making effort because of the contravention of superior norms, the final authoritative interpretation of which is constitutionally entrusted to the court. The political-question doctrine is a qualification on this qualification. It seemingly asserts that some actions, practices, or determinations by legislature or executive are not reviewable in the courts. But the precise status and nature of the doctrine are much in dispute.

Under one view, espoused notably by Professor Wechsler of Columbia Law School, the application of the doctrine amounts to a determination of constitutional law that a question has been reserved by the Constitution for a branch of government other than the judiciary. To say that a question is a political question would thus be a legal decision about the jurisdiction of the Court. This is not to say that the challenged action of the executive or legislature did not involve a matter of constitutional interpretation, but rather that the decision of the executive or legislature under whatever constitutional provision may be in issue is one that is not open to challenge in the courts. Professor Wechsler writes:

The only proper judgment that may lead to an abstention from decision is that the Constitution has committed the determination of the issue to another agency of government than the courts. Difficult as it may be to make that judgment wisely, whatever factors may be rightly weighed in situations where the answer is not clear, what is involved is in itself an act of constitutional interpretation, to be made and judged by standards that should govern the interpretive process generally. That I submit is *toto caelo* different from a broad discretion to abstain or intervene.[6]

An example cited by Professor Wechsler is a judgment of impeachment.[7] In the course of an impeachment trial questions of a constitutional nature may clearly arise, but it seems equally clear that such a judgment cannot be reviewed in the courts in the light of Article 1, Section 3 of the Constitution, which declares that the "sole power to try" is in the Senate.

A different view has been put forward by Professor Bickel of the Yale Law School. Professor Bickel is willing to agree that sometimes the determination that an issue is not within the jurisdiction of the court is a matter of constitutional interpretation, but he argues that often the determination that an issue is not justiciable because it is a political question is rather an exercise of prudential discretion and is not a determination about the constitutional allocation of decision-making power to different branches of government. In his book, *The Least Dangerous Branch*, he has written:

Only by means of a play on words can the broad discretion that the courts have in fact exercised be turned into an act of constitutional interpretation governed by the general standards of the interpretative process. The political-question doctrine simply resists being domesticated in this fashion. There is . . . something different about it, in kind not in degree; something greatly more flexible, something of prudence, not construction and not principle.[8]

Professor Bickel later speaks of the foundation of the political-question doctrine as being

The Court's sense of lack of capacity, compounded in unequal parts of (a) the strangeness of the issue and its intractability to principled resolution; (b) the sheer momentousness of it, which tends to unbalance judicial judgment; (c) the anxiety, not so much that judicial judgment will be ignored, as perhaps that it should but will not be; (d) finally . . . the inner vulnerability, the self-doubt of an institution which is electorally irresponsible and has no earth to draw strength from.[9]

This paper is not designed as an essay in constitutional law to make any judgment about the rival merits of the views advanced by Professors Wechsler and Bickel as descriptions of the practice of the Supreme Court in the political-question area. Material can indeed be found in the opinions of the Court that touch on the political-question doctrine that lends support to either view.[10] My purpose is rather to consider some of the general implications of both views for legal philosophy with particular reference to their impingement on the issues that surround civil disobedience.

At the outset it may be helpful to make a distinction between norms of competence and norms of adjudication. By this I mean that if we should ask ourselves whether designating something as a political question involves the application of legal norms, the enquiry would be unfortunately telescoped, producing an ambiguity. Certainly the federal courts under the norms of the legal system are the competent organs to decide whether they will hear certain cases. It is perhaps possible to imagine a rule under which some decision-maker other than a court would be empowered to decide whether a court had power to make some kinds of decisions; we could have a procedure by which the President might issue a certificate to the effect that a dispute involved a matter of supreme political importance and therefore was not to be submitted for judicial determination. But that is not the rule in our legal system, and the norm is clearly established that the courts themselves determine the limits of the range of justiciable issues. A decision by a court that it cannot or will not hear a dispute is clearly then a legal application of norms of competence in the sense that there can be no doubt that the court is designated by the norms of the system as the proper organ to make such decisions.

But real issues for debate do remain, for the obscurity does not have to do with norms of competence but rather with what norms of adjudication are employed by the court as a basis for deciding that it will not or cannot hear a case. The court may indisputably be the proper organ to make such decisions, but is there something about its practice in this area of the political-question doctrine that departs in any significant way from that familiar judicial working with rules and principles which characterizes the everyday business of the courts? It is in this context of norms of adjudication that the political-question doctrine may pose fundamental and disturbing interrogatories.

Under Professor Wechsler's view, the holding that something is a political question is a decision on a matter of constitutional law that seems to place us in the comfortably familiar world of norms of adjudication. But the position seems more difficult of analysis under Professor Bickel's view of things. His presentation confronts us with the question of what kind of a legal system we might have when a court has a discretion not to decide cases. Suppose we were playing football and the captain of one team claimed to the referee that a member of the opposing team was offside. We can well imagine the referee's rejecting the claim but what if, instead, he should say: "I just don't want to decide that question. It would be too embarrassing at the moment because tempers in both teams are high and whichever way I decided would be likely to provoke a fight." If we were told before playing the game that it was to be that kind of a game, one in which officials would only apply rules when they felt like it, we might be reluctant to play at all.

This would be a kind of a game, perhaps something like that kind of a game which Professor Hart, in another connection, has called "scorer's discretion," [11] but it would be less of a contest than a gamble and one that only gamblers would want to play. Does Professor Bickel's description of the political-question doctrine lead us to conclude that the American legal system at one of its most fundamental levels is a game of scorer's discretion? We have suggested that to say that the referee is the proper man to decide that he does not want to decide would establish a perfectly orderly norm of competence, but one that would be quite inadequate to ensure that kind of regular ordering of human behavior which would attract those who wished to participate in a contest of equal opportunity. Is the political-question doctrine a similar threat to that reliance on the expectation of principled decision-making, which is a part of what we have in mind when we speak of the rule of law?

If such an assertion were made, any attempt to comment on it would inevitably lead us to a very difficult enquiry into distinctions between principled decision-making and appeals to prudence and discretion. If we present the heart of the political-question doctrine as an unfettered discretion in the federal courts not to decide a case when decision is thought to be inexpedient, then it begins to look dangerously like our referee example. As the quotation above from Professor Bickel has indicated, there is certainly material in the pronouncements and actions of the courts that could incline one to this view. It will be remembered that he singled out the "momentousness" of the issue as one element that may justify a refusal to utter a decision. In the legislative reapportionment case of *Baker v. Carr* the Supreme Court enumerated a number of considerations, the presence of any of which might make a question political. They include the impossibility of judicial resolution "without expressing lack of the respect due coordinate branches of government" and "an unusual need for unquestioning adherence to a political decision already made".[12] These and especially the second certainly seem to imply *Inter arma silent leges* and to cast doubt on the aphorism that it is a Constitution that is being expounded.

On the other hand the Court also said in *Baker v. Carr*:

Deciding whether a matter has in any measure been committed by the Constitution to another branch of government, or whether the action of that branch exceeds whatever authority has been committed, is itself a delicate exercise in constitutional interpretation, and is a responsibility of this Court as ultimate interpreter of the Constitution.[13]

The Court itself thus seems not altogether sure about its role in the political-question area, talking sometimes as if it were doing a conventional job of constitutional interpretation and at other times as if it were merely recognizing reasons of sensitivity for holding its hand. But is there any kind of tension here anyway? Could reasons of political sensitivity not be assimilated into the notion of principled decision-making?

Certainly the practical prospects for enforcement of its decisions have long been familiar considerations that a court will take into account in certain areas of decision. Thus a petition for injunctive relief may be refused not because the plaintiff is unable to show a breach of duty towards him by the defendant, but because an injunction is not a suitable remedy, since there could not be effective enforcement. In the injunction example, however, the court does recognize a breach of duty in the defendant and only refuses a certain kind of remedy; other remedies, such as damages, are left for relief. The political-question example is more radical since it involves a general rather than a partial denial of action by the court.

One can imagine any kind of arbitrary and whimsical ground for a refusal of decision being built into a legal system in a quite explicit fashion. For example, the statute setting up a court and conferring jurisdiction on it might say that the judge could always refuse to hear a case when he did not like the appearance of the plaintiff. This would establish a perfectly clear norm of competence and would also give a simply expressed substantive ground for refusing a hearing. We would, of course, find it very objectionable for a number of readily apparent reasons, the chief of which would be the manifest injustice of setting up as a condition of obtaining a hearing a test which has no rational connection at all with the merits. But suppose we tried to defend such a provision in the following way: The operation of the courts in the community may have been gravely hampered by frivolous litigation that unduly consumes the time of the judiciary and hinders a proper determination of substantial suits. A class of vexatious litigants has appeared who are adept at initially concealing the frivolity of their claims. The judges, however, urge that from their long experience they can usually spot the kind of person who is bringing such a vexatious suit just by the look of him. The legislature, impressed by this judicial testimony, has enacted the hypothetical provision in order to give courts a speedy way to cut off potentially frivolous suits. Surely this would not silence our objections, though the explanation is now offered in a way that seems less arbitrary and has something of the air of a justification. Why exactly would we still object? I think because the provision would still quite fail to meet proper standards for a judicial determination in the sense that it still failed to *express* a good reason for denying or withholding what is being denied or withheld. Thus, when a judge cut off a suit under the statute he would be saying nothing about its frivolity but only that he did not like the look of the plaintiff, and that just will not do as a reason. We are not prepared to trust even our judges enough to allow them to make determinations unsupported by good reasons and to rely on the hope that good reasons lurk in the background. A central plank in our concept of a just legal system is that, though there may be some exceptions, judgments shall generally be supported by an opinion that is a public parade of the reasoning on which the judgment stands. The practical importance of this is to assure us and reassure us that the reasons are not unacceptable, as would be an assertion that the judge does not like the look of the plaintiff.

Nothing about the nature of the political-question doctrine precludes the possibility of the court's parading reasons in an opinion. Even if we accept Professor Bickel's characterization of the process as a prudential one rather than a matter of constitutional interpretation, then it is still perfectly possible to articulate what are felt to be the controlling prudential considerations in the form of an opinion. Hypothetically, the court might in effect say: "The processes of litigation and judicial determination are certainly capable of deciding whether there has been any executive encroachment on the reservation to Congress of the power to declare war, but we think the initiation of such processes is dangerous to the security and stability of the nation when questions about war are involved and we therefore hold that such questions are not within the province of a court's jurisdiction." Articulated heads of prudence of this kind could very well be developed and take their place in a body of constitutional law and practice. Rules and principles that are charged with policy and prudence in this fashion are perfectly familiar in a legal system. The first point that needs to be emphasized, therefore, is that the introduction of the concept of prudence as an underlying theme in the political-question doctrine does not in itself threaten values that we associate with the rule of law.

But suppose the court were rather to say: "Although we might sometimes be willing to decide questions about the alleged encroachment of the executive on powers reserved to Congress, we decline to make any determination in this case because we are of the opinion that the present President is an unbending man who would pay no respect to our judgment if it should go against him." This too could indeed be characterized as a prudential decision, but it would be much more obviously a threat to the rule of law. A general principle of rejecting a certain kind of question because it is the kind of question where a decision by a court would threaten national security may be acceptable, though of course open to criticism; but a declaration of an attitude that may shift from year to year according to the personality of an Executive

Officer is not acceptable at all as a justification for a judicial decision, even if it is a decision not to decide. For we expect courts to decide questions; we do not mind if they tell us that they cannot decide a question because they have no jurisdiction, because under the Constitution such questions are reserved for another branch of government. We can all understand that this is a kind of a decision, an answer that settles the matter and is properly responsive to our question. If such a constitutional interpretation is frankly grounded in prudential reasons, this does not in itself detract from its acceptability. However, a response which may change from case to case according to the personality of the protagonists deeply offends a demand that is part of the fabric of the concept of a just legal system. This is the demand that rules should not be put into abeyance because of the power or lawlessness of the parties to a suit. A general doctrine to the effect that courts ought not make orders that cannot be enforced because of the nature of the prescription contained in the order is perfectly proper; so orders of specific performance are not made in contracts of personal service. But where the prescription is of a kind that, in the ordinary course of things, is seen as proper to be included in a judicial order, then to refuse to do so because of the apprehended lawless power of the defendant would be at once seen as improper.

I do not want to suggest for a moment that the Supreme Court of the United States has indulged in the kind of evasion of decision-making that I have here characterized as improper. But a lack of clarity in the articulation of the political-question doctrine has, I believe, led to two connected areas of obscurity that are very relevant to the debate in which those who contemplate civil disobedience are engaged.

In the first place, it is not easy to assess the weight of precedent contained in a decision that a court will not interfere with a legislative or executive action on the ground that it involves a political question. If general heads of prudence were developed in this area in a body of opinions, lawyers could be just as comfortable as they are with that body of opinions that surrounds the question of when a contract may be void for offense against public policy. But in cases that touch fundamental concerns of many citizens, as in *Mora v. McNamara*, when the lower courts refuse the petitioner without a reasoned opinion, and the Supreme Court simply denies certiorari, we are left without any structure of argument in which to operate for the future. If certiorari had been granted in *Mora*, as the dissenting Justices thought it should have been granted, what would have been the controlling arguments that might have led the majority to hold that interference was improper under the political-question doctrine? Perhaps an argument might have been the Court's inability to enforce any decision that might hold against the executive; or the weakening impact on the political structure of the nation of a challenge by the courts to the executive; or the aspect of national security involved in questions touching on war and military powers; or perhaps some literal interpretation of the Constitution that made no reference to such broad notions of policy. We cannot tell and it is not healthy that we should not be able to tell. This refusal to expatiate, this failure to justify, deprives lawyers and the public of the opportunity to scrutinize and criticize reasons and argument, an opportunity that is most vitally necessary in such a fundamental and sensitive area of decision-making. At worst, the refusal to explain breeds suspicion that the Court shrinks from reasoned justification because of an apprehension of the difficulty of offering a good justification. Those who advocate civil disobedience have, I think, some warrant for saying that a dearth of reasoned opinions on the political-question doctrine in its application to issues that surround the war in Vietnam leaves them without a satisfactory response to their challenge. And by a satisfactory response I do not, of course, mean one that agrees with the petitioner nor one that will enable neat predictions to be made in the future, but only one that presents a reasoned justification for the denial of his claim.

A second source of confusion attends the status of the political-question doctrine. When in our referee example there was a refusal to decide whether a member of the opposing team was offside, the practical result, at least as far as the immediate consequences were concerned, would surely be much the same as if there had been a decision that he was not offside. How would this analogy carry over into the legal issue? Is a decision that a matter involves a political question equivalent to a decision that the challenged actions of the executive are legal? We should remember here that, under Professor Wechsler's view, a decision that a matter involves a political question is a decision in constitutional law that the question is to be decided by the executive or the legislature and not by the courts. It is true that this is not an express declaration that what the legislature or executive has done is legally proper. To say, "We will consider the legality of what has been done and we find it legal," is rather different from saying, "It is not within our jurisdiction to rule on the legality of what has been done." But does this have any implications for the judgment on legality? When a court declares that it has no jurisdiction to decide a question, then is this not a declaration that no power resides in anyone or any institution under any norm of the system to make a finding of illegality? If a court declares that it has no power to make a finding that the executive is under a legal duty to refrain from certain conduct, is this not equivalent to saying that the executive has a legal liberty to engage in that conduct?

The question here is about how a jurist can explain what the court has decided in the context of the whole normative structure of the legal system. It seems to me that, if we adopt Professor Wechsler's view of the political-question doctrine, then we cannot escape the conclusion that a decision by the court under this doctrine that it has no power to make a determination is tantamount to a finding that there is a legal liberty for the legislature or executive to perform the challenged act. The only alternative would be a position in which it was argued that the court's declaration of absence of jurisdiction merely shifted the question of legality to some other forum. But what could that other forum be? If the Supreme Court says it cannot decide whether the President has usurped the reservation to Congress of the power to declare war, then who is to decide it and what significance could legally be attached to any such decision? Congress, of course, might assert that the President has usurped such a power, but if the Court refused to resolve the dispute we could only conclude that in our legal system clashes may occur between President and Congress that cannot be resolved under the norms of the system. We might then be presented with a political choice about taking sides, but not with a legal question for resolution. If the Constitution reserves powers to Congress in such a way that dispute can be envisaged between Congress and the President, and if the Court tells us that it has no power to resolve such disputes, we can only conclude that such provisions in the Constitution are of no more than hortatory significance.

The position is perhaps not so clear under Professor Bickel's way of presenting the matter. Under his formulation the Court in advancing the political-question doctrine may not be saying that it is not within its jurisdiction to rule on the constitutionality of the challenged conduct but rather that, though the matter might be within its jurisdiction, it just does not choose to do so, at any rate at the moment. Professor Bickel appears to argue that this is a useful device in that it refrains from legitimating the actions of the other branch of government so that perhaps it leaves the constitutionality of these actions in abeyance, as it were. At this point we are forced into examining more closely what the real differences are between the positions of Professors Wechsler and Bickel. Courts, as we well know, can change their minds. They have changed their minds in the political-question area as in the celebrated shift of opinion in which they took jurisdiction of legislative reapportionment cases after having seemed to declare earlier that they would not. If we bear this in mind it seems that the difference between Professors Wechsler and Bickel is rather a subtle one and not the great chasm that it might first appear to be. Under Professor Wechsler's view the Court is taken to be saying that it has identified norms of the system that curtail its jurisdiction. Under Professor Bickel's view the Court is taken to be saying that it has identified a norm of the system that confers a discretion upon it to hold its hand from deciding certain questions. The latter view recognizes much more prominently the prospect of the Court's changing its mind and at the same time makes it easier for it to change its mind since it does not commit itself so squarely in a precedential sense. But, our system being what it is, the possibility of a change of mind is still present under Professor Wechsler's position.

Nevertheless, even under Professor Bickel's presentation, the legal liberty of the executive or legislature to perform the challenged act is still established by the decision of the court that the matter involves a political question. There is still no implication that some other forum is designated by the norms of the system for determining the legality of the challenged act. The court's decision that it will not interfere is still in the instant dispute a determination that the court will not act under any norm of the system to declare the challenged act to be illegal. It perhaps encourages the interested parties to believe that the matter may be more hopefully reopened in a similar case in the future than would Professor Wechsler's view but, as we have seen, this is a matter of degree and not one of a vital nature about the normative aspects of the holding.

These perhaps are rather subtle questions for legal philosophers that are not likely to make a great popular impact. It seems to me that some of those who oppose the actions of the executive with respect to the military operations in Vietnam believe that the courts have somehow abdicated their decision-making functions and so have left open the question of the legality of the acts of the executive to private determination by each citizen in his own legal conscience. I have tried to show above that such a view is untenable, but I do think that the courts have been imprudent in failing to give reasoned articulation to support their decisions in this area. Where feelings are high and the moral dilemma is acute, and where a lower federal court has declined intervention on what is essentially a political-question basis, then good sense and prudence might well be thought to demand that the Supreme Court should proffer an opinion on the propriety of the action in the court below instead of merely declining review. To decline review is certainly not to disturb the decision of the court below but neither does it offer it much real sustenance.

Certainly very delicate questions of prudence are here involved. In *Mora v. McNamara* the Supreme Court might have granted certiorari, might have held that the matter was within its jurisdiction, and might have determined that actions of the executive in the military operations in Vietnam were constitutional. It could be argued, however, that this would only further exacerbate the opponents of the policy reflected in those actions. If, on the other hand, the Court had held that the actions of the executive were unconstitutional, it might have precipitated a very grave constitutional crisis. For the executive might well feel that the vital interests of America were so at stake that it must defy the Supreme Court and persist in repeating the acts. No one can foresee the outcome of such a crisis. For these reasons it may well be that the most prudent path that the Supreme Court could take today in connection with questions about the legality of executive actions with respect to military operations in Vietnam would be to declare these to be political questions over which the Court has no jurisdiction. If this response were presented in a reasoned fashion it would be perfectly acceptable. But to deny certiorari, to dismiss suits without a reasoned opinion, has a tendency to arouse suspicion that the Court is simply shrinking from making pronouncements about the basic norms of the system. For those contemplating civil disobedience this can create the impression that they are operating in a limbo of legality. This is a situation fraught with some danger. If courts cannot decide questions about the legality of government action, then they have a public duty to give acceptable legal reasons for their inability to seize the issue. These reasons may quite properly be prudential, but they should be advanced for scrutiny by the profession and the public.

Up to this point I have been talking in terms of legality. We have to add the very important observation that it is quite possible to assert meaningfully, though it would indeed be strange to American ears, that the executive is acting unconstitutionally though not illegally. Suppose the Constitution required the President to report to Congress on the state of the nation twice a year and the President had made no such report for years. Suppose that this issue were somehow raised in the Courts, who declined jurisdiction on the ground that it was a political question. My argument above that this would establish a legal liberty for the President not to report to Congress clearly does not now imply that his failure to report is not a breach of the Constitution. He would be acting unconstitutionally though not illegally. This follows from the observation above that some sections of the Constitution are hortatory. This is not to say, of course, that they are insignificant. The fact that the President is acting unconstitutionally, though not illegally, is a powerful ground for criticizing him and opposing him politically. It would furnish exactly what is most relevant to the debate about civil disobedience, a moral reason for ignoring or disobeying executive orders that could not be declared by the courts to be illegal. In the example above the case would not be marginal, and it would be clear that the President was ignoring a constitutional demand that he should report to Congress. The issues that surround the war in Vietnam, such as the argument that the executive has usurped the power to make war, are of course more arguable. But this is not unfamiliar. We might often be called on in everyday life to debate whether a person has broken a moral obligation. So a man, in the presence of witnesses, may make a solemn promise to his dying father and later it may be in issue whether he has broken the terms of the promise. We would have to debate that in order to know whether there was any foundation for making a moral criticism of his behavior. In an institutional setting the President who violates hortatory provisions of the Constitution is in the same position. His conduct strengthens the moral case for disobeying executive orders that stem from his departure from constitutional demands.

The relevance of the political-question doctrine to civil disobedience is thus crucial. The institutional morality of a legal system such as that of the United States includes the demand that the Constitution should be observed even in cases where legal process is not available. Legal norms that spring out of unconstitutional action are morally tainted even if not legally void. The courts, in rejecting jurisdiction because of the political-question doctrine, may have spoken the last word legally in the instant dispute, but they have only initiated the moral debate.

NOTES

1. A. Cox, "Direct Action, Civil Disobedience, and the Constitution," in *Civil Rights, the Constitution, and the Courts* (Cambridge, Harvard University Press, 1967), pp. 3, 22–23.
2. People v. Ferguson, 134 Cal. App. 41, 24 P.2d 965 (1933); State v. White, 237 Mo. 208, 140 S.W. 896 (1911).
3. 355 U.S. 255 (1957).
4. 369 F.2d 323 (1966), cert. denied, 386 U.S. 972 (1967).
5. Reported as Luftig v. McNamara, 252 F. Supp. 819 (D.D.C. 1966), aff'd, 373 F.2d 664 (D.C. Cir.), cert. denied sub nom., Mora v. McNamara, 389 U.S. 934 (1967).
6. Wechsler, "Towards Neutral Principles of Constitutional Law," 73 *Harv. L. Rev.* (1959), 1, 9.
7. *Id.* at 8.

8. A. Bickel, *The Least Dangerous Branch* (Indianapolis, Bobbs-Merrill, 1962), pp. 125–6.
9. *Id.* at 184.
10. For a comprehensive survey of the merits of the two views, see Scharpf, "Judicial Review and the Political Question: A Functional Analysis," 75 *Yale L.J.* (1966), 517. After the decisions in Baker v. Carr, 369 U.S. 186 (1962), and Powell v. McCormack, No. 20,897 (D.C. Cir., Feb. 28, 1968), it seems that Professor Bickel's presentation best matches the present practice of the courts.
11. H. L. A. Hart, *The Concept of Law* (New York, Oxford University Press, 1961), p. 141.
12. 369 U.S. 186 (1962).
13. *Id.* at 211.

A THEORY OF CIVIL DISOBEDIENCE

Ronald Dworkin

I

Introduction

The literature on civil disobedience seems to me deficient in two respects. The first represents a conceptual block. Lawyers and philosophers have been careful to separate the legal issue of whether the law is valid from the moral issue of whether it should be obeyed. They argue in the alternative: If the law is invalid, then no problem of civil disobedience arises. If the law is valid, then the moral problem is presented of whether it is ever proper to disobey a valid law. The structure of this argument hides the fact that the validity of a law may be in doubt. The dissenters may believe that the law they break is invalid, the officials who judge them may disagree, and both sides may have plausible or colorable arguments for their positions. If so, then the issues are different from what they would be if the law were clearly valid or clearly invalid, and theories designed for these alternatives are irrelevant.

The case of doubtful law is by no means a special or exotic case. On the contrary. In the United States, at least, almost any law that would tempt a significant number of people to dissent would be doubtful—if not clearly invalid—on constitutional grounds. The Constitution makes the essentials of our conventional political morality relevant to the question of validity; any statute that appears to compromise that morality raises constitutional questions, and if the compromise is serious, the constitutional doubts are serious also.

Certainly the constitutional standing of the present draft laws is doubtful. Congress did not declare war in Vietnam; the national interest there may not be great enough to justify risk of life under the due pro-

225

cess clause; the draft as administered discriminates among citizens in a way that might be condemned by the due process and equal protection clauses, taken together; and the law that forbids counselling draft resistance hampers speech on a vital political issue, contrary to the policy behind the first amendment. These doubts are strong enough for dissenters to reasonably believe that the laws are invalid, though I think a majority of lawyers would hold, on balance, that they are not. We need a theory of civil disobedience (if that is the right phrase) that covers this sort of case.

The second deficiency in the literature is a matter of standpoint. Almost all of it speaks to the issue of what a man should do who thinks that a law is immoral. It does not speak to the decision the government must make if someone does break the law out of conscience. When should the government stay its hand and tolerate rather than punish dissent?

The theorists have said little about this, I suppose, because they think there is little to say. They believe that a government can do nothing but enforce its laws once these have been enacted and until they have been repealed. They assume that a citizen who disobeys out of conscience is necessarily pitted against the rest of society. Even when he is justified in breaking the law, the majority is justified, at least according to its own standards, in prosecuting him. Indeed, some of the dissenters themselves assume that punishment is appropriate; they feel almost cheated if they are not prosecuted, because this implies that they have been evasive or clandestine, or that the community has not taken note of their act.

These two gaps in the literature are connected. The case that the government should stay its hand is obviously stronger when it is arguable that the law is invalid, and the failure to make that case may be traced to the traditional structure of argument that focuses on the rare occasion when it is not. I shall therefore attempt to answer this question: If it is unclear whether a criminal law is constitutional, in the sense that a reasonable lawyer might think it is not, and someone breaks that law out of conscience, how should the state respond? In Section II I shall argue that the state has a general responsibility of leniency in these circumstances, because our practices encourage men to follow their own judgment when the law is unclear, even though we do not guarantee immunity from punishment if they do. In Section III I shall consider how the state might acquit this responsibility in the case of draft offenses, consistently with other policies it thinks it ought to pursue. I do not mean to suggest that a man should never disobey when the law is clear, or that the state should always punish him when he does. But those are the special cases, and I am anxious to avoid the limitations that preoccupation with these cases has imposed.

II

The Responsibility of Leniency

There are practical reasons for not prosecuting conscientious dissenters. These men are rarely enemies of the state; they are often among its most loyal and dedicated citizens. Jailing them solidifies their alienation, and the alienation of many who are thereby deterred.

What objection could there be to tolerating rather than prosecuting dissent? The most powerful objection, many people think, is that a policy of tolerance would be unfair to the majority of citizens. It would be unfair, so the argument goes, because the bulk of our citizens "play the game," by obeying even those laws that they themselves disapprove or find disadvantageous. If those who will not play the game go unpunished, then they are allowed to secure the benefits of deference to law, without shouldering the burdens. It is no answer to this argument that the system might change so that everyone had the privilege of disobeying laws he believed immoral. The majority wants no such change; the present system will continue, and those who do not want to keep its rules should quit the community.

This argument is limited, however, by the hidden assumption I mentioned, the assumption that the law is clear. We cannot apply the argument to cases like the present draft until we confront this further question: What should a citizen do when the law is unclear, and he thinks it allows what others think it does not? I do not mean to ask, of course, what it is *legally* proper for him to do, or what his *legal* rights are; that would be begging the question, because the answer depends upon whether he is right or they are right. I mean to ask what his proper course is as a citizen, what we would consider to be "playing the game."

There is no consensus on this question—no obvious answer on which most citizens would readily agree—and that fact is itself significant. If we examine our legal institutions and practices, however, we may find support for one or another position. I shall proceed by setting out three possible answers, and then attempt to show which of these best fits our practices and expectations. The three possibilities I want to consider are these:

(1) If the law is doubtful and it is therefore unclear whether it permits someone to do what he wants, he should assume the worst and should act on the assumption that it does not.

(2) If the law is doubtful, he may follow his own judgment; that is, he may do what he wants if he believes that the case that the law permits this is stronger than the case that it does not. But he may follow his own judgment only until an authoritative institution, such as a court, decides the other way, in a case involving him or someone else. Once an institutional decision has been reached, he must abide by that decision, even though he thinks that it was wrong. (There are, in theory, many subdivisions of this second possibility. We might say that the individual's choice is foreclosed by the contrary decision of any court, including the lowest court in the system if the case is not appealed. Or we may require a decision of some particular court or institution. I shall discuss this second possibility in its most liberal form, namely that the individual is free to follow his own judgment until a contrary decision of the highest court competent to pass on the issue, which in the case of constitutional issues involved in draft refusal, is the United States Supreme Court.)

(3) If the law is doubtful, he may follow his own judgment even after a contrary decision by the highest competent court. Of course, he must take the contrary decision of any court into account in making his judgment of what the law requires. Otherwise the judgment would not be an honest or reasonable one, because the doctrine of precedent, which is an established part of our legal system, has the effect of allowing the decisions of courts, and particularly high appellate courts, to *change* the law. Suppose, for example, that a taxpayer believes that he is not required to pay tax on certain forms of income. If the Supreme Court decides to the contrary, he might, taking into account the practice of according great weight to the decisions of the Supreme Court on tax matters, decide that the Court's decision has itself tipped the balance, and that the law now requires him to pay the tax.

Someone might think that this qualification erases the difference between the third and the second models, but it does not. The doctrine of precedent gives varying weights to the decisions of different courts, and especially great weight to the decisions of the Supreme Court, but it does not make the decision of any court conclusive. It is distinctly possible that even after a contrary decision an individual may still reasonably believe that the law is on his side. This is especially likely in the fields of constitutional law that are relevant to civil disobedience. The Supreme Court has shown itself more likely, in this area than in any other, to overrule its past decisions if it is persuaded that these have unduly limited personal or political rights.

We do not follow the doctrine, in other words, that the Constitution is always what the Supreme Court says it is. Oliver Wendell

Holmes followed no such rule in his famous dissent in the *Gitlow* case. A few years before, in *Abrams*, he had lost his battle to persuade the Court that the First Amendment protected an anarchist who had been urging general strikes against the government. A similar issue was presented in *Gitlow*, and Holmes once again went into dissent. "It is true," he said, "that in my opinion this criterion was departed from in [Abrams] but the convictions that I expressed in that case are too deep for it to be possible for me as yet to believe that it . . . settled the law." Holmes voted to acquit Gitlow on the ground that what Gitlow had done was not criminal, even though the Court had recently held that it was.

Here, then, are three models we might choose in attempting to specify how a dissenter should behave. Other models are possible, of course, but these three may serve as paradigms.

I think it plain that we do not follow the first of these paradigms, that is, that we do not expect citizens to assume the worst. If no court has decided the issue, and a man thinks that the case that the law allows him to do what he wants is better than the case that it does not, we think it perfectly proper for him to follow his own judgment. It is worth pausing a moment to consider what society would lose if it did follow the first paradigm or, to put the matter the other way, what society gains from the fact that people follow their own judgment in cases like this.

When the law is uncertain, in the sense that the lawyers can reasonably disagree on what a court ought to decide, this is generally because different legal principles and policies collide and it is unclear what the best accommodation of these conflicting legal principles and policies would be. Our practice, in which different parties are encouraged to pursue their own understanding, provides a means for testing hypotheses that are relevant to this issue. If the question is whether a particular rule would have certain undesirable consequences, or whether these consequences would have limited or broad ramifications, then it is useful, before the issue is decided, to have the experience that is provided if some people proceed on that rule. If the question is whether a particular solution would offend principles of justice or fair play deeply respected by the community, or how grave the offense to these principles would be, it is useful, again, to test the community's response on an experimental basis.

If the first paradigm were followed, we would lose the advantages of these tests. The law would suffer, particularly if this paradigm were applied to constitutional issues. When it is doubtful whether a statute, particularly a criminal statute, is constitutional, the doubt can often be traced to the fact that the statute strikes some people as being unfair or unjust, because it infringes some principle of liberty or justice or fairness which they take to be built into the Constitution. If our practice were that whenever a law is doubtful on these grounds one must act as if it were valid, then the chief vehicle we have for challenging the law on moral grounds would be lost, and over time the law we obeyed would certainly become less fair and just, and the liberty of our citizens would certainly be diminished.

We would lose almost as much if we used a variation of the first paradigm, that a citizen must assume the worst unless he can anticipate that the courts will agree with his view of the law. If everyone deferred to his guess of what the courts would do, society and its law would be poorer. Our assumption in rejecting the first paradigm was that the record a citizen makes in following his own judgment, together with the arguments he makes supporting that judgment when he has the chance, are helpful in forging the best judicial decision. This remains true even when, at the time the citizen acts, the odds are against his success in court. We must remember, too, that the value of the citizen's example is not exhausted once the decision has been made. Our practices require that the decision be criticized by the profession and the schools, and the record of dissent may be invaluable here.

Of course a man must consider what the courts will do when he decides whether it would be *prudent* to follow his own judgment. But it is essential that we separate the calculation of prudence from the question of what, as a good citizen, he is entitled to do. We are investigating how society ought to treat him when its courts believe that he judged wrong, and for that reason we are asking what he is entitled to do when his judgment differs from others. We will beg the question if we assume that what he may properly do depends on his guess as to how society will treat him.

We must also reject the second paradigm, that if the law is unclear a citizen may properly follow his own judgment until the highest court has ruled that he is wrong. It fails to take into account the fact that any court, including the Supreme Court, may overrule itself. In almost every case, when a court does reverse its prior decision, it applies its new decision retroactively. If the Court should hold a particular criminal law unconstitutional, for example, it would almost certainly extend its decision backwards and hold that citizens who had infringed that law before the new decision were not guilty of any crime.

In 1940 the Supreme Court decided that a West Virginia law requiring students to salute the flag was constitutional. In 1943 it reversed itself, and decided that such a statute was unconstitutional after all. What was the duty, as citizens, of those people who in 1941 and 1942 objected to saluting the flag on grounds of conscience, and thought that the Supreme Court's 1940 decision was wrong? We can hardly say that their duty was to follow the first decision. They believed that saluting the flag was unconscionable, and they believed, reasonably, that no law required them to do so. The Supreme Court later decided that in this they were right. Some will say that they should have obeyed the Court's first decision, meanwhile working in the legislatures to have the law repealed, and in the courts to find some way to challenge the law again without actually violating it.

That would be, perhaps, a plausible recommendation if conscience were not involved, because it would then be arguable that the gain in orderly procedure was worth the personal sacrifice of patience. But conscience was involved, and if the dissenters had obeyed the law while biding their time, they would have suffered the irreparable injury of having done what their consciences forbad them to do. It is one thing to say that an individual must sometimes violate his conscience when he knows that the law commands him to do it. It is quite another to say that he must violate his conscience even when he believes that the law does not require it, because it would inconvenience his fellow citizens if he took the most direct, and perhaps the only, method of attempting to show that he is right and they are wrong.

Since a court may overrule itself, then those same reasons we listed for rejecting the first paradigm count against the second as well. If we do not have the pressure of dissent from those who think that the law has been misunderstood, we will not get the most effective presentation of the view that it has been. We will not have a dramatic statement of the degree to which the earlier decision coerces conscience, a demonstration that is surely pertinent to the question of whether the first decision was right. We will increase the chance of being governed by rules that offend the principles we claim to serve.

These considerations force us, I think, from the second paradigm, but some will want to substitute a variation of it. They will argue that once the Supreme Court has decided that a criminal law is valid, then citizens have a duty to abide by that decision until they have a reasonable belief, not merely that the decision is bad law, but that the Supreme Court is likely to overrule it. Under this view the West Virginia dissenters who refused to salute the flag in 1942 were acting properly, because they might reasonably anticipate that the Supreme Court would change its mind. But if the Supreme Court were to hold the draft laws constitutional, it would be improper to continue to challenge these laws, because there would be no great likelihood that the Court would soon change its mind.

The same objections apply to this suggestion as applied to the comparable variation of the first paradigm. Once we say that a citizen may properly follow his own judgment of the law, in spite of his judgment that the courts will probably find against him, there is no reason why he should act differently because a contrary decision is already on the books.

I conclude that the third paradigm, or something close to it, is the fairest statement of a man's social duty in our community. A citizen's allegiance is to the law, not to any particular person's view of what the law is, and he does not behave improperly or unfairly so long as he proceeds on his own considered and reasonable view of what the law requires.

Let me repeat that this is not the same as saying that an individual may disregard what the courts have said in deciding what to do. The doctrine of precedent lies near the core of our legal system, and no one is making a reasonable effort to follow the law unless he grants courts the general power to alter it by their decisions. But this aspect of the doctrine of precedent varies in its force, as I said, and someone who believes that a Supreme Court decision wrongly infringed fundamental personal rights need not regard that decision as conclusive.

One large question remains before we can apply these observations to the problems of civil disobedience. I have been talking about the case of a man who believes that the law is not what other people think, or what the courts have held. This description may fit some of those who disobey statutes out of conscience, but it does not fit most of them. The bulk of dissenters are not lawyers or political philosophers; they believe the law contradicts our legal ideals, but they may not have considered whether it is invalid for that reason. Of what relevance to their situation, then, is the proposition that one may properly follow one's own view of the law?

To answer this, I shall have to return to a theme I mentioned at the outset. Our Constitution injects an extraordinary, and increasing, portion of our political morality into the issue of whether a law is valid. Anyone who believes that a law is profoundly immoral, on the ground that it is grossly unfair or unjust to some of our citizens, would be almost certain to think it unconstitutional if he understood the present reach of the due process and equal protection clauses. (I use this strong language—"profoundly immoral" and "grossly unfair"—because these clauses are complex, and someone who thought a law mildly unfair might hold this outweighed by other considerations and therefore believe the law valid.)

Let me list some of the grounds on which the dissenters believe that the present draft is immoral. They believe that the United States has no legitimate interest at stake in Vietnam, certainly no interest large enough to justify forcing immense personal sacrifice upon a selected segment of our population. They believe that if an army is to be raised to fight that war, it is immoral to raise it by a draft that defers or exempts college students, and thus discriminates against the economically underprivileged. They believe that there is no morally relevant difference between objection to all wars on religious grounds, and objection to a particular war on moral grounds, and that the draft, by making this distinction, implies that those who hold the second view are less worthy of the government's respect than those who hold the first. They believe that the law that makes it a crime to counsel draft resistance stifles those who oppose the war, because it is morally impossible to argue, with sincerity and passion, that the war is profoundly immoral, and stop short of encouraging and assisting those who refuse to fight it. Not everyone who holds the draft laws immoral believes all of this, but most of them believe at least some of it.

Lawyers will recognize, in these moral positions, arguments that the laws in question are violations of due process, of equal protection, and of freedom of speech. The statement that the majority of draft dissenters believe they are breaking the law therefore needs qualification. They hold beliefs that, if true, very strongly support the view that the law is on their side; the fact that they have not reached that further conclusion is traceable, in at least most cases, to their lack of legal sophistication. If we believe that people who follow their own judgment of the law are acting properly, it would seem wrong not to extend that view to those dissenters whose judgments come to the same thing. No part of the case that I made for the third paradigm would entitle us to distinguish them from their more knowledgeable colleagues.

We might draw these tentative conclusions from the argument so far: When the law is uncertain, in the sense that a plausible case can be made on both sides, then a citizen who follows his own judgment is not behaving unfairly. That privilege extends to those who believe that the law is clear, but also believe that it is deeply immoral because grossly unfair to some citizens. The argument we began by considering—that it would be unfair to tolerate draft dissenters because they are not "playing the game" of American society—is therefore invalid. On the contrary, this feature of our practices places on our government an affirmative responsibility of leniency, because if we believe that those who follow their own views are behaving properly, we ought to protect them.

It does not follow that we are never justified in prosecuting and punishing dissenters. Obviously we could not follow the simple practice of acquitting everyone who thinks the law is on his side. But we can follow the more complex practice of attempting to accommodate those whose views of the law are plausible, even though our officials think they are wrong, so long as we can do this without great damage to other policies.

In Section III, I shall describe the techniques available for accommodating dissent, and the limits of these techniques. Before turning to these practical questions, however, I want to consider a philosophical objection to my argument so far.

Someone will say that I think that law is a "brooding omnipresence in the sky." I spoke of people making judgments about what the law requires even in cases in which the law is unclear and undemonstrable. I spoke of cases in which a man might think that the law requires one thing even though the Supreme Court has said that it requires another, even when it was not likely that the Supreme Court would soon change its mind. I will therefore be charged with the view that there is always a "right answer" to a legal problem, to be found in natural law, or locked up in some transcendental strongbox.

Of course the strongbox of law is nonsense. When I say that people hold views on the law when the law is doubtful, and that these views are not merely predictions of what the courts will hold, I intend no such metaphysics. I mean only to summarize as accurately as I can a host of the practices that are part of our legal process.

We make claims of legal right and duty, even when we know these are not demonstrable, and we support these with arguments even when we know that these arguments will not appeal to everyone. We make these arguments to each other, in the professional journals and the classroom, and we make them to courts. We respond to these arguments, when others make them, by judging them good or bad or mediocre. In so doing we assume that some arguments for a given doubtful position are better than others, and that the case on one side of a doubtful proposition may be stronger than the case on the other, which is what I take a claim of law in a doubtful case to mean. We distinguish, without too much difficulty, between these arguments and predictions of what the courts will decide.

These practices are poorly represented by the theory that judgments of law on doubtful issues are nonsense, or are merely predictions of what the courts will do. Those who hold these theories cannot mean to deny the fact of these practices; perhaps they mean that these practices are not sensible, because they are based on suppositions that do not hold, or for some other reason. But this makes their objection mysterious, because they never specify what they take the purposes underlying the practices to be, and unless these are specified, one cannot decide whether the practices are sensible. I understand the policies behind the practices to be those I described earlier, having to do with the development and testing of the law through experimentation and through the adversary process. We pursue these policies by inviting our citizens to make determinations about the strength and weaknesses of legal arguments for themselves, or through their own counsel, and to act on these judgments, though we qualify that permission by the limited threat that they may suffer if the courts do not agree. Our success depends on whether there is sufficient agreement within the community on what counts as a good or bad argument so that, although different people will reach different judgments, these differences will be neither so profound nor so frequent as to make the system unworkable, or overly dangerous for those who do act on their own lights. I believe there is sufficient agreement on criteria of argument to avoid these traps, although it remains one of the outstanding tasks of legal philosophy to exhibit and clarify these criteria. In any event, the practices I have described have not yet been shown to be misguided, and we may therefore properly take them into account in determining whether it is just and fair to be lenient to those who break what others think is the law.

III

How Should the State Respond?

In the remaining section of this paper I want to consider the important practical question I mentioned a moment ago. Granted that the government has what I called a responsibility of leniency to those who break the law out of conscience, what steps should it take to acquit that responsibility? I shall make some suggestions, using the draft cases as examples. I cannot explore any of these in detail; my purpose is rather to indicate the variety of techniques available.

The legislature can repeal or amend the statute that purports to make the dissenter's act a crime. Every program our legislature adopts is a medley of policies and restraining principles. We accept loss of efficiency in crime detection and urban renewal, for example, so that we can respect the rights of accused criminals and compensate property owners for their damages. A legislature may properly defer to its responsibility of leniency, therefore, by adjusting or compromising its other policies. The relevant questions are these: What means can be found for maximizing tolerance while minimizing impact on policy? How strong is the responsibility of leniency in this case, that is, how deeply is the conscience of the minority involved, and how strong the case that the law is invalid after all? How important is the policy in question? Is the interference that a compromise would cause too great a price to pay? These questions are no doubt too simple, but they suggest the nerve of the choices that must be made.

They argue, I think, for repeal of the law that makes it a crime to counsel draft resistance or aid draft resisters. If those who want to counsel draft resistance are given free reign, the number who will resist induction may increase, but not, I think, significantly beyond the number who would resist in any event. If I am wrong, then the fact of this residual discontent is of importance to policy makers, and it ought not to be hidden under a ban on speech. Conscience is deeply involved—it is hard to believe that many who counsel resistance do so on any other grounds. The case is strong that the laws that make counselling a crime are unconstitutional; even those who do not find the case persuasive will admit that its arguments are substantial.

If we turn to draft resistance itself, however, the state's response becomes more problematical. Those who believe that the war in Vietnam is itself a grotesque blunder will favor any change in the law that makes peace more likely. But if we stick to the standpoint of those who favor the war, then we must admit that a policy that continues the draft but wholly exempts dissenters would be unwise. The responsibility of leniency supports two alternatives that have been mentioned, however: the volunteer army, and an expanded conscientious objector category that includes those who find this war immoral. There is something to be said against both of these proposals, but once we recognize the principle that requires respect for dissent, that may tip the balance in their favor.

If Congress does not amend its laws to accommodate dissenters, the executive branch of government may respond by exercising its discretion not to prosecute. Many non-lawyers are unaware of the practice that lawyers call prosecutorial discretion. Under that practice, it falls to certain public officials (the Justice Department or the District Attorney, for example), to decide whether to prosecute someone believed guilty of a crime. Practice varies from jurisdiction to jurisdiction; some prosecutors pay more and others less attention to such factors as whether the accused is young, inexperienced, or ignorant, what damage he caused, the likelihood of his reforming without correction, and so forth.

I do not suggest that prosecutors ought to exercise this discretion in favor of anyone who acts out of conscience. If failing to prosecute would jeopardize what the law recognizes as the moral rights of other citizens, that is a strong argument for prosecution. The law may be wrong, but the government must act on the assumption that it is not, and the force of this assumption can be shown by an example. There are many sincere and ardent segregationists: their view is that the civil rights laws and decisions are unconstitutional, because they compromise principles of local government and of freedom of association, and this is a colorable, though not a persuasive, view. But if we tolerate the man who blocks the school-house door, then we violate the rights of the school-girl he blocks. The nation has decided that she has the right to enter and it must act consistently upon this confrontation.

The draft laws, however, do not rest on a presumption of underlying moral rights. A great deal of flexibility and discretion is built into the draft: no one is entitled to have his draft board classify others in particular ways, or to have the army use any particular system for assigning men to dangerous posts once drafted.

If there is no question of jeopardizing legal rights, then the decision whether to prosecute a dissenter must rest on practical considerations similar to those that the legislator had to face. The prosecutor has much less flexibility, of course. His is a yes-or-no decision; he cannot accommodate conflicting policies through such devices as a volunteer army or alternative service. Still, he is able to weigh these conflicting policies, and he must make the limited choices he has in the light of his judgments. He must weigh the long-term impact of rending the society, and the strength of the responsibility for leniency, against the damage to the policies represented by the law.

These factors suggest that those who counsel resistance should not be prosecuted, provided, of course, that the means they use do not encourage violence or otherwise trespass on the rights of others. The calculation is more complicated in the case of those who refuse induction when drafted. The crucial question is whether a failure to prosecute will lead to wholesale refusals to serve. It may not, for there are social pressures, including the threat of career disadvantages, that would operate to force many young Americans to serve if drafted, even if they knew they would not go to jail if they refused. If the number would not much increase, then the state should leave the dissenters alone, and I see no great harm in delaying any prosecution until the effect of that policy becomes clearer. If the number of those who refuse induction turns out to be large, this would argue for prosecution. But it would also make the problem academic, because if there is sufficient dissent to bring us to that pass, we will not be able to pursue our policy in any event.

Perhaps these recommendations of prosecutorial discretion are surprising. It goes against our traditions to leave crime unpunished. But if discretion not to prosecute is ever proper, and if I am right that we owe leniency to those who break doubtful laws on grounds of conscience, I cannot see why that discretion is not appropriate here.

There is a trace of paradox in the suggestion, however. I argued earlier that when the law is unclear citizens have the right to follow their own judgment, partly on the ground that this practice helps shape issues for adjudication; now I propose a course that eliminates or postpones adjudication. But the contradiction is only apparent. It does not follow from the fact that a practice facilitates adjudication, and renders it more useful in developing the law, that a trial should follow whenever citizens appeal to that practice. It remains an open question whether, in the particular case, the issues are ripe for adjudication, and whether adjudication would settle these issues in a manner that would decrease the chance, or remove the grounds, for further dissent.

In the draft cases, the answer to these questions is negative. There is considerable ambivalence about the war, and considerable uncertainty and ignorance about the scope of the moral issues involved in the draft. It is far from the best time for a court to pass on these issues, and tolerating dissent for a time is one way of allowing the debate to continue until it has produced something clearer. It is plain, moreover, that an adjudication of the constitutional issues now will not settle the law. Those who have doubts that the draft is constitutional will have the same doubts even if the Supreme Court says that it is, and our practices of precedent, as Holmes said, will encourage them to hold these doubts. Certainly this is so if the Supreme Court appeals to the "political question" doctrine, and refuses to pass on the constitutional issues at all. Under this waning but still powerful doctrine the Court denies its jurisdiction to consider matters seriously affecting, for example, foreign and defense policy, and it seems likely that the court would appeal to that doctrine in the draft cases.

Suppose, finally, that Congress refuses to amend its statutes to accommodate dissenters, and that the prosecutor refuses his discretion in their behalf. This, after all, is what has and probably will happen. What ought the Court to do?

This is a complex question, and I shall deal with it too shortly. If the acts of dissent occur before the Supreme Court has held the laws valid, or before it has ruled that the political question doctrine applies, then the courts should acquit. The Supreme Court has often reversed convictions on the ground that the criminal law in question is too vague, and there seems little difference in principle between a criminal law whose terms are vague and a criminal law whose terms are precise, but whose constitutionality is in doubt.

If the acts of dissent occur after the Supreme Court has ruled, then acquittal on the ground of vagueness is no longer appropriate. The Court's decision will not have settled the law, but the Court will have done all that it believes can be done to settle it. The courts may still, however, exercise their sentencing discretion, and use light or minimal sentences as a mark of respect for the dissenters' position.

PHILOSOPHY, LAW, AND CIVIL DISOBEDIENCE

Tom C. Clark

The *Acts* XVII, 18, records a statement of which perhaps each of you is reminded as I appear before you tonight. It relates: "Then certain philosophers of the Epicureans, and of the Stoics, encountered a speaker. And some said: 'What will this babbler say?' " First, let me say that though I have founded a school, I am no philosopher. Nor have I made any imaginary laws for imaginary commonwealths, as Francis Bacon used to say philosophers did; but I do know less and less about more and more, as some philosophers do. For example, I do know: Philosophy is not only the law of life; it is the life of law. As Mr. Justice Cardozo said:

Implicit in every decision where the question, so to speak, at large, is a philosophy of the origin and aim of law, a philosophy which, however veiled, is in truth the final arbiter. It accepts one set of arguments, modifies another, rejects a third, standing ever in reserve as a court of ultimate appeal. Often the philosophy is ill coordinated and fragmentary. Its empire is not always suspected even by its subjects. Neither lawyer nor judge, pressing forward along one line or retreating along another, is conscious at all times that it is philosophy which is impelling him to the front or driving him to the rear. None the less the good is there. If we cannot escape the Furies, we shall do well to understand them.[1]

Frankly, we have neither escaped the Furies nor understood them. Most lawyers think of philosphy as "dwelling in the clouds," and mostly on cloud nine.[2] But both philosophy and law are deeply concerned with the study of ultimates of which Cardozo said, "there is little that is profitable in the study of anything else." [3] Truthfulness is an ultimate aim of law, and justice is but truth in action. To stand the test of truth an idea must not only have proper content but entail practical consequences and useful results. The law distrusts the nebulous. Rather than discoursing on abstractions, it deals with the concrete.

From the ideas of jurisprudential thinkers, the action of lawgivers and jurists and the activity of practitioners there have evolved legal philosophies, theories, and systems. This is because law is a human contrivance; men are of many minds, of many ends, and of many countries. Whether or not men count in philosophy, theory, or jurisprudence found in the books they count powerfully in the law in action. Therefore, juridical science must be multiform to fit the varying needs of multifarious peoples. In this manner it has grown up over the centuries, mirroring the conscience of the peoples which it governs. On the whole, law changes slowly, depending upon whether its activists prevent change, hasten it, or cushion the fall of the system. But law keeps rolling along perhaps changing from one school of thought to another, but in any event gaining its strength from its sister sciences as well as from its own sources, its assumptions, its experiences, its accommodations, its aims, or its necessities. As Dean Pound often said, "the exigencies of justice" have written many new chapters in jurisprudence despite the adage that "necessity knows no law."

This is not to say that the law has grown in terms of insularity. History shows us that there is just as truly a world commerce in juristic ideas as there is in goods. This exchange in the concepts of jurisprudence, this dialogue of ideas and conclusions about the purposes and background of law and its place in governing, and this diffusion of the methodology of effective justice knows no frontiers on land or sea. It has been borne from generation to generation, and from nation to nation by many ways and various means. By such processes throughout the centuries many of the legal theories, philosophies, and systems have had their origin and development. The speculations of a Kant or a Hegel about right and truth have from book to book and mouth to mouth influenced legislation, adjudication, legal theories, philosophies, and systems throughout the world. As a result, the grist of many a legal system's mill has been blended with much diverse jurisprudential thought. For example, the deadening effect of the teaching that law is found, but never made, may well be paired with the thought that law must grow to meet the expanding social needs of an explosive society. Even *stare decisis*, which Dr. Wigmore characterized as "an unreal fetish—the government of the living by the dead, as Herbert Spencer has called it," may find itself blended with Thomas Jefferson's philosophy that "the earth belongs in usufruct to the living; . . . the dead have neither rights nor power over it."

This is not to say that we have reached the point in time where judges of different national states can sit in exchange and participate in the disposition of cases in their respective jurisdictions. This proposal was advanced a few days ago by a distinguished Indian trial judge. From a philosophical standpoint it may have merit. Perhaps the exchange would result in the tempering of justice, the widening of the law's horizons at least for some national states. Certainly it would promote better judicial relations. As in the case of Selden's doctrine of the unity of law, some good may come by its recognition. If nothing else, it would bring world renown to the rule of law and through state sanctions perhaps bring greater respect to human dignity and individual freedom. But as distinguished as Selden was and as Americanized as was his experience, his articulated doctrine just does not wash in our nationalistic world. Aside from analytical considerations, it is clear that while during this century more and more national legal systems have been patterned from the American plan, the tendency is toward proliferation. Indeed, there are almost as many systems today as there are countries, and few, if any, would be willing to embrace Selden's syllogism. In fact, the United States has again and again negated the acceptance of such a theory through the Congress.

The pluralistic doctrine that laws belong solely to their own system and that each nation's judicature makes up its own peculiar disciplines is as American as apple pie. Our legal system is individuated not only by the principle of judicial review, the federal-state relationship, and the constitutional requirement of Article VI, cl. 2, that all treaties made under the authority of the United States are the supreme law of the land; but it is distinguished by a philosophy unknown to others, such as separation of church and state, etc. Other structures have differing identifying characteristics that readily afford criteria for determining to which system laws belong, i.e., civil law as opposed to common law, etc.

Moreover, the Kelsen doctrine is opposed to common sense. Even though a country adopted another's system *in toto*, it does not follow that the system as administered in the adopting state would be a part of the country's system from which it was borrowed. It is not what is written in the books that makes law; it is what is enforced on the countryside. The country of adoption alone could enforce the adopted system which necessarily makes it its own. While there are isolated examples to the contrary, international law *per se* imposes no general obligation on the individual citizen of a national state. The "completion relationship," as identified by Mr. Hart, is in my view state, not international, action. It was Kant who said: "So act, that thy rule of conduct might be adopted as a law by all rational beings." But even if such a norm was universally adopted and assuming, but not agreeing, that there was a logical necessity that simultaneously valid norms belong to the same system, still that would not necessarily be true. The practical and realistic approach would be that the norm belongs in each of the respective legal systems of the adopting states.

In any event, despite its laudable purpose to soften conflicts between state and international law, I submit that the recognition of Selden's doctrine, in the light of the stuff of what human beings are constituted in our world, would cause more heat than it would give light.

Let us now pass from the discussion of the unity of law to the disunity of people—civil disobedience. Raghovan Iyer, a contemporary student of Gandhi in his "an occasional paper" on civil disobedience for the Center for the Study of Democratic Institutions, 1966, referring to his experience in the field, said:

Broadly, we might say that there are two familiar types of infuriating people. One is the moralist; the other is the legalist. The moralist is infuriating when he wants to raise every single issue, however local and specific, to the status of an eternal principle; the legalist is infuriating when he wants to reduce an important matter of moral principle involving basic human rights and human dignity to mere formalism or sheer expediency.[4]

It is well for us to first get oriented. In my view civil disobedience necessarily involves legal and moral considerations. It has legal aspects because it openly dishonors law, and it deals in morals because it has to do with personal or collective passion. Any theory that interprets the problems of civil disobedience into traditional norms of law and order must be based on both law and morals.

At the outset it is well to say that no one denies the right of any person to dissent—to differ with the government, or to petition for a redress of grievances, or to express his views in speech or by press or in assembly. But disobedience is a far cry from dissent; it involves a deliberate and punishable breach of a legal duty. It matters not that the disobedient is passive in his conduct; while that may go to the punishment, it bears not on the breach. Civil disobedience does not arise from the belief in the immorality of a relevant governmental policy unless it is coupled with the disobedient's conscious choice to violate a law. If he refuses to obey because he verily believes the law unconstitutional—which he has a right to do—then he is not in civil disobedience until the law is finally declared valid and he thereafter continues his defiance. This distinguishes challenges to the validity of a law as a test case from disobedience to a law on moral or conscientious grounds that are personal to the disobedient.

Throughout history many people have contended that man has a right to disobey any law to which he is conscientiously opposed. A well-known American remonstrance—and the first against governmental interference with the liberty of conscience—was issued by the people of Flushing in 1657 and, being addressed to the Governor, read:

You have been pleased to send up unto us a certain prohibition or command that we should not receive or entertain any of those people called Quakers because they are supposed to be by some, seducers of the people. . . .
[O]ur desire is not to offend one of his little ones. . . . Therefore if any of these peoples come in love unto us, we cannot in conscience lay violent hands upon them, but give them free egresse and regresse unto our Town, and houses, as God shall persuade our consciences.[5]

To theologians conscience is the exercise of a man's judgment as to the morality of an action, such as a judgment that the Viet Nam conflict is immoral. Conscience can be either right or wrong. But, it is said, man is justified in following his conscience even when it is erroneous, if he has no authoritative information to the contrary. Some extrinsic norms for judging whether an action is morally obligatory are recognized, but theologians are not agreed upon them even among themselves, for example, the confusion over contraceptives, the use of nuclear weapons, the performance of abortion, etc. Those supporting the conscience theory assert that the state must respect any reasonable claim of conscience. However, the state may require evidence of circumstances beyond the mere assertion that a law conflicts with conscience. The resulting problem of proof admittedly has its difficulties just as in conscientious objector cases under the draft law. But since the state has the obligation and duty to defend its citizens against foreign and domestic enemies, it is conceded that it has the right to reject the claim. The same dictates of conscience, according to the theory, also extend to the unjust exercise of jurisdiction under an otherwise just law, i.e., the action in Viet Nam is immoral and unjust; therefore, the draft law may not be utilized to service it. Likewise, court sentences and military commands are included within the *verboten*. The right to disobey *just* laws, commands, sentences, etc., however, would be outside of its scope. The civil disobedient in those cases must claim that the law is unconstitutional; a situation to which we have already adverted. In sum, a disobedient may claim the right to disobey on two independent grounds, i.e., conscience and constitutional illegality. Let me say, however, that before one embarks on the nullification of any law he must be ready to pay the penalty. And he must appreciate that his judgment cannot be purely personal, for in our society it inevitably has grave consequences on others. Disobedience should, therefore, be carefully, prayerfully, and only as a last resort embraced.

The papers on law and philosophy raise many questions—both legal and philosophical—which, for the purposes of discussion, I narrow to the following: Whether one motivated by a conflict of conscience may be justified in not obeying a law, and, if not, in the event of a finding of guilt, should his moral motivation be taken into consideration on sentence? Next, would a sincere belief that a law was unconstitutional warrant a breach of it? Professor Hughes seems to answer all three questions in the affirmative but places four "restrictions" on the latter, i.e., was the purpose to demonstrate unconstitutionality rather than disobedience; was the constitutional doubt legitimate; was there another method open to test unconstitutionality; was the disobedience non-violent? The draft and the Viet Nam conflict seem to furnish the basis of the dissertations. The political question issue involved in the recent denial of *Mora* v. *McNamara* by the Court is the "smoldering volcano" to which Professor Hughes gives emphasis. Assuming *arguendo* that the Court did not base its denial in *Mora* on a resolution of the constitutional question, fault is found with the 40-year-old certiorari system of the Court, which recognizes the exercise of the individual discretion of the Justices to deny a petition for certiorari unless four Justices vote to grant it.

On the merits, Professor Dworkin takes a more positive position. He says: "In the United States at least, almost any law that would tempt a significant number of people to dissent would be doubtful—if not clearly invalid—on constitutional grounds." He reasons that the "essentials of our political morality" are written into the Constitution, and "any statute that appears to compromise that morality raises constitutional questions." From this he proceeds to find the validity of the draft laws doubtful and concludes that one who believes the law immoral may, therefore, follow his own conscience as to obedience, "even after a contrary decision by the highest competent court." I, of course, disagree with all of this. I find nothing in the First Amendment or, for that matter, any clause of the Constitution, that supports it. I say that such a doctrine would promote sheer anarchy. The specific burden of Professor Dworkin's paper is, if it is unclear whether a criminal law is constitutional and someone breaks it out of conscience, how should the state respond? He suggests that the government not prosecute on the basis of the exercise of the "prosecutor's discretion." This would include, in addition to the civil disobedient, those who counsel resistance, both on the basis "that the laws that make counselling a crime are unconstitutional" as well as on the "prosecutor's discretion." In any event, Professor Dworkin finds, the prosecution should hold its hand until the effect of such a policy "becomes clearer." If "wholesale refusals to serve" in the armed services result, this would make the problem academic, it is concluded, "because if there is sufficient dissent to bring us to that pass, we will not be able to pursue our policy in any event." Finally, if Congress, the prosecutor, and the Court all decide against the disobedient, then the judge shall "use light or minimal sentences as a mark of respect for the dissenter's position."

First, let us nullify the applicability of the few authorities cited by my learned friends. Reliance is placed on the Nuremberg trials where sanctions were imposed for waging an illegal war and the theory of unjust or immoral action gained some recognition. I submit that it is hardly fair or even helpful to analogize the Viet Nam conflict to the outrages of the Nazis. Moreover, the Nuremberg trials have little, if any, precedential value. They have been repudiated again and again as a valid sanction for the offense of waging illegal war. Indeed, many distinguished jurists deplore such use of *ex post facto* prosecutions on the basis that the judicial process is not a part of the spoils of war.

Next, it is elementary that mistake of law is no defense in a criminal prosecution. The principle of estoppel has at times been applied where a person was advised or required by a government official to commit the act complained of. However, this is not invariably true. One should compare some of the *Madison Oil* case language. Nor has the old rule that ignorance of the law is no excuse been overruled. *Lambert v. California*, 355 U.S. 225 (1957), is no "new doctrine." As Mr. Justice Douglas clearly points out where the obligation of an act is to require one to register, it must be brought home to him and an opportunity afforded to do so. While I heartily agree with the proposition that existing law does not permit one to escape punishment on the mistaken belief that a statute is unconstitutional, I would not whittle down this doctrine as Professor Hughes does in his proposed restrictions which I mentioned before. In my view the disobedient must be ready to suffer the consequences of his illegal act when he takes the law in his own hands. A standard reference is the fine of two million dollars imposed on John L. Lewis and the United Mine Workers back in 1946.

Furthermore, in my view, disobedience directed against the conflict in Viet Nam, on the ground it is immoral, cannot furnish a valid defense to prosecution under the draft law. The inductee may never be sent to Viet Nam and, even should he be, he might never participate in the conflict. The claim is therefore premature as well as improperly taken because it is not aimed at the invalidity of the draft but at the Viet Nam program. To permit such a defense would place all of the various federal social projects in jeopardy at the hands of their detractors.

Professor Hughes takes particular umbrage at the decision in *Mora v. McNamara*, where the Court refused certiorari, without noting any reason. Thousands of cases have been handled by the Court in its identical fashion. For forty years the Court has operated—after full notice to the Congress—on a system that where less than four Justices vote to grant a petition for certiorari, it is summarily denied. He analogizes this to the action of a referee in a football game refusing to pass on a violation of the rules of the game. The judicial process is not a game but it does act under rules. What the good Professor wants in *Mora* is to have five quarters of play, not four. In *Mora* he has already played the full "game" under the rules, namely, he has filed his suit, tried it in the District Court, appealed it to the Court of Appeals, filed his petition for certiorari, and he has lost the game. Why another quarter? The referee in the football game does not give any reasons why the losing team lost the game! And the certiorari system's rule does not require that any reasons for denial be noted. Indeed, during my eighteen years on the Court I never once noted my vote on a petition. The denial of a writ of certiorari has no legal effect, no precedential value. See the opinion of Mr. Justice Frankfurter in *The Baltimore Radio* case. Moreover, traditionally no authority is cited to support the denial of certiorari. However, in Mora's case the Court might well have cited *Johnson* v. *Eisentrager*, 389 U.S. 763 (1950), where the Court said:

Certainly it is not the function of the judiciary to entertain private litigation—even by a citizen—which challenges the legality, the wisdom or the propriety of the Commander-in-Chief in sending our armed forces abroad or to any particular region.

Or the Court might have listed *Baker* v. *Carr*, the apportionment case. Whether the denial was based on *Eisentrager* or *Baker*, or gone off on the political question doctrine, or on discretion, we do not know. But we do know that the Court has not been slow in hearing and deciding political questions where invidious discrimination existed, such as *Baker* v. *Carr* and other cases. But there is more to the case posed here than a political question. It also involves foreign affairs, which are peculiarly left with the Chief Executive under our Constitution, as well as Supreme Court procedures.

It is said that the failure of the Court to act is approval *sub silencio* of the President's action. This, however, is not true. The Court has put its approval on nothing when it denies a certiorari. The denial merely means that the Court is permitting the judgment of the court from whence it came to stand. The judgment of that court becomes the law of the case. And in *Mora* the District Court held that the issue raised was a political question. *Mora*, therefore, has a ruling to that effect in his case. The Supreme Court let that decision stand. It is the law of the case.

Furthermore, this action by the Court does not abdicate its function. It has considered the question fully and has ruled that the decision of the District Court shall stand. Nor does it leave the claim *in limbo* or leave it open to private determination. It leaves it for the President to decide. And if the Congress does not approve his decision, it can quickly stop the action in Viet Nam by cutting off the money. If it does approve, as it has again and again, it can either do nothing, or it can continue to appropriate monies for Viet Nam, or affirm the Tonkin Gulf Resolution. The President would be obliged to act accordingly and has so advised the Congress. This has happened, I understand, over one hundred times before and will, I am sure, happen again and again.

Moreover, if other disobedients feel that *Mora* and like cases of the Court afford them no answer to their dilemma, they are free to bring their own case. *Mora* is no precedent binding upon them; what's more, the Court may find something different in their case and grant their petition and decide their issue. All a disobedient need to do is to corral two additional votes to add to those of Justices Douglas and Stewart. Finally, not wishing to do this, the disobedients can take their case to Congress and avail themselves of that forum to control the action about which they complain.

Professor Hughes asks what kind of legal system we have "when a court has a discretion not to decide cases." That question assumes too much. It sets up a straw man. The Supreme Court decided the case: It decreed that the judgment of the District Court must stand.

Let us now turn to the argument of our learned friend, Professor Dworkin. His basic argument is that some laws are just and some are unjust; that each person may determine for himself, in accordance with his own conscience, in which category each law falls; and those that fall in the unjust basket may be freely violated; and, even though thereafter such laws are held valid, the disobedient may continue his recalcitrance if his conscience will not permit him to agree. Furthermore, if failing to secure relief from the prosecutor in the exercise of the latter's discretion and upon prosecution, the disobedient is finally found guilty, the court should either turn him loose or be lenient "as a mark of respect."

This remarkable position, unheard of in our jurisprudence, is, to me, incomprehensible. Lawyers, above all other people, should retain a wholesome degree of rational detachment in the face of emotional causes. The legal profession has a heavy responsibility for the preservation of the rule of law. The Dworkin doctrine has no historical antecedents. Some apologists of civil disobedience refer to totalitarian examples, the Nazis and Fascists; others mention the Freedom Fighters in Hungary, Thoreau, Gandhi, and even the American Revolutionists. But these are all inapposite. Despite injustices, which admittedly exist in America, they can be redressed through courts, legislatures and established political institutions. The victims of the Nazis and the Fascists, the Freedom Fighters, Gandhi and the American Revolutionists had no courts to which they could turn, no legislatures to petition, no elections through which to seek reform. And as for Henry David Thoreau, his thesis was that "government is best which governs not at all." He believed devoutly that each person should determine which laws were just and obey only those so found. His dogma was: "It is not desirable to cultivate a respect for the law, so much as for the right. The only obligation I have . . . is to do at any time what I think is right." He refused to pay taxes on the ground of "conscience," was convicted and jailed for one night. His conscience troubled him so deeply that rather than serve the rest of his sentence, he let his friends pay his taxes! His conscience stopped hurting when someone else paid his tax bill!

To me the philosophical justification for the Dworkin doctrine is equally unimpressive. In short, as I have indicated, it finds a higher law —the conscience of the individual. Its application is the "unjust law" that is out of step with morality. The test of enforceability is the individual's conscience. The disobedient is the prosecutor, the defense counsel, the judge, and the jury. He makes the first and the last decision, employing a Gertrude Stein logic—a conscience is a conscience is a conscience.

Now, I ask you, where does that doctrine lead a society as complex as ours? I say down a blind alley! One man's conscience is often another man's poison. Each one of us has a pet unjust law; such a doctrine would result in the tyranny of the "unjust." There would be no law, no order, and, soon, no society. A democracy is structured on the principle of voluntary compliance with law. To foster such disobedience could only result in chaos, mob rule, the overthrow of our government and the very Constitution that the disobedients claim as their protector. As Abraham Lincoln said 150 years ago, it leads only to despotism.

The doctrine of integration furnishes a good example of where the Dworkin doctrine leads us. Thousands upon thousands of our people believe the segregated life the better, not only for them but for the country; it was the backbone of the doctrine of interposition that once bloomed in the South; it sparked the program of "massive resistance" to the effort to integrate public schools; and it was based on what was claimed to be an unjust interpretation of the Constitution. No person believed and adhered so firmly to that doctrine than did Governor Ross Barnett of Mississippi. He said that his conscience told him that integration was an unjust and immoral rule. He disobeyed it. He lost and finally obeyed. Does the draft disobedient stand in a different position?

There remain a few odds and ends that should be corrected for the record. It is asserted that the constitutional standing of the present draft law is doubtful. However, the constitutionality of the law has been upheld again and again. *Lichter* v. *United States,* 334 U.S. 742 (1948); *United States* v. *Miller,* 367 F. 2d 72 (C.A. 2d 1966), *cert. den.* 386 U.S. 911. An equal protection argument—apparently based on the student exemption—is made. However, this exemption has been withdrawn. The question concerning those persons who are charged with "counselling draft resistance" is tied in with allegations that they criminally conspired. If this be true, the overt act would be outside the protections of the First Amendment.

I find little to quarrel about with regard to the proposals on sentencing. If a test case fails and the disobedient enters the service, I would see no harm in a suspended sentence or parole; if he refused to be indicted, that might well be ground for the imposition of a sanction. I leave the severity of the sentence to the sound discretion of the trial judge, within statutory limits.

Likewise, I agree that the prosecutor has broad discretion. However, I would leave it at large, the final decision as to prosecution being left to him rather than being controlled by regulation.

In conclusion, let me say that we live in a period of unrest and discord. The sparks of a riot can quickly develop into the flames of rebellion. The ultimate danger is to the rule of law and the framework of government which sustains it. It may be that I express undue alarm, but history teaches us that once a society condones organized defiance of law it will soon destroy itself. Indeed, just a few nights ago a graduate of one of our most distinguished military academies sadly said to me: "America has reached its crest; it is now at the beginning of its eclipse, which, if not arrested, will result in its downfall." And my thoughts went back only a score of years when America in the eyes of the entire world stood on the heights. What could have brought on such rapid deterioration? Demonstrations, draft card burning, "lay-downs" in the streets, seizure of public buildings, defiance of constituted authority, riots, pillaging, maiming, rape, crime and uncontrolled violence. And last night the murder of Dr. King. Ours is a country now gripped in the fear of rebellion! What has become of the noble ideals of our people, particularly our younger ones; of our great aspirations for their welfare; of our devotion to law and order and equality for all? Where is our patriotic fervor? Has it been turned into hate and passion, distrust and greed, and violence? If we ever doubted it, we know it now. To me the signal is clear: It is more necessary than ever that we stop, think and look more closely at where we are going!

NOTES

1. *The Growth of Law*, Yale University Press (1925), pp. 25–26.
2. *Id.* at 23.
3. *Id.* at 25.
4. *The Catholic Lawyer*, Vol. 13, No. 3, p. 198 (Summer 1967).
5. *University of Pennsylvania Law Review*, Vol. 106, 1957–58 (p. 806).

REFLECTIONS ON HUMAN RIGHTS

Sidney Hook

Social and political theory is often a preface to practice. But often theory lags far behind. The exigencies and opportunities of experience provoke responses which seem appropriate and desirable long before we can justify them. This seems particularly true about movements for human rights. Despite the widespread and growing consciousness of the importance of human rights, and the multiplicity of movements and causes in behalf of one or the other of such rights, there is a paucity of theoretical literature on the subject in comparison with the literature on other philosophical themes. The existing literature betrays a tentativeness and perplexity, and sometimes an outright skepticism, about the nature, reality, and so-called foundations of human rights.

Nonetheless, demands for the recognition of human rights proceed apace. Like the cry for justice in whatever idiom, they flow from feelings of deprivation and resentment which feed the judgment that things can be, and should be, better than they are. Their promulgation is not likely to be affected by difficulties in meta-ethical analysis. Nor does their realization depend upon such difficulties rather than upon the relative power of those who support, and those who oppose, these demands— something quite apparent in the agitation for the recognition of new welfare and housing rights in American communities.

To some extent, however, confusions in some interpretations of the meaning of human rights in political and legal discussions have an effect on the recognition of the grounds on which human rights are accepted or rejected. Some writers, interpreting claims to human rights literally as claims to inalienable rights, reject the whole notion as unintelligible. Thus, Santayana, in referring to the rights enumerated in the American Declaration of Independence, characterizes them as "a salad of illusions," and Bentham before him, as "nonsense on stilts." But once rights are cut free from the metaphysics of Blackstone or the religion of Deism—or of any other kind of metaphysics or theology—it can be shown that statements of and about them make perfectly good sense even in terms of Bentham's utilitarianism or Santayana's eudaemonism, albeit not free from some difficulties. At any rate with respect to the cluster of rights which are presupposed by a democratic form of political rule, Bentham's acceptance and Santayana's rejection of them flow not from differences concerning their alleged ontological foundations but from different estimates of their fruits in experience.

The most momentous consequence of skepticism concerning the intelligibility or validity of any theory of human rights is the tendency it encourages to regard them as ideological masks of sheer power relations.

I

A number of grounds have been offered to justify the denial that there are human rights or that we can know them. I wish briefly to consider them before discussing my conception of human rights.

(a) It is sometimes argued that "human rights" do not exist because there are no such things as moral rights altogether. And what this means is that we cannot ever supply a valid or objective foundation for any moral judgment. This wholesale moral skepticism takes two forms. Sometimes it asserts that the expression "right," to the extent that it is intelligible, is wholly reducible to might or power—the familiar Thrasymachian position. Sometimes it is argued that there are various systems of morality, all historically contingent, and that with respect to contrary or contradictory judgments about common practices either both are valid or none is. Nietzsche's philosophy is sometimes cited in support of both varieties of skepticism (the first may be considered a special case of the second).

It seems clear to me that these meta-ethical questions are really irrelevant to some questions that arise concerning the substantive nature of the rights which should be enumerated in a Declaration of Human Rights. For at any definite time there are more classes of actions that are considered right than can be listed in any Declaration. *Differences* concerning what should be listed as "rights" can be intelligently discussed without calling the whole of morality into question. The "right" thing to do in a situation does not automatically give rise to a class of rights. "It is right to speak the truth," "It is right to fulfill one's promises," "It is right to repay a debt," etc. But although these may be presupposed by any set of human rights, they are not listed among them. When differences about specific rights do arise, for example, on the right to inheritance, or the control of property, or the privilege against

self-incrimination; the determination can be, and is, made independently of meta-ethical considerations. The situation would be the same
were one to deny that we could have adequate grounds for distinguishing between proposed laws to effect certain purposes on the ground that
no definition of law has as yet been reached by jurists.

If the viability of the belief in human rights did depend upon the
rejection of the Thrasymachian position it seems to me to be refuted by
two considerations. The first is the linguistic fact that in none of the
major languages of the world are "right" and "strong," "wrong" and
"weak" used interchangeably, and that those who claim to do so are
never consistent in their usage. The second and more important consideration is this: Even if someone were to be found who sincerely and
consistently claimed that he could not distinguish between the concepts
of might and right, and that the authority of right was ultimately rooted
in the authority of might, a situation could be devised in which his
own experience would reveal that there was something askew, something that could not be explained in the equation. This evidence seems
to me just as decisive as that which leads to the acknowledgement by a
color blind person who has failed to distinguish between red and green
objects that something is lacking in *his* powers of color discrimination
—an acknowledgement induced not by the coercion of numbers but by
the deliverances of his own experience.

I can describe the situation only in barest outline. It requires a distinction which could hardly be challenged without abandoning the distinction between sane and insane, between blind *force* that has no direction, and therefore can rend the person who employs it, and *might*
whose direction is self-conserving. Let Thrasymachus be the almighty
conqueror strong enough to do anything he pleases. To profit by his
conquest and to make his rule more secure he lays down the harshest
rules imaginable of curfew or what not, rules which enable the population to know what it must do to avoid destruction. A man is brought
before him charged with violating the curfew. He denies it. Thrasymachus has the power to kill him whether he broke the rule or not, the
power to change the rule or to abolish it altogether. But under the rule
Thrasymachus has himself laid down, he knows that the question can
intelligibly be asked, whether *he* chooses to ask it or not: Guilty or not
guilty? This is not a question of who is stronger or weaker. But whoever
asks it or realizes that it can be asked, knows that might and right cannot be identified because questions of guilt or innocence are *in nuce*
questions of justice or injustice.[1]

As for the wider or more radical form of skepticism, the position
seems to me to rest upon a confusion between objectivity and universal-

ity. If it is possible to discover some shared interests among members of a community, one can find good and sufficient reasons in the light of those interests for choosing to perform some action, whose consequences have been carefully compared with the consequences of alternative actions, rather than others. If we encounter creatures on Earth or from Mars or Nietzschean supermen with whom we can share no common interest, whether of peace or survival, then we could not have a *common* morality. Nonetheless this does not entail that we cannot have an objectively grounded morality. If human morality is relevant to human interests, needs and desires, its objectivity is not affected by the existence of other creatures with irreducibly different interests, needs, and desires. There may be questions of how or whether and to what degree these differences are irreducible. These will define the limits of what is common. Before making inquiry into these questions it is as easy to be too pessimistic—and to see in every other man a wolf—as to be too optimistic and not envisage the possibility that we may have to fight to defend our way of life. But no matter what the theoretical foundations of morality are taken to be, secular or religious, formalistic or teleological, no morality can be set up as normative without assuming that with respect to some basic interests that they are shared or shareable. It is only because human beings build Gods in their own moral image that they can reasonably hope that the Divine Commandments can serve as a guideline in human experience.

The very language of those who argue from the theoretical *possibility* of a multiplicity of systems of morality to the denial of the objectivity of human rights within any one of these systems, often betrays confusion on this point. I have heard philosophers declare that they ardently wished to see the Universal Declaration of Human Rights "implemented and respected" by all nations at the same time as they asserted it was quite evident to them that we do not know that there are any such rights and that we have no ground for believing that they "ought to be both acknowledged and respected." Actually, for every one of the rights listed a variety of good reasons could easily be offered why it should be acknowledged and respected even though we cannot show that it should be acknowledged and respected for every manner of man and interest *conceivable.*

(b) It is sometimes argued that there are no human rights in any system of morals unless these rights are construed as absolute, unconditional, or inalienable. This view is implied in the position taken by some liberal minded jurists with respect to the rights listed in the American Bill of Rights (especially the First Amendment), a few of which appear in the UN Declaration of Human Rights. It is a position that makes no sense in its own terms except on the assumption that there is only one absolute right or, if there is more than one, that we can be provided with convincing reason to believe that all human rights are compatible with each other and that in no foreseeable or credible circumstances will they ever conflict. But this is implausible on its face. It is easy to show that the rights found in every Bill of Rights often conflict in specific situations. Freedom of speech may not only prejudice a man's right to a fair trial but in the mouth of a demagogue haranguing a lynch mob, imperil a man's right to life.

The illuminating distinctions between prima facie and absolute obligations and rights drawn by Ross and Ewing seem to me to constitute an adequate analysis of the problems we face. All human rights have a prima facie validity in situations in which they are relevant, but they are not absolutely or categorically binding on conduct in any specific case although they must always be considered. We are unable to say which rights are categorically binding not only because we cannot anticipate with what other rights they may conflict but because the consequences of abiding by or violating different prima facie rights and obligations are so complex and of such unequal and inconstant weight that no fixed hierarchy or rank can be established in advance to guide us in all situations. Reflection is required in all grave moral decisions. John Dewey defines the moral experience out of which a genuine quest arises for what is our moral duty to do here and now, as one in which good conflicts with good, or right with right, or good with right. This makes every right, every value, every principle, every rule which we bring to bear upon a moral problem, of presumptive validity until reflective inquiry into the specific situation settles on what is morally best, or at least better, here and now.

Intellectually the procedure is comparable to a decision that must be made in selecting the best or the least objectionable out of any collection in which all members vary in their qualities of shape, color, grace, light, etc., and in which no member excels all the others in most respects. But when we must decide between conflicting human policies, with their varied goods and rights, the choice is much more difficult because we cannot sum them up arithmetically or so clearly foresee the consequences of acting upon them.

There are some who believe that there must be, if not absolute rights, then absolute wrongs or absolute obligations of what not to do. Psychologically a powerful case can be made for this position and there are certain things that we may be asked to do in the interests of justice which would make life unendurable. Nonetheless the ironies and tragic cruelties of history create situations in which the choice is between lesser evils, and in which no matter what we do, we cannot avoid guilt. Here our categorical duty is to prevent situations from arising in which such choices must be made; but when they are thrust upon us we cannot say that all alternatives are equally bad. The holy man who refuses to kill the beast or the wicked man who has run amok and is about to kill hundreds of innocents, if killing him is the *only* way of preventing the outrageous evil, is in effect an accomplice in their murders. His holiness cannot wash him morally clean.

The only alternative to this approach, with which I am familiar, which seeks to avoid the fanaticism of absolutism, is to hold that the categorical assertion of inalienable rights presupposes that there are certain exceptions built into the universal judgment, that rules of conduct despite their linguistic form are not intended to convey what is communicated if they are interpreted literally. This has obvious difficulties. No one can foresee all the exceptions. Once it is admitted that all propositions about human rights are open-ended, it becomes semantically impossible to state them in universal form without appearing inconsistent or hypocritical. To attempt to derive the meaning and universal validity of moral utterances (of which statements about human rights are a particular class) from the conditions of linguistic significance under which they are learned so that we know when to disregard the obligation that flows from the statement, "He has a right to be told the truth," seems to me to be hopeless. The conditions of linguistic significance are not universal; and even where they are the same, they cannot by themselves enable us to understand the situations in which a man has a right to be told the truth and when not.[2]

(c) Another source of skepticism concerning "human rights" arises because of the differences in the lists of rights as they appear in various declarations of human rights. This objection testifies to a profound misconception of the purpose or point of listing such rights. Such lists are inescapably historical and functional. Any attempt to enumerate human rights without specific reference to a historical situation, or without such reference being presupposed, would give us a schedule of moral rights and duties of such variety and generality that they would be without bite, mere rhetorical pieties, reconcilable with any set of practices. Bills of Rights are always historically determined in the sense that their particular provisions depend upon the experience of specific deprivations or oppression or upon the felt need for some service or facility hitherto lacking or not previously acknowledged as a public responsibility. That is why out of an indeterminately large number of rights that are potentially eligible for inclusion, comparatively few are selected.

The fact that rights are always historically determined is apparent in two phenomena. As conditions change, the very meaning of the rights listed is often extended or reinterpreted to cover new situations. Justifications for actions deemed reasonable to meet present day conditions are read out of, or into, the old formulations. The history of the interpretations of the First Amendment to the United States Constitution is sufficient evidence. Even more striking, new human rights are found presumably carried in words that no one dreamed in previous centuries had such comprehensive connotations. Volumes have recently been published about "the right to privacy" as a fundamental human right enshrined in the American Constitution. Justice Douglas, for example, explicitly maintains that the First Amendment freedoms are derivative from the "right to privacy" which is nowhere mentioned in the text, despite its allegedly ultimate character, or in any of the discussions that accompanied its adoption.[3] It is notorious and yet unavoidable, because of the absence of explicit definition, that new and conflicting meanings have been read into key expressions like "due process of law," "cruel and unusual punishment," "self-incrimination," etc.

Secondly, when new Declarations or Bills of Rights are promulgated, new rights are often conspicuously added without the subterfuge of exegesis. For example, the right to rest, the right to work, the right to social insurance of various kinds, the right to a nationality, the right to leave one's country, were as a rule not found in earlier formulations because of the absence of the social and economic conditions, and sometimes political conditions, that make them relevant. Certain conditions, of course, are always relevant, especially threats or dangers of arbitrary and despotic government action. This accounts for the presence of some basic human rights in all declarations, e.g., the right to life, liberty, freedom of religious worship, speech, press, and assembly. Historical changes may make a profound difference to the meaning of a Bill of Rights because of the shift of emphasis from one subset of rights to another. In the United States today the right to property, which was the most fiercely defended right in the course of the last century and indeed up to 1936, no longer has the same urgency that it possessed in the days of Locke and even Jefferson, for a variety of reasons, most notably because of the bearing of new forms of social property, as distinct from personal property, on the exercise of the human rights of those who do not possess property.

Finally, whether a right becomes a "human right" does not depend upon whether it gets on a list or declaration. Any moral right can emerge as a focal human right in the course of social and political life. Where human rights are recognized and enforced this is evidence that they have legal force. But their validity does not depend upon their recognition or enforcement. It is or should be obvious that the whole point of asserting, or more accurately, *proposing*, human rights is to win acknowledgement of their validity wherever they are not exercised.

II

This brings us to the thorny and tangled question of the definition of human rights. Before we can define them we must identify them. There are certain expressions in use, "human rights," or their synonyms, and there are certain practices associated with them that can be described in ways that enable us to determine whether or not they obtain in the community. What definition will best do justice to the following true statements about them?

(a) Human rights are a "species" of rights. They are not synonymous therefore with rights per se. The genus of which "human rights" are a species is "moral rights" even when the "human rights" are recognized as legal rights too.

(b) When we speak of human rights, if the adjective "human" has any force, they cannot be the same as the rights of animals or the rights of angels, if any, or the rights of corporations or states as such.

(c) Although theoretically any moral right can become a human right, at any given time and place not everything which is a moral right or is morally right is considered a human right. This would be more manifest perhaps if we drew up a Declaration of Human Wrongs. Many things are wrong but only a few would figure in a significant and relevant way on a formal Declaration of Human Wrongs. Declarations of Human Rights have always been issued in the context of demands for the redress of *grievances*. Most actions which we consider right in a specific context would not be entitled to inclusion among "the rights of man" or "human rights." It is morally right to go out of my way to procure gasoline for a motorist stranded in the desert, but it is not something that can legitimately be included in a Declaration of Human Rights except under theoretically conceivable circumstances of a kind that explain, e.g., why the right not to have soldiers quartered in one's home in times of peace was included in the American Bill of Rights (3rd Amendment).

(d) When human rights are invoked they are cited as *warrants* or good reasons for action or forbearance from actions.

(e) Human rights are regarded as general rights as distinguished from special rights that are derived from special relationships to others whether of contract, status, or consanguinity. This is brought home by the question which Felix Cohen addressed to his fellow philosophers shortly after the Second World War: "What rights, if any, can a man [justifiably] claim of me not because he is my brother or my neighbor or my colleague or co-religionist or fellow citizen but just because he is human?" There are certain difficulties with the way in which this question is formulated. Depending upon whether we take the term "human" as a strictly biological characterization or whether we regard it as normative our answers may differ. Anyone who does not answer "none" to the question and enumerates one or more rights may be taken to subscribe to a belief in human rights.

(f) Human rights are always regarded as in some sense "basic," "fundamental," or "important."

If this is a sufficient identification of the expression "human rights," and the practices related to their use, how shall we define them? We are seeking a definition that will do justice to the widest variety of usages of the expression "human rights." A considerable number of definitions have been offered on which brief comments are in order.

There is a class of definitions which assert that human rights are "powers and securities" possessed by individuals. This is inadequate because we speak of the human rights of the powerless and insecure. Another class of definitions makes central the so-called "negative" freedoms from interference by others, and especially by the state. This is inadequate because we speak intelligibly of the human rights of individuals to an education, medical care, work, and not merely of the right to be left alone. There is also a class of definitions which define human rights as claims made by an individual which society stands ready to enforce. This fails to distinguish between moral rights and legal rights. Human rights are moral rights whether or not they are enforced, whether or not they are the law of the land. It is or should be obvious that some claims are enforced by law that are not considered human rights and many human rights are not legally enforced but should be.

Recently another class of definitions has been put forth by H. J. McCloskey and others, according to which human rights, like other rights, are defined as "entitlements." [4] Of all the single terms that one may substitute in English for "rights" without linguistic awkwardness "entitlement" is the least objectionable. But what illumination is added by the substitution? If one says: "I have a right to x," and one is asked for clarification and replies "I mean I am entitled to x," why is this any more satisfactory than if one says "I am entitled to x" and, upon being challenged, replies "I mean I have a right to x?" Like the word "title," the expressions "entitlement" or "entitled to" seem to suggest what is bestowed or conventional, what follows from a rule, and therefore something that may lapse or be cancelled whereas we tend to think of human rights as not so readily cancellable as titles or modifiable as rules. "Entitled" suggests more of a legal than of a moral term. The very nuance and ambiguities of the terms confirms this. Normally, if we say to someone: "You have no right to the rights you enjoy" it is clear that the first use is of a moral term and the second of a legal one and that we are expressing a moral judgment. If we say, however, "You are not really entitled to your titles," this suggests a legal defect in one's title, a legal judgment.

One of the most interesting definitions of human rights has recently been offered by B. Mayo: "A human right is a claim, on behalf of all men, to corporate action (or perhaps inaction) on the part of whatever institution is in a position to satisfy the claim." [5] Presumably, if no institution exists in a position to satisfy the claim there is an implied moral obligation on all who are in a position to do so, to bring it about.

There are certain difficulties about this definition. A minor one is that there is no limit placed on the scope of the claim. Theoretically it could cover everything or anything at any particular time whereas all human rights that have hitherto been articulated or sought for have been limited to claims of paramount importance. Secondly, it does not distinguish between rights that *are* claimed and rights that *could be* claimed—a distinction not identical with one that contrasts "claiming" and "being disposed to claim." As I understand this definition, if a person makes no claim for a right or no one else claims it for him or is disposed to do so, it makes no sense to speak of his having a right. On this view presumably, a hundred years ago a man being lynched by a crowd for killing another, who had resigned himself to his fate, had no right to a fair trial until or unless someone spoke up for him or made the claim on his behalf. So if we now say that the man had a human right to a fair trial, whether or not the law enforced it, the right comes into being, so to speak, as well as the violation of the right, with the present claim. A right that was not "possessed" could not have been violated. In defending this view, Mayo argues: "Certainly, an umbrella exists independently of my claiming it [but] it is hard to see that my right (of ownership) exists quite independently of my claims to it. Could an umbrella be *mine* if I never claimed it as mine or ever had the least tendency to do so?" [6]

The answer to this question is: "Of course! I could own the umbrella not only if I never claimed it as mine but even if I claimed it was not mine." To which Mayo retorts that "the only class of rights which can plausibly be detached from claims seems to be: rights (including ownership) which the *possessor does not know that he has.*" Suppose, however, a man knows that he has rights; can we separate them from his claims to them? Spinoza had both a legal and moral right to his bequest and he knew he had it, but in the end he did not claim what was his by right. In such cases, Mayo holds the rights "are claimed *on his behalf* by someone else." [7] What if they are not? Must Spinoza's rights depend upon the fact that he or someone else in his behalf actually claims them? Is it not necessary to say that the right *could* be claimed? Going further, is it not necessary to say that the existence of the rights does not depend upon whether someone *in fact* claims or *could* claim them, but rather upon whether someone could *justifiably* claim them?

Mayo denies this. There is something odd about a definition of human rights that leads to this denial. It stems from Mayo's belief that a reference to right is embedded in the very meaning of "claim." He asserts flatly that "all claims are rights" and dismisses the objection that only *justified or justifiable* claims are rights on the ground that these qualifications are otiose, i.e., futile or functionless and therefore unnecessary. This seems to me to be a piece of arbitrary semantic legislation. "A *demand*," he asserts, "can be (totally) unjustified and unjustifiable" but not a *claim.* Yet every time a host of claims are made to an estate to which there are no known heirs or to large sums of found money, most claims are dismissed as totally unjustified and unjustifiable, and some as fraudulent. Mayo seems to hold that no one uses the word "claim" unless he sincerely believes that his claim is justified or justifiable. This is empirically false. He asserts that the sentence: "I claim *x* but there is no reason at all why you should give me *x*," is self-contradictory. I can conceive of situations in which such a sentence would be true. In other situations it might be false. If there is a special sense in which it is self-contradictory, then the sentence in question is no more contradictory than one in which we substitute *demand* for *claim:* "I demand *x* but there is no reason at all why you should give me *x*." Actually, in ordinary life situations, no normal man ever makes a claim or demand or even a request without being able to back it up with a reason. The only question is whether the reason is a good one or a morally relevant one. Even in extreme situations where language takes on aberrant uses "demands" are as supportable as "claims." The demands of bank robbers are often supported by reasons (including threats) which may be no weaker than the "reasons" that back up claims.

I conclude therefore that a right is a justifiable claim and offer the following definition of a human right as more adequate to the widest use of the expression "human right" in contemporary discussion:

A human right is a morally justifiable claim made in behalf of all men to the enjoyment and exercise of those basic freedoms, goods, and services which are considered necessary to achieve the human estate. On this definition human rights do not correspond to anything an individual literally possesses as an attribute, whether physical or mental. Morally justifiable claims are *proposals* to treat human beings in certain ways. Human rights are not names of anything. They specify procedures —courses of action—to be followed by agencies of the government and community with respect to a series of liberties, goods, and services.

Before discussing the problem of justification of rights, several features of the definition should be noted. It is clear that the definition is normative or prescriptive in that it interprets human rights as moral rights. It is normative or prescriptive in another sense since the proposal to treat human beings in a certain way reflects a conception of what the human estate *should* be, an idea or ideal of what is worthy of man. It is highly misleading, a category mistake in Ryle's words, to say that man "possesses" his rights in the way he possesses the traits that identify him as a biological creature distinct from other creatures. It is often said that a man possesses his human rights in virtue of his inherent dignity. "Inherent dignity" is ascribed to man presumably in contrast to his acquired dignity. But it is far from clear that all men have "inherent dignity," or how it is to be identified among those who have it, and why it should be the justifying source of human right rather than human sensibility or intelligence. If it makes any sense to speak of human dignity in connection with human rights, it is not as a designation of a trait comparable to grace and style of gait, such as Aristotle's great souled man might have had, but as a method of treating human beings. It is more natural and less obscure to speak of the right of a human being to be *treated* with dignity whether he possesses it or not.

One of the advantages of putting the question: "What rights, if any, can a man claim of me just because he is human?" is that it leaves open the significant possibility that there are *no* rights a man can claim of me merely or just because he is a man. In other words, whatever the answer, it need not be construed as analytic. This can only be denied by overlooking the systematic ambiguity in the terms "man," "human," and cognate expressions. In some contexts, where "man" and "human" mean different things, it makes perfectly good sense to say "The man is not human." So long as any use of the term "man," or a derivative, refers only to membership in a biological species, I for one cannot see why that membership *alone* gives anyone a right he can justifiably claim of me. If I recognize a duty not to impose unnecessary suffering upon him in any of my relationships with him, it is not because he is a member of the species *homo sapiens* but because he is a creature capable of suffering. This would be true of my relationships towards any animal or other sentient creatures capable of suffering. However, if the term "human" or any of its synonyms or derivatives, refer to a member of a moral community, i.e., if these are normative terms, the nature and degree of right would depend on the kind of moral community that existed between him and me.

If the derivation of human rights depends upon a normative conception of man's estate it presupposes that we are committed to the view that one set of proposals for treating human beings is better grounded than others. What are these grounds? My answer, most simply put, is that they are of the same order as those invoked in the justification of any ethical judgment. That is to say, the anticipated *consequences* of treating human beings in accordance with the proposals put forward are, upon sustained and careful reflection, believed to fulfill the requirements of moral ideals accepted as valid within the problematic situation which is the context of the inquiry. This justification of human rights rests upon the *consequences* of our purported behavior and not on any presuppositions about the nature of man or antecedently accepted facts about him. This view seems both paradoxical and obviously circular, but I shall try to resolve the paradox and show that it is not viciously circular.

First a few words about an alternative view that argues that there are some theological or physical or psychological facts about human beings (e.g., he is created by God, he is a kin of all men, he is endowed with capacity for choice and intelligence, he shares a common fate with others) that presumably are sufficient to justify that he be treated *as* a human being, i.e., with the human rights we regard as intrinsic to our conception of a human being. But no one has been able to show why, from the acceptance of antecedent facts about human beings, they should be treated in some determinate way rather than another, although it does exclude some modes of treatment. At most whatever man is or is discovered to be, this must be compatible with the way he should be treated. Whether the characteristics of his existence are compatible with a proposed mode of treating him is something that depends upon experience, not direct or immediate inspection. It is obvious that whatever the nature of human nature is taken to be, it is compatible with at least several proposals of how to act. *Merely* on the basis of man's biological traits alone, one can, with as much or little warrant, derive "the right to kill" as well as "the right not to kill," "the right to eat" and "the right not to be eaten." Grant that all men are children of God or have immortal souls. These premises, although they would exclude some possibilities, would not determine in the least whether men should organize their society democratically or on the hierarchical model of Heaven itself.

The danger of looking for the justification of human rights—especially of equality of treatment which is integral to all proclamations of human rights—in antecedently given facts of equality is that it leads to an overstatement or inflation of the facts of natural equality. One of the great intellectual scandals of the times has been the emergence of political biology; and this is to be deplored whether it takes a reactionary or liberal form. The liberal form of political biology in the interests of a policy of racial equality postulates that the native capacities of intelligence of all branches of the biological human family are equal. This is a proposition which in some formulations is so vague as to permit no determinate answer; and where it is clear it requires suspended judgment until more trustworthy evidence may be had. But my main point here is that the proposal to treat human beings equally in certain respects does not rest upon any assertion of biological equality, but is advanced as a moral policy justified by its consequences. Even if it were established, which is far from being the case, that certain psychological and intellectual differences among the families of men were inherent and not all culturally acquired, this would not necessarily have any bearing on the validity of a policy of equality of concern for the members of all groups to develop themselves to their best capacities. Individual parents may have children whose I.Q.'s vary from the range of the mediocre to that of the genius, but would this fact justify denying the requisite food, clothing, shelter, and educational opportunity necessary for each child to develop his full stature as a person? The relevance of real or alleged facts of equality or inequality becomes apparent only when the consequences of certain policies and their alternatives are examined or envisaged.

It is undeniable that equality of treatment is in some sense central to the conception of justice but it seems to me to be a source of great and continuous error to ground this proposal of equality primarily on the equal possession of some antecedent property. This is apparent from the fact that no one really accepts, despite his profession, a completely formal conception of justice as consisting in equality of treatment. For in that case, as I have had occasion to point out elsewhere, we could not distinguish between "Everyone ought to be treated equally" and "Everyone ought to be *mistreated* equally." The just policy cannot regard the presence or absence of human happiness or welfare as irrelevant. And what will produce the acceptable balance of happiness and justice sometimes may depend upon our disregarding the facts of equality.

Actually in the concrete historical situations in which equality of treatment is demanded, the very starting point or presupposition of the demand is not a fact of equality but of inequality or difference. Whether we are urging that members of different races be treated equally, or that communicants of different religious faiths have equal rights of worship, or that men and women receive the same pay for the same work, our recommendations make sense because we are recognizing the fact of prima facie difference rather than of sameness or similarity.

The dialectical expansion of the concept of human rights seems based on a commitment to the *equality of difference* in some relevant respect. The quest for the common rights of man is a demand for the recognition of the right to be different or to remain different without forfeiting the right to equal and humane treatment in relevant respects. This is especially true with respect to natural differences for which human beings have been penalized, so to speak, by nature. With respect to social differences like religion or class, the right to be different and the extent of these differences depend upon the consequences of policies based upon them for certain shared or common values of overriding concern to the community as a whole.

From this point of view we must also consider the attempt to derive human rights from some metaphysics of desire as misconceived. Human rights are claims, and claims are rooted in interests and desires. We have already rejected the view that every claim is a right, but it reappears again in the attempt to find the warrant for a right in some antecedent feature of human existence. It is a position taken by William James and reaffirmed by some contemporary authors. It argues from the mere existence of a claim to an obligation toward it, from the mere fact of a demand to its justification. I would hold that the possibility of a claim or demand constitutes a necessary but not a sufficient condition of its validity, that it is only when we have seen and reflected on the consequences of gratifying the claims or demands in the moral community in which claims and demands are made that we can judge their validity. James, on the other hand, writes:

Take any demand however slight, which any creature, however weak, may make. Ought it not, for its own sake, to be satisfied? If not, prove why not? The only possible kind of proof you can adduce would be the exhibition of another creature who would make a demand that ran the other way. The only possible reason there can be why any phenomenon ought to exist is that such a phenomenon is actually desired.[8]

This view is obviously circular and also leads to conclusions which James would be among the first to reject. Its circularity is obvious when we are confronted with a desire or demand which not merely "ran the other way" but demanded the suppression of the desires of others. If the mere fact that another's demands run counter or different to our own deprives it of validity then *both* demands are invalid. Not everything desired ought to exist since one may desire what is false or foolish or fraught with the death of all desires. Even what is mutually desired may be mutually undesirable if it is unreflectively desired. The very conflicts among our actual desires make it impossible to give them legislative authority. For it is the conflicts among one's own desires, and the conflicts between one's desires and those of others, that provide the occasion for the quest of the desirable. The *de facto* strength alone of desires cannot give them *dejure* status. Only when this quest initiates a reflective inquiry and not merely a battle can desire acquire the patents of validity.

Further, if the ontology of desire were the source of the validity of desire why should it be restricted to demands or desires? Why not embrace needs, hopes, wishes, purposes, requests or commands? Can we not with the same show of tolerance and reasonableness ask not only of demands but of any power in the human psyche: "Ought it not, for its own sake, to be gratified? If not, why not?"

III

We must now face the problem of the justification of human rights more directly and grapple with the question: Is the view that human rights are reasonable proposals, defensible in virtue of the consequences of acting on them, any less circular or question-begging than other justifications?

There are three generic ways in which human rights have been or can be justified (assuming that nothing can be justified by postulation) —by logic, by immediate intuition, or by empirical inquiry.

(1) Logic obviously cannot carry us very far in justifying human rights. Contrary claims to "human rights" can be universalized and shown to be equally self-consistent. There are some specific rights in the American Bill of Rights like those involving church-state relations and the privilege against self-incrimination whose prima facie validity would be hard to establish. Any human right can be denied without logical contradiction. Only too often they have been denied in theory and violated in practice. If a human right follows logically from some premise about man, nature, or God, it is these premises that must be justified. And when the attempt is made to do so, invariably a value judgment is surreptitiously introduced into them.

(2) Neither the rights listed as human rights or any premises from which they are presumably derived appear to be self-evident. If they are self-evident, they can only appear so to specially qualified investigators

since so many millions of human beings have been unaware of them or have denied them—a fact which is not incompatible with their being valid but is incompatible with their being "self-evidently" valid. There is nothing self-evident even about so basic a right as the right to life, particularly when the loss or destruction of one life is a necessary condition of the survival of another. There are many worthy causes which argue that the right to die is coeval with the right to live, and neither one is self-evident. No rhetoric can conceal from us the fact that men and women do not have an equal right to life in any community in which men are conscripted for active military service in war but women are not.

There is the famous, if apocryphal, episode of the soldier who, in response to Napoleon's rebuke for having abandoned his post under fire, blurted out: "A man must live, Sire!" To which Napoleon is supposed to have retorted: "I do not see the necessity of it." Napoleon's reply, however callous, is literally valid if there is no logical or any other kind of necessity for life. But the soldier certainly had a good reason, if not a conclusive one, for leaving his post if he faced probable death holding it. Some might be tempted to argue that the right to life is not even a prima facie right in the same sense as the right to be repaid for a debt or to the fulfillment of a promise. No one promised the soldier his life. He hadn't paid for it. And if a volunteer, he has committed himself to taking certain risks. Nonetheless even recognizing that no absolute claim can be made for it, the right to life seems much stronger than the right to be repaid or to have a promise kept. It outweighs the other rights because of the intensity and multiplicity of the evil consequences of violating it.

(3) Does not this appeal to consequences founder because of its obvious circularity? I do not believe so, if we do not try to solve all problems at once or regard all problems as facets of one problem. The conventional wisdom on the question of justification of rights is that rights can be ultimately derived from some fundamental ethical principle or insight which is intuitively valid. The most promising, even if inadequate, approach along these lines is a qualified negative utilitarianism in which we justify the specific proposals or decisions we recommend on the ground that we thereby reduce and equalize human suffering in the world. In one form or another the twin principles of welfare and justice appear as ultimate.

It seems to me that there is an element of vagueness, irrelevant abstractness, indeed of unreality, about this whole approach. Very few persuasive cases can be made out on the basis of so-called *ultimate* principles, whether of happiness or justice or inherent dignity, for any specific decision to propose the recognition and adoption of a human right. Who can foresee all the consequences of an action or balance the disparate experiences of pain and pleasure in their various dimensions and qualities? Is it not true that there are moral qualities in experience that are not simply reducible to forms of happiness or welfare and justice—e.g., sincerity, kindness, truthfulness, nobility, friendliness—so that we must conclude either that there are many irreducible ultimate values, or, since they are in conflict when a moral situation is experienced, that there are no ultimate values?

It is a commonplace fact of our moral experience that we sometimes choose a just course of action rather than one that maximizes welfare. And it is also true that on some occasions we rationally prefer to forego the just solution if we can thereby raise appreciably the level of welfare for all, even at the cost of privileges for some. It is just as significant that we sometimes judge a kind act (which is not a mode of dispensing welfare) as more praiseworthy than a just act, and a noble or self-sacrificial act as more praiseworthy than one which increases the average or total welfare.

The truth seems to be that the demand for the recognition of a specific human right is justified not only by some envisaged consequences for weal or woe in adopting it or not adopting it, but also by implicit reference to other values accepted as valid or beyond question *at that point*. The demand for women's rights to suffrage, or for the right to a job, or for the right to insurance against want if a job is not forthcoming, or the right to medical insurance all presuppose changes in the structure of family life and in the industrial character of society, but their justification does not rest on such considerations alone. In every problematic situation in which these demands conflict with others, what is presupposed is not only the social-historical material context but the validity of certain ethical values, some of them *already* possessing the authority of human rights, whether it be the right to security, the right to fair procedure, the right not merely to life but to a decent life. Some of these rights may have a complex character like the right not to be punished by ex post facto laws.

To be sure, any one of these values, commitments, rights, which we bring—together with an analysis of the factual situation—into the process of justification can be challenged just as any statement about the factual presuppositions and consequences of introducing or not introducing the proposed new right may be challenged. But note: we do not challenge in one gush *all* the values we bring to the consideration of the specific proposal—else no moral questions would ever be settled, they would all become confrontations of ultimate values—and where we are moved genuinely to challenge some specific value-commitment taken for granted in resolving a problem, we meet it in the same way by reference to *both* fact and other assumed values.

Does this not raise the ghost of an infinite regress? No more so than does any process of scientific explanation. If I coherently explain the cause of a disease I do so only because I have made certain other causal assumptions that, although not in dispute in my inquiry, are theoretically challengeable. I do not have to explain the cause of the cause until I reach a first cause to accept a causal explanation as valid. Nor do I have to reach an ultimate value about which there is universal agreement in order to justify a given proposal to treat human beings in a certain way; so long as the consequences of the proposal are in accord with, or serve to further, the shared values on which, for the problem at hand, there is no dispute. The questions whether the values declared ultimate in specific situations of moral conflict are really ultimate rather than penultimate; and whether if we are committed to many different values, any one of which may be justified in terms of others, the apparent circularity is objectionable; I leave unexplored except to point to C. I. Lewis's reminder that a dictionary, however ideal its definitions, is still useful even if all of its words are defined in terms of other words in the dictionary. Nor am I overlooking the difference between the subject matters of scientific and ethical inquiry, but I am contending that just as we do not put everything we know into dispute in the process of scientific inquiry and confirmation, so we do not put all our values in dispute in the process of ethical validation. We no more have to solve all scientific problems to solve any than we have to resolve all moral conflicts to resolve any.

Actually in the process of reflective inquiry by which we seek to resolve moral conflicts we reach out to find the shared interests and values from which to survey our differences. If the ultimate inarbitrable values from which all our other values hang (as if from some cosmic hook) guided our deliberations, we could not explain so plausibly those agreements on proximate and intermediate goals on which ordered life in a community depends. To be sure, there are some who claim to invoke ultimate values as decisive, not merely as theoretical postulates dictated by dialectical necessity, but in concrete historical situations—e.g., with respect to the use of nuclear weapons or the choice of being red or dead. In every case that has come to light the discussion reveals either that some reason is offered in support of the alleged ultimate value, or more commonly, that the value(s) held and the way they are held depend upon some implicit assumptions of fact about the causes and/or consequences of believing and acting on them. Anyone in a genuine problematic context who espouses a value in complete independence of the factual presupposition of the causes of the conflict situation, or of the consequences of believing and acting on the value, in contrast with courses of conduct guided by alternative values, has offered us a paradigm case of an unreasonable, indeed, a fanatical belief.

The history of human reflection on the nature of values indicates that we are surer of the validity of at least *some* of our moral judgments than we are of the theories or principles we offer in ultimate justification of them. At any definite time there seems to be a set of moral judgments whose acceptance appears necessary for the conduct of civilized life and which function as "intuitive" checks upon proposals. We sometimes reject a theoretical position like that of unrestricted utilitarianism because it leads to conclusions that we find morally unacceptable. But these "intuitive" or "counter-intuitive" checks are not absolute, or eternal, or so certain as to be beyond possibility of rational doubt. We do not accept every pronouncement of our moral consciousness as valid without considering the wider context of moral judgments and principles in which it is embedded. We seek to make consistent, as integral to the process of justification, our moral judgments on different practical occasions. Here, too, there is an analogy with the process of verification. The truth of a judgment of fact depends upon observation, and we are more certain of our perceptions than we are of any theory which is tested by them. Nonetheless, any particular judgment of perception or of observation, no matter how certain we may feel about it, may have to be withdrawn if some assumption which guides our observation is challenged, or if some subsequent observation is incompatible with the truth of our previous perception.

On this view of the justification of human rights, they are *proposals* to recognize as binding, on all and sundry who are relevantly situated to defend and/or enforce them a set of rules which within the historical and cultural context in which they are enunciated are more reasonable. Rights are not derived from the state of affairs we start from. They are not derived from the reason of things or the reason in God, Nature or Man. They are justified by the consequences of rules of action. Nor can it be said that these consequences are such that they strictly *entail* any proposals or choices, but only that they render some more reasonable or less arbitrary than others. This pragmatic justification needs no metaphysical or theological proposition for logical underpinning any more than moral judgments in ordinary experience require such support. Whatever the incompatible over-beliefs or dogmas that human beings bring to the consideration of moral problems, in the end, if they go on living together instead of fighting each other, they have in effect indicated a working agreement as to what is, comparatively, better among the possible alternatives. That agreement is a necessary condition for the solution of the problem, even if it is not always sufficient.

There are some who have defended the belief in human rights as useful *fictions* justified by happy results. This seems to me just as inadequate as the view which asserts that statements about rights are as descriptive as statements about things and relations, and literally true. It is a belief that reifies valid proposals; that assumes that the attribution of rights could be literally true or false, in the sense in which the "mirage" of an oasis could turn out to be a real oasis; and that commits a category mistake under the guise of intellectual sophistication. It fails to explain why some rather than other rights are useful, thus losing an opportunity to stress the nonfictional reasons for the proposals in question. In addition, it is psychologically self-defeating to characterize beliefs in rights as beliefs in fictions, if it is expected that human beings will run great risks in defence of human rights. Men are not passionately concerned to defend anything publicly identified as "fiction" that shades into "myth" and then into "pious fraud" which, like plain lies, may also be useful. This is not to deny that men have fought and died for unanalyzable abstractions, for lost causes, for Gods that have not existed, for the honor of Kings and Countries that have had no honor, for unrealizable ideals. What I am contending is that to describe the objects of these struggles as "fictions" misconceives and misdescribes human behavior. For in all of these cases it is possible to find a good if not morally adequate reason for their action. Most men may be fools: they are not systemically deluded.

IV

This brings us to a cluster of related questions. How significant is the distinction between negative and positive rights or freedoms? Does it correspond to the distinction between civil and political rights, on the one hand, and social and economic rights on the other? Is it confusing to include both sets of rights in the UN Declaration of Rights? Are Maurice Cranston and other critics justified in charging that a fundamental incoherence was introduced by Roosevelt in the Atlantic Charter when he spoke of the four freedoms—a confusion perpetuated in the UN Declaration of Rights and carried to absurdity in some of the provisions in Articles 21 to 30?

There are distinctions between the so-called positive and negative freedoms or rights. But these do not require that we draw hard and fast lines of separation between them. If we recognize the historical character of human rights, we should be prepared to expand the list or schedule of rights regarded as not only relevant to, but of paramount importance in our conception of the kind of life deemed fit for man. Nonetheless, although the so-called negative and positive rights are interrelated, there is a sense in which we are justified in considering the traditional civil and political rights or freedoms as the most strategic. I believe that this is what the critics of the UN Declaration really have in mind when they object to the inclusion of other rights.

The so-called negative freedoms are ordinarily defined in terms of absence of restraints on human conduct. The right or freedom to speak is present whenever a person is free *from* the interference of others in speaking his mind. Positive freedom is ordinarily defined in terms of powers or guaranteed opportunity to achieve certain desired goals. This freedom "to" or "for" implies that the desire or willingness to do something, its voluntary character so to speak, is not enough, even in the absence of interference by others. There may be other obstacles to overcome. All rights or freedoms can be defined in negative terms if the interferences are not broken down into different types of interference—personal, natural, or social. All rights or freedoms can be defined in positive terms if the power to do what one desires is interpreted as the power to overcome all human obstacles or interferences or the power to prevent others from preventing our action. My point is that what is of the greatest issue here is not whether the analysis of rights is to be made in negative or positive terms, but the substantial question of the relative validity of the specific right at issue, and the difference between the different kinds of conditions preventing its fulfillment.[9]

Freedom from restraint may be freedom from constraint—from direct human interference—or from other preventing conditions. Preventing conditions may be of two kinds: natural and beyond the control of men; and social, for which institutions, and indirectly men, are responsible. To enjoy "the freedom to sail" I must be free from the interference of those who would prevent me from sailing, who would steal or damage my boat. My "freedom to sail," however, may also be frustrated by a storm or other natural conditions no one can do anything about. But, and this is the source of the grievance, even when I am not referring to vandals or pirates, my freedom to sail may be frustrated by the failure of the economy to manufacture boats, or the refusal of those who do to sell them to me at a price I can afford, despite the fact that my livelihood may depend upon the use of a boat. Only the historic context tells us whether the demand for "the right to sail" is a demand for the freedom of the seas or a demand for the acquisition of the means to sail.

The historic context shows that "freedom of belief," especially freedom of religious belief, is almost invariably a demand that there be no interference with religious belief, private or public; no punishment, persecution or, discrimination. On the other hand, where the cry of "freedom to eat" is heard, this is never intended as a plea for prevention of interference with our dietary freedom, but as a demand for positive, reconstructive measures for more food. Yet this positive freedom or right *to* or *for* more food, where its availability depends to some degree on social action, can also be described in negative terms as "freedom *from* hunger."

The rights enumerated in the UN Declaration of Human Rights make up a mixed bag. Articles 6 through 11 are designed to protect the individual's right to fair judicial process. This cannot be done *merely* by preventing other members of the community from interfering with the proper norms of due process. On the contrary, the implementation of these articles requires positive actions on an extensive scale by the institutions of the state—measures which would be comparable to those undertaken by the state in *behalf* of some social and economic rights. Think, for example, of what is required to protect a defendant's right to a fair trial. Surely a fair trial cannot be guaranteed merely by negative action, by stopping the use of illegal coercion against a defendant, as in dispersing a lynch mob. It may necessitate the performance of many positive, complex tasks—among them the careful selection of jurors to diminish the likelihood of discrimination, change of venue, the provision of competent counsel, and contribution to the costs of the defence. If the enumeration of human rights were to restrict itself to a statement only of freedoms which should never be invaded, of actions that should never be performed, of liberties that are inviolable and therefore "supremely sacred," it is difficult to understand how we can implement "the right to a fair trial" since this requires not leaving a man alone or refraining from violations of his personal property, but doing, positively, a great deal more than that.

Article 16, however, requires much less in the way of positive action on the part of the State—perhaps only the minimal, positive action of registration. This article gives men and women a right to marry and found a family. This obviously does not mean that the state or community will undertake to provide a wife or husband for those who wish to marry, but only that if they do find someone willing to marry them there will be no coercion permitted to prevent it and no legal hindrance of a discriminatory sort. In other words, what limits this right, as in the prevention of child-marriages, is the assertion or defence of another human right. In communities where custom requires, as a necessary condition of marriage, that the bride have a dowry, the spirit of the other articles of the Declaration would make it incumbent upon the states in question to provide for those economically disadvantaged.

Article 19 prescribes the right to complete freedom of expression. Here, too, this does not mean that the community is under an obligation to provide any individual with the means necessary for the public expression of his views but rather, once an individual possesses the means, it will prevent hostile actions designed to interfere with the expression. Under certain circumstances social control to forestall a monopoly of newsprint may be necessary in the interests of freedom of expression. On a priori grounds one might conclude that those who own the press have a greater freedom of expression and therefore greater political influence than those who have limited means. But actually this has not proved true. So long as there is no coercion against expression of opinion in *other* media, and no monopoly, there is no direct relation between political influence and press ownership. Roosevelt and Truman were violently opposed by most of the press.

There are other provisions of the Declaration which focus upon the responsibility of the community to bring into existence constructive and positive programs of action. Article 23 recognizes the "right to work." This obviously means more than if the individual finds a position, he will be protected against others who wish to take it away from him. Indeed, it will not protect him against others if they wish to deprive him of the position by peaceful competition or bargaining. It means that whatever the result of the competition, the community recognizes the obligation to create social conditions in which the individual can find a position, or failing that, in which he can receive unemployment insurance.

The responsibility of the community for even more comprehensive social action is implied in Article 26, on the right to an education. The right to an education was among the rights of citizens recognized as early as 1789. In its first intention it does not even remotely suggest that it is directed against those who would prevent children from attending school. Nor does it provide for an alternative comparable to unemployment insurance for those for whom it cannot arrange to find work. This article calls upon the community to accept the duty of compelling schooling of some sort for all, at least on the elementary level. Its positive enforcement is complex and widespread and cannot be interpreted as freedom *from* preventive human constraints but only as freedom from the preventing condition of ignorance.

The classification of rights as negative or positive is hardly illuminating. When negative rights are identified with the civil and political, and positive rights with the social and economic, and a plea is made to

exclude the latter from the list of genuine human rights, confusion results—because, as we have seen, all rights can be defined as either negative or positive; many are interrelated; and whatever sensible hierarchy
exists in the economy of values is independent of such classification.

The nub of the argument against including the so-called social and
political rights in the UN Declaration of Rights is put by Maurice Cranston as follows: "A human right by *definition is a universal moral right*,
something which all men, everywhere, at all times ought to have, and
something of which no one may be deprived without a grave affront to
justice, something which is owing to every human being simply because
he is human." [10] Consequently, Cranston argues that to refer to such
rights as those provided in Articles 23 and 24, which even go so far as to
mention the right to "provide holidays with pay" is simply nonsense.
Cranston does not agree with Bentham that all talk about human rights
is nonsense. It is only talk about social and economic rights that he dubs
nonsense—despite the fact that he acknowledges that under some circumstances they may be "morally compelling." The reasons he gives for
this critical judgment are that such alleged rights are neither practicable,
nor categorical, nor of paramount importance.

Let us grant that no community is obliged to do what is impossible. But to say that something is impracticable is not to say the same
sort of thing as that it is impossible. Practicability is surely a matter of
degree. The objective historical situation that determines whether a
right is realizable varies from country to country. In a country which is
very poor, very illiterate, and internally chaotic, how "practicable" is
"freedom of the press" or "a fair trial"? Certainly, not fully. Even so, so
long as a beginning can be made, its recognition is justifiable. Not all
the civil and political rights that Cranston endorses are fully practicable
in many of the new countries, but this does not testify against the desirability of emphasizing them, nor does it justify the abrogation of primitive beginnings of democratic participation in government, called for in
Article 21, on the ground that the country is not fully prepared for
them. In how many countries of Asia and Africa is it practicable to enforce the right to an education, or the civil right to marriage (Article
15), which specifies that it be entered into *only* with the free and full
consent of the intending spouses, who are to enjoy *equal rights* at marriage, during marriage, and upon its dissolution?

Further, it is clear that some social and economic rights are more
practicable, even if not completely practicable, than some civil and political rights. I cheerfully acknowledge that the reference to the right to
"periodic holidays with pay" (Article 24) is a supererogative demand. It
is much too specific. It need not have been listed. Whenever and wher-

ever a case can be made for it, it can be brought under the broader provisions of other articles (specifically Article 23, Sections 1 and 3). But if we look at Article 24, which concludes with the mirth-producing reference to "periodic holidays with pay," we find that it begins: "Everyone has a right to rest and leisure including reasonable limitations of working hours." It could have ended there without the addition of the phrase "and periodic holidays with pay," which, when it is feasible, can be construed as an application of the right to rest and leisure and a reasonable limitation of working hours. The right to rest and leisure seems to me as universal, practicable and relevant as any civil and political right. Labor *without* rest or leisure can kill. It is incompatible with the right to life. It is significant that the importance of this humane provision was recognized as long ago as the promulgation of the Decalogue and was invested with the authority of divine sanction.

If, by "categorical," is meant that human rights cannot ever be legitimately breached for any reason, this makes them "absolute" and "inalienable," and we have seen that no right has that character, not even the right to life which appears on all Bills and Declarations of Rights. If it is admitted that social and economic rights are moral rights, then they have the same categorical character as all moral rights including civil and political rights. To be sure they sometimes conflict with each other but so do the latter.

There remains then, the difference in their degree of urgency or paramountcy. What makes a right of paramount importance? If this is measured by the amount of suffering or the extent of injustice consequent upon the absence or denial of a right, I doubt whether it can be legitimately asserted that in all situations the violation of any civil and political right is productive of more evil than the violation of any social and economic right. Everyone can think of certain historical crises in which the pinch of hunger or hurt of social humiliation has led to a too easy sacrifice of civil and political liberties for the promise of security and welfare. And in times of great need, danger, or famine, the rights of due process are suspended.

If civil and political rights are, as I believe, of paramount importance, it is not for the reasons given by Cranston. Most simply put, the civil and political rights in any statement of rights are of paramount importance to all others in that without them all other rights could be easily ignored, abused, corrupted and ultimately lost. Without them the very right to eat—the bread-card of welfare—becomes a weapon of tyranny. Where they are present, the evils of monopoly of any kind may be curbed. And where they flourish, they make possible the discovery of other and new rights, and the recognition of these new rights by the moral conscience of the community. Civil and political rights are primary to all others in the same way as political democracy is basic to all other forms of democracy.

One of the unhappiest legacies of the vulgar-Marxist tradition, partly inspired by ambiguities in Marx's own writings, has been the tendency to infer from the fact that civil and political rights are not sufficient *by themselves* to guarantee human rights of a social and economic nature that they were therefore purely abstract and formal, irrelevant to historical progress, and functioning primarily as ideological masks to extend class privilege. The point of view is typified in a statement like this, explaining why "the classical framework of civil and political rights" was deemed inadequate: "The man who stole bread was sure of a fair trial and was free to speak out against the law that condemned him before he was hanged." [11]

When such things were possible, did the man who was *denied* a fair trial and the right to speak out against the law, escape hanging? The freedom to speak out was not the less important because it failed at once to put an end to such outrages. For the historical record shows that it was in virtue of the continued speaking out that the punishment of death for the theft of bread was first abolished, and then, more gradually, bread was supplied to all who needed it, making it unnecessary to steal it. On the other hand, where these scorned "bourgeois" freedoms of speech and press do not exist, it becomes quite easy for the rulers to promise bread to all but never deliver it, and to hang without trial or by means of rigged trials, innocent men who have violated no laws, not even laws against theft.

The history of the last two centuries has shown that respect for civil liberties has not in itself been sufficient to achieve a guranteed livelihood or decent minimum level of welfare for all without profound changes in the economic order and in the traditional conception of the role of the government. But the same history has shown with even greater vividness that where civil and political liberties have not been respected, the so-called social and economic rights have not been guaranteed to all, that they have always been in a state of precarious dependence upon the whim of a despot or a small political minority. Bread and circuses are notoriously uncertain if those whose decisions determine their distribution are not responsible to those they govern. The assertion that social and economic rights exist in such circumstances is far more of a "sham" and "pretence" than the assertion that civil and political rights can still function effectively in societies where social and economic rights are yet to be introduced. Only in a very Pickwickian sense can one say it is possible to enjoy social security without political freedom since such security cannot be guaranteed by powers that consider themselves above the law and can withdraw it on the merest suspicion that the citizens—really subjects—are not totally reliable.

The upshot of conceptual analysis reinforces the lessons that can be drawn from history. Unless civil rights and liberties are regarded as of *strategic* importance and become, so to speak, the ribbed frame of the ship of state and its political order, the social and economic rights that define the social order lack the proper safeguard against erosion, or still worse, perversion into support for tyranny. It is not necessary to conceive of civil rights and liberties as absolute: but it is necessary on historical, psychological, and ultimately moral grounds to give them priority of concern in building the social order to meet the needs of the whole man or ideal man or new man—however he be morally conceived. If this is not done, civil rights are easily sacrificed as too costly or inconvenient in the slow and painful progress towards the desirable social order. But once they are sacrified the shining goals of the new order become more remote. For there is no way now to safely evaluate the goals by criticism of the means used to achieve them, no freedom to expose the folly and even the madness of those who are implementing the goals, no mechanisms of press, radio or public debate by which the truth may be communicated.

One leading member of the European Commission of Human Rights which limits the jurisdiction of its inquiries only to reported violations of civil and political rights of the classical tradition is critical of the distinction which Cranston and others seek to uphold between these rights and social and economic rights. For he believes that such distinctions have an adverse effect upon their implementation. In the perspective of the unending task of making society more reasonable and humane, such a distinction "is a fixation of human rights in terms of a particular phase in the development of social ideas." [12]

A distinction, however, is not a separation. It is not necessary to confine a Declaration of Rights to civil and political ones alone. Others may be added. Moreover, an emphasis is not a fixation. Precisely because the development of new social rights is so important, the civil and political rights must be recognized as strategic or central or preferred. And Mr. Fawcett implicitly acknowledges this when he discusses the key question of the implementation of human rights. For unless the rights proclaimed in any Declaration can be at some point implemented, they are a cruel mockery of human hope and aspiration. In discussing the most effective method of implementing human rights, Fawcett says: ". . . fundamental to *all* effective methods of implementation of human rights is independent and objective fact-finding, and its ally, publicity; indeed, *publicity is perhaps the most decisive element of all.*" [13]

This admission sustains my point. If it is true that independent and objective fact-finding and publicity are the most effective methods of implementing rights, then surely the best guarantee that the conclusions reached will be broadcast in available media of communication, is the operating presence of civil and political liberties. All the more evident is this when the findings are critical of those in power and challenge entrenched privilege. I believe it is fair to conclude, therefore, that these rights or liberties are, to use Mr. Fawcett's expression, "the most decisive" feature in any declaration of human rights.

V

An obvious question which arises in this connection is: What is the point of the enunciation of a Bill of Rights whose most decisive provisions are violated by the signatory governments? Is it not gross hypocrisy for countries which declare their belief in the freedom of the press to jail those who try to exercise this freedom; or which, by total monopoly of the press, paper and printer's ink, reinforced by prior censorship, deny to anyone not approved by the government an opportunity to voice an opinion?

The obvious answer is provided by the influence of such declarations in the history of nations whose institutional practices violated both the letter and spirit of the rights inscribed in their constitutions. Their presence has an educational influence that in time undercuts the cynicism and Machiavellianism which inspired their adoption as a political manoeuvre. The disparity between the solemn words and the ignoble deeds, raises questions, creates puzzles, awakens doubts, in any reasonable mind. It has to be explained. And once an explanation is given, it invites belief or disbelief.

Nonetheless we must not make too great a claim for the effect of *mere* words. They tip the historical spears with which men do battle. But their force and penetration depends upon the length of the shaft— the social interests behind them. The Stalin Constitution with all its "guarantees" of civil rights was proclaimed at the very height of one of the bloodiest terrors in human history. There is no evidence that any group invoked these constitutional guarantees from 1936, when it was promulgated, to the death of Stalin. Even in the United States the educational influence of the Bill of Rights declarations, both in federal and state constitutions, has been slow, accelerating with the pace of events.

Nonetheless it remains true that if and when opposition movements develop against dictatorial practices or regimes in countries that formally profess allegiance to Bills of Rights, they can make tremendous headway by appealing to these official declarations. It becomes increasingly difficult to charge the champions of human rights with importing a foreign ideology when they use as their rallying cry the very formula which the representatives of legitimacy have used as rationalizations of their power.[14]

NOTES

1. Cf. Jonas Cohen, Theorie der Dialektik: Formenlehre der Philosophie (Leipzig, 1923), pp. 52 ff.
2. Cf. A. I. Melden, "The Concept of Universal Human Rights" in Science, Language and Human Rights (Philadelphia, Pa., University of Pennsylvania Press, 1952), pp. 167 ff.
3. Griswold v. Connecticut, 381 US 479 (1965).
4. Cf. H. J. McCloskey, "Rights," Philosophical Quarterly, Vol. 15, No. 59 (April 1965), pp. 115 ff.
5. B. Mayo, Aristotelian Society Supplementary, Volume XXXIV (1965), p. 231.
6. Ibid., p. 232.
7. Ibid.
8. William James, Essays on Faith and Morals, R. B. Perry, ed. (New York, Meridian Books, 1962), p. 195.
9. Cf. The illuminating essay by Gerald C. MacCollum, Jr., "Negative and Positive Freedom" in Philosophical Review, Vol. 26, No. 3 (July, 1967), pp. 312 ff.
10. Maurice Cranston, What Are Human Rights? (New York, Basic Books, 1962), p. 36.
11. J. E. S. Fawcett, Political Theory and The Rights of Man, D. D. Raphael, ed. (Bloomington, Indiana University Press, 1967), p. 133.
12. Fawcett, op. cit., p. 133.
13. Op. cit. pp. 132–133, italics mine.
14. I am indebted to Richard Brandt for criticisms of a draft of this paper. He is not responsible, of course, for any of its views or formulations.

SOCIOLOGY AND THE PHILOSOPHY OF HUMAN RIGHTS

Raymond Aron

In 1968, the United Nations celebrated the twentieth anniversry of the vote, by the General Assembly of the United Nations, of a universal declaration of the rights of man. *The United Nations* the organization which gathers together almost all of the States of the world (with the exception of China and various fragments of divided countries), but not humanity itself. The declaration, now twenty years old, was not accepted by member States as a basis for legislation, as regulating principles for judicial decisions; it remains, today as it was yesterday, a simple, solemn—and perhaps vain—enumeration of the rights which States judge theoretically desirable to grant to individuals but which they shun considering as imperatives. Intentions or objectives, perhaps; higher commands to a positive right, before which the leaders of States themselves must bow, certainly not. No State, not even the United States, has given the rights of man, as proclaimed in 1948 by this assembly of States, a status equivalent to that of the amendments to the American Constitution on the basis of which the Supreme Court of the United States makes its decisions. This anniversary—the year of the rights of man—cannot fail to arouse mingled emotions in all of us. Is it an occasion for sadness or for joy? Remembrance of a lost hope or of a work in progress? Is the century of concentration camps, of genocides, and the atomic bomb rendering the homage of vice to virtue when it evokes or invokes the rights of man? Or must we go still further: Do the rights of man appertain to the philosophy of our time? In the eighteenth century, they were intrinsically linked to the rights of the citizen; personal and political rights were expressed in a liberal and universalist conception of the social order. In the twentieth century, they have been enlarged by economic and social rights. Does this represent a progression, in conformity with the logic of the philosophy of the Enlightenment? Or perhaps, on the pretext that carrying bourgeois statements to their

282

completion by including in them the rights legitimately claimed by socialists, have the drafters of the 1948 declaration confused incompatible ideas, brought together desirable objectives and categorical imperatives, without distinguishing between them, and finally, emptied the concept of *right of man* of its content and its significance by giving to it an undefined extension?

These are the interrogations to which the following pages attempt to give an answer.

I shall take as a point of departure a comparison between the first French declaration of the rights of man (voted by the Constituent Assembly on August 23, 1789, accepted by King Louis XVI on October 3rd and promulgated on November 3rd) and the universal declaration of the rights of man voted by the General Assembly of the United Nations in December 1948. In such a comparison, two propositions stand out very clearly: *in essence, individual, political, and intellectual rights have not changed in the period from 1789 to 1948;* jurists or statesmen continue to formulate them in the same terms (though not without some significant exceptions). The 1948 declaration, however, devalues certain rights (such as property) which lie between political rights and economic rights, *and it includes a section on social rights to which the members of the French Constituent Assembly gave no thought.*

I shall make a distinction between four categories of rights in this French declaration—or perhaps it would be preferable to say between four kinds of articles.

1) The first category proclaims the *equalitarian* principle. Thus, in Article 1: "Men are born and remain free and equal in rights. Social distinctions can be founded only on common utility." Or again, in Article 6: "The law must be the same for all, whether it protects or whether it punishes. All citizens, being equal in the eyes of the law, are equally admissible to all public dignities, places, and functions, in accordance with their capacity and without distinction other than that of their virtues and their talents." Pareto or an analytical philosopher would have no difficulty in demonstrating that "common utility," for lack of a precise definition, does not make it possible to determine what "social distinctions" are justified. By the same token, there must be a standard of measurement for "virtue and talents" in order for society to reconcile equality and social distinction, in accordance with justice.

The equalitarian principle finds an equally strong and more precise expression in the 1948 declaration. "All human beings are born free and equal in dignity and rights." The term "dignity" belongs to the language of the twentieth century. It would be interesting to seek out its origin, the date on which it was incorporated into the classic terms (equality, liberty, fraternity). Article 2 reinforces the equalitarian principle even further: "Everyone is entitled to all the rights and freedoms set forth in this declaration, without distinction of any kind, such as race, color, sex, language, religion, political or other opinion, national or social origin, property, birth or other status . . ." Article 7 goes on to affirm equality before the law and explicitly proscribes all discrimination, while Article 16 sets down the equality of man and woman in matters of marriage or divorce, and Article 23, in paragraph 2, offers the following rule: "Everyone, without any discrimination, has the right to equal pay for equal work."

Obviously, formulas such as "men are born free and equal in rights" can not stand up under analysis ("to be born free," in the proper sense of the term, signifies nothing), but they draw their inspiration from a philosophy we will follow Parsons in terming *universalist*. Equality before the law excludes privileged classes and inherited status, even though it does not forbid the transmission of fortune or prestige from one generation to another. In 1789, of course, this equalitarian or universalist principle assumed a revolutionary impact, against the *Estates* of the old régime, since it included the "admissibility of all to all functions," and called for a reform of the tax structure, of which Article 13 ("A common contribution is indispensable to the maintenance of public authority and the expenses of administration. It should be equally shared among all citizens, in proportion to their abilities.") suggested changes that would bring about the liquidation of the fiscal privileges of the nobility and the clergy.

2) The articles which specify what I shall call in Gaetano Mosca's phrase, *the democratic formula*, belonged to a second category. Representative of this, in the 1789 declaration, are Articles 3 ("The source of all sovereignty resides essentially in the Nation.") and 6 ("The law is the expression of the general will. All citizens have the right to contribute to its formation, personally or through their representatives."). Article 21 of the 1948 declaration echoes this: "Everyone has the right to take part in the government of his country, directly or through freely chosen representatives. The will of the people shall be the basis of the authority of government, this will shall be expressed in periodic and genuine elections which shall be by universal and equal suffrage and shall be held by secret vote or by equivalent free voting procedures."

Even though each of these two declarations affirms the democratic idea, they differ in many respects. The 1789 declaration is manifestly directed toward a limitation of the action of the State (Article 5: "the law has the right of prohibit only those actions prejudicial to society") and draws its inspiration from a philosophy enunciated both by Rousseau ("The law is the expression of the general will.") and by Montesquieu (Article 16: "No society in which the guarantee of rights is not assured nor the separation of powers determined can be said to have a constitution."). The 1948 declaration seems more precise in its categorization of the democratic idea and in its reference to free elections. The latter represent another institutional translation of the democratic idea—more democratic, from some points of view—than separation of powers. But Article 12 of the 1948 declaration, which tends toward conservation of the rights to private life (". . . no one shall be subjected to arbitrary interference with his privacy, family, home or correspondence") does not suffice to conceal the gap between the *nomocratic* State envisaged by the members of the Constituent Assembly of 1789 and the *modern* State, in which achievement of social and economic rights is accorded a higher place than respect for individual rights.

3) Individual and intellectual liberties belong in a third category. They are summed up in articles 10 and 11 of the French declaration ("No individual shall be troubled because of his opinions, even religious opinions, provided that their manifestation does not disturb the public order established by law. . . . Free communication of thoughts and opinions is one of the most precious rights of man; every citizen, therefore, may speak, write, and print freely, with the exception of being answerable for abuse of this liberty in cases determined by the law."). Even the drafters of the 1789 declaration did not accept religious liberty without some difficulty and reticence (*"even* religious opinions"). By invoking disturbance of the publc order brought on by a manifestation of opinion, the authorities of the time found a facile argument for limiting or prohibiting such manifestations. And in the same manner, the expression "abuse of liberty" authorizes all of the abuses of repression.

The 1948 declaration has a more liberal sound: freedom of thought, of conscience, and of religion (Article 18); freedom of opinion and expression (Article 19); freedom of peaceful assembly and association (Article 20); freedom of movement and of residence within the frontiers of the State; freedom to leave one's own country or to return to it (Article 14), to find refuge from the persecution of a foreign State (Article 14). The representatives of the Communist nations were among those who signed this declaration: should this be considered a cause for rejoicing or indignation; should it be regarded as an expression of their ideal—extending beyond the despotism of the present time—or of their contempt for these bourgeois rituals?

4) Lastly, the administration of justice forms the subject of a fourth category of rights: Articles 7, 8, and 9 of the French declaration; Articles 9, 10, and 11 of the universal declaration: ("No man may be accused, arrested, or detained except in cases determined by the law, and in accordance with forms prescribed by the law."); nonretroactivity of laws (Article 8 of 1789; Article 11, paragraph 2, of 1948), presumption of innocence until a verdict of guilt (Article 9 of the French declaration; Article 11, paragraph 1 of the 1948 declaration). The universal declaration adds more of a supplementary formula than the element of a new idea: "Fair and public hearing by an independent and impartial tribunal."

The historic, social, and political import of the French declaration was not lost on the most farsighted and the most implacable of critics of the Revolution, Edmund Burke. *Analytically*, the article stating that men are born free and equal in rights presents nothing of significance. *Historically*, it excludes hereditary distinctions of classes or Estates. And, in the same way, other articles postulate the fact that functions prohibited to anyone by reason of birth, fiscal exceptions inherited through tradition, and, in the final analysis, monarchy by divine right, no longer existed. The author of *Reflections on the French Revolution* was, therefore, not mistaken when, in a certain sense, he encroached on the Marxist critique—although on a basis of judgments of value in only a contrary sense—and passionately denounced the revolutionary principles expressed in abstract language by the declaration of the rights of man. This declaration delivered the *coup de grace* to the hierarchic order of the old régime, by stripping it of all legitimacy. The relative permanence of individual, political, and intellectual rights, between 1789 and 1948, can also be explained by its context of history. The old régime, as Burke conceived it, with its reciprocal obligations, from above as well as from below, the rights and the duties defined by the place of each individual in the fabric of society, had been carried away with no hope of return by the revolutionary agony, although traces of it remained in Europe and in France throughout the nineteenth century and even during a part of the twentieth.

In terms of *ideas-as-power*, individual rights triumphed and destroyed institutions founded on contrary ideas. To what extent did they triumph in a positive sense, favoring or permitting the construction of a society in conformity with their demands or their logic? Marxists and democrats of liberal inspiration give contradictory answers to this interrogation. They reached agreement, sincerely or hypocritically, in drafting a declaration which adds economic and social rights to those rights whose four categories we have just summed up. But the democrat-liberals deny the fact that the democrat-socialists respect the individual rights of bourgeois tradition; and the democrat-socialists deny the idea that the society termed capitalist, whether bourgeois or liberal, achieves the economic and social rights which the authors of the universal declaration placed on the same level as those rights I shall call traditional.

Before attempting to interpret or comment on the dialogue between liberals and socialists relative to economic and social rights, a few remarks are necessary on the changes which took place between 1789 and 1948 in the matter of the traditional rights whose four categories we have summarized. The first such change concerns the right of property, and its significance must be readily apparent to any observer. In 1789, property formed a part of Article 2, between liberty on the one hand and security and resistance to oppression on the other. In 1948, it did not appear until Article 17, after an article relative to the family and to marriage and before an article relative to freedom of thought, of conscience and of religion. The right of property is expressed in ambiguous terms, acceptable both to the Marxists of the East and to the liberals of the West. "Everyone has the right to own property alone as well as in association with others. No one shall be arbitrarily deprived of his property." Even in a socialist régime, certain goods may be the object of individual appropriation: the Soviet representatives were thus able to subscribe to such an article without violating their own principles. But in spite of everything, the moral devaluation of the right of property between 1789 and 1948 emerges clearly from the comparison between the two texts. Even a text drawn up exclusively by the Western Powers and intended only for the use of the West would have marked more or less sharply a decline of the right of property in the hierarchy of values.

Even more than this devaluation of one right, it seems to me that a comparison between the two declarations makes clear the decline of *all* rights, of the very notion of the rights of man. The French declaration termed the right of property an inviolable and sacred right, which the drafters of the 1948 declaration would never have written. But neither would these latter have written that the aim of all political association is the conservation of the natural and unalienable rights of man. Such a formula, in effect, implies a philosophy of *natural right* and *individualist finality:* In other words, a philosophy by whose standards reason is called upon to determine the principles of the social order, valid everywhere and at all times; a philosophy which states as its final goal for the collectivity, a guarantee of the rights of individuals, with the individual appearing as the sole reality of which a society is composed and, simultaneously, as the ultimate finality of the collective organization. This individualist philosophy of natural right still survives here and there, but it no longer receives the assent of either legislators or influential thinkers, even in Europe or in liberal America. It is true that, in the United States, the amendments to the Constitution resemble a statement of the rights of man and give form to abstract principles in the light of which the Supreme Court decides the questions which are submitted to it. It seems to me, however, that, even in the United States, the amendments, like the rights of man, are considered as the supreme rules of a particular constitution and not as universal principles for humanity. Even the members of the American Congress would hesitate to take up again the French formula by which the goal of all political association is the conservation of the natural and unalienable rights of man. Moreover, if we suppose that they were to consider such an article, it would not have the meaning it assumed in the eyes of its authors at the end of the eighteenth century: those authors, in fact, did not confide to the State the responsibility for promoting what we call today economic and social rights. They were far more concerned with limiting the established power, that of the monarch at first, and that of the State in whatever form it might later take. The rights of man have not disappeared but they have changed in character: henceforth, they define or characterize the condition considered proper to assure to all members of the collectivity, if necessary, through the intervention of the State. From this, it is a logical step from traditional rights, restated from declaration to declaration, to the rights termed economic and social.

Before any study of the significance and status of these economic and social rights, I should like to pose a question which inevitably provokes contradictory replies. Were the socialists, by which I mean the representatives of régimes of the Soviet type, sincere in their agreement to traditional rights or were they not? When one half of the drafters of the 1948 declaration rendered only lip service to traditional rights and the other half was unresolved as to the meaning of the new rights, is there any cause for astonishment at the fact that it remains, twenty years later, what it was on the first day, a sort of appeal to the leaders of governments, a discourse which exhorts them to conduct themselves in a decent manner?

Of the four categories of traditional rights which we have surveyed, the Soviet régimes accept the first—that which translates into abstract language the idea of nondiscrimination and of equaliy before the law— without reserve. Not that the Soviets do not sometimes violate the rules of what Parsons calls *universalism*; but the Western nations do not do otherwise. The claims of racial, ethnic, or religious minorities invoke violations, both overt and covert, of the universalism proclaimed as a maxim for any modern society.

The second category, that which translates the *democratic formula*, is not foreign to the authentic philosophy of the Soviet leaders and the peoples of Eastern Europe. The Marxists-Leninists claim to express and interpret the will of the masses. They organize ceremonies of acclamation and christen them elections, as if to symbolize their respect for a formula they do not apply without repudiating it and which they probably hope to apply some day, after having long held it in contempt. The Soviet leaders offer multiple justifications for the rule of the single party, sometimes as the avant-garde of the proletariat, which is itself invested with a historic mission, and sometimes as the guide and representative of the entire people. Occasionally, they put forth other arguments, such as the futility of elections in a country in which there no longer exists a class conflict, or the greater importance of other forms of participation in the collective life, within the trade unions or the factories and farms. But, no matter what the justification finally adopted may be, the spokesmen for the socialist régimes—of tomorrow if not of today—do not reject the democratic formula, the origin of sovereignty in the people.

The attitude of the Soviet régimes with regard to the rights of the third and fourth categories—personal liberties and guarantees of impartial justice—seems to me more ambiguous. At the present time, full and complete freedom of expression has not been granted to the citizens of any of the countries of Eastern Europe. At the very moment in which I write these lines, the liberalization toward which the leaders of the Czechoslovak government are striving is spreading terror in Warsaw and Moscow, to such an extent that the men of the Kremlin are talking of a counter-revolutionary movement and of eventual action on the part of "fraternal countries" to reestablish or restore socialism. In the sense given to it by the Marxists-Leninists, socialism therefore seems to exclude liberty in the sense given to it by liberals of the entire world, and even in the sense given to it by intellectuals and ordinary men formed under socialist régimes.

Marxist-Leninist socialism does not, however, reject liberty in the manner in which fascism did. It does not deny personal and intellectual liberties—which the Stalin constitution of 1936 itself solemnly recognized and promised to all—any more than it denies the sovereignty of the people, as amended by the guiding role of the communist party. *Ideologically*, how is the reconciliation between principles and reality brought about? The arguments employed by the leaders of the régime oscillate between the old formula—no liberty for the enemies of liberty —and the pure and simple affirmation that the citizens of the Soviet Union effectively enjoy freedom of expression but that they have no desire to express anything which contradicts orthodox doctrine. To conclude on this point, let us say that the socialist régimes, which at first were ambitious to enrich formal *liberties* by real *liberty*, have not, a half century after the October revolution, succeeded in reestablishing the formal liberties whose insufficiency Marx proclaimed but whose decay he would have indignantly denounced.

The same contradiction exists to an even greater degree with regard to the exercise of justice in the socialist régimes. Concentration camps, condemnation, and execution of innocent people by the hundreds of thousands, confessions by individuals and groups accused of imaginary crimes: no régime before that of Stalin's had violated the rules of civilization relative to the administration of justice with so much brutality, so much cynicism, such enormous, Kafka-like lies. These violations of legality were attributed to the "cult of personality"—an expression devoid of meaning except in the sense that it imputes to a single man the responsibility for all of these crimes, and such an imputation, coming from Marxists, is not lacking in involuntary irony. The fact remains— and the evolution of the socialist régimes proves this every day—that here again adherents of the Soviet system subscribe to the fourth category of the rights of man without hypocrisy and without illusion. Without hypocrisy, since they are not actually opposed, in principle, to an administration of justice in conformity with the ideal of the bourgeois West of the eighteenth century. Without illusion, since they are well aware of the enormous gap between the reality and the ideal. Perhaps, for that matter, I am wrong in according them such an ideal. Despite all else, the "socialist legality" which they invoke more and more frequently differs in one essential point from liberal legality: the tribunals, even in theory, have no status of independence with relation to the State, which is itself in the service of the party. Insofar as minor offenses or common law crimes are concerned, socialist tribunals could be fairly close to tribunals of the liberal type; it would not, however, be the same in anything concerning crimes against the State—and this concept remains curiously elastic.

Such then, avoiding all polemics, is the manner in which I see the dialogue between a Marxist-Leninist and a liberal philosopher of the rights of man. Rights which the Marxist does not deny, even though he does not apply them: He respects the principle of universalism, common to all modern societies; he admits the democratic formula, while seeking a translation for it other than that of free elections; he does not definitively exclude intellectual or personal liberties, although he refuses the benefit of them to the citizens of today; he preaches socialist legality, but shows no sign of resigning himself to the independence of tribunals.

Does the dialogue between a philosopher of the rights of man, as they have been formed by tradition, and a champion of economic and social rights, take on a character comparable to the preceding dialogue? I do not think so. The liberal does not reject the majority of economic and social rights, either in principle or in fact. The crux of the debate seems to me essentially theoretical: can or should economic and social rights be placed on the same level as the rights I have termed traditional —those which express universalism, the democratic formula and personal or intellectual liberties?

Let us first recall the principal economic and social rights enumerated in the 1948 declaration: the right to marriage without "any restriction due to race, nationality, or religion." The declaration even adds to this the equality of rights of male and female with regard to marriage and divorce, by requiring the "free and full consent of the intending spouses." The declaration goes on to accord to each individual the right to social security (Article 22), the right to work with the free choice of employment and an equal wage for equal work, the right to form a trade union or to belong to one, the right to repose and to leisure, the right to a "standard of living adequate for the health and well-being of himself and of his family," the right to education (and even to an obligatory and free primary education). And finally, in Article 28, the declaration includes the following formula: "Everyone is entitled to a social and international order in which the rights and freedoms set forth in this declaration can be fully realized."

Does there exist a difference of nature or only one of degree between economic and social rights and the rights I have called traditional? In a little book entitled *Human Rights Today* (London, 1962) the English writer, Maurice Cranston, devoted some pages to this problem and came to the conclusion of a difference in nature. Economic and social rights, he wrote, constitute, so to speak, the "lofty ideals" of societies; they cannot be assimilated to categorical or unconditional rights. Two criteria permit and justify the distinction between *rights* and *ideals*: the criterion which Cranston terms *practicability* and that of *paramount importance*.

In order for one person to have a right, it is necessary that another has a duty—that of respecting or of carrying out that right. Any State can normally assure the right to life, to freedom of expression, to a trial of its citizens by a jury; it is not, however, the same when it comes to

the right to work, to social security, to paid vacations, to a decent standard of living, to obligatory and free primary education, etc. . . . The second criterion, which Cranston considers less decisive than the first, is
easily applied to certain cases: "Holidays with pay are excellent too; they
contribute to the greatest happiness of the greatest number. But they
are not a matter of paramount importance, like freedom of speech or
equality before the law."

Does this second criterion, which is obviously valid for the example
mentioned, have a general significance? Is there a distinction of decisive
importance in whether criminals are subject to the decision of a jury
rather than to that of a professional judge? And if so, for whom? There
are fewer criminals than workers. If importance is measured in terms of
the number of individuals affected, the jury has less importance than
holidays with pay. But, is it not true that since *anyone* may be called before a tribunal *everyone* is interested in the administration of justice?
Remembering the case of Russia under Stalin, let us admit this to be
true. But even in this hypothesis, it is a matter less of a difference of nature than of degree, unless we are to define *importance* in moral and
not in material terms. The equitable administration of justice concerns
us all because it calls into question *values* which are essential in our
eyes. It is no longer a question of happiness, but of morality. But in this
hypothesis, the criterion supposes something which remains in question:
the radical distinction between the *universal rights* of man and the
objectives which a social order should set for itself.

The first criterion, that of practicability, of a duty correlative to
rights, is also applicable at first estimate, once a choice has been made
of economic and social rights, expressed with excessive precision, and
personal or intellectual rights, expressed in vague and abstract terms.
The governments of the poorer nations do not have the material means
to assure a decent standard of living to all, or to guarantee a free and obligatory primary education to all children. How can we accord to all
men a right to which there is no corresponding duty, since no one can
be *held* to the accomplishment of what he *cannot* accomplish?

The argument loses something of its force if economic and social
rights are formulated in other, less precise, less restrictive terms. It would
suffice to suppress rights such as those to paid vacations (a desirable
objective but not a universal right of individuals or an unconditional
duty of government leaders or private businessmen), to suppose that the
right to work, to social security or to a decent standard of living are understood with a reserve of common sense "in terms of the resources
available to the collectivity," in order for the contrast to seem less sharp.
Why should the State not have the same obligation to assure to all the

standard of living compatible with the wealth (or the poverty) of the nation as to guarantee freedom of expression or equitable administration of justice? In what manner does the capacity or the power to accomplish these goals differ from one case to the other?

The question may be raised that the rulers of the State do not manipulate the sharing out of incomes in accordance with their own will, since such sharing out is probably subject to a determinism which economists strive to understand and the leaders of governments find difficulty in controlling. The objection is just, but are the leaders of governments any more capable, at all times and everywhere, of achieving the rights of man relative to freedom of expression and to the democratic formula? As soon as one attempts to measure the real capacity of the effective leaders of the régime, or the multiple pressures to which they are subjected, there no longer exists any radical difference between the economic order and the political order: the leaders do not completely control either the one or the other.

According to Maurice Cranston, "A human right by definition is a universal moral right, something which all men, everywhere, at all times, ought to have, something of which no one may be deprived without a grave affront to justice; something which is owing to every human being simply because he is human." In other words, Cranston is here taking up again, purely and simply, the philosophy of natural right, of the rights of man as a man. It is in terms of this philosophy that he establishes a discrimination of principle between political and individual rights on the one hand and economic and social rights on the other. The two criteria on which he supports his attempt to establish this discrimination theoretically are open to criticism. They are applicable to the simplest cases, to the most pronounced oppositions; they suppose essential discrimination, they do not establish it.

The distinction between universal and categorical rights on the one hand, and noble ideals on the other, marks a return to the very philosophy whose particular character, in spite of its pretension to universality, has been brought to light by all sociological thought and not simply by Marxism.

The French declaration of 1789 draws its significance less from its alleged universality than from the historic content which was both expressed and concealed in abstract formulas. Two centuries ago, the right to property was considered sacred; in our time, it has become relative, precarious and revocable; a universal right, on the condition that it is expressed in terms which condemn neither Soviet practice nor Western practice. Each régime determines what may be the object of individual ownership. Generally speaking, one could state the dilemma in the following terms: Either rights attain a certain sort of universality because, thanks to the vagueness of their conceptual structure, they allow of any institution whatever; or they retain some preciseness and lose their value of universality. The accused has the right to be judged according to fair procedures, but in every epoch and in every society the definition of fairness of procedures is subject to substantial variations. And in the same manner, participation in the government of the nation remains a universal right only on the condition that the institutions, through whose intermediary such participation becomes effective, are no longer specified. The principle of nonretroactivity of laws was violated at the Nuremberg trials.

The radical discrimination between *universal rights* and *lofty ideals* is vulnerable to the criticism which, from Nietzsche to Pareto, by way of Marx, brings to light the ruses of the will to power and of personal (or collective) interest. The Marxist thinks to *unmask* the predominant concern for personal liberties, which are vital to some, in the refusal to place economic and social rights on the same level as the rights of liberal tradition. Do those rights decreed as universal and categorical, and which act primarily to the profit of some, present a greater importance than social security or the standard of living, which are profitable to all? Is not the inequality of the statutes attributed to these two kinds of rights the conscious or unconscious expression of a policy, legitimate but not evident as such? A liberal policy is not a universally valid philosophy.

Lastly, the radical distinction between categorical rights and lofty ideals is open to a final and more serious objection. Whether it is a matter of universal suffrage, of freedom of expression or of guarantees of a fair justice, the rights of man demand an established order. They have not been conquered without violence and they are not respected in a period of violence. Revolutionaries forget or scorn them and they cannot always do otherwise. In certain circumstances, the transformation of the social order with a view toward achievement of *lofty ideals* demands a resort to force. In such a case, the means judged necessary—rightly or wrongly—to attain the objectives fixed by economic and social rights excludes respect for personal or intellectual rights, for a period of uncertain duration. The rights of these two categories are not *essentially* incompatible, but they become so under certain conditions.

Obviously, the experience of the twentieth century has taught us the perils of sacrifice of traditional rights in the hope of realizing the lofty ideals of economic and social rights. Formal liberties—the right to the vote, personal liberties—do not suffice to guarantee a decent existence to all; they can expand only in a climate of real liberties or, if you prefer, on condition of assuring security and a decent standard of living to the greatest number; the Marxists are right to remind us of this. But there is available to us in this respect a pertinent reply: The suppression of traditional rights, although proclaimed at the beginning to be provisional, may remain in effect for a long time, and the producer does not always gain in real liberty what the citizen loses in formal liberty.

However pertinent this reply may appear to me, it leaves intact a system of reasoning most often attributed to Marxism but renewed in one form or another by all sociological thought: As of the time when achievement of economic and social rights becomes the prioritary object of action on the part of the State, individual rights, far from retaining their sacred character, become or are in danger of becoming obstacles to be surmounted in order to attain the true goal, a reconstruction of the social order. Let us once again cite Article 2 of the Constitution of 1789: "The aim of all political association is the preservation of the natural and unalienable rights of man. These rights are liberty, property, security, and resistance to oppression." If the men who govern, even in the West, were to seek to define "the aim of all political association," what terms would they employ? Probably, they would refer to equality (nondiscrimination), to economic security, to the standard of living, but certainly not to the preservation of the natural and unalienable rights of man. Thus, we return to the opposition already mentioned between a philosophy of rights which tends to limit the power of the State and a philosophy of rights confused with lofty ideals, which confides to the State the crushing, perhaps unrealizable task of transforming the condition of man in society, in compliance with certain requirements which were never manifested in the course of preceding centuries.

This ambitious, sociologically inspired, philosophy prompts a refusal to hold strictly to the formal or the legal. Whether individuals are formally equal before the law signifies nothing so long as custom ignores this equality. In the United States, civil rights legislation tends not only to compel the states or the schools to put into practice the equality which is an integral part of the American credo; it also, on occasion, curtails certain traditional rights—that of the land owner for example—by prohibiting discriminatory practices. In this sense, legislation endeavors to alter customs.

Another example of this movement which extends from the formal to the real can be found in the realm of education. The right to education signifies nothing if the family does not have the financial resources without which it would be unable to exercise its right. This has already resulted in free primary and even secondary education and in the multiplication of scholarships. But, in a later stage, we might question the advantages derived from their environment by the children of privileged families: Might it not be advisable to reestablish real equality by doing away, insofar as possible, with advantages which are reflected by a certain correlation between educational results and the social origin of students? Until the present time, it seems that no government anywhere has given supplementary points to candidates coming from the lower classes of society. But such a project has nonetheless been evoked. Carried to its logical end, it could imply, in a case in which the number of places available for higher education was limited, a *numerus clausus* for the children of the upper classes, in order to augment the degree of social mobility.

But let us set aside these projects, which are Utopian at the present time, and which we have evoked here solely in order to shed light on the passage from the formal to the material. In poor societies, particularly in Africa, even a primary education for all is probably beyond the resources of the States. Thus, it will be the responsibility of these States to select those who are to receive a basic education. Of course, such a process of selection has also been at work in the past, but within and by society. Experience of the exclusion of the majority has not, in the common conscience, threatened the principle of the right of all to education. An unexercised right remained a right. Neither society nor the State were held responsible for furnishing to all the material means of exercising their rights. Sociological thought dispels this illusion of good conscience. And at the same time, it is concerned less with limiting the intervention of the State in order to protect the individual than with strengthening the public powers, in order that they may permit every individual to exercise his rights.

If we follow this line of thought, society or the State become, so to speak, the parties responsible for individual failures. American writers are already discussing formulas for a negative income tax: a contribution by the State to taxpayers situated below the line of poverty, of a sum which would raise the lowest incomes to the level estimated by opinion as the social minimum. Such a formula can be justified by reference to the classic conception of welfare payments or of social security. It seems to me however to have a more profound and richer significance: sociological thought has conferred on economic and social rights a status equivalent to that of traditional rights; it has transformed lofty ideals into unconditional imperatives. Some will conclude from this that the theory of the rights of man has become obsolete, others that it has become richer. In both cases, the State appears as the victor, since neither traditional rights nor economic and social rights restrict it or, possibly, condemn it.

If necessary, the wealthy societies can move through the successive stages of this dialectic without sacrificing either the liberties of the liberals or the ideals of the socialists. It is not the same in poor societies. So long as legislators and philosophers refrain from establishing a hierarchy between civil and political rights on the one hand and the conditions of existence of the masses on the other, what reason is there for astonishment that the latter should be considered more important than the former? Can the underdeveloped countries make the passage from the formal to the material without recourse to violence? In a revolutionary age, do the rights of man represent something more than a luxury of wealthy nations?

What conclusion is suggested by these brief analyses? Should we rejoice at the extension of the traditional idea of the rights of man into the political and social realms? Or should we deplore the fact that these rights have lost or seem to have lost their unconditional, almost sacred character? Probably, we should accept both conclusions at the same time: our epoch has the merit of having enlarged the number of subjects and the scope of objects of those rights which are stated to be universal, but this enlargement is accompanied by a compensating depreciation.

In a certain sense, sociological thought has consecrated Nietzsche's, Marx's or Pareto's criticism of eighteenth-century philosophy. It accepts historic relativism: Every society organizes itself in accordance with a certain system of standards or values, which are termed culture. The so-called universal rights merit this qualificative only on condition of being formulated in a language so vague that they lose all definite meaning. Of what significance is the right to property so long as the nature of the property open to individual ownership remains undetermined? Of what significance is political liberty so long as, from one epoch to another, there are constant changes in the institutional translation of participation of all in the government of the nation? This historic relativism, now becomes an integral part of the common conscience and, profoundly marked by the sociological mode of thought, entails the technique of "debunking," of bringing to light the interests or passions concealed behind these supposedly disinterested, passionless resolutions. But at the same time, the rights of man, stripped of their false universality, recover a historic significance, indeed a historic efficacy. The 1789 declaration cannot be separated from the particular and nonuniversal philosophy which inspired it, or from the bourgeois revolt against the old régime. Logico-experimental thought, to use Pareto's expression, has no difficulty in bringing out the nonlogical character of the rights of man, the variation of formulas between an abstraction too vague to authorize any judgment, and a preciseness too great (separation of powers) to safeguard the claim to universality. But the analysis of historic origins restores their dignity to the rights of man by stripping them of their illusory universality. Any declaration of rights appears finally as the idealized expression of the political or social order which a certain class or a certain civilization is attempting to realize. It at least permits the condemnation of certain institutions (class distinctions) or the affirmation of certain principles (nondiscrimination), if not of a definition, on the basis of imperatives, of the precise make-up of social organizations.

It is in this manner that the ambiguity of the universal declaration of rights of 1948 can be explained. It borrows from Western civilization the very practice of a declaration of rights, while other civilizations, though not ignorant of collective standards or of individual rights, are unaware of the theoretical and pretendedly universal expression of such standards or rights. The Western origin of the declaration manifests itself, for example, in the articles relating to the family: nowhere is the free choice of a spouse or the equality of rights of male and female fully realized; in a strict sense, perhaps, Westerners play out for themselves the comedy of subscribing to such an ideal of the family. It is not the same thing for the men or women who belong to other cultures. If so many delegates from five continents did, in appearance, subscribe to this article relating to the family, it is because it too expressed, in an extreme form, the philosophy of individual rights or of the equality of all—a Western philosophy granted lip service as an exemplary pattern. Another ambiguity of the 1948 declaration stems from the attempt at synthesis between Marxist-Leninist conception and liberal conception. The juxtaposition of traditional rights and economic and social rights was and remains acceptable to both the representatives of the Soviet Union and to those of the Western nations. Both parties, in effect, set themselves the objective of accomplishing both forms of rights. But this reconciliation leaves unanswered the real question, that of the relative importance of the two forms of rights.

Among the liberals, some, such as Cranston, would like to reserve for the traditional rights a status different from that of economic and social rights. Others accept the theoretical equality of status but maintain the decisive importance of traditional rights on the level of political strategy. Still others—and I am among these—reject both the one and the other of these discriminations, even if they personally accord a higher place to traditional rights; even if they judge that, for the moment, the régimes of political democracy offer the least defective synthesis between the double ideal of bourgeois liberalism and of socialism.

Interpreted thus, the 1948 declaration, through its very ambiguity, fulfills the historic function of any such declaration: it criticizes modern society in the name of the ideals which this society has set for itself. According to sociological thought, all philosophy of natural right expresses and denies at the same time the society from which it emanates. It borrows its values and reproaches it for having betrayed them. The 1948 declaration, sometimes exaggeratedly concrete, sometimes falsely universal, takes its place in the line of earlier declarations, in spite of the defects natural to a collective work; it enjoins modern societies to maintain the traditional rights of individuals and to give to all the material means to make use of these rights. The drafters of the 1789 declaration wanted to limit the State in order to liberate the individual. The drafters of the 1948 declaration, without being fully aware of it, were prepared to give all powers to the State in order that it might assure the security and the standard of living of all.

The declaration of rights criticizes positive right in the name of the ideal to which the society subscribes. The 1948 declaration criticizes liberal society in the name of the socialist ideal and socialist society in the name of the liberal ideal. Which of the two societies offers the greater resistance to this criticism? This is a question which each individual must decide for himself. In any event, to the pessimist who rightly deplores the excessive interval between proclaimed rights and respected rights, the optimist may reply that men have never before been so ambitious: they wish to conciliate the ideals of enemy régimes; simultaneously or at intervals, they grant their confidence to the State or they mistrust it. Through impatience or through necessity, they often prefer violence to reforms. In a revolutionary age, is there cause for astonishment that States so often violate the rights of man or that the representatives of these same States pretend to retain both the memory of and respect for these rights?

PHILOSOPHY AND HISTORY IN THE DEVELOPMENT OF HUMAN RIGHTS

Richard McKeon

Human rights are natural, inborn, inalienable; yet they have a history, they are acquired, and they are increased and developed. Human rights have a universal common basis in human thought and community; yet they are differently interpreted, and their recognition and practice depend on the development of a common understanding of rights and freedoms. For this reason the Preamble to the Universal Declaration of Human Rights, adopted twenty years ago, proclaims "recognition of the inherent dignity and of the equal and inalienable rights of all members of the human family"; it recognizes that in the Charter of the United Nations "Member States have pledged themselves to achieve, in cooperation with the United Nations, the promotion of universal respect for and observance of human rights and fundamental freedoms"; and it declares that "a common understanding of these rights and freedoms is of the greatest importance for the realization of this pledge."

Human rights have a philosophy as well as a history; and the acquisition, extension, increase, and exercise of human rights depend on the historical situation in which they are asserted and achieved, and on the views and convictions which make statement of them, and actions in accordance with them, possible. The historical situation conditions the conception of human rights developed in those times and circumstances; and in turn, the conception of human rights and of human nature and society conditions the statement of the history of human rights and the varieties of historical accounts in which knowledge of the past and of the present is set forth. Philosophy and history are inseparable in the development of human rights. Ideas and values are ingredients in recognized or *known facts*; what is the case, and true statements about conditions and needs, are both determinants and consequences of accepted or *sought values.* The history of human rights must be rewritten, at each stage of its progress, from the point of view of the ideas and values, the philosophy, of that period. The philosophy of human rights must be reformulated from the point of view of the problems and opportunities presented by the facts and desires of the historical situation in which oppositions and agreements constitute the community of a people and of a time, and form their philosophy in action.

The investigation of the philosophy and history of human rights has been an integral part of the formulation and promulgation of a declaration of human rights, and of conventions to advance human rights, in the United Nations. An inquiry into the theoretical problems raised by the preparation of a universal declaration of human rights was part of the program of UNESCO in the first year of its operation. A Committee on the Theoretical Bases of Human Rights (it was also referred to as the "Committee on the Philosophic Principles of the Rights of Man" in UNESCO documents) was established in 1947, a month after the ratification of the Constitution of UNESCO. The Committee was convinced that the perspectives open to men, both on the planes of history and of philosophy, are wider and richer today than ever before, and that the hopes that emerge as possible become greater the deeper the reexamination of the bases of human rights that is made. A series of questions was prepared in March 1947 "concerning the changes of intellectual and historical circumstances between the classical declarations of human rights which stem from the eighteenth century and the bill of rights made possible by the state of ideas and the economic potentials of the present," [1] and was circulated to a select list of scholars of the world. The Committee met from June 26 to July 2, 1947, to study the replies to the questionnaire that had been received and to draw up a history of human rights and a theoretical schematism of rights based on that history.

Replies to the questions concerning the theoretical bases of the rights of man had been received from scholars and statesmen in many of the major parts of the world in the few months between March and June 1947. The selection of replies later published by the Committee included letters or essays by Mahatma Gandhi, Benedetto Croce, Teilhard de Chardin, Aldous Huxley, Salvador de Madariaga, Jacques Maritain, E. H. Carr, Harold J. Laski, F. S. C. Northrop, and Humayun Kabir. The Committee made use of these replies in drawing up its Report on "The Grounds of an International Declaration of Human Rights," but presented its report as conclusions concerning the history and nature of human rights which did not represent the opinions of all the scholars who had contributed to the Symposium.

It is the conviction of the UNESCO Committee that these inquiries into the intellectual bases of human rights may contribute to the work of the Commission on Human Rights in two fashions: first, by a brief indication of the places at which the discovery of common principles might remove difficulties in the way of agreement and the places at which philosophic divergence might anticipate difficulties in interpretation and, second, a more precise and detailed examination of the common principles that may be formulated and the philosophic differences that have divided men in the interpretation of those principles. The document which is here presented is an attempt to perform the first and preliminary task. The Committee is convinced that UNESCO will be able to muster the scholarly resources necessary for the accomplishment of the second task.[2]

The celebration of the twentieth anniversary of the adoption of the Universal Declaration of Human Rights can take no more fitting form, it seems to me, than a review and extension of the history of human rights and a reexamination and restatement of the philosophy of human rights sketched by the UNESCO Committee twenty-one years ago. In what follows I shall divide that review and reexamination into two parts: first, a statement of the ideas and the situation twenty years ago, and second, what has happened in thought and practice in the twenty years since the Declaration was made, including changes of ideas, attitudes, and relations which have resulted from the Declaration.

1. The United Nations and Human Rights, 1948

"An international declaration of human rights must be the expression of a faith to be maintained no less than a programme of actions to be carried out." [3] These are the opening words of the Committee's Report, "The Grounds of an International Declaration of Human Rights." The Committee argued, therefore, that the preparation of a Declaration of Human Rights faces fundamental problems concerning principles and interpretations as well as political problems concerning agreement and drafting. The task which scholars might undertake to assist the Commission on Human Rights of the Economic and Social Council of the United Nations was the examination of the intellectual bases of a modern bill of rights to uncover common grounds for agreement and to explain possible sources of differences. Members of the United Nations share common convictions on which human rights are based, but the Committee was also convinced that those common convictions are stated in terms of different philosophic principles and on the background of divergent political and economic systems. Examination of the grounds of a bill of rights should reveal common principles and anticipate differences of interpretation. The common faith of the United Nations in freedom and democracy and its determination to safeguard their power to expand is recorded in the Charter of the United Nations. That faith in freedom and democracy is founded on the faith in the inherent dignity of men and women.

It is this faith, in the opinion of the UNESCO Committee, which underlies the solemn obligation of the United Nations to declare, not only to all governments, but also to their peoples, the rights which have now become the vital ends of human effort everywhere. These rights must no longer be confined to a few. They are claims which all men and women may legitimately make, in their search, not only to fulfil themselves at their best, but to be so placed in life that they are capable, at their best, of becoming in the highest sense citizens of the various communities to which they belong and of the world community, and in those communities of seeking to respect the rights of others, just as they are resolute to protect their own.[4]

In the United Nations the nations of the world combined in their expression of a philosophy of human rights and in their efforts to contribute to the history of the advancement of human rights. The history of the philosophic discussion of human rights, of the dignity and brotherhood of man, and of his common citizenship in the great society is long, but, the Committee pointed out, the history of declarations of human rights and of institutions established to protect them is short, going back no further than the British Bill of Rights and the American and French Declarations of Rights of the seventeenth and eighteenth centuries.

The first question considered by the Committee was the philosophy of human rights. Does the fact that human rights depend on ideas and on a philosophy mean that men must come to agreement on a common philosophy before they can make a Declaration of Rights, or does the philosophy of human rights take a more flexible form congruent with the freedom to philosophize which is a basic human right? After long and detailed discussion the Committee agreed that the recognition of common grounds of human rights, the enumeration of particular rights, and agreement on the actions required to achieve and protect them, do not require a doctrinal consensus or agreement concerning the philosophic definition of basic terms. There was no "natural law" philosophy in the seventeenth and eighteenth century: Philosophers as different as Hobbes, Spinoza, Locke, Puffendorf, Bellarmine, and Grotius made use of the term "natural law" without sharing a philosophy or ideology; and the statesmen who borrowed the term when they drew up Declarations of Rights or interpreted them did not define natural law more rigorously than had the philosophers.

The Committee is convinced that the philosophic problem involved in a declaration of human rights is not to achieve a doctrinal consensus but rather to achieve agreement concerning rights, and also concerning actions in the realization and defense of rights, which may be justified on highly divergent doctrinal grounds. The Committee's discussion, therefore, of both the evolution of human rights and of the theoretic differences concerning their nature and interrelations, was intended, not to set up an intellectual structure to reduce them to a single formulation, but rather to discover the intellectual means to secure agreement concerning fundamental rights and to remove difficulties in their implementation such as might stem from intellectual differences.[5]

The Committee therefore agreed on working definitions of "right," "liberty," and "democracy," susceptible of divergent particularizations. They were definitions which contained a deliberate, pragmatic, and productive ambiguity.

For the purposes of the present inquiry, the Committee did not explore the subtleties of interpretation of right, liberty, and democracy. The members of the Committee found it possible to agree on working definitions of these terms, reserving for later examination the fashion in which their differences of interpretation will diversify their further definition. By a right they mean a condition of living, without which, in any given historical stage of a society, men cannot give the best of themselves as active members of the community because they are deprived of the means to fulfil themselves as human beings. By liberty they mean more than only the absence of restraint. They mean also the positive organization of the social and economic conditions within which men can participate to a maximum as active members of the community and contribute to the welfare of the community at the highest level permitted by the material development of the society. This liberty can have meaning only under democratic conditions, for only in democracy is liberty set in that context of equality which makes it an opportunity for all men and not for some men only. Democratic liberty is a liberty which does not distinguish by age or sex, by race or language or creed, between the rights of one man and the rights of another.[6]

In terms of the living and developing philosophy of human rights and liberties in which these working definitions were formed and used, the Committee examined the broad lines of the history and evolution of particular rights.

a. The History of Human Rights

(1) Civil and Political Rights

The rights of man have moral and social foundations which were discussed in all cultures and societies, Eastern and Western, ancient and modern, in literature, religion, and philosophy. In the West the growth of universities and the diversification of higher education, the proliferation of popular religious movements, and the development of national states, focused attention on action needed to free man from unwarranted interference with his thought and expression, and a series of freedoms were formulated more and more precisely and insistently from the late Middle Ages to the eighteenth century: freedom of thought and expression, of conscience, worship, speech, assembly, association, and the press, gradually took definite form. Legal implementations for their protection, by the institution of courts or the extension of the jurisdiction of existing courts, associated these rights and other personal rights with the right to justice by appeal to law and in that appeal to be protected from summary arrest, cruel treatment, and unjust punishment. As civil rights these rights were closely related to political action by which the function of citizens in states is defined. *Political* rights were written into instruments and institutions of government. *Civil* rights, protected from interference by governments by recourse to courts, were written into bills of rights. Political rights were discussed in the eighteenth century in close connection with the right to rebellion or revolution and with the right to citizenship, and in the nineteenth century the dependence of political rights on the right to information became increasingly clear.

(2) *Economic and Social Rights*

The development of industry and technology in the nineteenth century, by making the means of livelihood potentially accessible to all men, led to increased recognition that to live well and freely man must have at least the means requisite for living. Economic and social rights were sometimes treated, as in the Anglo-American constitutional tradition, as extensions of civil and political rights. They were sometimes treated, as in the French and Continental political tradition, as distinct rights, and since the achievement of political rights had required political revolutions, their achievement seemed to depend on further economic and social revolutions carried out by planned violent action or gradual reform, or by unplanned chance or necessity, or by rhetorical persuasion or manipulation, incitation or deception. In the Anglo-American tradition, the right to property was closely associated, in statement and conception, with the right to the pursuit of happiness. The evolution of economic and social rights depended on the discussion of the ownership and use of property, of private and common ownership, and of private rights and public responsibility. Recognition of the right to education led to the institution of public systems of education; the right to work was a freedom consequent on the right to property and led to legal provision for bargaining and arbitration; the right to the protection of health was first given institutional form in pure food and drugs legislation under the provisions of police power, was extended to minimum medical and dietetic services, and finally in the twentieth century to provisions for social security.

(3) Cultural Rights

With increasing technological advances, the right of all to share in the advancing gains of civilization and to have full access to the enjoyment of cultural opportunities and material improvements came to be recognized and to be extended. Since the ideals and accomplishment of an age find their expression in art and literature, a new emphasis has been placed in the rights of the mind, on the right to inquiry, expression, and communication. Whether the purpose of communication be the expression of an idea or an emotion, the furthering of an individual or social purpose, or the formulation of an objective and scientific truth, the right is grounded both in the purpose of developing to the full the potentialities of men and in the social consequences of such communications. Moreover, much as the development of economic and social rights transformed and enlarged the interpretation of civil and political rights and the number of men and women who exercised them, so the development of cultural rights has transformed civil, political, economic, and social rights by an increase of mutual understanding and cooperation and an appreciation and development of the values which are accessible to men associated in the community of mankind and humanity.

b. The Fundamental Human Rights

The evolution of men's conception of human rights clarifies not only the problems which man and society faced at each stage of the formation of the idea of human rights, but also the means that have been found in the institution of human rights for the solution of those problems.

Human rights have become, and must remain, universal. All rights which we have come slowly and laboriously to recognize belong to all men everywhere without discrimination of race, sex, language or religion. They are universal, moreover, not only because there are no fundamental differences among men, but also because the great society and the community of all men has become a real and effective power, and the interdependent nature of that community is beginning at last to be recognized. This universality of the rights of man, finally, has led to the translation into political instrumentalities of that close interdependence of rights and duties which has long been apparent in moral analysis.[7]

All the rights which men have acquired through the centuries are important in the life of man and in the development of human communities and a world community. New rights, made possible by advances in knowledge and technology and by the institution of the agencies of the United Nations, have assumed priority in the development of rights and in the extension of rights—those long recognized and those newly conceived—to more and more people, for the new rights have not only added to the list of rights, but they have also made clear the full sense of the older rights and have made them universally practicable. The UNESCO Committee was therefore convinced that it is possible to draw up a list of fundamental rights on which all men are agreed. They may be viewed as rights implicit in man's nature as an individual and as a member of society, and therefore they all follow from the fundamental right to live. The Committee therefore organized a list of fifteen rights under three headings.

(1) The right to live is the condition and foundation of all other rights. The first group of rights are specifications of the right to live as they bear on man's provision of means for subsistence, through his own efforts or, where they are insufficient, through the resources of society: (2) the right to the protection of health, (3) the right to work, (4) the right to maintenance in involuntary unemployment, infancy, old age, sickness and other forms of incapacity, and (5) the right to property. The right to live is more than the right to bare living, and the first group of rights designed to safeguard bare living is supplemented by a second group of rights "providing intellectual foundations for living well, training for the proper use of human abilities, as well as the opportunities for self-development and the advancement of the common good:" [8] (6) the right to education, (7) the right to information, (8) freedom of thought and the right to free inquiry, and (9) the right to self-expression. A third group of rights bear on man's participation in society and his protection from social and political injustice: (10) the right to justice, (11) the right to political action, (12) freedom of speech, assembly, association, worship, and the press, (13) the right to citizenship, (14) the right to rebellion or revolution, and (15) the right to share in progress. These rights are of fundamental importance not only to the enrichment of the human spirit but to the development of all forms of human association, including the development of national cultures and inter-national cooperation. The Committee laid particular emphasis on "the dynamic character of the interrelations of human rights and the need, therefore, to explore and control the basic ideas which are in the process of being fitted to new industrial and technological means for the achievement of the human good." [9]

2. The Philosophy and History of Human Rights, 1948–1968

The Preamble of the Universal Declaration of Human Rights recognizes that the Charter of the United Nations established institutional arrangements to promote fundamental human rights, and the Declaration itself states in specific detail the rights which are referred to in the

Charter. The Declaration is a statement of principles. As such it has been influential in the last twenty years, but it has also been the basis for international conventions and covenants, for national declarations of rights in new constitutions of new states, for new laws and radical changes in social and economic conditions and relations, and, finally, for increased opportunities and increases in the number of people who can make use of those opportunities as well as in the scope and variety of aspirations which color and guide the lives of man. The Universal Declaration of Human Rights has had an educational effect on the lives of individual men and of societies and associations of men, on nations, and on the community of mankind. It has also had a direct effect on the Conventions and Protocols instituted by the United Nations and its Specialized Agencies. The history of human rights during the last twenty years, as well as the philosophic problems encountered in that history, may be seen in institutionalized form in the development of conventions which have restated the principles of the Declaration as law, much as the Declaration had restated the objectives of the Charter as principles.

The Universal Declaration of Human Rights was adopted by the General Assembly of the United Nations on December 10, 1948, by a vote of 48 to 0 with eight abstentions and two absences. The Commission on Human Rights started at once to work on the draft international conventions. They were divided into two conventions based on the distinction of kinds of rights suggested by the philosophic principles that had emerged in their discussion. In 1954 the preliminary texts of a draft covenant on civil and political rights and a draft convenant on economic, social, and cultural rights were completed and sent through the Economic and Social Council to the General Assembly where they were considered article by article from 1955 to 1966. The two Covenants and an Optional Protocol were adopted by the Assembly on December 16, 1966—the Covenant on Economic, Social, and Cultural Rights by a vote of 105 to 0, the Covenant on Civil and Political Rights by a vote of 106 to 0, and the Optional Protocol to the Covenant on Civil and Political Rights by a vote of 66 to 2 with 38 abstentions.

Although it took eighteen years to come to agreement on the overall covenants which give a legal or treaty status to arrangements by which the principles stated in the Declaration might be made operative, a whole series of conventions had been formulated, adopted, and ratified during that period. A convention or convenant differs from a declaration because it requires not only approval by the General Assembly but also ratification by the member states which decide to become parties to the covenant. The declarations are statements of position on which *member states* take a stand and vote; the conventions or covenants are international treaties which *states parties* to the convention ratify and undertake to follow. There have been declarations and conventions on many of the varieties of rights stated in the Universal Declaration: a recognition of self-determination as a human right, a declaration on the granting of independence to colonial countries and peoples, campaigns to promote freedom from hunger and the right to health by the Food and Agriculture Organization and the World Health Organization, and programs to promote education and reduce discrimination in education by UNESCO as well as a Convention and a Recommendation against Discrimination in Education and a Protocol instituting a Conciliation and Good Offices Commission. There have been conventions on Genocide, on the Status of Refugees, on the Political Rights of Women, on Slavery, and on Statelessness.

Part of the philosophical and practical problems of human rights and their implementation and advancement may be seen in the problems encountered in securing ratification of conventions. It is, for example, proper and fitting to note, at this celebration in the United States of the twentieth anniversary of the Universal Declaration of Human Rights, that the United States has not ratified any of the Conventions or Covenants—not even the Convention on the Prevention and Punishment of the Crime of Genocide adopted in 1948 and ratified by 71 states by the end of 1967, or the Convention on the Political Rights of Women adopted in 1952 and ratified by 55 states by the end of 1967, or the Convention against Discrimination in Education adopted by UNESCO in 1960 and ratified by 41 states by the end of 1967. The two Covenants and the Optional Protocol on Human Rights adopted in 1966 are not yet in force because each of the Covenants must be ratified by 27 states, and the Optional Protocol by 18 states, before it goes into force. The United States has ratified none of them.

Why is it easier to vote for a declaration than to ratify a convention? It is customary to find reasons in considerations of power. Responsible Bar Associations have published committee reports which support the position that ratification of a United Nations Convention would diminish or endanger national sovereignty. This is a dubious argument since ratification of the conventions does not grant rights of inspection or policing, or agree to submission to judgments pronounced by an international body, and even the protocols require only answers to complaints and charges. The conventions provide means to implement the rights set forth in the Universal Declaration as well as some few which are not explicitly contained in the Declaration. They are implemented by a system of reporting. Thus in the two Covenants on Human Rights, the States Parties undertake to submit reports every three years on the measures they have adopted and the progress they have made in achieving observance of the rights recognized in the Covenant. In the Covenant on Civil and Political Rights there is also a system of state-to-state communication and conciliation. The Optional Protocol to the Convention on Civil and Political Rights adds a third method of implementation. A State Party recognizes the competence of the Human Rights Committee to receive and consider communications from individuals subject to its jurisdiction who claim to be victims of a violation by the State Party of any of the rights set forth in the Covenant. The Committee is required to bring the communication to the attention of the State Party, which in turn undertakes to submit to the Committee written explanations or statements clarifying the matter and the remedy undertaken. The question is considered at a closed meeting. The implementation of the covenants is by report; the implementation of the protocol is by replies to charges. It would be desirable and wise for member states to undertake such stock-taking as regards progress in human rights even if they decided not to ratify the covenants and the protocol. The question of power and sovereignty is less meaningful—both in the sense of corresponding to objective reality and in the sense of adapting to the situations and processes of change—than the question of discovering and achieving realizable values and effective rights. In a period of social and cultural revolution violent change can be avoided only by institutionalized revolution; and the only stable society is a self-renewing society.

a. Philosophy in the Development of Human Rights

The history of the development of human rights is more than an account of "facts." Facts are contingent and particular. Human rights have a history, but it is neither necessary nor fortuitous. The evolution of human rights is not a "necessary" process, but the rights which evolve are "unconditioned" and they are claimed "unconditionally." The rights which are achieved are "particular" rights of particular men, but they are inborn, "universal" to all men, and they are attributed "universally" and fully to each man. The structure of the history of human rights is a structure of particular events and ideas which give concrete application to a "universal declaration of human rights." As a history of rights, it is a history of unconditional universality; its necessity and essentiality are linked to the nature of man; and like other powers and functions of man, the rights of man are used and developed in the midst of contingencies and discriminations. The unconditional universal structure is manifested in the universalization of existing rights to all men, of new rights essential to existing rights, of transformation of existing rights in the light of new rights "which have made clear the full sense of older rights and have made them universally practicable," [10] and of action in a context of increased material resources which bear on the life of man and the development of human communities and the world community. The history of human rights may easily be reduced to a game of random chance or a mystery of divinely imposed destiny when it is recounted as a report of what has happened or as a myth of what men have done, without recognizing that it is also a history of ideas and that the structure of a continuing argument and inquiry enters into the structure of the empirical narration and of the impassioned myth. The history of human rights is paradoxical, because it embodies concretely all the great antitheses and paralogisms explored by philosophers—the problems of the whole and the part, the universal and the particular, the internal and the external, the apparent and the real.

When the UNESCO Committee examined the history and philosophy of human rights in 1947, the members of the Committee recognized that their task involved both the discovery of common principles which might remove difficulties in the way of agreement, and the places at which it might be anticipated that philosophic divergences might lead to differences and difficulties in interpretation. They also anticipated a second step in which a more precise analysis of the common principles and philosophic differences would be made. The Committee recognized that the ambiguity of the terms in which human rights and policies for their achievement are stated is the source both of agreement and differences at each stage of discussion and action. They therefore laid down working definitions of "right," "liberty," and "democracy." They interpreted the ambiguity ideologically in the fashion of the 1940's, and classified rights as civil and political, economic and social, and cultural, and worked out questions of priority and interrelations among the kinds of rights and liberties in a democracy. These are still ambiguous terms today, twenty years later, but the discussion of human rights now centers on a different set of basic terms which uncover new meanings and applications for right, liberty, and democracy which continue and enrich their ambiguity.

The relation between rights, liberty, and democracy depend on the relation between "right" and "law," and problems of right and law have moved to the center of debate and agitation as questions of particular rights have taken more concrete form in the context of universal rights during the last twenty years. Right and law provided the basic distinction in the brief history of rights and conventions sketched in the preceding pages, as well as in the antithesis between power (sovereignty is the power to make binding laws) and justice (the just is the right, and justice protects rights from impositions of power, including the power of the state), and within states the opposition between rights and interests, public good and private advantage. The determination of the hierarchies of rights and their limitations and negations reflects a continuing structure of philosophic interpretations in which a succession of basic terms is taken as fundamental in stating, understanding, and acquiring rights. Changes in the vocabulary, brought about both by adding new words and by changing the meanings of retained words, complicate the recognition of common principles and of differing philosophic interpretations, and the ambiguity opens the way to the use of interested misrepresentation as an instrument of power and the distraction of irrelevant quibbling advanced in lieu of rational analysis. John Stuart Mill makes a suggestive distinction in tracing the history of liberty between the problems presented when rulers and the ruled are thought to be distinct, and the problems presented in a democracy in which the ruled rule. The characteristics of recent discussions of liberty may be understood by adding a third relation, since the statement of the claims of many of the new freedoms are made in terms of situations in which the ruled oppose the rulers. The different forms of the statements of right may be given systematic form by considering them in terms of schemata of rights in which civil and political, economic and social, and finally cultural rights are in turn taken as fundamental.

When ruler and ruled are conceived to be different in nature in the analysis of liberty and rights, their differences are found in the character of those who rule or should rule, and of those who are ruled or should be ruled, and those differences are institutionalized in constitutions, monarchical, aristocratic, and democratic. Natural law takes its significance from these conceptions; the true forms of government are directed to the good; and the chief danger to liberty and rights is in the tyranny of the ruler. When the ruled are conceived to be the rulers in the analysis of liberty and rights, the basic problems of liberty and rights are not found in nature or in the nature of men, but in the relations between the individual and society. Responsibility takes its significance from the difference between actions for which the individual is accountable only to himself and those for which he is accountable to others and to society; and the chief danger to liberty and rights is in the tyranny of the majority or of common opinion. When the ruled are conceived to be the antagonists of the establishment, the basic problems of liberty and rights are not found in generalizations like nature or convention but in the inequities of current situations and in the lack of recognition, by themselves as well as others, of the victims of injustice. Assertion and initiation take their importance from the need to bring the situation to awareness and to do something about it; and the chief danger to liberty and equality is in the tyranny of the unrepresented minority.

We have not yet taken seriously or examined rationally the grounds or the consequences of the third way of formulating rights. We tend to translate it into the first vocabulary and to argue about right and wrong in terms taken from the vocabulary of civil and political rights, or to translate it into the second vocabulary and to argue about the ideologies of the cold war or the class war or some like confrontation in terms taken from the vocabulary of economic and social rights. We have not yet listened to the statements of action which translate civil and political, economic and social rights into a vocabulary based on terms taken from cultural rights. Instead of listening, we react with perplexity or indignation to "resistance" (nonviolent and violent), to "demonstration" (manifestation and disalienation), and to "imperialism" (military, political, economic, colonial, social, and cultural). We continue to talk in terms of old conceptions of nature and the good, or of power and sovereignty instead of adapting our vocabulary to new conceptions of revolution and relevant change.

The hierarchy of human rights formulated by the UNESCO Committee had made use of the new cultural rights to transform and order the older civil and political, economic and social rights. Cultural rights were treated as the last historical development and as the apex of the hierarchy which ranged from needs and wants to aspirations and wishes, from external undergoing to internal impulsion, from rights dependent on protection from external restriction of liberty to rights whose attainment would depend on the attitudes and actions of all people. Therefore, in sequence and in hierarchy, human rights were rights of living (the satisfaction of needs), of living well (self-development and advancement of the common good), and of living in society (justice and protection from the varieties of injustice). The recent emergence of rights which depend on the action of other men and eventually all men is symbolized in the prepositions of the four freedoms of the Atlantic Charter: freedom of thought and expression, which requires institutions to protect men from interference, and freedom from want and fear, which depends on a society of men who produce the requisites of life and do not resort to violence in the solution of problems. But cultural rights—the conception but not the fact—were new in 1947. The UNESCO Committee described cultural rights briefly in the traditional terms of the arts and sciences: the emerging cultural rights, their problems and their potentialities, were not investigated and the nature of their effect on the other rights was not elaborated.

The twenty years since 1947 suggest the need of a restatement of the philosophy of human rights and therefore, since the facts of history are affected by the philosophy of the time of the historian, a retracing of their history. Conceived in terms of cultural rights, neither men nor the rights of man can be ranged significantly or usefully in hierarchies: all rights are cultural rights, and cultural rights contribute to the satisfaction of needs, aspirations, and justice as well as (or more correctly, as instances of) the creation and appreciation of values; and in the history of mankind, justice and the enjoyment of truth and beauty were sought as early as the satisfaction of any other needs and wants. In the same fashion, freedoms *of* and freedoms *from* have been transformed by new developments of freedoms *to*—freedoms to participate in the values of culture and the fruits of progress. Cultural freedoms contribute to relating rights to the right and to the good, and to relating desires to what is desirable and what is possible. Their nature and effects are in part philosophic problems and in part empirical and practical problems, which are profoundly affected, like all empirical and practical facts, by the philosophical perspectives and conceptions in which they are encountered and experienced.

b. *Philosophy in Conception and Action in Human Rights.*

Problems arise from difficulties in action and ambiguities in thought and statement. The ambiguities of philosophic problems are frequently stated as paradoxes. One of the most persistent paradoxes which men have faced has been the paradox of right and law. It has found profound and suggestive formulation in myth, religion, poetry, law, and philosophy. If the historical and current statements and manifestations of the paradox of right and law are examined formally (to clarify the meanings and applications of rights and laws) it is apparent that four relations are possible between them as between any pair of terms. All four sets of meanings have been advocated by men in all periods of the discussion of rights and laws, and all four are still advocated in discussions and arguments today. Two of the possible relations may be called *ontic*, since they imply and depend on something real grounding the diversity of forms of rights in actual situations or institutions: either *transcendent*, inborn, or inalienable rights which provide the grounds for *laws* and constitutions, or *underlying* laws of the universe and of the nature of man which provide grounds for the assertion and pursuit of *rights*. Two of the possible relations may be called *phenomenal*, since they deny transcendental and underlying groundings and make rights and laws dependent on what men do and what they institute, and they place rights and laws in two possible relations as a result of the actions of men: *mutually exclusive* actions by which *rights* are freedoms and *laws* obligations, and rights are consequently found in actions concerning which laws are silent; or *mutually implicative* or dependent actions in which *rights* acquired in society and associations carry with them obligations, and *obligations* undertaken in law and custom carry with them rights. The "common principle" of human rights is stated in all four of these formulations of the relation of right and law, and all four conceptions have entered into the institution of human rights at all stages of their development. The divergent philosophic interpretations of the common principle have been the source of differences and oppositions; they have also been the source of ongoing progress in understanding and acquiring human rights.

Two dimensions of rights have been made apparent from the oppositions of the two fundamental pairs of relations between right and law: in phenomenal conceptions, freedom is the right to do as one pleases whether or not it is thought for any reason that one should do what one chooses to do; in ontic conceptions, freedom is the right to do as one should whether or not one wishes to do what is right. Justice has a place in each of these conceptions of right (as is apparent in the etymologies of right and justice in the ancient languages from which Western discussion of philosophy and politics derived its vocabulary: *dikaiosune* and *dike, justitia* and *jus*), since justice is a formulation of the relations of rights to the right and of the desired to the desirable in each of the philosophic conceptions of right; rights are conceived and sought in a context of power of action and of judgment or jurisdiction, and judgment takes the form of expressing what men think to be honorable or good and useful or effective; the inclusive context of practical thought and action is power and justice.

The evolution of human rights in the history sketched by the UNESCO Committee in 1947 is a history of rights stated in bills of rights since the seventeenth and eighteenth centuries. It was carefully separated from the history of philosophic conceptions of rights developed prior to the seventeenth century or expressed in parts of the world which drew up bills of rights only on the model of Western institutions. When the importance of cultural rights is recognized, that history must be reconsidered because the very conception of law and of constitution is changed in the context of cultural rights, and the possibility of the development of the rule of law, and of human rights and international obligations, must not be limited to the legislative powers of an international assembly, or the police powers of an international force, or the compulsory jurisdiction of an international court. As in the case of other transformations of human rights in the light of cultural rights, the

main lines of the history of rights may be made the basis for the restatement of the institutional history of rights in the broader framework of
the philosophy of rights and laws.

The first human rights to emerge in law were civil and political
rights. The conception of justice in terms of which their formulation
was made, "rendering to every man his due," was borrowed from
Roman law. When the pattern of the evolution of this conception of
justice is sought, it is worthy of note that it was given expression earlier
by a philosopher who undertook to show its insufficiency as a definition
of justice. Plato puts this definiton in the mouth of Polemarchus in the
first book of his *Republic*. It is refuted by Socrates, and in its place Socrates established, in the fourth book, a definition in which justice consists in each man performing his appropriate function in the state. The
passive conception of *rendering* to men gives way to the active conception of each man *doing*, and the division of men into friends and enemies, or classes based on considerations of benefit and harm, yields to
the division of men according to functions and work, or classes based on
contribution to the common good. The definition of justice as rendering
to every man his due was refuted by Socrates, but it was installed in
Roman Law and in the legal systems of the West and it was declared in
the Universal Declaration of Human Rights.

The second group of human rights to emerge in law were economic
and social rights. The conceptions of the division of labor and reward
and of the status and relations of men, which were used in the development of economic and social rights after the industrial and technological revolutions, had earlier philosophic beginnings. When Socrates constructs a series of states in which to find and define justice in Book II of
the *Republic*, the division of labor is the principle which guides the
formation of the successive states, and his definition of justice in Book
IV reflects that principle. Similarly, Aristotle, having defined justice as
the virtue which renders men apt to do just things, and having differentiated between legal justice, which is exercise of virtue as a whole relative
to others, and equal justice, which is a particular virtue relative to the
state, and between distributive and rectificatory justice as kinds of equal
justice, treats the distribution of honor, wealth, and other divisible as-
sets of the community, which may be allotted among its members
in equal or unequal shares, argues that there are as many kinds of
justice as there are kinds of constitutions of states, and relates legal to
equal justice by arguing that the different kinds of justice proper to each
state reflect natural justice which is the same in Athens and in Persia.
Even in Greece, the consideration of economic and social rights transformed the meaning of civil and political rights. It is frequently said

that Aristotle was no lover of democracy, yet he defines the state in terms of citizens, and he defines citizens as those who share in the administration of justice and political functions—that is, as the ruled who rule—remarking that his definition might seem best adapted to the citizen of a democracy; and when he distinguishes between good constitutions, which are directed to the common good, and bad constitutions, designed to further private interests, the name which he uses for the good form of democracy, is "polity," *politeia*, the word which means "constitution."

The final human rights to emerge in law are cultural rights. The objects cultivated by man, which give content to the conception of "culture" and "cult," include fields and herds, God and man's own mind and capacities. We are once more brought today, as were the Greeks and the Romans, to a recognition of the pluralism of justice, the pluralism of legal justice and also of equal justice, to borrow and adapt Aristotle's terms. It is a pluralism which has been in effect in economic and social rights, and it reflects a pluralism of philosophic interpretations in any policy proposed to extend and broaden the equality of equal justice. Before we draw up, or in the process of drawing up, a new legal formulation of the justice of equality we must reexamine, rethink, and restate the philosophic conception of man's function or his task in human societies and in the community of mankind. The philosophic problem of the paradox of rights and laws is at the bottom of the puzzling paradoxes encountered in efforts to define and advance human rights. It is at the bottom of the paradoxes of our hesitations over conventions, which are laws to implement and enforce rights we have already approved in a universal bill of human rights. It turns up again—in a particular form in the United States—in the need for a "civil *rights law*" to put into effect rights already guaranteed in an amendment to the Constitution. It is the paradox of the need of obligations to be free, of heteronomous laws to enforce autonomous rights and freedoms, of passionate attachment to principles warranted by cognitive analysis, of using legal equality to state equal rights. It is a paradox which appears in the terms we have been using to restate the philosophy and history of human rights: We have seen that all rights—civil, political, economic, and social—have become "cultural" rights, yet we watch new movements to advance rights, which state their objectives, and indicate the means that must be used to achieve them, by reducing all rights to "civil" rights.

The paradoxes are not ambiguities resulting from confusion or contradiction; they are productive ambiguities which embody the knowledge and experience men have acquired in the long history of rights, and which provide the beginning points for further advances. They encapsulate the history of the language of human rights as well as the history of the rights themselves, and they are restated in the language of the cultural revolution which is the present stage of the advancement of rights. Bills of rights are universal; conventions and laws are particular to circumstances and to specific rights. The distinction between rights and laws bearing on rights can be made in terms of natural law and the good; it can be made in terms of sovereignty and power. It is also made forcefully and pertinently in terms of revolution, for the statement of common principles and ideals is indicative of injustices and wrongs. The importance of conventions or laws is that they are ratifications or enactions of means by which to remove particular injustices and establish conditions for the acquisition and exercise of particular rights, of "freedoms to do." Revolutions are violent or peaceful changes of those in power under a constitution, or of the interpretation of the constitution, or of the constitution itself; and the vocabulary and methods of revolution extend far beyond the devices of political or military revolution, to include industrial and technological revolutions, social and cultural revolutions. Colonialism has likewise been analogized, in statement and program, to more relations between peoples than merely political affiliation or dependence, or even economic interdependence or exploitation, or social development or stratification, and has been further extended to include relations of groups or classes within a single nation or society. The ideas and the histories of revolutions and constitutions are closely intertwined: appeals to innovation and progress are made in the name of both, as are appeals to tradition and renaissance. The constitutions of the United States and of France, which were the basis of the constitutionalism and the economic and social reforms of the nineteenth century, were based on revolutions. Political, economic, and social changes that affected the lives of hundreds of millions of people and the whole structure of their relations with the other people of the world, and the modes of life of those other peoples, were initiated in the twentieth century by the revolutions of Sun Yat-sen, Gandhi, and Lenin. Considerations of natural law and oppositions of power were modified in revolutionary consideration of means of removing inequities revealed by a common principle.

Revolutions, from the beginning of the use of that term and concept, could be violent or nonviolent. They could be brought about by direct action or by circuitous manipulation; they could result in changes in the organization of society and the state, or changes in the government and the officials of government. They could be exercised by overt changes, real or apparent, or by occult changes, real or apparent—as

Augustus preserved the forms of the Constitution of the Roman Republic when he set up an Empire, or Napoleon continued the innovations of the French Revolution when he set up an Empire which used forms and structures borrowed from the Roman model. They could be achieved by practical action directed purposively and causally to a ladder of values; they could be achieved by indicative action pointed demonstratively and manifestively to a list of injustices. "Demonstration" is used in many arts—in logic, rhetoric, poetry, geometry, politics. The semantic changes are not a play of games in which stakes are not for keeps or a use of words in which meanings are not for sense: "Demonstration" may be used for human rights, to prove that a given mode of action is an exercise or an instance of a right; to persuade that a given end is good or to be accepted as good, or that a given means is useful or to be accepted as practicable; to manifest or expose a given action or relation or institution or establishment as wrong; to impede or delay or prevent activities of a given kind or of any kind whatever until actions or policies are changed.

As part of the range of meanings of "demonstration," civil disobedience and nonviolent resistance may be interpreted, and may therefore be, consequences or contributions to maintaining the constitution or to furthering the revolution. The transition from acting as a good citizen in accordance with the law and the constitution and acting as a good citizen to change the law and to amend the constitution; or the transition from nonviolent demonstrations to performing or undergoing violent actions, is gradual and subtle. It is not treated adequately by appeal to established and rigid conceptions of natural law or of structures of social or political powers and functions, although adequate analysis and interpretation of the transition could be made if those conceptions of civil and political, economic and social rights were given the flexibility they acquire in a context of cultural rights. The revolution is no longer basically a political, economic, or social revolution; it is a cultural revolution. It is not a revolution to establish the rights of a people, or of the inhabitants of a region, or of a "class" in any of the many senses in which men may be grouped in genera or species; it is a revolution to establish the group and the consciousness of the group as a step to acting to secure the rights which the group, once constituted by action, seeks or claims, not wholly unlike the revolution by which the Jews became a people chosen by God and withdrawn from the esteem of other peoples, or the United States avoided the entangling alliances and enmities of Europe and offered mankind a model of democratic government for imitation. Gandhi's program of nonviolent action and resistance was a revolution which went through several stages: a first step to give the Indian people a sense of self-identity, a second step to lead them to act as Indians in ways not approved by society or common opinion and even to risk disapproval by imprisonment, a third step to risk economic disadvantage and loss of social status, a fourth step to secure political independence. With political independence, the Indian people had the opportunity to determine what ends to pursue and what to do to secure those ends, and even to discover that the political use of nonviolent resistance may lead to large scale violence. The adoption of the policy of nonviolent resistance by black people in the United States required adaptations: the group was marked for constitution as a group by the skin color of its potential members in a white society, and the rights they sought were stated in the Constitution of the nation. A hundred years of inaction modulated by minuscule and partial changes, however, provided a situation in which demonstrations and manifestations of injustices prepared for the broad recognition of a principle and for the formation of opposed and supplementary policies of what to do or not to do in order that black men might achieve opportunity and motivation for self-realization. Students in the United States and in many other countries, dissatisfied with educational and with political and international policy, sought in demonstration means by which to realize their identity as students, as young people, as members of universities or of the republic of science and letters, and to determine what ought to be done or what ought not to be done by those constituted groups in a world of change and revolution.

It is to neglect the semantic change of language and of situation to criticize such movements for lack of clarity in statements of purpose, if what is sought is the clarity of a preamble to a political constitution or to an economic or social manifesto. The relevant clarity will be found by examining what the movements are against, and what can be done to repair the indicated injustices and the felt wrongs. Action and statement are employed to bring unclearly defined but clearly sensed wrongs to attention. The revolution is not contrary to reason or to nature or against the constitution and the rule of law, for in the process of semantic change traditional values are preserved in changed formulation as part of the revolutionary innovation: For all our distress concerning the ambiguity of natural law we find ways of asserting inborn rights; for all our suspicion concerning the implications of consensus and sovereignty we find ways of seeking and asserting power; for all our emotive ambivalence concerning revolution we seek ways to institutionalize revolution in progress. The Constitution is based on and is an expression of the law of nature, the operation of sovereignty, and the institutionalization of revolution. Progress and revolution have become the basic terms from which nature and power derive their meanings as a result of our growing recognition of the importance and the priority of cultural rights.

.   .   .   .

Rights and the right are independent. In the light of cultural rights, freedom of thought and expression are rights of the wise and the foolish, and the right of the wise to be wise in fact and reality, in statement and action, depends on recognition of the right of the foolish to be foolish. There is no criterion antecedent to consideration and interpretation of their action and statement by which to determine which is wise and which is foolish, because the best attested and the most widely accepted criteria would impede the activities and forestall the statements which contribute to wisdom and knowledge and the realization of values. Freedom to philosophize, as a cultural right, is freedom of thought and expression, and the exercise of the right broadens philosophizing to include philosophies of life as well as the treatises which express the philosophizing of professed or recognized philosophers. A new mode of philosophy emerges as an instance of cultural rights and as a common principle of rights and the right, and of the organization of knowledge and wisdom and of values. A pluralism of philosophies parallels the pluralisms of societies devoted to and dependent on cultural rights.

The philosophic differences in the interpretation of the common principles by which men live, yield programs of action relative to selected aspects of common experience directed to selected values of common ends. If common problems are considered from a variety of basic philosophic orientations, common policies may be agreed on and common actions may be undertaken for a variety of reasons under the guidance of a variety of professed philosophies. Differences of philosophies and confrontations of groups lead to controversies of opposition. When action and policy are discussed in the vocabulary of the structure and oppositions of power, the differences are sought in differences of intention or differences of consequences, that is, in terms of imputation (as Kant and his continental predecessors analyzed problems of moral action) or in terms of accountability (as Mill and his English predecessors presented moral problems). The concept of responsibility which emerged from the reflexive joining of considerations of antecedent purposes and posterior consequences has moved the center of the application of responsibility from the responsibility of an agent who carries out the directions of his principal, to the responsibility of a representative who makes decisions for the people he represents, to the responsibility of an activist who acts to change the structure within which decisions are made.

Semantic controversies are concerning the proper, or the preferable, or the "relevant" formulation of the common principle. Discussion of the common problem might take the place of controversy concerning the formulation of, or orientation to, the common principles of the parties brought together to consider the common problem, and might shift the issue from oppositions of parties to applications of reasons for the actions formulated to resolve the problem, and might open the possibility of coming to agreement on common action or policy for the different reasons of the opposed formulations. Criteria in such a discussion would be sought in the actions proposed to resolve a concrete problem, rather than in the principles, or methods, or interpretations used in statements of the problem. Once the focus of the discussion is on concrete problems and concrete consequences of proposed actions, rather than on the intentions, ideologies, and beliefs of the parties to the discussion and to the proposed action, the movement of the exercise of liberty and rights might be an on-going confrontation of new problems and new opportunities. Within the peace and security of the common institutions of the pluralistic society built on the exercise of cultural rights, men would have the circumstances and incentives conducive to developing the implications and the consequences of the varieties of philosophies and of self-realizing activities, and in moments of leisure from creative inquiry and expression they would be free to undertake the task of refuting and converting each other. In such a society a new mode of philosophizing would take form by the addition of discussion of common problems to the continuing opposition of preferred positions and interpretations; and under the influence of such a philosophy, a peaceful and progressive society would take form by use of the diversity of philosophies to uncover and verify common principles and to test them by the falsification of proposed formulations and systems.

NOTES

1. *Human Rights: Comments and Interpretations*, A Symposium edited by UNESCO with an Introduction by Jacques Maritain (London, A. Wingate, 1949), p. 262.
2. *Ibid.*
3. *Ibid.*, p. 258.
4. *Ibid.*, pp. 259–260.
5. *Ibid.*, p. 263.
6. *Ibid.*, pp. 262–263.
7. *Ibid.*, p. 267.
8. *Ibid.*, p. 269.
9. *Ibid.*, pp. 271–272.
10. *Ibid.*, p. 267.

IS THE DECLARATION OF HUMAN RIGHTS A WESTERN CONCEPT?

Jeanne Hersch

If I were to consider this task in my personal capacity as a philosopher, I would conceive of it in a completely different manner. I would try to ask philosophical questions about the Universal Declaration of Human Rights, including the compatibility or incompatibility which might exist between different aspects of the Declaration. But I address myself to the topic under consideration, not primarily as a philosopher, but rather as the representative of an organization which has attempted to deal with human rights as a world problem.

UNESCO, as an organization, officially has two chief aims. These aims, *raisons d'être* of the organization, are first, the construction and safeguarding of peace, and second, the development and implementation of human rights. Some might not consider it to be evident that the defense of peace and the development and implementation of human rights always go hand in hand. But because UNESCO has been conceived in this way, it should be made clear that the peace which UNESCO is to defend may not be defined simply as the absence of armed conflict. Instead, it is a peace in which human rights must be, at least to a degree, respected. Such a concept of peace—a peace designed for the ultimate service of man—requires that peace and human rights be considered reciprocally necessary. One cannot implement and establish human rights if there is no peace, and there is not a true peace if it is not one in which human rights are implemented and established.

We are, this year, celebrating the twentieth anniversary of the Universal Declaration of Human Rights. I should like to stress some of the important differences which emerge when we compare the world situation of 1948 and the world situation of 1968. The Universal Declaration was adopted by the United Nations General Assembly in 1948, two years after the creation of UNESCO, and shortly after the end of the

Second World War and the defeat of Nazism. The Declaration was conceived in an atmosphere which encouraged the consideration that human rights and peace should be seen as interdependent, because the Second World War was born out of the violation of these rights.

The people who created UNESCO as well as the Declaration of Human Rights clearly were predominantly Western. Nontheless, it was intended that the Declaration should be taken as universal in application. The word "universal" was made a part of the title of the Declaration, and it is important to note that this was done deliberately. It was intended that the Declaration be both more *universal* and more *concrete* than such former declarations as the French and American ones, which were written by particular groups of national citizens. It was conceived as applying to all nations, and it attempted to take into account those material and economic conditions under which human rights take on meaning, and without which they cannot exist. But in spite of all this, it still remains that those who created the Universal Declaration of Human Rights were predominantly citizens of the Western states.

The differences between 1948 and 1968 are huge. There are more than twice as many member states in UNESCO now than there were in 1948. We now have one hundred and twenty-two member states. New countries from the developing world, including former colonies, have gained their independence and become member states. In considering the total world situation, it is vital that one take into account the concrete presence of these new nations. The chief features which characterize the current situation, include the following. First, there is an obvious inequality between rich countries and poor countries, and despite all efforts, this inequality is growing every day. Second, huge, endless appetites and desires arose. In poor countries which are reached by mass media it now is possible for all people to know how well human beings can live in the twentieth century if they possess the economic and material means of technological development. Third, not only are the inequalities between rich and poor countries growing, but the awareness of these changes is growing as well. All three factors serve to test the principles of the Universal Declaration of Human Rights and raise the basic question: Can it stand? It is, in a way, as though the world finally has reached a point in which the question of human rights has been put to an ultimate test. Is the concept of human rights something to be realized in this world, or is it simply a dream? This is a most essential question. Because of the current situation, new poor countries tend to believe that such Universal Declarations of Human Rights are the invention of people who are well fed, and have no meaning for those who are not. As Gandhi once put it, "Freedom of spirit begins with butter at breakfast." It is appropriate, I think, that a man like Gandhi should express himself in this way. Ideas are matters of the spirit, but they take on reality by forming and shaping the material reality. That is why the literal, concrete situation becomes the testing ground for the best dreams of humanity.

This is the situation we now have. The people from the developing countries must see declarations of human rights as changing reality wherever it needs changing, and not simply as applying to the economically mature Western world. Many in the Western world used to accept the view that the concept of human rights is a Western invention; indeed, not simply Western but only Christian. It is something, they say, which only the Christian Western era has created. Others, however, would claim that there is another interpretation, i.e., that human rights are the creation of an anti-Christian tradition. For instance, the concept of human rights has served as the flag of the French Revolution, and one cannot say that the French Revolution is to be taken as a typically Christian event, in spite of the fact that you can find the intellectual roots of the French Revolution in Christianity. All this is extremely ambiguous, for there has been a fight between the Christians and Church tradition on the one hand, and the liberal human rights tradition on the other. I want to tell you something about an experiment which we in the Division of Philosophy of UNESCO have conducted to try to answer the question which is the title of this paper, "Is the Declaration of Human Rights a Western Concept?" It was thought that the Division of Philosophy should prepare a book for the twentieth anniversary of the Universal Declaration of Human Rights, which would be a collection of texts dealing with different aspects of these rights and proving that they belong to all mankind.

We thought we would do something which only UNESCO *could* do, something which other people somewhere else could not. Since UNESCO was represented in one hundred and twenty-two member states, we thought we would ask the national commissions for UNESCO in all one hundred and twenty-two member states to send us texts from their traditions which they considered had something to do with human rights—human rights in a very broad sense, and not necessarily declarations or codifications; any kind of text, from any epoch in their history in which could be found a sense for the dignity of the human being, which is the central point of the Universal Declaration of Human Rights. Thus we asked the one hundred and twenty-two national commissions, as well as some thirty cultural experts and a number of nongovernmental organizations (in fact, we asked all the sources we could get in touch with) to send us texts. We asked them to send us anything—a piece of an epic, proverbs, a fragment of a play, a tale, an inscription on a rock or stone, a song or some piece of old legislation which reflects a sense for human rights. In fact, we said, send us any kind of literature you want; we are curious about anything *you* consider to have a relationship with or a sense of human rights.

This was our starting point, and we waited. We had set up a huge net. It was our way of fishing all around the world and we didn't have the slightest idea what we would come up with, or even if we would come up with anything at all.

The first thing which came, came from Burundi. Burundi sent us some proverbs and two tales. This seemed to be a very good beginning. In the end, we were confronted with a mountain of texts from all time and all parts of the world.

When these texts arrived, I noted the themes that were touched on in them. Without any preconceived schema of evaluation, I noted what they were talking about. By this completely empirical method we discovered an unbelievable richness of many themes implied in these texts. We then composed the book, not by countries or culture—these are intermingled. Rather, the book is organized around different themes. We came to see that for most people, human rights are not primarily a juridical matter, but rather something which is alive at all levels of human existence. Without any comment, simply by putting one text after another, all the issues can be seen.

Let me tell you something about the various themes we found. There are a great many texts which deal with relationships between human beings; texts which deal with the solidarity between others and myself; texts which deal with the value of every life and those which deal with the respect and protection necessary to a weak human being. This last is a feature which, to my astonishment, one finds nearly everywhere. The idea that the human being needs and deserves protection, especially when for some reason he is weak, a child, or a very old person, or a sick one, or a woman with a child, or a foreigner without a family, or an exile, or a defeated warrior. Some sort of protection is needed in all these cases.

Yet another theme found in many different regions is the responsibility an individual bears. Still another is the right of a human being to choose death rather than being forced to do something he does not want to do. Here then, is a basis of human rights which I believe is at least as important as those social or economic bases of human rights that are so often cited. There is here a feeling of what is irreducible in man—when you cannot force somebody to speak, when you cannot force somebody to submit. You might kill him but you cannot force him.

Another group of themes was concerned with power. From many different areas there are texts which are concerned with the problem of the sources of power—chiefly coercion or the delegation of power to somebody. The difference between these two types of power is not at all only Western. The texts are concerned with the idea of the legitimacy of power, i.e., under what conditions is power accepted as legitimate? For instance, power goes with protection. When power no longer protects, it becomes illegitimate. It is not usually said in these abstract words which I now am using in order to summarize. Rather, it is said by concrete example, for instance in the ritual words which an African king must pronounce when he is taking power, words which show that the power is of a conditional rather than an unconditional sort. The sovereign has duties which, if not fulfilled, will cause him to lose his sovereignty.

The notion of justice as the expression of human rights is found everywhere. It is found in the right for any subject to take the king by the sleeve and to say, "Now you are going to say what is just—you must judge, and you must judge in an impartial way." We find this expressed in the rule that you cannot give presents to judges. The idea of the impartial judge is very general and quite fundamental.

We then find a whole group of themes about the limitations of power. It is not true that a large part of the world has admitted that power is boundless, limitless, and that only the West has invented constitutional limitations on power. Everywhere we find texts that are against the arbitrariness of princes or the arbitrariness of states. Nearly everywhere there are texts which state that a rule or a law is above personal power. (There are, though, other texts which say the contrary, texts which state that a law which is not served by a moral power cannot be morally applied. But though relations are conceived both ways, there is at the heart of each a fight against arbitrariness and a sense of human rights.)

Not only is the law taken as superior to power, but so is the conscience of the individual. There are limits to obedience and people have a duty to disobey if someone else demands what is wrong, arbitrary, or false. Then there is not only a right to revolt or to rebel, but there is a duty. It seems to me that the *duty* to rebel is much more understandable than the *right* to rebel, because the right to rebellion ruins the order of power, whereas the duty to rebel goes beyond and breaks it.

Next, we found a group of themes which are about civil freedoms, individual freedoms in very different forms. Freedom to move, freedom to go to another place, freedom to change work, etc., are found in many places.

Now I come to a part which is more Western in orientation: the reflection about the constitutional organization of power, about democracy and republic, about forms of government and formally guaranteed fundamental rights.

The problems one encounters when freedom is linked with truth, are many. There is no freedom when you cannot speak what you consider the truth to be. The importance of the right to think, of the right to free expression and criticism might be thought of as a modern invention, but this is not quite so. There is a story from Old Egypt that takes place about two thousand years before Christ, of a very poor man who is treated unjustly by a vassal of the king, and who complains about his treatment. Because of his complaints he is threatened, yet he goes on complaining and complaining. Still the threats continue, but still he continues to complain about abuses which he finds in the kingdom. For many pages of the story he denounces all kinds of powerful people in the most violent terms. In the end, this man is rescued and all the injustices to him are corrected, because he has had the courage to complain until something was done. I am not saying that this is typical of behavior in ancient Egypt; rather, what the story shows is that as far back in time as two thousand B.C., people thought they had a duty to denounce abuses and summoned the courage to do so. The right to object, the right to doubt, the right to speak out, the right to write, and so on, are stated in civilizations which are very old, or very far away from the West.

Themes of tolerance or dialogue between particular absolute beliefs are found in texts of very different religious origins.

Next, there is a rich group of social rights—statements about social equality or inequality, about property and limits of property, about the right to work. Ancient Egypt is well know for the slaves who constructed the pyramids. But in spite of this you find inscriptions on the pyramids where the pharoahs said that the people who worked for them had been well paid, and had been satisfied by the salary given to them. So even as far back as ancient Egypt, the necessity of an agreement, of consent between employer and employee, was already recognized, even if it was not always respected. Even at that time, it was conceived as being necessary and just. The right to strike and other social laws, expressed in juridical terms in the West, are found in different forms in older traditions.

Now we come to the concept of concrete liberty, the conjunction of political rights with social rights. Because this is a theoretical concept, it is found chiefly in the recent West. Yet, in spite of that, in ancient Rome we find statements saying that, if more power is given to the plebes without at the same time freeing them from their debts, nothing has really been given to them. As far back as ancient Rome, then, the connection between minimal economic conditions and freedom were already conceived.

Continuing our examination of the various themes from around the world, we next turn to those dealing with education, science and culture. The right to know, the right to read, the right to write, instruction for all, the essential function of the teacher, teacher-pupil relationships, all are found in very different traditions. The relationship between acquiring knowledge and using that knowledge to feed hungry people, between acquiring knowledge and curing the sick, between knowledge of poetry and knowledge of freedom, are found in all parts of the world.

Next we found old texts about slavery and violence, which state that the only way to correct unbearable conditions in which slaves may find themselves is to employ violence, and that under the conditions where violence is found to be the only way out, it then becomes legitimate. The idea of slavery being contrary to human nature is present in many parts of the world. Another group of themes maintain that the only weapon against force is the concept of human rights: one does not give up or give way, but constructs laws and guarantees. We find again and again the right of any man to be respected, even in war, by the enemy.

Many texts state that every group of people has a right to its own identity, to its own existence. They claim there is equality between different nations and between different groups, and the rights to their own traditions and language should not be threatened or destroyed. Defeat should not go hand in hand with slavery; defeat of a group should not mean that that group is to be enslaved. In very different traditions, too, men have thought that a judge or arbiter is necessary in international conflicts, as well as some concrete form of international law, that there is a universality of being a human being, that there is the same birth for all people, the same death, the same needs, and that fraternity is implied in all this.

We found in some texts no talk of social justice *per se*, but rather a simple saying which comes to the same thing, i.e., if somebody is eating alone when another one does not eat, it makes for a stomach ache.

In the end, texts from the most varied traditions refer to the sources and ends of the rights and the dignity of man. Some refer to a moral absolute, others to natural rights. Some refer to God as being the common Father or the common Creator, others refer to nature as common to all people. Thus, though the justifications may be very different, in all cases the human being as such, conceived in a fraternal way, is the source from which all justifications of rights spring.

From this mountain of texts we received, a book of more than five hundred pages has been printed, with more than a thousand fragments from all sorts of sources, times, and places. The current that runs through these texts is a very deep sense of brotherhood, a sense of what a man is *qua* man, not only as a biological being. There is always in a man a mysterious possibility which remains open, so that one can never reduce a human being to a fact. Every human being, as long as he is breathing, has a possibility to create himself in another way. Thus there are legends and stories in which somebody who may always have been despised grows in a certain way, or does something which is absolutely unexpected, so that one wonders at the development of man through himself. So it is that human rights are grounded not on facts, but on the possibility of man's freedom.

What strikes one when reading these texts is seeing that most human beings and most cultures contain something of the Kantian idea, that the human being should never be used only as a means, but always taken also as an end. And this is proposed not because he is such a perfect being, but because he can change, he has the ability of becoming. That is why he deserves and he requires respect, why he has rights. In very different ways, the necessity for this respect is recognized everywhere, even when it is violated, and even if its only expression is a cry of despair. The sense for this respect, in one way or another, is both more common and more different than one would think before looking into the texts. It seems to me, then, that in order to understand this, we must make use of a faculty other than reason. We need imagination, the kind of sympathetic imagination which enables us to understand different cultures and what it means to be respected and treated like a human being in all of them.

We turn now to the use of such a book. I would like to say very quickly what it is not. It is not a reflection of the factual, literal history of humanity, which is full of crimes and contempt and offense. It is, of course, not an idealization of human history. Rather, it contains what men from everywhere have conceived as being right, and how they have reacted against what they have believed was wrong.

There is a very important fact we must take into account, i.e., when people complain about offenses to human rights, that is proof that they are not the worst victims, for the worst victims are silent. Those people who have been most severely smashed historically have been silent. They have no place in history and no voice in such a book.

What can be found in this book are the contradictory aspects of human nature. For instance, there are texts which demand unwritten laws, while others state that those people who speak of demands for unwritten laws are mad: they are burying laws, burying rights and re-creating a situation of force. And neither view is wholly wrong.

What is the function of the Universal Declaration today? First of all, it is a kind of moral charter which is common, at least theoretically, to all nations. It is not univocal, but it at least gives to people a minimum common reference so they may talk together and prepare for the future. It also is an instrument for victims everywhere, whose rights have been offended. The victims can use, at least to a degree, the Universal Declaration to defend themselves. Another function which is most important is the following: there must be a minimum of common air which international civil servants and international organizations can breathe in order to be able to think. No one has the right to make use of his personal ideas when he is working on the level of an international organization. But the Universal Declaration of Human Rights provides the base upon which international organizations may flourish and develop. It is also the point of departure for more precise juridical conventions, i.e., it provides the clear possibility of applying the pressure of international opinion upon absolute sovereign states. When states have signed and ratified a convention, for example the convention against discrimination in education, the international organization asks the member states to give a report every second year saying what is done in their country towards the implementation of the conventions they have ratified. They are required to report and the report is read and discussed in public, on the international scene. Here we have the pressure of international opinion, which, though not juridical, is still somehow above national absolute sovereignty.

I think also that the Universal Declaration may play a very important role in each nation's self-examination, in helping each country to control itself and to ask itself what it is doing towards the implementation of human rights, This is really an exercise which I think should be widespread in international life. Usually people believe, especially if they are citizens of old democracies, that they have an innate respect for human rights—that at worst there are only details which are not in proper order, at least in their own soul, if not in their own country. Now that is not true at all. As soon as there is a lack of apartments, or a lack of work, or a lack of anything essential to your own life, your family, or the people you love, you at once find a good reason for exercising your rights against those who are living next door, especially if the person next door is not a citizen of the country, or is not of the same race.

So human rights seem to be a very fragile thing to maintain, and it seems to me that human rights are not, in this sense, natural. I think they are very much against nature. It is natural to use all means, when essential things are at stake, to save oneself, or if not oneself, the people one loves or the ideas one cares for, or the beliefs one lives for, or the country one loves. There always seem to be very good reasons to violate human rights. That is why I think that *if human rights are to stand, they have to be conceived in an absolute way.* No good reason then could justify their violation.

There must be no excuse for any violation. Otherwise, from compromise to compromise, from one excuse to another, human rights will never persevere. They are too much against nature, though they are *in* human nature. But human nature itself is not nature, and there is something in it which is against nature. The implementation of human rights is a task of human nature against nature.

NOTES

1. *Birthright of Man* (New York, UNESCO Publications Center).

NOTES ON CONTRIBUTORS

CHARLES FRANKEL Professor of Philosophy, Columbia University, former Assistant Secretary of State for Educational and Cultural Affairs. Publications include: *The Faith of Reason* (1948); *The Case for Modern Man* (1956); *The Democratic Prospect* (1962); *The Love of Anxiety and Other Essays* (1965); *The Neglected Aspect of Foreign Affairs* (1966); *Strange Country* (1969).

WALTER KAUFMANN Professor of Philosophy, Princeton University. Publications include: *Nietzsche* (1950); *Critique of Religion and Philosophy* (1958); *From Shakespeare to Existentialism* (1959); *Hegel: Reinterpretation, Texts, and Commentary* (1963); *Tragedy and Philosophy* (1968); translator and editor, *Basic Writings of Nietzsche* (5 complete books) (1968).

F. E. SPARSHOTT Chairman, Department of Ethics, Victoria University of the University of Toronto. Publications include: *An Enquiry into Goodness* (1958); *The Structure of Aesthetics* (1963); *A Divided Voice* (1965); *The Concept of Criticism* (1967); "Socrates and Thrasymachus", *The Monist* (1966).

JAMES GUTMANN Professor Emeritus of Philosophy, Columbia University. Publications include: *Spinoza's Ethics* (1955); *Marcus Aurelius* (1964); "Cassirer's Humanism", *Philosophy of E. Cassirer* (1949); "Mystical Experience and Human Values", *Horizons of a Philosopher* (1962); "Post-Kantian Romanticism", *Dictionary of History of Ideas* (1969).

SIDNEY HOOK Professor of Philosophy, New York University; Guggenheim Fellow (1928–1929); Fellow, Center for Advanced Studies (1960–1961); President, Eastern Division, American Philosophical Association (1959–1960). Publications include: *From Hegel to Marx* (1936); *Heresy,*

Yes—Conspiracy, No (1953); *The Quest for Being* (1959); *The Place of Religion in a Free Society* (1967).

GEORGE McGOVERN United States Senator from South Dakota. Publications include: *War against Want: America's Food for Peace Program* (1964); and numerous contributions to professional and popular periodicals.

KURT BAIER Professor of Philosophy, University of Pittsburgh, President, Australasian Association of Philosophy (1961). Publications include: *The Moral Point of View* (1958).

ANTHONY QUINTON Fellow, New College and University Lecturer in Philosophy, University of Oxford. Publications include: contributions to *Philosophy, Politics and Society* (1956); *The Nature of Metaphysics* (1957); *Mind, Proceedings of the Aristotelian Society* and *Victorian Studies*.

PAUL W. TAYLOR Professor of Philosophy, Brooklyn College. Publications include: *Normative Discourse* (1961); Editor, *The Moral Judgment* (1963); Co-editor, *Knowledge and Value* (1959); *Problems of Moral Philosophy* (1967).

JOSEPH GILBERT Assistant Professor of Philosophy, State University College, Brockport, New York, Assistant Director, International Philosophy Year (1967–1968).

H. L. A. HART Former Professor of Jurisprudence, University of Oxford and Fellow of University College, Oxford. Publications include: *The Concept of Law* (1961); *Punishment and the Elimination of Responsibility* (1962); *Law, Liberty and Morality* (1963); articles in numerous philosophical and legal journals.

RONALD DWORKIN Professor of Law, Master of Trumbull College, Yale University, 1966–1969; Professor of Jurisprudence, University of Oxford, 1969. Publications include: "Judicial Discretion", *The Journal of Philosophy* (1963); "Wasserstrom: The Judicial Decision", *Ethics* (1964)—reprinted as "Does Law Have a Function?", *Yale Law Journal* (1965); "The Morality of Law (A Symposium)", *Villanova Law Review* (1965); "Lord Devlin and the Enforcement of Morals", *Yale Law Journal* (1966).

GRAHAM HUGHES Professor of Law, New York University School of Law. Publications include: *Law, Reason and Justice* (1969); "Rules, Policy and Decision", *Yale Law Journal* (1968); "Civil Disobedience and the Political Question Doctrine" and "Reparation for Blacks?", *New York University Law Review* (1968).

TOM C. CLARK   Associate Justice, United States Supreme Court (1949–1967); Attorney General of the United States (1945–1949). President, Institute of Judicial Administration (1966–1967); President, Federal Bar Association (1944); American Bar Association Gold Medal (1962); American Judicature Society (first annual award, 1962).

RAYMOND ARON   Professor of Sociology, University of Paris. Publications include: *France: Steadfast and Changing* (1960); *Introduction to the History of Philosophy* (1961); *Main Currents in Sociological Thought* (1965).

RICHARD McKEON   Charles F. Grey Distinguished Professor of Philosophy and Greek, The University of Chicago. Publications include: *Thought, Action and Passion* (1954); ed., *Medieval Philosophers, Selections* (1959); ed., *Aristotle, Basic Works* (1941).

JEANNE HERSCH   Director, Division of Philosophy, UNESCO; Professor of Philosophy, University of Geneva, Switzerland. Publications include: *Birthright of Man—A Selection of Texts* (1969).